MILTON'S CONTEMPORARY REPUTATION

MILTON'S CONTEMPORARY REPUTATION

An Essay
together with *A Tentative List of Printed Allusions to Milton, 1641-1674*, and facsimile reproductions of five contemporary pamphlets written in answer to Milton

By

WILLIAM RILEY PARKER
Assistant Professor of English
The Ohio State University

31213

HASKELL HOUSE PUBLISHERS LTD.
Publishers of Scarce Scholarly Books
NEW YORK. N.Y. 10012
1971

First Published 1940

HASKELL HOUSE PUBLISHERS LTD.
Publishers of Scarce Scholarly Books
280 LAFAYETTE STREET
NEW YORK, N. Y. 10012

Library of Congress Catalog Card Number: 70-122996

Standard Book Number 8383-1129-6

Printed in the United States of America

Not to know mee argues your selves unknown
—Paradise Lost, IV, 830.

PREFACE

Confession is good for the preface. With Milton's unfailing candor to comfort me, I admit that I am writing here "out of mine own season, when I have neither yet compleated to my minde the full circle of my private studies, although I complain not of any insufficiency to the matter in hand." I have long had such a book as this in mind, and for some years have been left-handedly gathering materials for it; but the opportunity for publication, afforded through the generosity of the Graduate School of the Ohio State University, came so unexpectedly that I was unable to make the list of Milton allusions as full as I had wished. The time, moreover, is out of joint.

Acknowledgment is also good for the preface, because research proceeds by accumulation. In common with all who study Milton today, I am standing like a pigmy on the shoulders of David Masson, and if I see a few things which he has missed in his great *Life*, it is because I am later born. The generosity of Professor J. Milton French in making his valuable notes available to me has both added to my list of allusions and confirmed my faith in the nature of scholarship. Professor Douglas Bush kindly sent me an allusion which I had overlooked. Friends helped in last minute checking of references, and I must thank Mrs. Josephine W. Bennett, Professor Ruth Hughey, and Dr. Francis Lee Utley in particular for bringing the Huntington and Harvard Libraries to my door. Dr. James G. McManaway of the Folger Shakespeare Library, Miss Caroline Jakeman of the Treasure Room at Harvard, Mr. John Pendleton of the University of Rochester, Professor August C. Mahr of Ohio State University and Dr. Earl Wasserman of the University of Illinois were helpful and kind. It is a melancholy pleasure to recall, as well, the many courtesies of officials of the British Museum, the Bodleian Library, and the Cambridge University Library; in these treasure-houses, in quieter times, most of the work for this book was done. Even while Nazi bombers roared over England, Messrs. F. C. Francis and Victor Scholderer of the British Museum helped me to check references in books which had been removed to Wales for greater safety. To them I am perhaps most grateful of all, for their action taught me that the spirit of Milton is still alive in a nation which now views his broken statue at St. Giles Cripplegate.

The essay on Milton's contemporary reputation was read in manuscript by various friends and colleagues. Professors H. R. Walley, J. H. Wilson, and William Charvat made many stimulating suggestions. The essay, in its early stages, also passed under the vigilant eyes of four distinguished Miltonians, who were as provocative as they were generous in their criticisms; and I am proud to acknowledge the assistance of Harris Fletcher, Allan H. Gilbert, J. H. Hanford, and Merritt Y. Hughes. These scholars have saved me from many a slip; but the errors that remain, and the opinions here expressed, are my own.

If the pages to follow need justification, it is best expressed in Milton's own words, from the *Defensio Secunda*: "Is solus magnus est appellandus, qui res magnas aut gerit, aut docet, aut dignè scribit."

CONTENTS

	Page
Milton's Contemporary Reputation: an Essay	1
List of Printed Allusions, 1641-1674	69
A Modest Confutation, 1642	123
An Answer to The Doctrine and Discipline of Divorce, 1644	170
Filmer, Observations on Milton against Salmasius, 1652	218
The Censure of the Rota upon Milton's Book, 1660	229
L'Estrange, No Blinde Guides, 1660	245
Notes on A Modest Confutation	263
Notes on An Answer	270
Notes on Observations on Milton against Salmasius	278
Notes on The Censure of the Rota	280
Notes on No Blinde Guides	284
Index	293

MILTON'S CONTEMPORARY REPUTATION:
AN ESSAY

MILTON'S CONTEMPORARY REPUTATION: AN ESSAY

I

Who would not sing for Lycidas?

 He who seeks the bubble of another's reputation must beware, not of the cannon's mouth, but of the mouths of idolaters. Of all the subtle dangers to be faced, most insidious is that error of anachronistic judgment which has been called "the superstition of masterpieces." When men put their great upon pedestals, it sometimes pleases them to imagine that they were always there, and any attempt to achieve historical perspective is bitterly resented. We tend to forget that many a "minor" writer has had his day, and many a "masterpiece" has had to earn its status slowly. Today, for example, all men admire "Lycidas" and "L'Allegro"; their artistry is so perfect, their appeal so inevitable, that we find it difficult to imagine a time when most lovers of poetry failed to discover their beauty. The realization that there is apparently not one printed reference to these lyrics during the entire period of Milton's life comes as a shock. If, that is, the realization comes at all. We have had no Milton Allusion Book. We have had, instead, the idolatrous Masson, whose collection of allusions scattered through six monumental volumes is constantly interpreted in a mood of hero-worship.

 Masson is often guilty of the anachronistic error,[1] whether he be discussing Milton's poetry or the prose. Furthermore, his interpretation [of printed allusions] . . . suffers egregiously from the Carlylean attitude of mind by which he was obsessed, and from his failure to do justice to what he regarded as the lower and less pleasant aspects of Milton's contemporary background. The inferences to be drawn in the light of the time from the paucity of allusions to Milton

---

[1] I have thought it absurd, in this essay, to quarrel specifically with Masson's interpretations of Milton's fame. Anyone interested in comparisons may turn to the *Life*: III, 51-2, 186-7, 232, 431, 434, 445, 673; IV, 316, 350, 428; V, 574, 657, 663-4, 666n., 675; VI, 165-6, 558, 636, etc.

in the pamphlets and from the character of those few that do occur run plainly counter to the impression conveyed by Masson in the third volume of his *Life*.[2]

Professor Haller, who wrote these sentences, has done more than anyone else to clarify Milton's reputation during the early years, 1643-1647, and his recently published conclusions are sobering. For more than two centuries *Areopagitica* has been hailed as a work of noble reasoning and eloquent prose; today Milton's impassioned plea for liberty of the press calls more powerfully than ever before to the English-speaking peoples of the world; and yet, incredible as it may appear, there seems to have been not a single reference to this masterpiece in the thousands of books and pamphlets printed at the time, some of them dealing with the same subject.

It is an illuminating experience for a literary student to sit for months in the British Museum and to read in the thousands of Civil War and Commonwealth tracts which the bookseller, George Thomason, had the foresight to collect for posterity. If one labors under the anachronistic error, he may expect constantly to see the name of the author of *Paradise Lost* appear on the printed page. Many names do recur—Prynne, Lilburne, and Needham, for example—but if one is judging reputation solely on the evidence of such allusions, he will probably conclude that most contemporary writers were hardly aware of Milton's existence.

On the other hand, whereas Masson is a victim of "the superstition of masterpieces," Professor Haller is equally a victim of what might be called "the clipping bureau error." There is more than one kind of evidence for contemporary reputation. The present writer thinks it only fair, therefore, that he explain, at the outset, some of the considerations which have influenced the conclusions hereafter to be presented.

The "reputation" enjoyed by any author in his own age is a sociological fact upon which the artistic or literary value of his work may, or may not, have a bearing. We must not assume, without evidence, that our own taste in such matters has been anticipated by others. We must remember that the religious and political scruples of the public are sometimes as powerful

---

[2] William Haller, *Tracts on Liberty in the Puritan Revolution* (Columbia U.P., 1934), I, 128-9.

factors in the making of "reputation" as their artistic scruples. Actually, the words "reputation," "success," and "popularity" are dangerous words, because ambiguous. They raise questions. Reputation with what type of reader? Success where? Popularity with how many persons out of a potential reading public? What *kind* of reputation? There is gossip and there is fame. There is curiosity and there is interest. Centuries blur the picture, and students too easily forget sociological factors. In considering Milton's reputation, for example, one must remember the comparative concentration of English printing within the confines of one city. One must remember, not only the higher percentage of illiteracy in the seventeenth century, but also the fact that many readers of English pamphlets could not cope with Latin. In any age there is a limited audience for men who choose to write on certain subjects. And in any age there are more readers for topical pamphlets than for poetry.

In many of his works, Milton deliberately and knowingly limited his own audience; hence it is absurd to call him "ignored" if he presumably reached that audience and no more. Like all authors (even modern scholars), Milton could count on readers from his own widening circle of friends and acquaintances; for there have always been, besides gift copies and off-prints, delightful creatures who feel a social compulsion to con the printed words of persons they know. When I discuss Milton's contemporary reputation, therefore, I am assuming this audience, although I may seem to ignore it. "Reputation," in the sense employed in these pages, is taken to mean the common estimate of a writer held by those people who are uninfluenced by *personal* liking or hostility.

How may one determine such "reputation" after three hundred years have passed? Let us consider first the problem offered by a writer of verse. There are various tests that may be applied. Obviously printed and manuscript allusions tell us something; scholars have found profit in compiling and studying Allusion Books for Shakespeare and Jonson. Tributes from other contemporary writers are revealing if we interpret them cautiously. Remembering Donne, we know that a poet can exert influence merely by the circulation of his verses in manuscript; remembering the numerous reprints of *The Temple* even before Walton published his life of Herbert, we realize that multiplicity of editions can be an index of popularity. But then four folios of the works of Shakespeare sufficed for almost ninety years, and the verse of Robert Herrick, although it knew but one edition, found its way into countless manuscript collections and miscellanies. Clearly, no single test is enough; printed allusions must be checked by unprinted allusions; editions, by inclusion in manuscript commonplace books. Furthermore, while success and influence are not synonymous, influence is a partial indication of success. The vogue of Spenser may have passed, but his reputation is not eclipsed while Jonson and Donne are in conscious revolt, and while Milton, Cowley, and a pair of Fletchers are finding in him their inspiration. Translation and adaptation, too, are significant indexes of fame—as significant in their way as imitation of style and phraseology. All of these factors must be carefully balanced, then examined in the light of the poet's harmony with literary trends of his day, before we can submit a judicious estimate of his contemporary reputation. Catering to popular taste is more likely to bring immediate applause than creating popular taste. Sylvester's translation of Du Bartas was once a successful poem, but the sonnets of Milton had to wait one hundred and fifty years for an appreciative audience.

The writer of prose offers equal difficulties to the student of reputation. The number of editions or reprints of any given work tells us something, but to judge success on this evidence alone is hazardous. Editions are not all of the same numerical size; all copies of any given edition may not have been sold; books are sometimes bought and not read; moreover, books are sometimes read and not bought. The *spread* of editions, over both years and places, is an important factor. Too, we should consider whether the edition is private or limited, as Milton's *Of Education* and *Epitaphium Damonis* were, public like most of his pamphlets, or official like the *Eikonoklastes* and *Defensio Prima*. A writer holding a public position is more likely to attract a wide audience than a writer in private life. Contemporary printed allusions constitute a valuable index to popularity and influence, but they should be carefully checked by manuscript allusions and other forms of evidence. The periodical press was just beginning in the seventeenth century, and should not be overlooked. With the prose-writer as with the poet, success and influence are not inseparable, but indications of influence can tell us much. Did the pamphlet achieve its end, in whole or in part? Did it meet with printed approval, or provoke refutation? Again, all these matters must be carefully considered, and then checked by the writer's conformity with the spirit of his age. Did he express prevalent ideas and ideals, or was he thinking in advance of the time? Was his prose style current, or eccentric, or difficult? Did he meet the interests of his public, or did he try to create a new interest?

There are doubtless other considerations as important as some of those I have mentioned, but I have sought an adequate rather than an exhaustive check for the problem of Milton's reputation during his own lifetime. A full history of that reputation is not my intent, and I beg that this essay be read as suggestive rather than definitive. Some of the argument is from negative evidence—always dangerous and easily upset— but most of it is from the kind of evidence which I have sketched above.

II

Fame is the spur

It was probably in the autumn of 1620 that Milton's tutor, Thomas Young, sailed eastward for Hamburg to make arrangements for a permanent home.[1] Like many English Puritans of the day, he had found his own country *dura parens*; on September 6, from Plymouth, the *Mayflower* had sailed westward with a whole boatload of people like Young, seeking peace in a new world. For Milton, aged eleven, this same year probably brought a voyage from the island of domestic adulation to the colder continent of society. He entered St. Paul's School in London, and remained there until his admission to Christ's College, Cambridge, February 12, 1625. In those years, his brother Christopher later told John Aubrey, he "composed many copies of verses which might well become a riper age";

---
[1] See the present writer's "Milton and Thomas Young," *MLN*, LIII (June, 1938), 399-407. For an eloquent commentary on Young's exile, see Milton's *Elegia Quarta*.

"early in that time," declared the anonymous biographer[2] more specifically, he "wrote several grave and religious Poems, and paraphrased some of David's Psalms." If, however, he enjoyed any celebrity at St. Paul's as either a student or a youthful poet, there is no record of the fact—and probably we should expect none. We may note, however, that Alexander Gill the younger, a minor Latin poet of the time, was one of Milton's teachers at St. Paul's (and a good friend), but among all of his printed verses he left nothing in praise of his gifted pupil.[3]

At the University Milton was for some time, according to his own account, unpopular; and eventually he was given the nickname of "Lady." There may be no connection between these two facts, although it is tempting to see one.[4] Indeed, because he was at all times sensitive to the opinion that others held of him, we may discount somewhat his references to his unpopularity. He later confessed that he was endowed with "a certain niceness of nature, an honest haughtiness, and self-esteem either of what I was or what I might be"; and such a person might easily have considered himself unpopular, or the object of hostility, if his abilities were not instantly recognized or his ideas generally accepted. We know that he quarrelled with his tutor, William Chappell, and suffered rustication as

[2] One of Aubrey's most provocative notes to Wood is this: "Q. Mr Allam of Edm: hall Oxon. of Mr J. Milton's life writt by himselfe v. pagg." Andrew Allam (1655-1685) helped Wood considerably with biographical researches on contemporary writers. He was young enough to admire Milton without the usual political prejudices, and the anonymous life may well be from his pen. This life, however, consists of five *leaves*, not *pages*; and the formal hand in which it is written bears no resemblance to the handwriting of Allam's letters preserved in the Bodleian Library. Further evidence of Allam's authorship is needed, although, until it is found, the fact of a life of Milton by Allam remains to be reckoned with. Professor A. R. Benham's recent argument (*ELH*, VI, Dec., 1939, 245-255) that the anonymous life was subsequent to Wood and perhaps to Edward Phillips, is weakened by the anonymous writer's statement: "But that this Age is insensible of the great obligations it has to him, is too apparent in that hee has no better a Pen to celebrate his Memory."

[3] See in particular Gill's *Parerga, sive Poetici Conatus* (London, 1632), which contains various verse tributes to others. Although there is the evidence of Milton's own letters that he and Gill exchanged poems in 1628 and 1634, Milton was not one of the ten contributors of commendatory verses to Gill's 1632 volume. Nevertheless, the possible influence on Milton of Gill's Latin poetry deserves study; and some manuscript notes in one of the Bodleian copies of the *Parerga* (Malone 924) might furnish a beginning.

[4] In his sixth prolusion (1628?) Milton says that he has lately (*"nuper"*) heard the epithet, and in the same speech he comments with pleasure on his recent discovery of friendly feeling toward him in the college. Is it possible that he misunderstood what most of us would recognize as a familiar practice among young men: the giving of unkind nicknames to persons of whom we have grown fond? I recall a "Goofy" of my own college days who is now a highly regarded educator.

punishment. This was hardly a promising beginning for one's academic career. Later he seems to have involved himself in controversy over educational theory. The remainder of the story, as he naively relates it, is sketchy but highly interesting. He stood before the members of his own college to deliver his first academic prolusion, and, having anticipated hostility on the part of his audience, he spoke words "steeped too much in vinegar." To his great surprise, everyone, including those who had heretofore seemed most unfriendly, greeted his prolusion with "unusual applause." Soon he was being called "the Lady," and finally he was chosen master of ceremonies at a banquet (1628?) for which he wrote a heavily humorous speech and a revealing English poem. Milton reacted as quickly to friendliness as he did to what he considered its opposite; his praise of his audience, in the Vacation Exercise oration, is both extravagant and ingenuous. Biographers like to imagine the young poet winning, at last, the recognition and comradeship of his fellow students; but, unfortunately, there are some additional facts to consider. There is the fact that, in after life, Milton had little that was kind to say about his Alma Mater. There is the fact that, during the very summer of the Vacation Exercise, he wrote bitterly to Gill about the limitations of Cambridge students, complaining that he found "almost no real companions in study." Apparently he made no friendships at Cambridge that survived graduation. There is even a hint of mystery in his being chosen "Father" for the vacation banquet.[5] We may believe Milton when he states that he took his degree "with applause," and left Cambridge "accompanied by the regrets of most of the Fellows of the college, who showed me uncommon marks of friendship and esteem." He had earned the respect of those with whom he had associated. If he won affection as well, no evidence has come down to us.

During his university career he wrote some twenty or thirty poems, among them verses which the world will not willingly

---

[5] He does not mention the banquet in his letter to Gill of July 2, or in his letter to Young of July 21. From the prolusion itself we learn that the summons came suddenly and unexpectedly, that the real leader of the Sophisters ("an eager candidate for the post") had recently "departed" as a result of an undergraduate prank, and that the annual banquet had not been held the preceding year, perhaps because the prospective "Fathers" had been taking the title too literally in the town. From the evidence, Milton seems to have been chosen for his character and his scholarship more than for his popularity. Note, too, that the actual choice of the annual "Father" seems to have been in the hands of one person—*cujus interest*—and not of Milton's fellow undergraduates.

let die. Did these go unappreciated? It is extremely difficult to judge, now, what reputation the young poet had in university circles, but his *juvenilia* give ample evidence of a social Muse, from the conventional tears for departed worthies to the assured tone of "L'Allegro." We may be certain that he found an audience, and that part of it, at least, was appreciative. The best known evidence still bears repetition: in 1628 an unnamed Fellow of the college who was to participate in a philosophical disputation at the Commencement, "being himself long past such frivolous trifles and occupied with serious business," asked Milton to write for him "the verses which have to be composed for the disputation in accordance with the yearly custom." These verses were printed for that occasion, and so constitute a "first edition" of the first of Milton's poems to be "published," but no one in our time has seen the precious sheet. The fact that Milton sent a copy to Alexander Gill implies that the poem's authorship was not a strict secret; on the other hand, Milton may later have felt some reluctance about including among his published verse a piece which had passed as the work of another, and the usual guess—that "Naturam non pati senium" is the poem in question—may or may not be correct. The incident proves that Milton was known to some as a capable versifier. Of the extent of his reputation it tells us nothing.

One expects to find Milton in the verse collections of his university, and it is difficult to explain his absence. Late in 1631, for example, Cambridge poets celebrated the births of Prince Charles and the Princess Mary, and among the contributors to the printed collection were Edward King ("Lycidas") and Robert Pory, both of Christ's College and the latter an exact contemporary of Milton. One may say, but not very convincingly, that the future author of *Eikonoklastes* would never stoop to honor royalty. If this is the only explanation, one must then explain why the future author of five tracts in the Smectymnuan controversy wrote verses, as an undergraduate, in praise of two Anglican bishops,[6] and actually printed those

---

[6] The verses may have been mere exercises, as some suggest, but he was not parodying "with tantalizing exaggeration the fashions of his college." (Raymond, *Oliver's Secretary*, p. 13). To save someone else the labor, let me confess that I have looked into all early editions of Andrewes to be found in the British Museum, in the vain hope of seeing Milton's *Elegia Tertia* printed or mentioned. Eight lines of verse by Ge[orge] Wi[ther] are engraved under the portrait of Andrewes in *The Morall Law Expounded* (1642), and Ja[mes] Howell contributed six lines for the portrait in *The Private Devotions* (1647 and 1648); but nothing of Milton is to be found.

verses in 1645. Perhaps more to the point, in the year 1631 Milton penned tears of perfect moan for the deceased wife of a Roman Catholic Marquis of Winchester,[7] and not long after composed *Arcades* and *Comus* for the entertainment of noble families. While the young poet was deliberately experimenting, he turned his talents to many uses; but he does not appear in the published anthologies of Cambridge University until 1638, six years after his graduation. Is it heresy to suggest that he was not invited to contribute?

Among the very few poems of Milton's Cambridge career which attracted enough notice to circulate in manuscript and find their way into commonplace books were his "Epitaph on the Marchioness of Winchester" and his two humorous epitaphs on old Hobson the carrier.[8] One of the Hobson poems appeared in the *Banquet of Jests* (1640) and both appeared in *Wit Restored* (1658)—in each instance without their author's name. There were other Hobson poems by other hands, and if the evidence of surviving manuscript collections means anything, some of these others were better liked because more often copied. Even if Milton's verses were better known than now appears, they were probably known apart from their author and added little or nothing to his reputation.

In 1630, according to his own dating, Milton composed his now famous tribute to Shakespeare, which was printed in the Second Folio of 1632. It is difficult to interpret the significance of this well known event. Even the date has been questioned by scholars, although there is some bibliographical confirmation of Milton's accuracy.[9] It is hard to believe that the young poet submitted the verses on his own initiative; he contributed no commendatory verses to the 1632 collection of his friend Gill; indeed, he is conspicuous in his abstinence from the poetical back-scratching customary in his time. Furthermore, there is

---

[7] Besides the well known elegies by Jonson and Davenant, there is an epitaph on this estimable lady by Walter Colman, a Roman Catholic poet, in his *La Dance Machabre or Death's Duell* (1633?), p. [70].

[8] Some admirer of the "Epitaph on the Marchioness of Winchester" not only copied the poem but also noted the author: "Jo Milton of Chr: Coll Cambr." B. M. Sloane MS 1446 ff. 37b-38. See also my "Milton's Hobson Poems," *MLR*, XXXI (July, 1936), 395-402.

[9] It was in 1630 (a plague year) that the publishers seem to have made their arrangements for printing the Second Folio. On November 16, 1630, Blount assigned his share in eighteen of Shakespeare's plays to Robert Allot, in accordance with an agreement of June 26, 1630. (*Stationers' Register*) Thomas Cotes was probably the publisher who invited Milton to contribute verses; the evidence, however, is slight.

nothing in Milton's career up to 1630 to suggest that a London bookseller would hear of him as a poet without being personally acquainted with either him or his scrivener father. Probably the lines "On Shakespear" were written at the suggestion of the Second Folio's publisher, who may have wished to do the Cambridge student a favor. The conventionality of the poem suggests, at least to one critic, a job performed rather than a creative achievement.[10]

If Milton's acquaintance with the musician, Henry Lawes, began as early as 1630, Lawes may have had a hand in the publishing of the tribute to Shakespeare. He seems to have been the only admirer of the youthful poet who went out of his way to encourage and publicize the latter's writing. *Arcades* must have been composed at Lawes' instigation; we know that *Comus* was. Both of these poetical entertainments are important in the history of Milton's reputation, for they mark his introduction to an audience outside his immediate academic circle.

Nevertheless, Milton himself was acutely conscious of his comparative obscurity and, more particularly, of his failure to live up to his own high expectations. Abraham Cowley's *Poetical Blossoms* was registered for publication October 24, 1632, and about two months later Milton lamented:

> My hasting days fly on with full career,
> But my late spring no bud or blossom shew'th. . . .
> And inward ripeness doth much less appear
> That some more timely-happy spirits endu'th.[11]

In a letter to a friend, enclosing this sonnet, he says that his life is "as yet obscure." It is not modesty that causes Milton, at the close of "Lycidas" (1637), to speak of himself as an

---

[10] Consider the poem's vagueness. There is not the slightest suggestion that Shakespeare is a dramatist; in fact, Milton's tribute was found quite appropriate for the 1640 edition of Shakespeare's *Poems*. Apart from the contrast briefly drawn between "thy easy numbers" and the "slow-endeavouring art" of others, the sixteen lines of the poem merely develop the conceit of a monument built of admiration—a conceit suggested by Jonson's tribute in the First Folio, and already elaborated by William Browne in his elegy on the Countess of Pembroke and by the author of an epitaph on Stanley. See Hanford's *Handbook*, 3rd ed., pp. 146-7, and Todd's 1801 ed. of *The Poetical Works*, VI, 85. As Hurd declared long ago: "This is but an ordinary poem to come from Milton."

[11] For the dating of Milton's Sonnet VII see my "Some Problems in the Chronology of Milton's Early Poems," *RES*, XI (July, 1935), 276-83. On the early reputation of Cowley's first volume see Arthur Nethercot's "Milton, Jonson, and the Young Cowley," *MLN*, XLIX (March, 1934), 158-62.

"uncouth" swain. Even *Comus,* which Lawes published during this same year, appeared anonymously, "not openly acknowledged by the Author." And "Lycidas," when it was printed in the memorial volume to King (1638), was signed only "J.M." Six years had passed since Milton had left Cambridge; even if he were invited to contribute the elegy, how many people, apart from his contemporaries at the university, would recognize those initials? One imagines, now, that the authentic voice of great poetry would have been instantly remarked, and that the appearance of "Lycidas" at the end of an otherwise unnotable volume would have created a stir; but there seems to have been not a single printed reference to the elegy in the whole period of Milton's life. One assumes from Lawes' statement about *Comus* —"the often Copying of it hath tir'd my Pen to give my several friends satisfaction"—that the masque had given its author a reputation of a sort; but it is equally significant that Sir Henry Wotton, who had noticed *Comus* soon after its publication, did not know the "true Artificer" until Milton revealed himself modestly in a letter. When the young poet departed for Italy in 1638, he was, as he told his father in an undated Latin tribute,[12] "a figure obscure" except to a very few people. He had himself encouraged this obscurity by deliberate and purposeful retirement.

The Italian journey widened his experience and inflated his ego. English friends had assured him that his style, "by certain vital signs it had, was likely to live"; but the more effusive Italians sent him home glowing with extravagant compliments and doubly convinced that he "might perhaps leave something so written to aftertimes, as they should not willingly let it die." They presented him, moreover, with written tributes in the same strain, which, six years later, he apologetically printed with his *Minor Poems.* His public use of these rhetorical and eulogistic *testimonia* is interesting for the light it

---

[12] I agree with Grierson, Tillyard, and Hughes in putting *Ad Patrem* late in the Horton period, not only because an apology for poetry would come more appropriately after the production of *Comus,* but also because the implied objections of Milton's father are (within the limits of our biographical knowledge) best explained by the latter's financial difficulties in 1637. Lines 12-16, 57, 68-71, 93-94 of the poem suggest that the scrivener had complained of his son's failure to support himself. If this interpretation is pertinent, the poem and the successful termination of the law suit combined to remove the father's objections, for less than two months after the scrivener's vindication in the courts (February 1, 1638), young Milton started his Italian journey.

throws on Milton's character. He lets them introduce the Latin, not the English, poems; he explains that friends have urged him to print them; he reveals himself sensitive to the conventional exaggeration of his talents. It was probably as early as 1640 that Milton had sent printed copies of his *Epitaphium Damonis* to various Italian acquaintances, and thus far he had received no acknowledgment from any one of them.[13] Nevertheless, in 1645, for reasons which we shall soon understand clearly, he wanted Englishmen to know that he enjoyed the esteem of notable persons elsewhere.

III

But the fair guerdon when we hope to find

When Milton finally made his entrance into public life, with the publishing of his *Of Reformation* early in 1641, it was modestly, by the side door of anonymity. He was thirty-two years of age, but painfully conscious of his own immaturity and lack of reputation. Some years before, he had confessed a natural "desire of honor and repute and immortal fame," but his thoughts had been exclusively (if we may judge from the words that have survived) of immortality as a poet. For this he had been "growing wings and learning to fly"; for this he had abandoned all hopes of riches, all idea of service in the ministry or the law. In 1640 he was engaged in the congenial task of teaching, and his mind, when he was out of the classroom, was full of plans for dramas and epics. His was "a calm and pleasing solitariness fed with cheerful and confident thoughts." A friend—the "Freind" to whom *Of Reformation* is dedicated—may have been responsible for Milton's abrupt plunge into "a troubled sea of noises and hoarse disputes." One remembers the friend (perhaps the same) who, about eight years earlier, had piously urged the youthful poet to come out of "the arms of studious retirement" at Horton and to give his

---

[13] His first word from Italy was a letter from Carlo Dati in 1647, as his reply, April 21, 1647, makes clear. The *Epitaphium Damonis* was written during the summer of 1640 (see lines 9-12 of the poem), and probably printed in a limited edition soon afterwards. Copies were sent to his Italian acquaintances as a substitute for prosaic "bread and butter" letters.

talents to the Church. Milton had then argued in reply that he was waiting "with a sacred reverence and religious advisement how best to undergo." In 1641, when Thomas Young[1] was giving his initials to SMECTYMNUUS and his energy to the great struggle against the bishops, Milton's conscience was suddenly smitten and, sadly but reverently, he lent his pen to the controversy:

> neither envy nor gall hath entered me upon this controversy, but the enforcement of conscience only, and a preventive fear lest the omitting of this duty should be against me when I would store up to myself the good provision of peaceful hours. So lest it should be still imputed to me, as I have found it hath been, that some self-pleasing humor of vainglory hath incited me to contest with men of high estimation, now while green years are upon my head, from this needless surmisal I shall hope to dissuade the intelligent and equal auditor.... If I hunted after praise by the ostentation of wit and learning I should not write thus out of mine own season.... If I were wise only to mine own ends, I would certainly take such a subject as of itself might catch applause, whereas this hath all the disadvantages on the contrary.... Lastly, I should not choose this manner of writing [that is, prose], wherein knowing myself inferior to myself, led by the genial power of nature to another task, I have the use, as I may account it, but of my left hand.... But were it the meanest underservice, if God by His secretary conscience enjoin it, it were sad for me if I should draw back. (*Reason of Church Government*).

In his five tracts against Episcopacy, Milton often alludes to his desire for fame as a poet, and he says nothing of a similar ambition as a pamphleteer. On the contrary, he anticipates little but envy and recrimination. It is true, nevertheless, that as time passed, and as his early "call" to fight for Presbyterianism grew into a God-inspired passion for all forms of liberty, his early longing for poetic immortality was extended to include prose. The development of this hope was slow and gradual; it suffered set-backs in periods of disillusionment; but it reached a climax with the publication and celebrity of the *Defensio Prima*, when, as Professor Grierson has observed, Milton's dream of writing a national epic seemed, through God's myste-

---

[1] Although there is no direct evidence, I suspect Young of being the "friend" in both instances. See my note in *TLS*, May 16, 1936, p. 420.

rious providence, fulfilled. The writer who five years before had presented his collected prose to the Bodleian Library, hoping for both immortality and a vacation from calumny, took undisguised pleasure in having the power of his left hand recognized. As a deeply religious person, Milton probably never wrote anything, prose or poetry, without feeling that it was God's bidding. As a man of the Renaissance, he probably never wrote anything without feeling that God's work should be applauded by "the wise and right understanding handful of men."

Unfortunately for those who would now study the reception of Milton's pamphlets, the printed allusions to them by his contemporaries contain few compliments; most are devoted to reviling and ridiculing him; even the number of serious rebuttals is small. If we judge his reputation on this evidence alone, we shall have a strangely distorted picture—one which leaves out of account the private applause of friends and the approving nods of mute, inglorious strangers whose thoughts he has expressed. To say this is not to sentimentalize; it is to take a realistic view of human nature. We must believe Milton when he declares that "divers learned and judicious men testified their daily approval" of his books,[2] even if these persons have left no trace of themselves. Then, as now, consent usually gives silence, while disagreement is vocal.

Milton's first pamphlet, *Of Reformation*, having been published anonymously, could not have contributed much to his reputation, except among those persons who already admired him for his learning. It was read by others, but how widely, there is no way now of knowing. A writer who called himself "Peloni Almoni" noted the tract immediately upon its appearance, and took exception to views expressed by its "late unworthy Author" on Irenaeus, who happened to be the subject of Almoni's *Compendious Discourse*. In the following year Thomas Fuller, mentioning the disesteem in which Cranmer, Ridley, and other protestant martyrs were currently held, instanced the author of *Of Reformation*—"whosoever he was" —as traducing them in reprehensible language. Bishop John

---

[2] He said this of his *Doctrine and Discipline of Divorce*, which, on the evidence of print, seems to have met with almost unanimous disapproval. One may assume that among these "judicious men" were friends such as Margaret Ley's husband (John Hobson), Henry Lawes, Samuel Hartlib, Patrick Young, the bookseller Thomason, and William Thomas—most of whom would be acquainted with Milton's domestic difficulties.

Bramhall also noticed Milton's disrespectful comments on these worthies and, in a paragraph pleading for England to acknowledge its blessings from them, damned the "young novice" for his loose tongue. All three writers ignored the main thesis of Milton's pamphlet; all three used part of it, a moment only, as a springboard for some argument of their own. It was many years before anyone else mentioned it, even incidentally, in print. Even so, it provoked more of a response than Milton's second pamphlet, which was also anonymous; for *Of Prelatical Episcopacy* seems to have inspired no allusions, condemnatory or otherwise.[3]

In his first two tracts Milton was helping his friends the Smectymnuans indirectly, but in his third, perhaps at their request, he entered their controversy with Bishop Joseph Hall. *Animadversions upon the Remonstrants Defence against Smectymnuus* was a direct attack upon a specific pamphlet by Hall, and it invited a reply. It received one—although not from Hall himself. Milton had again written anonymously, and the anonymous rebuttal pretended to deduce his character from the language of his pamphlet, while it extolled the virtues of the Bishop from personal knowledge. The result amounts almost to a new *Characters of Virtues and Vices*. However unfair, the portrait of Milton from "internal evidence" is appropriate in the face of his anonymity; and the writer was, of course, but half-serious in his inferences.[4] Nevertheless, Milton was outraged by such treatment, and felt the necessity for replying in an angry defence of himself called *An Apology*. Meanwhile, he also published his *Reason of Church Government*, a pamphlet which, like the *Apology*, is highly treasured today for its autobiographical passages. It is a significant commentary upon the reception of both of these tracts that unsold copies of each were reissued under a new title-page about 1654, when their

---

[3] To be sure, G. W. Whiting (see p. 71, note 1) argues at length that Almoni's pamphlet, although it cites only *Of Reformation*, is actually a reply to *Of Prelatical Episcopacy*. A detailed refutation of this argument would be inappropriate here, but I must briefly record my own scepticism. The few remarks about Irenaeus in *Of Reformation* would account for Almoni's reference, for he has an axe to grind. He would hardly answer Milton's second pamphlet point by point without making a single allusion to it or quotation from it. Furthermore, Milton's quarrel against Irenaeus, says Almoni (and Whiting omits these words), has already been "well answered" by Fevardentius.

[4] For a more detailed discussion of this *Modest Confutation* of Milton's *Animadversions* see pp. 263-270.

author had received some measure of fame.[5] The publisher who thus sought a return on his seemingly worthless stock was John Rothwell, and one wonders how he fared. He did *not* venture a second edition of the two—nor did anyone else in Milton's lifetime. Apparently there was not enough interest.

In that pamphlet age a printed attack often, if not usually, met with a printed rebuttal. Milton was quick to defend himself against the *Modest Confutation* of his *Animadversions*, and Smectymnuus carried on a pamphlet war with Bishop Hall and Archbishop Ussher. But although Milton attacked Ussher directly in *Of Prelatical Episcopacy*, the renowned Irish primate did not reply. Milton attacked him again (along with others) in the *Reason of Church Government*—with the same result. "I held myself ready should they thenceforth make any reply," he explained in the *Defensio Secunda;* but with five vigorous assaults on Episcopacy, he drew but one real answer. True, he was "bitten at," as he complains, by some "envious" men who read his tracts, but he held it "no honour to deal against such adversaries." It would have been an honor to deal against Ussher and Hall themselves, but these worthies ignored their young antagonist. Hence, although it may well be, as Milton later affirmed, that he "brought timely succor to those ministers [Smectymnuus], who had some difficulty in maintaining their ground against the bishops' eloquence," his opponents can hardly have taken his rôle in the controversy so seriously as do some of his biographers.

It may seem surprising, on the other hand, that Milton's identification of himself with Smectymnuus did not bring him more into public notice. The Smectymnuan controversy was certainly well known: *Smectymnuus Redivivus* was published in 1654 and again in 1660; and, quite apart from such revivals, printed references to the controversy persist throughout the period and even after the Restoration. But Milton was rarely mentioned in connection with the affair, even after 1654, when he made a public statement of his participation. To be sure, the Smectymnuans themselves did not mention either Milton or his pamphlets in print. Moreover, he was late in entering the controversy proper, and did so anonymously. His *Reason of*

---

[5] See my "Milton, Rothwell, and Simmons," *The Library*, XVIII (June, 1937), 89-103.

Church Government was the only one of these early tracts to which he signed his name. The general subject of all five of his pamphlets was the subject of hundreds of other pamphlets of the day; as he said later, every man was aiming his arrow against the bishops. In his *Apology* he admitted that his name was "of small repute." Smectymnuus, Bishop Hall, and their friends eventually learned something about him, but to the ordinary pamphlet-reader in London the name "John Milton" must have conveyed little. As we have already noticed, there were enough unsold copies of the signed *Reason of Church Government* and the autobiographical *Apology* to reissue a dozen years later. William London offered all save the *Animadversions* for sale as late as 1658. The anti-prelatical tracts doubtless had their readers; there was a section of the public with a lively interest in everything published on the subject of Episcopacy; but Milton's association with Smectymnuus appears to have contributed little to his contemporary reputation.[6]

IV

Nor in broad rumour lies

The first of Milton's pamphlets to catch the attention of the public was his *Doctrine and Discipline of Divorce*. It brought him nothing but grief. It completely failed to accomplish any of its avowed purposes, and it succeeded in giving him a measure of notoriety which was extremely distasteful. Its central thesis was one easily distorted: to the conservatively orthodox, to the casual reader, and to the person who knew the tract only by hearsay, a "libertine" author seemed to be advocating "divorce at pleasure." To heresy-hunters of all sorts

---

[6] When later Milton came into more prominence, a few men, like John Hacket (an Episcopal member of the Westminster Assembly), recalled that he had written "with all Irreverence against the Fathers of our Church," but they were more interested in damning him for subsequent and more heinous crimes. See John Hacket's *Scrinia Reserata: A Memorial Offer'd to the Great Deservings of John Williams*, London, 1693, part II, pp. 161-2. This allusion, written in the 1650's although not printed until 1693, concerns the attack upon *Eikon Basilike* by "that Serpent *Milton*, that black-mouth'd *Zoilus*." There are some additional epithets, and the inevitable reference to the divorce doctrine. By way of contrast, consider Henry Stubbe's quotation, in 1659, from *Of Reformation*, by "the excellent Mr. *J. Milton*." See p. 98.

(and the woods were then full of them) Milton seemed fair game. *The Doctrine and Discipline* was the first of his writings to need more than one edition; in three years it was revised once, and altogether there were four editions.[1] In his thirty-three years of public life, Milton wrote nothing else—except only his *Defensio Prima*—which demanded so many editions and which provoked so much comment. His political and religious opponents seldom failed to use it against him, and his friends referred to it cautiously when they mentioned it at all. If I may interject a personal judgment, Milton probably never made a greater mistake in his literary life than by publishing such views, in English, at such a time. While he was actually writing it, he felt that "it might perhaps more fitly have been written in another tongue." By 1654 his ideas on divorce were unchanged, but he declared ruefully: "I could wish only that I had not written it in English, for then I would not have had vulgar readers, who are usually unconscious of their own good fortune and ridicule the misfortune of others." In the following year, writing to Leo de Aitzema, who was planning to have the tract translated into Dutch, he reiterated: "I should myself have preferred that you had it translated into Latin, for I know only too well how the common rout usually receive uncommon opinions, through my experience with these very books."

The student of Milton must understand, however, that the author of *The Doctrine and Discipline* did not wake one morning and find himself infamous. In comparison with many other pamphlets of the period, the sensational tractate on divorce appears phenomenally slow in finding a printed reaction, although it had a good sale from the start. Its author was, of course, almost totally unknown; and news of his strange ideas seems to have spread entirely by word of mouth from July 1643 until January 1644, when the first edition was exhausted and the revised edition appeared. This revised edition, according to Milton himself, was "bought up" before August 1644—and, if so, the author for some reason did nothing about reprinting it immediately. Perhaps the explanation is to be found in his *Judgement of Martin Bucer concerning Divorce*, which was out in London August 6, 1644, and which describes the recep-

---

[1] For bibliographical evidence see pp. 270-273 following.

tion given the first two editions. He is annoyed because there has been a clamor of vague and loose talk, but no definite criticism, no printed reply. He has been "lavishly traduc't," has been made the victim of "odious inferences," of "blind reproaches and surmises," but no one has taken his views seriously enough to try to refute them. He has succeeded in stirring up gossip, but not, as he had fondly hoped, controversy. Particularly is he annoyed at the clergy, who "inveigh and exclaim on what I am credibly inform'd they had not read." Furious at this "inadvised rashness," this "indiscreet kind of censure," he accuses the ministers of envy and ingratitude. Had he not "done good service to the Church by their own confession"? Those "of whose profession and supposed knowledge I had better hope" had stood a "whole year clamouring a farre off," muttering that the doctrine was lewd, scandalous, "licentious, new and dangerous"—in short, "Libertinism." The first edition was published anonymously, but the style was, he is confident, "known by most men"; the second edition was signed and addressed hopefully to Parliament; but the author finds himself living in a "wild and calumnious world," "a world of disesteem."

One must allow for some exaggeration in Milton's account of his book's reception. Not many people can have recognized the style, for obvious reasons. Those who did must have been chiefly the Smectymnuans and their party,[2] and it is hardly surprising that they muttered, at a safe distance, about the unorthodox and somewhat impractical views of their young friend. Perhaps they thanked God that they had not publicly acknowledged his recent association with them. The muttering probably seemed to Milton, hating his sudden isolation, far more widespread and violent than it actually was. The most interesting aspect of his remarks is the irritation he exhibits at having had no definite answer. And now, in July 1644, a new and more disturbing factor had arisen: there was some danger of his book being suppressed. In the postscript of his *Martin Bucer* he mentions this with undisguised concern.[3] Four months later he published his *Areopagitica*.

---

[2] Bishop Hall later (1649) attacked Milton's views at some length, but did not name their author. Is it possible that he did not recognize the writer "of those too-well-penned pages"? See pp. 79 and 102 following.

[3] At this time he may have written his undated Greek verses, "Philosophus ad regem," the tone of which fits both the situation and Milton's state of mind. The verses,

In the latter part of 1644 the Presbyterian group in Parliament actually considered the problem of censoring Milton (along with some others), but, either impressed by the authority of Martin Bucer or influenced by more lively factors, it let the matter drop. The threat of being silenced must have given Milton some anxious moments, but certain new aspects of that threat probably afforded him a grim satisfaction: he was beginning to be attacked, at long last, in print! Most of the attacks were unflattering in their brevity as well as in their tone, but they were attacks. The crusading William Prynne was aware of a late increase in dangerous pamphlets—among others, one on "divorce at pleasure"—and he thought they should be speedily suppressed. In the text of Dr. Daniel Featley's long attack on contemporary heresies, entitled *The Dippers Dipt*, the topic of divorce was mentioned but Milton was not. However, Featley seems to have heard of some new heresies before writing his dedicatory epistle, for there "a Tractate of Divorce, in which the bonds of marriage are let loose to inordinate lust," is cited along with other recent pamphlets. On August 13, the Rev. Herbert Palmer preached a sermon before Parliament, condemning, among other things, "an universall Toleration." By way of illustrating his point, he mentioned the second edition of Milton's tractate (which shamelessly bore the author's name) as a wicked book "deserving to be burnt." Later in the year his sermon was printed. Milton's reaction to these almost casual attacks was to answer them in print, each and every one.

In the signed preface to *Tetrachordon* (published on or before March 4, 1645) he took care of Palmer and Featley. In *Colasterion* (published at the same time) he took care of Prynne. He also publicly thanked Parliament for its "incorrupt refusall of what ye were incens'd to," namely, "a hard censure of that former book." He likes to think of himself as in one of "our great controversies at this day," but still complains bitterly that "sound argument and reason shall be thus put off, either by an undervaluing silence, or the maisterly

---

which were printed with the 1645 *Minor Poems*, could not have been composed during the period 1625-1634 (see Milton's letter to Gill, December 4, 1634); and they constitute an appeal against hasty and unjust punishment. As Masson suggests, "The piece has a touch in it of the peculiar spirit of Sonnet VIII., beginning 'Captain or Colonel' "; but it was not until 1644-5 that Milton found himself innocently condemned along with "some robbers."

censure of a rayling word or two in the Pulpit." He is annoyed, too, at another attack which he has heard but evidently not read: some men "confesse that wit and parts may do much to make that seem true which is not," this being "their excuses to decline the full examining of this serious point."

When finally a genuine reply to *The Doctrine and Discipline* appeared, late in 1644, Milton could scarcely conceal his vexation and disappointment. The anonymous *Answer* was palpably by an unworthy opponent; it seemed unaware of the revised, second edition of the tractate, and of the *Judgement of Martin Bucer*; it ignored many of Milton's arguments and misunderstood others.[4] Nevertheless, it had to be answered, and Milton poured his growing rancor into *Colasterion*. He was particularly annoyed because the licencer, the Rev. Joseph Caryl, had not been content merely with signing an *imprimatur* for the *Answer* but had conspicuously expressed his approval of its message; hence Caryl is castigated along with the nameless pamphleteer, and is even accused of helping to write the rebuttal. In the *Colasterion* Milton is abusive, incoherent, illogical, and very, very angry.

There were no more full-length replies to *The Doctrine and Discipline*; there were no replies at all to the other three divorce tracts; but their author was never allowed to forget any of them. Men who knew nothing of John Milton heard rumors about a sect of "Divorcers" and solemnly listed this heresy in their catalogues. Men who were quarrelling with Milton on quite different grounds continued to taunt him with his views on marriage. A royalist poetaster, Christopher Wase, coined a phrase: "the froward Miltonist." After 1645 no more editions of the tractate were called for; the times were exciting, and new sensations captured the popular interest; the doctrine of "divorce at pleasure" soon became a half-remembered, half-legendary heresy of the age. It was recalled when *Little Nonsuch* created a momentary stir in 1646; it was recalled, sometimes, when preachers warned against the dangers of toleration; but, if one may judge from its publishing history and from contemporary allusions, it was quickly forgotten by most of the reading public. After 1646, if anyone were seriously interested in the problems of divorce, there was the *Uxor*

---

[4] The *Answer* is discussed at more length on pp. 273-277.

Hebraica of the learned Selden to consider, a work of scholarship dwarfing the mere pamphlets of a John Milton or a Daniel Rogers.

To Milton, who had hoped to effect a great reform and also to engage in a great controversy, all this constituted a crushing disillusionment, though he paid tribute to Selden's "copious elucidation," in the *Defensio Secunda* and elsewhere. *The Judgement of Martin Bucer*, his trump-card, tardily but triumphantly produced, seems to have been completely ignored. Even John Wilkins, who (somewhat inaccurately) listed the other three divorce pamphlets in his *Discourse concerning the Gift of Preaching* (1647), apparently missed this one in which Milton took such pride. *Tetrachordon*, which was "wov'n close, both matter, form and style," walked the town awhile and then vanished into temporary limbo; the Greek title was too much for the stall-readers. A critic of Milton observed in 1660 that he had "always been very unfortunate" in his choice of titles, and instanced that "learned Labor of yours, which you style *Tetrachordon*." But Milton was sometimes unfortunate in his choice of subjects as well. His disappointment and anger at the reception of his pamphlets are eloquently expressed in some of his poems. He tried to bring about a reasonable reform and was immediately environed with "a barbarous noise" of gossip and recrimination: "got by casting Pearl to Hogs." The Latin ode to Rouse, dated January 23, 1647, reveals him as hating the general public, considering himself unappreciated, feeling somewhat older and more experienced. After the pleasant sensation of being a valued supporter of Smectymnuus, he found himself popularly linked with absurd fanatics. After the glowing anticipation of helping to create a finer world, he found himself regarded as a nuisance, as an irrational element in society. It was the beginning, as Grierson has clearly put it,

of Milton's isolation, his quest of other allies, his movement more and more towards what we might call "the left", the Independents, the Army and its leaders, a movement which is to lead him from one disillusion to another until at the Restoration he sits alone, allied to no church and no party, disillusioned but undiscouraged and unrepentant and ready in his poems to put on record his reading of man's character and history.

No wonder that he closed the first phase of his career as pamphlet-writer by publishing his *Poems!* No wonder that he included in the volume the tributes of his Italian friends as proof "that the esteem of judicious and famous men contributes highly to his honour." At the moment he may have supposed that his public life was at an end. However that might be, the time had passed when he was "still untainted of the people." But poetry has cleansing power; his little book, safely enshrined in the Bodleian Library at Oxford, might yet bring him the fame which his pamphlets had failed to bring. "When envy has been buried, a sane posterity will know what my deserts are."

Moseley introduced the *Poems* with a typical bookseller's puff (which, long after Moseley and Milton's death, posterity considered no exaggeration), but the truest words in his somewhat anxious commendation were these: "the slightest Pamphlet is nowadays more vendible than the Works of learnedest men." More than a dozen years later, copies of the first edition were still to be bought; a second edition was not attempted until 1673. This comparative neglect should not be laid to political events, or to the lack of an enterprising publisher, for in 1645-46 Moseley also first published the poems of Waller, Crashaw, and Suckling; and the volumes of these poets went through three or four editions before Milton's book saw a second. The latter's verse found admiring readers, of course: in addition to Lady Margaret Ley, Henry Lawes, Samuel Hartlib, and other friends and acquaintances whom one may reasonably assume, there were also William Sancroft[5] (later archbishop of Canterbury), Joshua Poole,[6] and Robert Baron. It seems impossible now to name more, but with this much smoke visible on Parnassus, one may suspect a little fire. However, of contemporary poets, Baron seems to be the only one who paid Milton the compliment of imitation, and from the easy-fingered author of *The Cyprian Academy* and *Pocula Castalia* it is a dubious compliment.[7] Manuscript collections[8] and printed

---

[5] Warton discovered among Sancroft's MSS in the Bodleian Library transcripts of the "Nativity Ode," and Milton's "version of the fifty-third [*sic*] Psalm." (1785 ed., p.v.)

[6] Milton's 1645 volume is one of sixty collections named as having been used in the compilation of *The English Parnassus*, 1657. On Poole's use of Milton's words and phrases, see R. D. Havens' *The Influence of Milton on English Poetry* (1922), p. 423, no. 3.

[7] Warton noted Baron's indebtedness, or plagiarism, in his second edition of the *Minor Poems*, 1791, pp. 403-7, and gave two dozen parallels. Todd, in an appendix to

miscellanies of the period have been ransacked by modern scholars, but little or nothing has been found to suggest that the 1645 *Poems* were known to many poetry-readers. Beyond the praises of Wotton, Lawes, and a hopeful bookseller—all included in the volume itself—no printed or manuscript allusions to the minor English poems seem to exist.

Oddly enough, the momentary notoriety of the divorce pamphlet appears to have done nothing for the sale of the verses; most of the persons who attacked Milton then, and later, were evidently unaware of the fact that he was a poet. Salmasius was one of the few exceptions, and he procured a copy of the Latin poems for the sole purpose of ridiculing them. The ignorance of Milton's other opponents, in the face of his repeated statements and hints in the various tracts, is difficult to explain. Whatever his reputation up to the time of publishing *Paradise Lost*, it was clearly not as a poet. He may have attributed this to envy, or the dullness of his hearers, but part of the truth seems to be that his verses were as untimely in their appeal as the 1646 *Poems* of Henry Vaughan, which suffered the same oblivion.

We have failed to consider two other pamphlets that belong to this early period. The little letter, *Of Education: to Master Samuel Hartlib*, was clearly intended for a limited, almost private circulation, and doubtless had it. The first edition (1644) is a single sheet of eight pages, without title-page and without imprint. Although Milton's earliest publisher, Thomas Underhill, registered the tract for him, apparently no arrangements were made for its sale; and, unfortunately, we do not even know what Hartlib and other interested persons thought of it. We do know that it was heard of outside the Hartlib circle, for as late as 1670 John Eachard announced that he was none "of those occasional Writers, that missing preferment in

---

his first edition of the *Poetical Works*, 1801, VI, 401-6, added exactly eight parallels to Warton's collection. Since then, no, one seems to have bothered much about Baron, although Havens, *op. cit.*, pp. 427-8, reviews the case. It is surely significant that, in all the annotation on Milton's contemporaries done by modern scholarship, only a few, very doubtful echoes in other contemporary poets have been found. Marvell was almost certainly acquainted with his patron's early verse, but his debt to it is negligible. The case for Henry Vaughan's indebtedness, which has been several times urged, is even less convincing.

[8] See G. B. Evans' forthcoming "Two New MS Versions of Milton's Hobson Poems." The three versions now known—Bodleian Malone MS 21 f. 69^v, Folger MS 1.21 ff. 79^v-80^r, and Huntington MS H.M. 116 pp. 100-1—all seem earlier than the 1645 volume.

the University, can presently write you their new ways of Education; or being a little tormented with an ill chosen Wife, set forth the Doctrine of Divorce to be truly Evangelical." The great significance of this slur lies in the fact that Eachard does not mention Milton's name; he expects his readers to understand the allusion. He himself was a Cambridge man (not of Milton's college), and he was aged about eight on the appearance of the two pamphlets to which he alludes.

Unlike the tractate on education, *Areopagitica* was intended to have as wide a circulation as possible, and hoped to be the daring stimulus to a reform of the press. No reform followed, and no second edition followed. Professor Haller, remembering Masson's blithe assumptions, puts the situation bleakly. He finds that the pamphlet

seems to have contributed nothing to Milton's contemporary reputation and influence. . . . *Areopagitica*, notwithstanding its author's divorce heresy, seems to have gone completely unnoticed. It appears incredible that Milton's great plea for freedom of the press should have failed of any mention whatever in the thousands of pages printed at the time and abounding in specific references to hundreds of other publications, but the present writer is constrained to report that after a protracted search he has failed to find a single one. Surely, if the appearance of *Areopagitica* were ever to be noted, it should have been by Prynne in that chapter of his *Fresh Discovery*, written according to Thomason's dating about six months after the publication of *Areopagitica*, and devoted to the recent attacks upon the printing ordinance. But Prynne assails Henry Robinson, Lilburne, and the anonymous tracts of Overton, completely ignoring Milton. In the light of these facts, we must dismiss the notion that *Areopagitica* had any appreciable effect on the situation in 1644.[9]

To agree with part of this statement is necessary, for, historically, *Areopagitica* had no immediate effect and no allusions to it in the period 1644-1650 have come to light. But we need not agree that the pamphlet "contributed nothing to Milton's contemporary reputation" or went "completely unnoticed." There was, as we have said, no second edition of it during Milton's lifetime, yet in 1673 two of Marvell's opponents cited passages from it to embarrass Milton's protégé. One of them called it

[9] William Haller, *Tracts on Liberty*, I, 134-5. Compare Masson, III, 431-4.

"fustian bumbast," but conceded that it "past for stately wit and sence" in an age of reformation. As early as 1651, when Milton was newly *celebris Populi Anglicani defensor*, Christopher Arnold wrote a long letter to a friend about English personalities and books of the day; and closing a paragraph devoted almost entirely to the writings of the learned Selden, he cited and described *Areopagitica*. It was the only one of Milton's books so noticed, and he commented: "It seems to me that this very curious author had early thought upon the present freedom."[10] Still earlier, in 1649, Gilbert Mabbott asked the House of Commons to discharge him from the office of licencer, and his arguments were the arguments of Milton even though the latter was not directly quoted.[11]

While these allusions do not tell us directly what we should like to know, their implications are important. The *Areopagitica* had no practical effect, but it was known. Its poetical appeal to reason and idealism, its failure to descend to plans and expedients, account perhaps for its being ignored by the tooth-and-nail pamphleteers of the decade. But Milton's noble plea for liberty must have been known to a statesman like Henry Lawrence, and to a foreigner like Arnold it seemed almost prophetic. The Council of State is certain to have read it before hiring their Latin Secretary, and it is not fanciful to suppose that members of the Stationers Company had also made its acquaintance. Most significant is the fact that the author was not punished. Milton was always breaking rules, in a deliberate and meaningful, if sometimes paradoxical fashion. In the years 1643-1645 he dutifully registered his *Martin Bucer* and letter *Of Education*, but rebelliously failed to register his other three divorce pamphlets and his *Areopagitica*. In many tracts he boasts that he is not being suppressed, that Parliament is allowing him the freedom of speech which he demanded. Indeed, it seems likely that some persons in authority had an eye on him from the start, regarding him as an eloquent *enfant terrible*, impractical but sincere, and not to

---

[10] Arnold's letter was not printed until 1662. See p. 108.

[11] See p. 79 following and Masson, III, 432. Mabbott's reasoning cannot be quickly dismissed as mere coincidence, for Toland, although he has both name and date wrong, has heard something of Mabbott's indebtedness to *Areopagitica*. He writes: "Such was the effect . . . that the following year *Mabol*, a Licenser, offer'd Reasons against Licensing; and, at his own request, was discharg'd that Office."

be treated like an ordinary ink-stained fanatic. It is otherwise difficult to explain, not only his own claim to being a privileged author, but also his several escapes from official censure during the autumn of 1644 when both the Commons and Lords, acting under outside pressure, ordered him investigated. It is otherwise difficult to account for the choice of the Council of State in 1649, when they sought a scholarly and articulate Secretary, and selected a law-breaker and Divorcer.

V

And think to burst out into sudden blaze

For three years, 1646-1648, John Milton published nothing. This interval Grierson has called "the crisis of Milton's life." Controversies raged; the pamphlet wars continued; burning issues were being decided—issues to which he was surely not indifferent. But the man who had printed eleven separate tracts within the space of five years, sat back now as a spectator and passively watched history being made. Eager to assist in great reforms, passionate in his love of freedom, he had anonymously helped the Presbyterians to put down the bishops, had seen those same Presbyterians label his views on other subjects (proudly printed under his own name) as heresy, had made the disillusioning discovery that "New Presbyter is but Old Priest writ Large." His accomplishments to date, then, were nothing; his fame, a vulgar scandal of the moment. He felt dirty, and betrayed. His state of mind explains the publication of the *Minor Poems* (containing only three or four pieces written after 1640); and it may also explain, in part, his three changes of address within a five year period. But Milton was not nearly so conspicuous as he probably felt himself to be. It is noteworthy, for example, that none of the scattered attacks on his divorce pamphlet mentions the fact that he was separated from his own wife—and it is incredible that the fact would not have been used against him had it been known to those who condemned his ideas. One has only to recall Milton's treatment of Salmasius, which a witty royalist dubbed "that admired piece, which you writ to confute his Wife and his Maid." Few Londoners could have heard much about Milton personally. To most people he was a name connected with a heresy, and little more. During the period of his reconciliation with Mary Powell, his subsequent domestic trials and approaching blindness, only a small company of men encouraged him with their admiration to resume his quest of influence. For three years he waited.

Early in 1649 he reappeared in the stormy arena. His immediate provocation was presbyterian opposition to the trial and execution of King Charles. Milton, now thoroughly disgusted with his former allies, sought to expose their hypocrisy, and this time he chose the right moment and a popular cause. Even so, whether advised by friends or warned by bitter experience, he approached his problem in a mood of scholarly objectivity. Charles was executed January 30; *The Tenure of Kings and Magistrates* was on the book-stalls of London two weeks later; but the pamphlet did not once mention the late King's name. Milton explained later:

I neither wrote nor advised anything concerning Charles, but simply showed in general what may lawfully be done against tyrants, adducing in confirmation the authorities of no small number of the most eminent divines, inveighing at the same time almost with a preacher's zeal against the egregious ignorance or impertinence of those men [the Presbyterians], who had promised better things. *(Defensio Secunda)*

This statement is but half true, for Milton did not altogether avoid references to a particular King recently under trial or to the immediate crisis; but he made perhaps the greatest effort of his public career to achieve detachment.

Modern critics have suspected that persons high in authority asked him to write this defence of regicide, but there is little evidence to support the conjecture except the prompt sequel.[1] One is not surprised that John Goodwin, a prominent Independent, quoted from the *Tenure* at great length in his *Obstructours of Justice* and spoke of its author with respect; or

---

[1] Grierson argues that an official request "is almost proved by its careful printing, with more than ordinary attention to Milton's peculiar spellings, by Matthew Symmons, the printer in chief, as he soon became, to the Commonwealth." *Milton & Wordsworth*, p. 61. But Milton had been training Simmons in his eccentricities as early as 1643, and abandoned him, in 1650, for Thomas Newcomb, perhaps because of his carelessness in printing *Eikonoklastes*.

that Clement Walker, a Presbyterian leader, angrily identified "J. M." as "a Libertine that thinketh his Wife a Manacle"; but how shall we explain the fact that exactly one month after the publication of *The Tenure of Kings*, the newly chosen Council of State voted to offer the post of Secretary for Foreign Tongues to John Milton?

The appointment could hardly have been inspired by Milton's latest pamphlet alone. As Goodwin makes clear, it was but one of "some pieces published of late" on the same subject; and if the scarcity of printed allusions to it means anything, it was not much noticed at the time. On the other hand, there was a second edition within twelve months. We are confronted with some sort of mystery here. The Anonymous Biographer explains:

Upon the change of Government which succeeded the King's death hee was, without any seeking of his, by the means of a private Acquaintance, who was then a member of the new Council of State, chosen Latin Secretary. In this public Station his abilities & the acuteness of his parts, which had lyen hid in his privacy, were soon taken notice of . . .

Wood tells the same story, and one would give much to know who this "private Acquaintance" was and what influence, if any, he had in the composition of the *Tenure*. Certainly the decision of the entire Council to make Milton its Secretary for Foreign Tongues was based more on an inquiry into the latter's scholarship than on appreciation for his defence, in English, of the execution of tyrants. Also significant is the fact that, although in 1644 Milton had thought himself living in "a world of disesteem," his notoriety was so slight and so limited that he was acceptable as a public official within the space of a few years. True, it was a non-Presbyterian Council that selected him, but he must have had (as he affirmed shortly later) "a fair repute among good men." In spite of the anti-climax of his quarrel with the bishops, in spite of the divorce scandal, in spite of the futility of *Areopagitica*, Milton had attracted to himself persons who not only believed in him but also possessed the power to actuate their faith.

That the Council had read the *Tenure* and was aware of Milton's gift for polemics in his native tongue, is suggested by the first uses to which it put its new Latin Secretary. He was ordered to write, in their name, some official *Observations* upon the Irish situation; and this task occupied him during April 1649. Later in the year (after a taste of routine work) he was ordered to publish, this time under his own name, a semi-official reply to the troublesome and ubiquitous *Eikon Basilike*. The King's Book so called was making matters difficult for the struggling young republic; Parliament had tried in vain to suppress it; the *Princely Pelican* and *Eikon e Piste* had appeared in its support, and *Eikon Alethine* had appeared against it. Milton had his *Eikonoklastes* ready by October of 1649, and it was "Published by Authority." Doubtless a great many copies of the first edition were printed, for Parliament wanted it to have as wide a circulation as possible.[2] Nevertheless, in the following year, there were second editions of both *Eikonoklastes* and the *Tenure*.[3]

With his attack on the King's Book, Milton found himself again participating in a real controversy. He had fought, anonymously, on the edges of the Smectymnuan affair in the early 1640's; now he was part of a battle royal, with a government behind him, and with great issues at stake. But he was not happy about it. His earlier experiences had left a scar. The preface to *Eikonoklastes* is revealing if one reads it with those earlier experiences in mind. He still desires fame, but doubts that this pamphlet will bring it; indeed, he is not "destitute of other hopes and means, better and more certaine to attaine it." The refutation of *Eikon Basilike* is "a work assign'd rather, then by me chos'n or affected." He makes it clear that he dislikes his subject—chiefly because he anticipates the response. "Considering the envy and almost infinite prejudice likely to be stirr'd up among the Common sort, against what ever can be writt'n or gainsaid to the Kings book," he approaches his task with sadness and apprehension, hoping, almost pathetically (if one dare use such a word about Milton), for his "own read-

---

[2] For whatever the evidence is worth let me point out that, although *Eikonoklastes* was later called in by proclamation and copies of it burned (1660), the first edition is today one of the most available of Milton's early tracts. Most important libraries contain it, and (despite the prices asked) it turns up in booksellers' catalogues more frequently (or so it has seemed to me) than any of the other prose pamphlets. On the other hand, the second edition, judged by the same evidence, seems quite rare.

[3] Milton presented a copy of the second edition to the Bodleian Library June 11, 1656. Following his uncle's example, Edward Phillips presented the Library, on this same date, with copies of his recently published translations of *The Illustrious Shepherdess* and *The Imperious Brother*. One can imagine that there were mixed emotions on the banks of the Isis concerning these gifts.

ers; few perhaps, but those few . . . of value and substantial worth."

He was half right. The *Eikonoklastes* did not bring him sudden fame. Royalists were indignant, but there was no immediate reply. *Mercurius Pragmaticus* cried "Shame!" and reminded its readers that this was Milton the Divorcer; but few other voices seem to have been raised in printed protest. Milton himself interpreted the silence as meaning that he had, single-handed, refuted and set aside the King.[4] After the lapse of more than a year, there was a royalist attempt to counter-attack, interesting, to the student of Milton's reputation, for the things it does *not* say. The *Eikon Aklastos* is a long, tedious, point by point refutation, full of pious horror and abuse; but its anonymous author (Joseph Jane) says nothing about Milton. His book is full of tiresome references to "this Author" and "the Libeller" (with occasional adjectives), but there are no references to "J.M.," or to the divorce tracts, or even to the *Tenure of Kings*. To Jane "this Author" was somebody "hatcht by Rebellion," a mad tool of his masters, but otherwise without personality. Jane mentions John Lilburne (p. 41), but not John Milton.

Yet in 1651, the year in which *Eikon Aklastos* was published, the name of Milton suddenly became well known to Jane and to other royalists living on the continent. Soon there were many allusions to *Eikonoklastes,* and soon many people identified it with its author. Jane even tried to have his *Eikon Aklastos* published in a French translation, although copies of the first edition in English were still unsold. The explanation of all this lies in the simple fact that *Eikonoklastes* was the pamphlet which Milton wrote just before his *Defensio Prima.*

---

[4] See the opening of his *Defensio Prima,* Columbia ed., p. 9.

VI

Comes the blind fury

Milton loved controversy not wisely but too well. His intelligence (and, on several occasions, his friends) told him that a dramatic struggle must have mighty opposites, but he could seldom resist the temptation to answer a noisy scribbler who through malice or fury descended to personalities. He guarded savagely the reputation which he hoped, someday, to own. In his *Apology* of 1642 and *Colasterion* of 1645 he had the unpleasant suspicion that he was slashing away at nonentities, but tried to persuade himself that he was really fighting Bishop Hall and the Rev. Joseph Caryl. Time and events, moreover, forced him into awkward positions. In the Smectymnuan controversy he had supported the Presbyterians; in his *Tenure of Kings* he attacked these same Presbyterians. Ordered to write *Eikonoklastes*, he declared in his opening sentences, with a frankness that infuriated royalists: "no man ever gain'd much honour by writing against a King, as not usually meeting with that force of Argument in such Courtly *Antagonists*, which to convince might add to his reputation." Milton, however insulting, was perfectly sincere; he had never met a worthy antagonist in print. Still confident of his powers, he was also aware of the fact that while he had been writing for eight years and was "known to no small number of persons," he was far from famous. Explaining his comparative obscurity to an opponent who had taunted him with it, he said:

The truth is, I had learned to be long silent, to be able to forbear writing, . . . and carried silently in my own breast what if I had chosen then, as well as now, to bring forth, I could long since have gained a name. But I was not eager for fame, who is slow of pace. . . . It was not the fame of everything that I was waiting for, but the opportunity. *(Defensio Secunda)*

Early in 1650 came his great opportunity. During 1649 the Council of State had been sorely vexed by the demoralizing influence of two extraordinary books. The new republic had conquered by the sword, but the pen was threatening its victory. Countless copies of the King's Book were circulating throughout the country, making a sentimental appeal to the vulgar populace and arousing abhorrence at the brutal execution of Charles the Martyr. A wave of royalist sympathy and an irrepressible outburst of royalist pamphlets were the result. Among the educated classes of England and the continent another sort of book was also causing trouble. The celebrated classical scholar, Claudius Salmasius, had been commissioned by Charles II to write a learned *Defensio Regia pro Carolo I*, aimed at an international audience and shrewdly calculated to discredit the upstart English government in the council chambers of Europe. Although the *Defensio Regia* had but few editions[1] in contrast with the dozens published of *Eikon Basilike*, it was regarded as an equal, if not a greater menace. Where in England could anyone be found to answer it?

Milton's commission to write came on January 8, 1650, and he gave nearly a year to the task. On the last day of December the result was registered for publication in both Latin and English; but it was probably the author, remembering certain unhappy experiences, who decided that it would appear only in Latin.[2] The subject was impressive: "a defence of the English people." The title of the book was: *Johannis Miltoni, Angli, pro Populo Anglicano Defensio*. This time he was addressing, not the stall-readers of London, but the learned men of the world. This time he was answering, not a pamphleteer, but one (to use Milton's own words) "of whose erudition the opinion of mankind could go no higher." John Milton, Englishman, proudly accepted what seemed his destiny. He recognized it fully. The recognition rings in the tone of his prose, is patent in the high words that he chooses; and in his later *Defensio Secunda* he acknowledged that at last "the fit opportunity" had been given him.

Although Milton's *Eikonoklastes* had but two editions in English, his counter *Defensio* against Salmasius was many times

---

[1] The *Defensio Regia* was first printed by Elzevir in 1649; there were at least three editions during this year. In 1650 French and Dutch translations, and at least two new reprints of the Latin versions, appeared. In 1651 Salmasius' tract and Milton's reply were bound together, with a joint title-page, at Paris. There was at least one edition of the *Defensio Regia* in 1652, and then none (so far as I have observed) until 1684. Salmasius' name first appeared in the title in a Paris edition of 1650.

[2] That an English version was intended by the authorities is proved, not only by the registration of the book, but also by the report in *Hollandse Mercurius* for February, 1651, that it was actually available.

reprinted and twice revised.³ He had written a book "Of which all Europe talks from side to side." Salmasius was not without enemies on the continent, who chortled at Milton's unexpected rebuttal and sought for personal reasons to publicize the unknown Englishman. Their efforts, however, did not appear in print but were limited to private letters and conversation. *Mercurius Politicus*, an English news-sheet, carried about a dozen references to the success of Milton's book and Salmasius' discomfiture.⁴ *Hollandse Mercurius* reported Dutch, English, and French versions of the valiant defence to be available. An English royalist, John Rowland, quickly published an anonymous answer to Milton, which was twice reprinted in the following year (1652). An anonymous *Regii Sanguinis Clamor ad Coelum Adversus Parricidas Anglicanos* (actually by Peter du Moulin) had at least three editions during 1652. One— and only one—Englishman, Sir Robert Filmer, wrote a dispassionate analysis of Milton's argument. There was an anonymous Latin attack printed in Dublin (1652). John Phillips, Milton's young nephew, wrote a *Responsio* to Rowland, which was quickly reprinted. A German scholar, royalist in sympathy and impressed by the controversy, defended a dissertation confuting the English *Defensio*. In 1653 Rowland acknowledged his earlier rebuttal, and renewed the attack. Verse lampoons against Milton appeared on the continent and found their way to London. There was much talk, at home and abroad. Bishop Bramhall, angry at finding himself supposed to be the author of Rowland's poor pamphlet, wrote a sharp letter to Milton. Salmasius himself, indignant at being handled so rudely and amazed at the hornet's nest he had stirred up, began a devastating answer which he never lived to publish.

Part of the success of Milton's book was due to stirring up feelings of surprise and curiosity in his readers: Who was this unknown Englishman who had dared to answer "an adversary

---

[3] The most complete bibliographical study is F. F. Madan's "Milton, Salmasius, and Dugard," *The Library*, IV (1923), 119-45. See also Maurice Kelley's "Note" on this article, *The Library*, XVII (1937), 466-7. Madan lists thirteen different editions.

[4] J. M. French infers "that to the sponsors of *Mercurius Politicus* Milton was a figure of real importance . . . as a literary champion, a political spell-binder, a propagandist," and he speaks, moreover, of "the intimate fashion in which he lives in the pages of *Mercurius Politicus*, where he is like a gladiator in the arena or a halfback carrying the ball for the winning touchdown." "Milton, Needham, and *Mercurius Politicus*," *SP*, XXXI₁I (1936), 252. However, only eleven brief references to the *Defensio* occur in more than fifty numbers of *Mercurius*, Jan. 1651-Jan. 1652.

of so great a name" (the phrase is Milton's own)? "Who I was, scarcely anyone in those regions had ever heard." Part was due to the cross-currents of Salmasius' career: Wonderful that this Milton should refute the haughty scholar in his own language and with his own weapons! Part, also, was due to the contents of the *Defensio* itself; for its author, trained by a divorce "controversy" that had sputtered out, and fresh from ridiculing the *Eikon Basilike*, mixed exalted sentiments with gross scurrility[5] in profuse confusion. The book was designed to stimulate gossip among the sophisticates in the capitals of Europe, and it succeeded—for a time. Gossip quickly exhausts itself; ideas have more endurance.

Today it is easy to exaggerate the effect and influence of the *Defensio Prima*. Milton himself did so; and we are more familiar with his own account than with the evidence for it. The government had encouraged his sense of importance by making him their official spokesman, and his book held the stage for the moment.[6] But its publishing history tells a significant story. Ten or eleven reprints appeared on the continent, but two editions seemed to suffice for England until Milton himself revived it in 1658.[7] All but two of these editions, at home and abroad, were confined to 1651; and after 1652 they ceased. With one unimportant exception the replies were all confined to the period before 1654. Moreover, after an initial period of insecurity the English government was commanding increased respect on its own account and was less in need of literary support. There is no evidence that Milton earned more than perfunctory thanks from officialdom for his efforts. He probably refused a financial reward if any were

---

[5] The idolatrous will not like this word, which I use deliberately. Scurrility is scurrility, even if it is conventional, even if it is seemingly justified. A republican contemporary admitted: "Some perhaps may finde fault with the personall jerks therein." See *Mercurius Politicus* for April 10-17, 1651.

[6] There were other, unofficial, replies to Salmasius. For example, in 1653 Peter English published *The Survey of Policy: or a Free Vindication of the Commonwealth of England against Salmasius*, of which David Pierson said in a preface: "hitherto it hath been hindered."

[7] These figures assume the completeness and accuracy of Madan's list. I have never seen a copy of Madan no. 8 (which he himself had not seen), but I have examined the others and have found no new editions. Madan nos. 5, 8, and 10 may possibly be unauthorized English reprints, but I doubt it. Some copies of the official revised edition (1651) were printed on special, heavy paper, doubtless for presentation; the Harvard Library has one copy on ordinary paper, and two on the heavy paper; one of the latter (14496.13.4.11 F*) was a gift from Milton to Vane, the other (14496.13.4.10 F*) a gift from Samuel Hartlib to Peter Pels, February 17, 1652.

offered, but one expects him to have been honored in some conspicuous public fashion, and one is disappointed. Foreigners came to visit him, but doubtless as much out of curiosity and diplomacy as out of respect. (Milton was so rightly certain of his own ability that he was sometimes unable to recognize flattery.) To a visitor like Christopher Arnold he seemed a celebrated and *percuriosus* writer, with odd opinions. Apart from his own nephew's words (which he may actually have dictated) and his own account, there seems to be no printed acknowledgment of the great service he had done the Commonwealth. Nevertheless, he had acquired fame.

The fame might have been increased and prolonged if only Salmasius had published a reply. It was rumored that one was in preparation, rumored even that it was in the press; and Milton must have waited anxiously, throughout 1651 and 1652 and the first half of 1653, for its appearance. With restraint he ignored the attacks upon his book by a half dozen lesser opponents; "I did not feel myself injured," he explained later. Injured or not, his health was bad and he was reserving his energy for the struggle with someone worthy his steel. His name might yet be greater than that of Salmasius if he could emerge triumphant from a conflict in which the two were really pitted against each other. Salmasius had rebuked a nation; Milton had rebuked Salmasius; now, if Salmasius addressed himself to Milton, and Milton replied successfully, the whole world would applaud. He knew himself equal to the test, though now ill and blind. The growing strength of the Commonwealth, the rapid changes in political events, assured England's champion of the rightness of his cause. Next time he would overwhelm his antagonist. For more than two years he held his peace, writing little, publishing nothing. He could serve his God and country best by standing and waiting. Then, in September of 1653, Salmasius died. Immediately it became evident that the long-awaited reply would not be published.[8]

Milton reacted swiftly. A luckless Frenchman, Alexander Morus, had helped to publish the anonymous reply to Milton

---

[8] The interpretation in this paragraph is based upon Milton's full account of his waiting, in the *Defensio Secunda*. For example: "I thought it best to wait that I might reserve my whole strength against the more powerful adversary. But with Salmasius I suspect my fighting is at an end." There is a corroborative account in the *Defensio pro Se*.

called *Regii Sanguinis Clamor* (1652), and while the author, Peter du Moulin, had kept himself well concealed, Morus was less careful. Gossip inevitably had it that the book was entirely his. Word of this had crossed the Channel long ago, and apparently a rebuttal was sanctioned if not ordered by the English authorities. Milton, however, wrote nothing, choosing to wait on Salmasius. At last, cheated by death of a decisive encounter with the great man, he turned with fury upon the lesser.

> Considering myself relieved from a certain portion of my task by his [Salmasius] sudden death, and being somewhat restored in health . . . I commenced my attack upon him [Morus], in order that I might not altogether disappoint the expectations of important persons, and amid so many calamities appear to have abandoned all regard for reputation.

Morus made desperate attempts to halt the attack, for he rightly guessed its nature and knew himself vulnerable. But Milton was determined,[9] and pressed ahead with his violent and abusive *Defensio Secunda*, having been, or so it seems, relieved of his official duties so that he might write it. The title of this second book, *Joannis Miltoni Angli pro Populo Anglicano Defensio Secunda*, is in some ways a misnomer, because the volume is more a defence of Milton himself than of the English people and Milton admonishes his government while he defends it. But the title was obviously intended to remind readers of the more important defence against Salmasius and to suggest that England's champion had once more been called in a crisis. Milton addressed the same wide audience, but he failed to attract its attention. The book, which appeared in May of 1654, seems to have had only one edition at home,[10] and was reprinted by Vlaccus for readers in Holland who might want to amuse themselves with the mud-slinging between Mil-

---

[9] Did Milton know the real author before publishing his reply? The answer to this persistent question probably lies somewhere between love and Liljegren. The problem has been most clearly resolved by those scholars who understand Milton's character, and do not presuppose either Milton or Morus to be a liar. Milton's faith in his informants was obviously shaken by the time he wrote *Defensio pro Se*, but, as he interpreted the situation, Truth would suffer by a sudden deference to Fact. In his second and third defences he obviously identifies himself with England; hence Morus is a symbol of the enemies of England whether he wrote the *Clamor* or not, and England's enemies must be defeated.

[10] Catalogues sometimes mention a duodecimo London edition, but I have seen only the octavo, pp. ii + 173 + iii.

ton and Morus. Morus himself published a frantic and furious reply, protesting at the selection of the anonymous *Clamor* from all the answers to the *Defensio,* and vowing his own innocence. The bookseller, Vlaccus, shrewdly bound the *Fides Publica* of Morus with a reprint of Milton's book, and offered the whole quarrel for sale under one cover. No one else entered the controversy, and, although some people were interested,[11] the *Defensio Secunda* made comparatively little impression. This, if he fully realized it, must have been annoying to Milton, for he had fondly addressed himself to the "so many excellent and learned men throughout the neighboring nations who are now reading my writings and are disposed to think favorably of me." At least one well-wisher, Henry Oldenburg, hinted strongly that he was wasting his time on inconsequentials, and urged him to do something else. But Milton promptly "stooped again to this contention" with a third defence, this time calling it frankly *Defensio pro Se.* Again one edition sufficed for England, and again the book was reprinted abroad for whatever readers it might find. There were no more answers. The great controversy fizzled out in a dull exhibition of name-calling. Milton himself was now aware of the anticlimax, but tried to give it a dignified interpretation:

Englishmen! . . . Against you the fury and violence of the enemy have abated. To me alone, apparently, it remains to end this war. . . . I am now forced to stoop from relating most lofty and glorious achievements, to things of no note or lustre. . . . I should have quite spared myself this trouble if my enemy had not thrown out against me accusations and lies of such a sort that I could not bear adhering as a stain and suspicion to my character. Forced, then, by necessity to undertake this task, I trust I shall be pardoned by everyone if I show, just as once I was not found wanting to the people and the Commonwealth, so now I am not wanting to myself.

Brave words, but before he published them Milton must have known that Europe no longer talked of him "from side to side." Still, he had obeyed the voice of conscience; and this knowledge, together with a secret in his heart, gave him the courage to face the future.

---

[11] See, for example, B. M. Sloane MS 649 f. 30ᵛ.

VII

Alas, what boots it . . . ?

The first *Defensio* had brought Milton a certain celebrity, more among Europeans than among his own countrymen. His conflict with Salmasius had its elements of drama; his book had circulated widely, in Holland, Sweden, Germany, and France; public burnings at Paris and Toulouse, with other efforts to suppress it, had resulted in much publicity. A Leyden correspondent of *Mercurius Politicus* observed: "This policy of the Court, in burning the Book, will make it a Martyr, whose ashes will be scattered far and wide, and the Cause and Book be more inquisitively desired." Such proved to be the case. Interest may have died after a few years, but Milton had made an impression; and in the 1650's—and thereafter—he was one Englishman whose name was recognized by many learned men on the continent. He may have been more notorious than famous, but the point is that he was known. The *Eikonoklastes* was officially translated into French, not immediately after publication, but after the *Defensio Prima* was beginning to attract attention abroad (1652). In 1655 there was a move to translate Milton's tractate on divorce into Dutch, but the project was abandoned. The *Defensio* itself was translated into Dutch for the benefit of unlearned but interested Hollanders (1651). A French version was talked of, but seems not to have materialized. A few people even sought out copies of the Latin section of the 1645 *Minor Poems*, and read them with more curiosity than appreciation.[1] Naturally all opinions of Milton were colored by political sympathies, but among educated Europeans who were following international affairs he was considered a person to be reckoned with—whatever his faults, a scholar and a man of courage.

In his own country the attitude toward Milton was almost purely a matter of political feeling. Every literate Englishman

---

[1] Nicolas Heinsius had heard of Milton's Latin poems (presumably from Elzevir) as early as May 1651, but it was not until he was visiting Holstenius in Italy, in February of 1653, that he actually saw them. He reported: "They have no pretence to elegance. He blunders frequently in prosody." Masson, *Life*, IV, 318 and 475. Elzevir offered the 1645 *Poemata* for sale in his catalogue of 1674.

interested in international politics must have been aware of Milton's existence; and while the learned among Commonwealth men doubtless praised and admired him, learned royalists decried his scholarship. To John Hacket, for example, he was "a petty School-boy Scribler, that durst graple in such a Cause with the Prince of the learned men of his Age." Hobbes, whom Milton respected but did not like, came the nearest of anyone to leaving an unbiased opinion on record; of the rival books of Salmasius and Milton a colloquist in the *Behemoth* says: "Both are very good Latin so that I know not which is best, and both are very bad reasoning, so that I know not which is worst." But this is more an epigram than a judgment.

For three years after August 1655 blind Milton played again the rôle of spectator in a rapidly moving world. Oliver Cromwell was Protector; England flourished; the former champion of the Commonwealth stuck to his routine as one of the Latin Secretaries (there were others now), composing letters of state for the signatures of other men. Thomas Young and Stephen Marshall, of Smectymnuus, both died in November of 1655; James Ussher and Joseph Hall died during the following year. Late in 1656 Milton married Katharine Woodcock, and after little more than a year of life with her devoted husband, she died. In May of 1658 there were royalist uprisings in England. Early in September Cromwell died. Milton felt the moment propitious for a revival of his first *Defensio*, and in October 1658 it appeared. It is a clear bid for remembrance, issued at a critical time when the government had changed hands and men might forget past deeds. In a postscript Milton explains that he had always had in mind a more thorough revision than the one presented.[2] He is grateful for the commendation he has received for this service to his country, at home and abroad, and is fully cognizant of what he has accomplished. He chooses this means of letting his well-wishers know that he has now in prospect "yet greater things" and is considering how he "may bear best witness—not only to my

---

[2] Masson, V, 572-3, noted his impression that "differences from the original edition through the body of the work can be but slight." Thanks to the critical notes by C. W. Keyes in the Columbia edition of the *Defensio*, it is now possible to study these differences in detail. Lines are dropped, and new lines are added; altogether there are well over 250 small verbal changes and corrections, not counting about 700 differences in spelling and punctuation. The most conspicuous additions come in chapter five and at the very end. The revision deserves some study. Compare Tillyard, *Milton* (1930), pp. 205-7.

own country, to which I have paid the highest I possessed, but even to men of whatever nation, and to the cause of Christendom above all."

Masson interprets this passage as a reference to *Paradise Lost,* then presumably in preparation; Tillyard thinks that Milton has, instead, his *De Doctrina Christiana* in mind. The words clearly promise a work which will do for religion what the *Defensio* did for government, only not for religion in England alone, but throughout the world. Milton has in mind, I submit, the subject matter of his next two pamphlets; and if his real meaning has thus far been obscured, it is probably because these tracts did not create any impression and have, for this or some other reason, been neglected by students. The new Parliament met January 27, 1659; it was called *after* Milton's hint of "yet greater things." The times were critical, and the blind secretary was forced to hurry his project. Since the great work on religion should logically be addressed *first* to the legislators of his own country, and since there seemed to be urgent need for it, he abandoned his original plan and divided the book into two parts. His words in the dedication of the first part (registered February 16) are significant:

I have prepar'd, supream Councel, against the much expected time of your sitting, this treatise; which, *though to all Christian magistrates equally belonging, and therfore to have bin written in the common language of Christendom,* natural dutie and affection hath confin'd, and dedicated *first* to my own nation; and *in a season* wherin the *timely* reading therof, to the easier accomplishment of *your great work,* may save you much labor and interruption. [my italics]

This dedication, which is proudly signed "John Milton," also makes clear the parallel with the last sentence of the revised *Defensio:* "Of civil libertie I have written heretofore by the appointment, and not without the approbation of civil power: of Christian liberty I write now." He titled the first part of his book *A Treatise of Civil Power in Ecclesiastical causes.* The second part was probably delayed, for events were moving faster than Milton could compose. It was not to Richard's Parliament, but to the restored Rump Parliament that, six months later, he addressed *Considerations touching The likeliest means to remove Hirelings out of the church.* In the second dedication he reminds the Rump that since he was once trusted with the representment and defence of your actions to all Christendom against an adversarie of no mean repute, to whom should I address *what I still publish on the same argument*, but to you . . . [my italics]

The confidence which Milton expressed in this book was unwarranted, as he was quickly to learn. England was already moving steadily toward the Restoration; the short-lived Rump was unimpressed by the arguments of its champion on the subject of religious liberty. There is no evidence that either part of Milton's book had the slightest effect, and it is certain that the two parts were never combined in a single volume or translated into "the common language of Christendom" for the benefit of other nations. The dearth of contemporary allusions to them indicates, not only that they were lost in the swirling tide of events, but also that their author's prestige among his countrymen was not what his own statements would suggest. There is something truly pathetic about Milton's references, in 1659-1660, to his great controversy with Salmasius. Can anyone read the proud words, and then note the neglect of his pre-Restoration pamphlets, without a profound sense of the irony of Milton's public career? By August of 1659 he himself was beginning to realize that he was a prophet without honor in his native land: "If I be not heard nor beleevd, the event will bear me witnes to have spoken truth: and I in the mean while have borne my witnes not out of season to the church and to my countrey." "Borne my witnes . . . to the church"! Note the words. He had fulfilled the promise of the postscript to the *Defensio*.

Poetry stirred in the heart of Milton, and the knowledge of it was always a source of strength; but the thought that he was an influential statesman filled his mind, and this illusion was a source of weakness. By October of 1659 the Rump was dissolved, and Milton, sensing the implication of events, had a feeling of disaster and uselessness. In "A Letter to a Friend," written October 20 but unpublished, he resigned himself to the wisdom of those in authority, "not finding that either God, or the Publick requir'd more of me, than my Prayers for them that govern." Disillusionment had come to the old warrior;

but his fighting spirit was not altogether extinguished: he was still ready "in the midst of my Unfitnes, to what ever may be requir'd of me, as a publick Duty." Sadly he waited for the inner voice.

The sequel is stirring, although it would be hard to parallel as an example of apparent futility. The man who had checked Salmasius, the man who had caught the attention of learned Europe, suddenly commanded the waves to be still—and the scornful laughter of Englishmen rang about his ears. Milton proposed a *Ready and Easy Way to Establish a Free Commonwealth*, and Roger L'Estrange mocked: "I could only wish his Excellency [General Monk] had been a little civiller to Mr. Milton; for, just as he had finished his Modell of a Common-Wealth, ... in come the Secluded Members, and spoyle his Project." Someone else jeered that the Rump's "Goos-quill Champion" had "run himself into the bryers" and will soon "travel to Tyburn in a Cart." Send him to Bridewell or to Utopia, suggested another. Milton, by thus calling attention to himself on the eve of the Restoration, was inviting a terrible punishment. Ironically unaware that he was emerging from something like obscurity,[3] he struggled for influence and became the target, not only of rebuttal, but of suspicion and abuse. The divorce tract and *Eikonoklastes* were recalled. He was accused of writing other, anonymous pamphlets against the King. Linked with various political visionaries, he was ridiculed in a pasquinade called *The Censure of the Rota*.[4]

Milton may have realized—and if so, he was right—that this was a war of public opinion and the royalist pamphleteers were helping to win it. Thurloe later told Clarendon, in all *post facto* seriousness, that the books of the Cavaliers had brought about the Restoration. Many of these books were using a weapon which Milton had used effectively in the past, but which now, perhaps in his urgent haste, he neglected. The weapon was mockery, and his failure to use it was fatal, for he himself—perhaps of all men—was most vulnerable. His lofty claims,

---

[3] A new crop of pamphleteers had arisen, and they were concerned more with immediate problems than with past offences. William Colline, for example, although he knew Harrington, did not recognize the initials with which the *Ready and Easy Way* was signed. Others, of course, remembered Milton, but might have been disposed to neglect him if he had kept silent.

[4] This pamphlet is discussed on pp. 280-283.

his solemn advocacy of sweeping reform, his idealism and optimism in the face of the approaching storm—these things were easily turned to ridicule, and he was overwhelmed with a terrible laughter. Taunts and obscene mirth poured from the jaws of asses, and Samson missed his opportunity.

Near the end, Milton knew that a long "Lent of servitude" was approaching, but used the "little shroving-time" to speak freely and to take his leave of liberty in his own way. An impulsive but unimportant clergyman, Matthew Griffith, preached a violently royalist sermon that disturbed even royalist sympathizers; and Milton, apparently not alive to all the political implications, answered it as though it were an important declaration. "Sedition!" cried L'Estrange, anticipating the mood of a new Parliament about to meet. Let us have *No Blinde Guides!*[5] But the blind guide, calm in the sense of God's protection and his own inexorable destiny, dictated and published a revised edition of *The Ready and Easy Way*. Men were still laughing at the incredible title when the Commonwealth came abruptly to an end.

VIII

That last infirmity of noble mind

Milton firmly believed that he had saved his country in 1651, but it is exceedingly doubtful that many Englishmen of his own day, or many historians of ours, could agree with him. Such a view of the matter does not discredit the author's honesty or deny his continental celebrity; it only reminds us that Milton had an exaggerated notion of his own achievement. He had met and crippled the foremost ship of an invincible Armada, but in his natural exultation he ignored the lesser battles and the destruction wrought by wind and wave. Parliament and the people, without meaning to seem ungrateful, evidently took a larger view of the conflict. Hence, although some of his opponents treated him (for good controversial reasons) as a literary leader of the rebellion, the Council of

---

[5] L'Estrange's pamphlet is discussed on pp. 284-289.

State thanked him formally for his services and then proceeded to issue routine orders as before. He was, indirectly, "Oliver's Secretary," but there is no sign that Cromwell ever regarded him as more than a useful scribbler in business which required Latin. We know that Milton several times attempted to advise the Protector, and we know that none of his advice was taken. We know also that he offered political counsel to General Monk, and that Monk ignored him. In 1659 Milton reminded Parliament of its former confidence in him, and Parliament took no notice. In 1660 he and a few others tried to rally the forces of the republic, and the Restoration swept over them.

After the King's return, therefore, the blind rebel was conspicuous enough to be imprisoned and to have two of his books suppressed by proclamation, but inconspicuous enough to escape additional punishment. Had it not been for his inflated notion of his own prestige and influence, he might have escaped altogether. On the other hand, had the new authorities agreed with his own opinion of his reputation, he would have been among the first to be hanged. Little wonder, as Richardson relates, that "he was in Perpetual Terror of being Assassinated . . . So Dejected he would lie Awake whole Nights." Toland reports some people to have been of the opinion that Milton "was more oblig'd to" Charles II's forgetfulness "than to his Clemency," but the King probably had nothing to do with the outcome. The picture is a confused one which has long troubled biographers, and it may never be seen whole; but the important facts, from one student's point of view, are these:

Milton's possible judges *among royalists living abroad* had once noted for punishment his *Eikonoklastes* and his *Defensio* against Salmasius. They knew little and cared less about his Smectymnuus pamphlets and his views on divorce. His defence of regicide, *The Tenure of Kings*, apparently escaped their notice.[1] His quarrel with Morus was more amusing than serious. His tracts of 1659-1660 they may never have seen. And after eight long years, even the *Eikonoklastes* and *Defensio* were, if not forgotten, at least not quite so important as they had once seemed; and the author, already punished by blind-

---
[1] Milton mentioned *The Tenure* in his own *Defensio Secunda*, under the impression that the author of the *Clamor* had attacked it. Du Moulin, however, may have been talking about something else in the passage involved. There are surprisingly few printed allusions to the *Tenure* during the entire period 1649-1674.

ness for his sins, was not marked out for revenge as were the actual regicides.

The attitude of Milton's possible judges *who had remained in England* was somewhat different. The period before the Restoration had seen a struggle of pamphlets, and the blind man had suddenly come to the fore, uttering preposterous claims and making seditious proposals. To these people—whose point of view is represented by a writer like L'Estrange—Milton was a half ridiculous, half dangerous figure, who certainly deserved some sort of punishment. Perhaps not death, but punishment nevertheless. The influence of this group was doubtless counter-balanced by Milton's powerful friends, among them, probably, Davenant, Marvell, Sir Thomas Clarges, Arthur Annesley, and Secretary Morrice. Hence, the name of the old rebel might never have come under consideration at all had not his reputation suddenly and ironically received a fresh impetus. *The Dignity of Kingship Asserted*, a long and impressive reply to the *Ready and Easy Way*, probably written by Gilbert Sheldon, was awaiting the exiled royalists on their return to London. Early in June L'Estrange reissued the unsold copies of his *No Blinde Guides* as part of a book containing other damaging references to Milton. A few more pamphleteers and rimesters helped to make a chorus, and during June it was necessary for Milton to go into hiding. A proclamation dated August 13 announced that all efforts to arrest him had failed. This was the season, of course, for his friends to do everything in their power for him. On August 29 the Act of Oblivion passed, and the blind man was presumably safe. But during the next month a hand was lifted from the grave to point an accusing finger at those who had shown such clemency. In Europe and in England the *Responsio ad Johannem Miltonum* of Salmasius was published posthumously. This was the long-delayed rebuttal which the English champion had awaited so eagerly during 1652 and 1653. Alas, he could not answer it now, and he must have listened anxiously for popular reaction to it through the month of October, when the execution of the regicides began and feeling ran high. Parliament reassembled on November 6, but apparently did nothing about Milton. (Is it possible that most of the worthy members could not cope with Salmasius' heavy Latin?) At some unknown time before the middle of December, Milton was arrested and imprisoned, but released on the fifteenth. His enemies had either decided to spare him or had felt that he was not worth bothering with.

After the crowded year of the Restoration, Milton deliberately sought oblivion.[2] He was aided, of course, by the swift changes which the new regime effected, and by the blessed alchemy of time. He seems not to have been without good friends in his solitude, and we are told that curious foreigners continued to seek him out on visits to London. Certainly he was not altogether forgotten in Europe, where the names of only a few celebrated Englishmen had penetrated and these few were likely to be remembered. His own countrymen, however, absorbed in the exciting affairs of a new era, alluded but rarely to the former opponent of royalty. A few over-zealous but unimportant persons expressed themselves as dissatisfied with his continued liberty. One James Heath, in his *Brief Chronicle*, noted parenthetically that "one Milton, since stricken with blindness," had been defeated by the pen of Salmasius! *Sic transit gloria*.

Although there are no printed allusions to prove the fact, it is highly probable that Milton, living more or less in seclusion, became an almost legendary figure to those Englishmen who remembered but did not know him. Men who do sensational things, and then drop completely out of sight, frequently become strange monsters to some, saints to others. Young Samuel Parker, in the days before he turned reactionary, "frequented *J.M.* incessantly and haunted his house day by day." Young Thomas Ellwood was thrilled to sit at the feet of the man whose scholarship had stood up to Salmasius. There were others, no doubt, who thus indulged in hero-worship, and there were persons who wondered what had become of the fiend who had dared to blaspheme against *Eikon Basilike*. At the time of the Great Plague it was rumored on the continent that Milton was among the dead.

Meanwhile, Milton had tried to put politics out of his

---

[2] He did little which might bring him into contact with the authorities. Toland, however, states that "in the latter part of his Life, he was not a profest Member of any particular Sect among Christians, he frequented none of their Assemblies." The poet may be the unidentified Milton who, September 24, 1664, had to explain his non-attendance at church (*CSPD*, 1664-5). Milton was also in arrears in his taxes, September 1665.

mind and had resumed the composition of *Paradise Lost*. Writing brought relief, but it was no anodyne. Into the throbbing words the poet poured both art and heart—to the everlasting confusion of romantic critics. He wrote eloquently of rebellion and frustration because he had lived them. He wrote serenely of the justice of God because he still believed in it. He was, in proof, through an all-wise providence, fulfilling a promise. As early as 1641, interrupting his mockery of Bishop Hall for a devout prayer, he had covenanted with his Maker:

He that now for haste snatches up a plain ungarnished present as a thank-offering to Thee, which could not be deferred in regard of Thy so many late deliverances wrought for us one upon another, may then perhaps take up a harp and sing Thee an elaborate song to generations.

In 1641 he had also told his fellow men: "It might be worth your listening, readers, as I may one day hope to have ye in a still time, when there shall be no chiding." The "still time" had come perforce, but it had come. He had known that it would.

The epic, written in blank verse and offered to a public then chuckling at the escapades of rakes and applauding the plays of Davenant and Dryden, appeared in 1667, one year after the Great Fire of London. In 1667 Wither, Cowley, and Jeremy Taylor died. In 1667 Swift and Arbuthnot were born. The stories about the early praise given *Paradise Lost* by Denham, Dryden, and the Earl of Dorset may be true, or they may be legend; but such a poem, appearing at such a time, probably created no sensation. There is, to be sure, some evidence that the first edition of about 1300 copies was exhausted in under two years, but if so, there is also the fact that no second edition was called for until five additional years had passed. Of course the book found its readers, some of them enthusiastic, some puzzled. The lack of rime bothered the first purchasers, and Milton added a note explaining his choice of blank verse. Thus he arose, for the third time in his life, from a period of silence and retirement into the critical eye of the English public. Again he appeared conscious of a great mission; only now he reminded no one of services past, now he demanded no radical reform. An artist had emerged from the chrysalis of controversy.

Although *Paradise Lost* was licensed according to law and formally registered, its publisher, Samuel Simmons, was probably relieved to learn that a volume bearing the name of Milton could really be offered for sale with impunity.[3] In 1669 he undertook to sell an innocuous Latin Grammar by his notorious author. In the next two years the *History of Britain, Paradise Regained* and *Samson Agonistes* appeared. In 1672 a publisher of the *History*, Spencer Hickman, offered the public Milton's textbook Art of Logic, a little volume with a title which must have evoked mingled emotions in those who recalled the proudest moment of its author's life: *Joannis Miltoni Angli, Artis Logicae*. In 1673 there seemed to be justification for bringing out a new edition of the *Minor Poems* (first printed in 1645), and Milton took this opportunity to reprint his letter *Of Education*.[4] In 1674 there was a second, revised edition of *Paradise Lost*. By this time publishers were evidently believing that anything from the pen of Milton would have readers, and one enterprising bookseller, having failed to obtain permission to print the Latin letters of state composed under the Commonwealth, went so far as to print Milton's personal letters and undergraduate exercises. This tiny book, one of the very last to appear in its author's lifetime, also had a title

---

[3] This is an inference from several facts. The book was formally registered as by "J.M." (initials only). Simmons omitted his own name or initials from the imprints of the first three title-pages (1667-8), but announced "Printed by *S. Simmons*" in all thereafter. Moreover, the first three title-pages declare prominently that the book was "Licensed and Entred according to Order," but this notice is dropped when Simmons decides to put his name in the imprint. One of the early title-pages contains Milton's initials instead of his name. Copies of the first edition were sold by six different booksellers, a rather large number for a book of poetry, especially since Simmons himself was a bookseller as well as a printer. He had been in business only about a year. When Matthew Simmons (Milton's publisher 1643-50) died in 1654, the printing establishment next door to the Golden Lion in Aldersgate Street was kept up by his widow, Mary Simmons, whose name or initials are found in books from 1655 until 1670 or later (a book printed *for* her was advertised in the Hilary Term Catalogue for 1672). Samuel Simmons (probably a son) was taken into the business in 1666, when he and Mary Simmons printed jointly the last part of Joseph Caryl's *Exposition* on the Book of Job. Samuel started printing independently during this same year, and since the agreement between him and Milton was dated April 27, 1667, the poet must have been one of his first customers. In the circumstances it seems more than likely that Mary Simmons was consulted about the publishing of *Paradise Lost*. Masson, VI, 509, is inaccurate in saying that Simmons was "in a far inferior way of business" compared with Herringman, for in the Hearth Tax Roll for 1666 the Simmons establishment is returned as having thirteen hearths, a greater number than that for any other printer on the roll. Said Jacob Tonson: "he was lookt upon as an able & substantial printer & I think his father a printer before him." Samuel Simmons was still in business late in 1677.

[4] Thomas Dring, the publisher, changed his address at some time between the Easter and Michaelmas Terms of 1673; hence the earlier issue of the *Minor Poems* contains the address "at the White Lion" in the imprint, and the later issue was to be sold "at the Blue Anchor." Both shops were on Fleet Street. Dring's father had published a good many books together with Humphrey Moseley, 1652-60.

that may have aroused memories: *Joannis Miltonii Angli, Epistolarum Familiarium Liber Unus.*

Milton's revival of the form of identifying himself which he had used in the three Defences probably had its significance in his state of mind. Having published several books without incurring the wrath of the authorities, having dutifully registered some and undutifully failed to register others, he was beginning to feel again the old urge to improve his native land. Not satisfied with having achieved "Things unattempted yet in prose or rhyme," with two mighty epics and a great dramatic poem behind him, the unreconstructed rebel was yearning once more for the excitement of controversy, the plaudits of men across the Channel. The last infirmity of noble mind was an insatiable longing for immediate fame through political reform.

In 1673, for example, there appeared a slim, badly printed tract entitled *Of True Religion.* It was unlicensed; it had in the imprint no indication of bookseller or printer; it was signed merely "J.M." There is nothing treasonable in its contents; but to anyone who read it,[5] it may have suggested that an aged fighter was back on the firing line, and that his publisher was frightened at what might happen next. Nothing happened. Taking courage, the bookseller, Thomas Sawbridge, ventured to advertise the tract in the Easter Term *Catalogue of Books,* giving the author's full name. Somewhat later another bookseller, Brabazon Aylmer, had Milton translate into English the *Declaration* of the election of John Sobieski as King of Poland. This was a noble document, with sentiments about popular rights and the true nature of kingship, and doubtless the translator derived real satisfaction from making it available to his countrymen. It was his last piece of writing and, like his first, anonymous.

Edward Phillips, telling about the closing years of his uncle's life, has a story that shows us another old impulse reviving in the battle-scarred veteran:

He had, as I remember, prepared for the press an answer to some little scribing Quack in *London,* who had written a Scurrilous Libel against him; but whether by the disswasion of Friends, as thinking him a

---

[5] An anonymous letter of April (?) 1675 contains the following allusion: "J. Milton has said more for it in two elegant sheets of true religion, heresy and schism than all the pr[elates] can refute in 7 years . . . " *CSPD,* 1675-6, p. 89.

Fellow not worth his notice, or for what other cause I know not, this Answer was never publisht.

One would give much to see this Answer (which may yet come to light); and one would like to know more about the "scribing Quack" who, like the mud-slinging critics of *Animadversions, The Doctrine and Discipline,* and *Defensio Prima,* had provoked Milton into making a reply. This person was almost certainly the anonymous author of *The Transproser Rehears'd,* 1673, who, in attacking Andrew Marvell, devotes a conspicuous amount of space to Marvell's patron and friend. The remarks on Milton are truly "Scurrilous," the more so because the writer, young Richard Leigh, has an extraordinary acquaintance with Milton's literary output, from the Smectymnuus and divorce controversies to *Paradise Lost* and the Latin Grammar. Here we have unexpected corroboration of a truth which Milton's booksellers were evidently discovering: that *all* the writings of their author were becoming of interest to readers. The references to Milton in the whole Marvell-Parker controversy did nothing to help the poet's reputation, and must have proved very embarrassing to Marvell himself; but they reveal several persons who had read Milton and had a lively recollection of what they had read.

One notes with disappointment, but hardly surprise, the dearth of printed allusions to *Paradise Lost* in the period 1667-1674. Except for Edward Phillips' praise in 1669, the poisoned criticism in *The Transproser Rehears'd,* and the commendatory verses of Marvell and Barrow, nothing has yet been found. But the facts that a second edition appeared in 1674 and that Dryden asked permission to "tag" Milton's blank verse indicate that the epic gained steadily in popularity. Critics are in the habit of saying that *Paradise Lost* "was most unfortunate in the time of its appearance," and, properly qualified, the statement is true. Nevertheless, it is interesting to speculate on what would have been the fate of the poem if it had been published in the period 1640-1660, when men had their minds, not on heroic couplets, but on heroic deeds. True, a handful of minor poets seemed to thrive in that clamorous atmosphere, but an epic on the Creation would probably have been lost in Babel. Let us not forget that Milton *did* publish verse in 1645, but it was during the Restoration that he first, *as a poet,* found an audience. The literary taste of his readers was not Milton's literary taste, but that is comparatively unimportant; the important fact is that literary taste had become again a reality, a subject to be argued, a force to be felt. Some Restoration readers found in Milton the charm of contrast—as eighteenth century readers were later to find. But others heard in him the authentic voice, the unmistakable word of genius. Within a year after his uncle's death Edward Phillips declared it to be "the opinion of many both Learned and Judicious persons" that Milton was "the exactest of Heroic Poets . . . either of the Ancients or Moderns, either of our own or whatever Nation else."

Milton's reputation after 1674 is not the concern of this essay, but it is impossible to understand the last phases of his contemporary fame without a glance at the sequel. William Winstanley in 1687 growled: "his fame is gone out like a candle in a snuff and his memory will always stink"; but Winstanley included him, nevertheless, among his one hundred and forty-six *Most Famous English Poets,* and thus gave the lie to his own prejudice. In the following year, that of the Revolution, an edition of *Paradise Lost* was published by popular subscription, more than five hundred distinguished Englishmen lending their names to the printed list—among them Milton's old enemy, Roger L'Estrange. I have a copy of the *History of Britain,* 1670, on the title-page of which a contemporary owner expressed the situation nicely: "A good Author though an ill subject to his Prince."

Although Milton was far from the important figure during the Commonwealth that Masson and other biographers have asked us to imagine, although his influence in the moulding of events, during his lifetime, was negligible, it is none the less true that political sympathy and antipathy were to color for more than a hundred years the biography and criticism devoted to him. How shall we account for this paradox? Furthermore, how shall we explain the fact that, before the close of the century, the legend of Milton the Statesman was already finding believers, whose names, in our own day, are legion?

Between the year in which *Paradise Lost* was published and the year of its author's death, two distinct (although not mutually exclusive) attitudes toward Milton were born which were to spread during the remainder of the century, and result in the deception of posterity. One attitude was to see Milton the Statesman through the "optic glass" of his art; thus a growing audience, willing captives to the poet, looked also into the prose and began to accept his achievements in controversy at his own proud evaluation. The other attitude was to see Milton the Statesman through the misty eyes of political nostalgia. In 1667 Samuel Pepys found it strange that everybody was thinking about Cromwell and singing his praises; but it was not strange, and some of these people yearning for "the good old days" seized upon Milton, the most articulate man of his generation, as a symbol of all that England had lost and might have again. Whig interests found him surprisingly topical; disgruntled republicans read him with satisfaction. His eloquent sentences expressed a lost cause that was still alive in the hearts of many of his countrymen.

One can trace the tangible results of these two attitudes in the twenty-five years that followed Milton's death. The attitudes come together at various points, most conspicuously with the 1688 edition of *Paradise Lost*. Although Aylmer had vainly tried as early as 1674 to publish the State Letters, two unauthorized editions did appear in 1676; and a reprint of these followed in 1690. In 1682 and again in 1694 these letters were translated into English for the benefit of readers whom Milton had despised. *Eikonoklastes* was reprinted in 1690; and in 1692 there was an English translation of the great *Defensio* against Salmasius (reissued in 1695). A second edition of the *History of Britain* appeared in 1677 (reissued in 1678 and 1695.[6] As a fitting climax to all this interest, the last decade of the century saw two separate editions of the Complete Prose Works (1697 and 1698). Meanwhile, *Paradise Lost*, through sheer artistic prestige, was adding to Milton's political stature. We have already noted his reputation on the continent, and we remember Wood's rather grudging admission that "he was more admired abroad, and by Foreigners, than at home"; it does not surprise us, therefore, to find two early attempts to translate the epic into German, and at least one attempt to

---

[6] Milton's *History* was taken very seriously by some persons in the seventeenth century, and was used for subsequent histories. My own copy is heavily annotated on both front and back fly-leaves in what appears to be a contemporary hand. B. M. Sloane MS 1030 f. 90^v is an early extract in French; Sloane MS 1506 contains notes taken from it.

translate it into French.[7] A German translation was actually published in 1682.[7] In 1690 and in 1691 two admirers tried their hands at putting it into Latin.[8] While the original was being reprinted (1674, 1678, 1688, 1691), imitations and adaptations were slowly appearing.[9] In 1695, fourteen years before Rowe published his edition of Shakespeare, three hundred and twenty-one closely printed folio pages of annotation on *Paradise Lost* were offered the public as a desirable supplement to an edition of the *Poetical Works*. This monumental tribute, the most voluminous notes on any English poet produced before modern times, indicates that Milton was regarded as a "classic" within twenty years after his death.

In the seventeenth century, biography was beginning to flourish as an art, but this fact alone does not begin to explain five separate lives of one man written or published before 1700. Aubrey diligently collected notes for Wood, who, although he hated Milton's politics, respected his reputation as a writer enough to include him—a Cambridge graduate—in a history of Oxford worthies.[10] An anonymous biographer paid a similar tribute to Milton's learning and character. Edward Phillips,

---

[7] A fragment of the French translation survives in B. M. Sloane MS 3324 ff. 273-288. Aubrey notes that "Theodore Haak R.S.S. hath translated halfe his Paradise lost into High Dutch in such blank verse, wch is very well liked of by Germanus Fabricius Professor at Heidelberg." This, evidently, was before 1681; and Ernst Gottlieb vom Berge's translation was printed at Zerbst in 1682.

[8] The Latin version of Book I, 1691, was by T. Power. In the previous year William Hogg had published a Latin version, not only of *Paradise Lost* complete, but of *Paradise Regained* and *Samson Agonistes* as well. He later published Latin versions of "Lycidas" (1694) and *Comus* (1698).

[9] Havens, Good, and others have examined and disproved the legend of the early neglect of *Paradise Lost*. John Dennis and Sir Richard Blackmore were largely responsible for the notion that Addison's *Essay* marked the turning point in Milton's fame, a notion encouraged by eighteenth century lack of sympathy with Restoration politics and morality. How *could* Milton have been appreciated in such an age? Yet adaptation of *Paradise Lost* begins with Dryden, and acknowledged imitation of Milton's blank verse begins with the Earl of Roscommon's *Essay on Translated Verse*, 1685. See Havens' *Influence of Milton* for a very full list of early imitations. I own a scarce volume of occasional verse, dated 1699, by an unknown author who wrote smart, polished heroic couplets, some of them obscene—but who sincerely acknowledges the greatness of Milton in a printed poem and in an autograph letter on a fly-leaf of the book. In John Hopkins' preface to his imitation of two books of *Paradise Lost* in rime (1699), there is an interesting confession: he began the paraphrase, he says, for the ladies, who found Milton too difficult, but "when I did it, I did not so well perceive the majesty and noble air of Mr. Milton's style as now I do; and were it not already done, I must confess I never should attempt it."

[10] Wood explains that Milton was incorporated Master of Arts at Oxford in 1635. This information came, not from the University Register, but from Aubrey, who said that he heard it from Milton himself. In any case, Wood could easily have omitted Milton from the *Fasti Oxonienses* if he had wished.

MILTON'S CONTEMPORARY REPUTATION

in a life prefixed to his translation of the Latin Letters of State (1694), emphasized his uncle's fame both as a writer and as a statesman. John Toland's biography, first printed with the 1698 edition of the prose, combined the three dominant attitudes of the age toward Milton: to Toland his subject was a man famed for his learning, for his writings on liberty, and for his poetry.[11] This biography was sufficiently in demand to be reprinted separately in 1699.

Thus the irony of fame. Dead Milton, who had vainly hoped to be a leader of thought in his own age, rose from the grave to stir the minds and hearts of his countrymen. The brave, futile words, the challenging ideas that his own contemporaries had ignored, walked the earth again and helped to create a world which the blind dreamer imagined but never saw. In 1666 he had written sadly to a friend: "the virtue which you call statesmanship . . . after captivating me with her fair-sounding name, has almost left me without a country." But men and women of after-days, dazzled by majestic verse, deceived by nostalgic admiration, and accepting the poet's own estimate of his contemporary prestige, fancied that he had been an important and influential figure in his time. This was not the fact, but faith in the living word gave it a measure of truth.

IX

As he pronounces lastly

In 1642 Milton declared that, while writing prose, he had the use, "as I may account it, but of my left hand." His statement has become so well known that it has obscured the truth, for he quickly learned to forge "this manner of writing" into a two-handed engine. Not enough study has been given his prose style, as style. The most pointed and significant criticism is to be found in *The Censure of the Rota* (1660), which students, regarding as ephemeral satire, have more or less ignored. The analysis there is, of course, limited, but it can help us to

---

[11] See the opening sentence of Toland's *Life*, where the three attitudes are nicely distinguished and balanced.

understand the contemporary reputation of Milton's pamphlets. For example, although Milton often addressed himself to "the elegant and learned reader" and often expressed his disdain of the "common sort," his opponents sometimes considered him a rabble-rouser. This wide divergence in point of view must be explained, and the explanation is to be found in the quality of Milton's prose. He wrote prose like a poet. In saying this I do not mean merely that his prose is often rhythmical and is frequently adorned with figures of speech, although both of these things are true. I mean also that he writes with a constant awareness of the emotional values of words, that he appeals to the idealism of his readers more often than he appeals to logic, that he translates practical problems of the moment into universals, that he dresses reason in robes of eloquence, that the mood of prophecy is often upon him. He speaks, in an early pamphlet, of "the cool element of prose," but his own style is sensuous and passionate. His tone is that of a learned and idealistic philosopher, something far removed from the persuasive writing of a pamphleteer. Milton preferred Queen Truth to King Fact. He grappled with facts when it seemed to him necessary; time and again he wrangled like a politician, chopped logic like a Schoolman, clubbed quotations with men whose learning and belief lay in marginal stuffings; but always, when the opportunity afforded, he lifted the debate out of the realm of practical details into the exalted air of ultimate reality as he conceived it. *Areopagitica* is deliberately cast in the form of an oration, but most of his pamphlets, though lacking the form, have the spirit of oratory rather than debate.

Milton wrote prose like a poet because, of course, he was a poet born. For those who regard such statements as romantic nonsense, there are other explanations, such as the psychological fact that, like most young persons, in his speech and thought he had imitated the speech and thought of his closest companions. I do not mean Diodati or Gill, his university friends or his London neighbors; I mean the poets and orators and historians of antiquity. The first half of Milton's life was spent largely in books. Physically he had lived in London and Cambridge and Horton, but his soul had been like a star, dwelling apart, holding high converse with the best minds of the past. He was at home with master spirits; painstakingly he learned to talk their language, to understand their ideas. Books did not think for him, as they did for Burton (and, later, for Lamb); he was always too strongly individualistic and too confident of his own powers. Without conceit, with a calm realization of his destiny, he taught himself to live on terms of familiar equality with the best that had been said and thought. To call such a purposeful reader a "bookworm" would be abysmal folly. To expect such a man to talk the low language of politicians and pamphleteers would be folly almost as abysmal. One of Milton's favorite quotations was from *Second Corinthians*: "My strength is made perfect in weakness."[1] Truly, his greatest limitation is also his everlasting glory as a writer: he was comparatively ignorant of the sloth and pettiness of the rest of us. Such ignorance constitutes a challenge.

To most of his contemporaries, however, Milton seemed impractical because he was concerned with eternal verities; he seemed a foolish dreamer because he looked beyond the fact to the justifying principle; he seemed a rabble-rouser because his words took on beauty and magic as the thought lifted them. His contemporaries were, of course, both right and wrong, as contemporaries usually are. Milton was, indeed, a visionary in his own age, but time can turn impracticality into prophecy, and time has abundantly vindicated the man who fought for human liberty without ever stating prosaically what he meant.

The author of *The Censure of the Rota*, for example, is shrewd and accurate, if we make some allowance for polemical exaggeration. His analysis of Milton's "admirable eloquence" is quite correct from a narrow point of view. "No Conjurer's Devill is more concerned in a spell, then you are in a meer word, but never regard the things which it serves to expresse." "You fight always with the flat of your hand like a Retorician, and never Contract the Logicall fist." "You trade altogether in universals the Region of Deceits and falacie, but never come so near particulars as to let us know which among diuerse things of the same kind you would be at." "All your politiques reach but the outside and circumstances of things and never touch at realities." "All your Politiques are derived from the works of Declaimers." The anonymous critic makes an even more

---

[1] *II Cor.* XII. 9. Milton twice used it for entries in autograph albums (1651 and 1656), and he alluded to it in the *Defensio Secunda*.

damaging assertion: "your stiffe formall Eloquence . . . you arme . . . with anything that lies in your way, right, or wrong, not onely begging, but stealing questions, and taking everything for granted, that will not serve your turn." Milton was not dishonest, but it is true, nevertheless, that his fervor or his indignation did, at times, thus blind him. Observe, too, that this contemporary criticism of Milton's style would serve for today if Milton had not succeeded in expressing, to a large extent, the slowly awakening ideals of his race. If his vision had proved narrow and personal, if his impracticality had not given courage to the dreams of later men, we should now agree that "it is all windy foppery from the beginning to the end, written to the eleuation of that Rabble and meant to cheat the Ignorant." A Milton is rightly a fanatic and a crack-pot until his voice awakes an echo—until humanity acknowledges him to be a Milton. Moreover, the man who keeps his eyes steadily upon his goal instead of upon the road to it will frequently stumble, and Milton frequently stumbled. Let us not blink the fact, and let us not condemn too airily his fellow travellers who laughed at his awkwardness and cried, "No blind guides!" Their eyes, through no faults of their own, were not so keen as his, and the goal toward which he urged them might well have been a mirage. Ordinary men must judge by ordinary lights, and so the author of *The Censure of the Rota* was, within his limitations, justified in wondering why Milton "did not give over writing, since" he had "always done it to little or no purpose."

There is another aspect of the problem which neither space nor knowledge permits me to treat adequately here. Milton was as much an individualist and a rebel in the techniques of prose style as he was in everything else. The unaccustomed does not inspire immediate confidence, and contemporary readers, used to the rough and practical sentences of Prynne and Needham, Walwyn and Overton, must have found Milton's rhetorical experiments somewhat difficult. Even viewed in perspective, his style is impossible to pigeon-hole. He was an independent, like Sir Thomas Browne, using in general a modified and personalized form of Ciceronian rhetoric; but he departed from it freely whenever he pleased. He had obviously studied various styles, and he dared to adjust them to his purposes. Professor Gilman has demonstrated his debt to Aristotelian rhetoric,[2] but has done nothing to account for the un-Aristotelian style of, say, *Animadversions* or *Colasterion*. The trend of the time was toward the anti-Ciceronian or Attic prose of Dryden and the journalistic prose of L'Estrange, but Milton ignored both as inadequate vehicles for his thought. Just as he insisted that Ellwood first learn the unusual form of Latin pronunciation before lessons could begin, so he demanded that his English readers accomodate themselves to his highly individualistic style so that he might speak to them. Such high-handed tactics do not make for contemporary popularity,[3] though they sometimes result in classics.

When the Restoration manacled Milton's "left hand" and compelled him to use his right, the audience that he had alienated in prose gradually came to him, and wonderingly admired his verse. I have already suggested certain reasons for this; let me now offer another. As the Ciceronian movement slowly died (making, like a character in Elizabethan tragedy, many farewell speeches), man's conception of the uses of prose slowly altered, and the artificial line between poetry and prose was drawn. The seventeenth century, the age of Bacon and the Royal Society, came to think of prose as a utilitarian vehicle for the clear expression of facts and workaday ideas. Let a pamphleteer lose himself in an *O altitudo!* and he invited suspicion of his common sense. Let the same writer express the same thoughts in poetry, however, and he might find an appreciative audience, perhaps even a convinced audience. Verse was becoming the proper medium for everything from sheer fantasy to challenging idealism. The more Truth, the more necessity for putting it into poetry. When Milton, therefore, turned from pamphleteering to *Paradise Lost*, the same man was expressing many of the same fundamental truths, but the same audience was more disposed to listen.

---

[2] Wilbur E. Gilman, *Milton's Rhetoric*, 1939 (University of Missouri Studies, vol. XIV, no. 3). This is a study of six "representative" pamphlets.

[3] The qualities of Milton's style did not, of course, go completely unappreciated by his contemporaries. "In truth its very hard to write good English, & few have attain'd its height in this last fry of bookes but Mr Milton," declared one admirer in 1650 (B. M. Sloane MS 1325 f. 13^r). Bishop Hall, hardly an admirer, remarked the "too-well-penned pages" of the divorce tract. My comments above are generalizations and permit of a good many exceptions, some of which the reader will notice in the collection of printed allusions.

The most important single event in Milton's life was the event against which he struggled most: the Restoration of Charles II. Had it not come, we might never have had *Paradise Lost* and *Samson Agonistes*; certainly we should never have had them in their present power and significance. The preceding twenty years were not wasted years; they, too, contributed to the wisdom and artistry of the great poems; but they also developed certain dominant traits in Milton's character which threatened both the composition and the human value of the verse which, early in his career, he had resolved to leave to posterity. The last words in this study of Milton's reputation must be, therefore, on the subject of the man's personality as it was affected by forces beyond his control.

Within him was the vast, ruthless energy of what we call the Renaissance, an energy which could and did shift its direction from time to time, but whatever way it moved, bowed everything before it. Milton probably wrote so much about the virtues of temperance because, in a sense, he had so little. He was an extremist, a perfectionist. Professor Hanford, with real insight, speaks of "the characteristic zeal which leads him to suppress one part of his consciousness while another is momentarily engaging his attention." This is a kind way of saying that he had a one-track mind. Students have seen this energy in the stubborn composition of *Paradise Lost* and in the five-year self-imposed sentence of private study at Horton (at the end of which he considered himself still unprepared for poetry); but they have sometimes ignored it in other periods of his life.

It is all very well to accept, remotely and academically, Milton's statement that his various pamphlets were integral parts of a carefully planned design: the defence of religious, domestic, and political liberty. Perhaps they were, and perhaps they were not; Milton, when under attack, was not divinely immune to rationalization. One thing, however, is certain: in the course of writing his pamphlets Milton discovered several things about himself.[4] He not only had a sincere interest in

---

[4] I merely glance here at the legend, now encouraged by many scholars, to the effect that Milton's life was preternaturally consistent: that he knew early what he intended to do, set about it simply and directly, never swerved from his determined course, and died with every item on his mental list neatly ticked off as completed. This is a fascinating theory, and, since too many persons find Milton almost inhuman to begin with, it has

different forms of liberty; he also had a growing desire for reputation in reform, and a genuine talent (God-given, he sincerely believed) for the vigorous, vituperative give-and-take of controversy. His bad manners in debate were, of course, not unique; they were his heritage as a child of his age; but he took his heritage, unsheathed it, sharpened it, and wielded it so enthusiastically that his own contemporaries found his language unusual, and today his more squeamish admirers avert their eyes from the unpleasant spectacle. The former Lady of Christ's could, and did, justify himself;[5] he felt, among other things, that only those who lived in glass houses had a moral right to throw stones. Viewing his practice historically or, some would agree, ethically, we cannot condemn him; but there is significance none the less in his calling one of the leading scholars of Christendom (and a man whom he was proud to meet in argument) a fool, monster, pimp, parasite, Judas, mongrel, slave, buffoon, scarecrow, liar, turncoat, midget, madman, coward, slave-dealer, pander, purse-snatcher, scoundrel, and a variety of birds and beasts including cuckoo, dunghill cock, and filthy swine. With these epithets Milton was not only voicing his hatred of a symbol of falsehood; he was also revealing a nature over-strong in combativeness. The replies, of course, were almost as harrowing, for Milton spat into a strong wind. And discovering what he had done, he spat again.

Today, looking down the cool corridor of history, we can discuss dispassionately Milton's theories of religion and govern-

enjoyed a real popularity. But, unfortunately, lives are not lived that way, even if a Milton is doing the living. The academic mind—reading into and between the lines, analyzing and systematizing—is one thing; the artistic mind is another. For example, thinking aloud in 1641 Milton expressed his genuine uncertainty as to whether he could best devote his energies to epic, or drama, or ode; and, alas for his biography, he mentioned the book of Job as a kind of small epic. A distinguished American scholar, knowing that Milton actually wrote a large epic, a small one, and a drama, ignored the ode as irrelevant and called the poet's expressed uncertainty "his plan of life endeavor." Not satisfied with this inference, the same scholar thought it "unlikely that Milton would ever have considered a further addition to his poetical works." Another example: writing a personal verse-letter to his best friend, one who like himself was still a college student, Milton cheerfully debated the relative virtues of feasting and fasting—arguing the case in the manner of an academic prolusion; and, alas for his biography, he mentioned the epic poet as an illustration of the latter (his friend is cited as an illustration of the former). Modern scholars, knowing that Milton later wrote an epic, ignore the friendly tone and the eloquent defence of feasting, and find "a definite resolution regarding his life work," a dedication to "earnest asceticism," a determination to write an epic. A distinguished English Miltonist, accepting this inference, argues further that the "Nativity Ode" and "Passion" were conscious studies for the future epic. And so it goes. For an unorthodox interpretation of the *Elegia Sexta*, see *MLN*, LV (March 1940), 216-7.

[5] See particularly his *Apology*, 1642, and *Defensio pro Se*, 1655. But the theme is recurrent in Milton. For contemporary reactions see pp. 86 and 116 following.

ment; but Milton, while expressing those theories, was smelling blood. There was a chip on the sturdy shoulder of his prose, a fanatic challenge in his ideas, an invitation to battle in his choice of subjects. Like the preacher in Shaw's *Devil's Disciple*, he suddenly found another calling, not only expedient, but much to his taste; he doffed the gracious robes of poetry and descended into the arena. He wrote five tracts on Episcopacy, four on divorce, and ten on politics and religion. Disillusionment over the progress of his reputation stopped him but temporarily; with his two-handed engine he struck once—and continued to strike long after striking was useless. One admires his courage in publishing *Brief Notes upon a late Sermon* and the revised *Ready and Easy Way* within the very month that King Charles was invited home; blessed with perspective one may praise the latter for its almost prophetic conception of an aristocratic democracy; but in publishing it he did not spit against the wind—he spat into the everlasting sea. Still, it was typical of the man; he loved an unequal struggle, and felt that "when God commands to take the trumpet and blow a dolorous or a jarring blast, it lies not in man's will what he shall say or what he shall conceal." If England had not positively tired of a Commonwealth, Milton might have gone on quarreling with human nature, planning utopias, and defending himself against the mud he was throwing at others.

The Restoration changed all that. It changed it because it came with a unanimity that even Milton realized could not be resisted. The return of Charles resulted, therefore, in Milton's being forcibly restored to his own destiny. The same power that disinterred Cromwell and Ireton, only to disgrace the remains, unwittingly disinterred the buried spirit of poetry in Milton, to revive and honor it. We can only guess at his thoughts in the year 1660, but decisions certainly had to be made. He could flee the country, and with his pen carry on a guerilla warfare from the continent; Aubrey tells us that he was mightily importuned to go into France and Italy. Or, now that Birnam Wood had really come to Dunsinane, he could stand his ground and try the last, going perhaps to a martyr's death. Both of these alternatives must have occurred to him, and it is significant that he rejected them. He rejected them because his destiny was still unfulfilled and still lay at home. He had done his patriotic best for the people of England, and the people had expressed their will, clearly, inexorably. But if divinest Melancholy came, uninvoked, she brought with her retired Leisure.

Milton's ideas did not greatly change after 1660, but they acquired depth and overtones which they had lacked before. One might almost say that the Restoration was good for Milton, intellectually. He was late in maturing, as he himself realized and confessed, but he was later than he thought. There is a facile idealism, an unrealistic conception of human nature, in much of his prose which hardly seems to promise a great poet. Read at a distance of three centuries, and removed from political and literary astigmatism, the early Milton is an high-minded and a plausible young man; but if we look beyond the great quotable passages, and close our ears to the background of familiar organ music, we find much to remind us that for thirty-three years (about half of his days upon this earth) he had tasted life from a silver spoon. He needed the vast illumination of a major disillusionment. He needed the terrible fire that turns knowledge into wisdom. The Restoration provided it.

Of course he had learned wisdom before. Life had been trying to teach him in the fashion it teaches ordinary men—through Mary Powell, through the divorce scandal, through the Presbyterians, through Cromwell's dictatorship, through the deaf ears of Parliament and General Monk in those last eventful months. Indeed, if one reads closely, one detects a gradually increasing realism and disillusionment in the pamphlets and poems. In Everyman's youth all things are either black or white; slowly there is recognition of gray. The immature Milton strictly meditated the thankless muse, and provoked his friend Diodati to exclaim: "I, in all other things your inferior, both think and know myself superior to you in this: that I know a measure in my labors." But after the Italian journey, he permitted himself (says his nephew) an occasional "Gawdy-day" with "some Young Sparks of his Acquaintance," and still later in life he advised his young friend, Cyriack Skinner:

> For other things mild Heaven a time ordains,
> And disapproves that care, though wise in show,
> That with superfluous burden loads the day,
> And when God sends a cheerful hour, refrains.

The immature Milton whole-heartedly supported the Presbyterians in an effort to end the evils of Episcopacy; but it is a considerably chastened Milton who wrote, a few years after he and others had thrown off their Prelate Lord: "New Presbyter is but Old Priest writ large." The immature young Puritan hated both Catholics and Catholicism, and his hatred put a strain on the hospitality of his hosts in Italy; but it is an urbane and wiser person who, writing to Carlo Dati in 1647, apologized for the violence of his poetical allusions to the Pope, calling it "the way which is customary among us." Life in those chaotic years was an active pedagogue for him, and the pupil learned to make distinctions. He wrote to Jean Labadie in April 1659: "I am fully aware that I have obtained a considerable reputation far and wide ... but it is my conviction that the only real fame is the good opinion of good men." Nevertheless, in respect to the major lessons of life, Milton remained as ever in his great taskmaster's eye: uncompromising, romantic in his views, egocentric and eager with his pen. Strong religious conviction strengthened an impervious optimism; even the curse of blindness became a mild yoke imposed by a wise providence.

But after the Restoration, faith, removed from the hothouse, took root and grew strong in the rich soil of reality. Milton remained hopeful until the end, but it was a hope conceived in painful knowledge of man's weakness, life's irony, and the inscrutable ways of God. Samson is victorious over his enemies, but (to borrow Milton's words from the *Defensio Secunda*) he has "purchased a less good with a greater evil— glory with death"—and this only after the Chorus has cried:

> God of our fathers, what is man!
> That thou towards him with hand so various,
> Or might I say contrarious,
> Temper'st thy providence through his short course,
> Not evenly, as thou rul'st
> The angelic orders and inferior creatures mute,
> Irrational and brute.
> Nor do I name of men the common rout,
> That wand'ring loose about
> Grow up and perish, as the summer fly,
> Heads without name no more remembered,
> But such as thou hast solemnly elected,

> With gifts and graces eminently adorned
> To some great work, thy glory . . .
> Nor only dost degrade them, or remit
> To life obscured, which were a fair dismission,
> But throw'st them lower than thou didst exalt them high,
> Unseemly falls in human eye,
> Too grievous for the trespass or omission,
> Oft leav'st them to the hostile sword
> Of heathen and profane, their carcasses
> To dogs and fowls a prey, or else captived:
> Or to the unjust tribunals, under change of times,
> And condemnation of the ingrateful multitude. . . .
> Though not disordinate, yet causeless suff'ring,
> The punishment of dissolute days; in fine,
> Just or unjust, alike seem miserable,
> For oft alike, both come to evil end.

The final chorus:

> All is best, though we oft doubt
> What th' unsearchable dispose
> Of highest wisdom brings about,
> And ever best found in the close

becomes then, neither an easy and pietistic optimism, nor a scholarly echo of Euripides, but a profound, personal affirmation. Milton seeks to justify the ways of God to men, and his illustration is the loss of Paradise. The theological problems of the Fall had long interested him, but the epic finished after the Restoration has a "new acquist of true experience from this great event" which makes it more than a masterpiece of language and technique, more than a rich mine of learning. One may say of it what Matthew Arnold said of *Samson Agonistes*: it is great with all the greatness of Milton. "He who would not be frustrate of his hope to write well hereafter in laudable things, ought himself to be a true poem."

A TENTATIVE LIST
OF PRINTED ALLUSIONS TO JOHN MILTON
1641-1674

A TENTATIVE LIST
OF PRINTED ALLUSIONS TO JOHN MILTON
1641-1674

It is hardly surprising that the mass of Milton biography and criticism lacks an Allusion Book. Such a collection, if it pretended to completeness, would run to several bulky volumes, for it must include such formidable works as *Eikon Aklastos*, *Regii Sanguinis Clamor*, the *Responsio* of Salmasius, and *The Dignity of Kingship Asserted*, to say nothing of various brief pamphlets directly answering Milton. But there is something to be said for reprinting as much as possible of this almost inaccessible *Miltoniana*, without a knowledge of which no one can adequately understand Milton's contemporary reputation or (in a number of instances) his own writings. There is also something to be said for collecting the shorter references to Milton or his work which appeared during his lifetime. The present volume represents a beginning only, and its editor regrets that he was unable to include more; he would particularly have liked to make available the lengthy but significant *Dignity of Kingship Asserted*.

A good many contemporary allusions to Milton have been noticed by scholars, who have all too frequently quoted but little or nothing at all. This is sad for students to whom the relevant books and pamphlets are inaccessible. Todd was the first to find a number of the more familiar references. Masson did an even more remarkable job of finding them, but he omitted several mentioned by Todd, and so scattered the remainder through six long volumes that they are difficult to locate and, indeed, seem to assume a significance which in fact they do not have. Stern was successful in discovering some additional allusions, which, because his *Life* is dwarfed by Masson, are often overlooked. Mrs. Raymond was even more successful than Stern, but inaccuracy and vagueness of reference mar her otherwise valuable book. More recently, Professor French has collected the various references to Milton in *Mercurius Politicus*.

My own search for allusions has not been systematic, and I have been able, with the help of friends, to add only about a dozen to those already noted. With real diffidence, therefore, I present this tentative list as a basis for a collection which I hope will grow rapidly, and I invite all students interested in Milton's contemporary reputation to send me additions. I doubt that much more will be found for the earlier period, which has now been rather thoroughly combed; but a more careful search through the years 1653-1674 should prove rewarding.

The following list may contain a few surprises. As one might expect, almost half of the allusions mention the *Defensio* against Salmasius; but Milton's views on divorce attracted more attention in print than his *Eikonoklastes*. His first pamphlet, *Of Reformation*, received as much notice as his *Tenure of Kings*, and almost as much as his *Ready and Easy Way*. There are three or four references to *Areopagitica* and one to *Of Education*, all of these, however, coming rather late. *Of Prelatical Episcopacy*, *The Reason of Church Government*, *The Judgement of Martin Bucer*, and *A Treatise of Civil Power* seem to have gone unremarked in print.

Of the 113 allusions, nineteen are advertisements for Milton's books and about sixteen might be classed as "news" or impersonal statements of fact. Of the seventy-eight that remain, only about fourteen are favorable to Milton. In other words, about eighty per cent of the contemporary notices of Milton were printed out of indignation or disapproval. The year which saw the most of these was 1660. There are references to either Milton or his writings, however, in every year from 1640 until 1664; the apparent absence of them in the period 1664-1668 is a tribute to his deliberate search for oblivion.

A word about the quotations. I have included in the numbered list only *printed* allusions to Milton by *name* or by *writings unmistakably his*. I have arranged these allusions in chronological order, with the help of Thomason's dating. In the case of pamphlets devoted entirely or largely to Milton's writings, I have given the title only and attempted no quotation. Nearly all quotations are from the original editions, and in most instances two or more copies have been examined for possible variants. Footnote references to Masson and others will enable the curious to check the completeness or accuracy of excerpts previously available. I have also put into footnotes bibliographical and other comments which I trust will prove useful. A few references, which for one reason or another I had been unable to verify before the book went to press, are noted within brackets. I regret the presence of these, but thought it better to expose my difficulties than to deprive students of useful references.

The following short titles are used in the footnotes:

French: J. Milton French, "Milton, Needham, and *Mercurius Politicus*," *Studies in Philology*, XXXIII (1936), 236-252.

Masson: David Masson, *The Life of John Milton*, 6 vols., London, 1859-1880.

Raymond: (Mrs.) Dora Neill Raymond, *Oliver's Secretary*, N.Y., 1932.

Stern: Alfred Stern, *Milton und seine Zeit*, 4 books in 2 vols., Leipzig, 1877-1879.

Todd: Henry John Todd, ed., *The Poetical Works of John Milton*, 4 vols., London, 1842.

Thomason: *Catalogue of the Thomason Collection*, 2 vols., London, 1908.

1) 1641: "Note then his [Irenaeus] *quality*. He was an holy man, a learned man, a peaceable man (as it may appear by his Epistles addressed unto *Victor*, Bishop of the Church of Rome) a constant defendour of the truth, and finally a patient sufferer for the same. What is your exception against him? The late unworthy Authour of a booke intituled, *Of Reformation*, &c. hath found some quarrell against him: but *Fevardentius*, in his apologeticall preface (in the defence of

---

[1] G. W. Whiting first called attention to this allusion in "A Pseudonymous Reply to Milton's *Of Prelatical Episcopacy*," *PMLA*, LI (June 1936), 430. He did not give the complete passage above. Almoni's 14-page tract confines itself to "one important Testimony," that of Irenaeus, which "is so cleare and ponderous, that it may sufficiently determine the whole cause." The preface is dated "Lond. *May* 31. 1641." Whiting's article was reprinted, in part, in his *Milton's Literary Milieu* (U. of N. C. Press, 1939), pp. 293-301. In connection with Almoni's comment on Milton, note the following from *Of Reformation*: "yea *those that are reckon'd for orthodox* began to make sad, and shamefull rents in the Church about the trivial celebration of Feasts, not agreeing when to keep Easter day, which controversie grew so hot, that Victor the Bishop of Rome Excommunicated all the Churches of Asia for no other cause, and was worthily therof *reprov'd by Irenaeus*. For *can any sound Theologer think that these great Fathers understood what was Gospel*, or what was Excommunication?" (my italics).

Irenæus) hath well answered such exceptions."—Peloni Almoni, Cosmopolites, *A Compendious Discourse, Proving Episcopacy To Be Of Apostolicall, And Consequently of Divine Institution*, London (E.G. for Richard Whitaker), 1641, p. [3].

2) 1642: [Joseph Hall and son?], *A Modest Confutation of A Slanderous and Scurrilous Libell, entituled, Animadversions upon the Remonstrants Defense against Smectymnuus*. [London], 1642.

3) 1642: "Since that, one might have expected that these worthy men should have been re-estated in their former honour, whereas the contrary hath come to passe. For some who have an excellent facultie in uncharitable Synecdoches, to condemne a life for an action, & taking advantage of some faults in them do much condemne them. And one [marginal note: "*Authour of the book lately printed of Causes hindring Reformation in England, lib.* I. *pag.* 10."] lately hath traduced them with such language, as neither beseemed his parts (whosoever he was) that spake it, nor their piety of whom it was spoken. If pious Latimer, whose bluntnesse was incapable of flattery, had his simplicity abused with false informations, he is called *another Doctour Shaw, to divulge in his Sermon forged accusations.* Cranmer and Ridley for some failings styled, *the common stales to countenance with their prostituted gravities every politick fetch which was then on foot, as oft as the potent Statists pleased to employ them.* And, as it follows not farre after, *Bishop Cranmer, one of King Henries Executours, and the other Bishops, none refusing (lest they should resist the Duke of Northumberland) could find in their consciences to set their hands to the disenabling and defeating of the Princesse Marie, &c.* Where Christian ingenuity might have prompted unto him to have made an intimation, that Cranmer (with pious Justice Hales in Kent) was last and least guilty, much refusing to subscribe; and his long resisting deserved as well to be mentioned, as his yielding at last. Yea, that very Verse, which Doctour Smith at the burning of Ridley used against him, is by the foresaid Authour (though not with so full a blow, with a slenting stroke) applyed to those Martyrs, *A man may give his body to be burnt, and yet have not charity.* Thus the prices of Martyrs ashes rise and fall in Smithfield market."—Thomas Fuller, *The Holy State*, Cambridge (Roger Daniel for John Williams), 1642, Bk. IV, Chap. 11, pp. 291-2.

---

[2] This anonymous reply to Milton is reproduced on pp. 123-168 of the present volume. An introductory note follows on p. 263.

[3] Masson, II, 359-60, gives only half of this quotation. The whole occupies about two-thirds of a folio page in Fuller. The second, third, and fourth editions of *The Holy State* (1648, 1652, and 1663) contain only trivial variants. In all of these the quotation is on pp. 279-80. Masson quotes from the 1841 edition.

4) 1643: "Sixtly, those Blessings which the English Nation have received from that Order, do deserve an acknowledgement. By them the Gospell was first planted in the most parts of *England:* By their Doctrine and Blood, Religion was reformed and restored to us: By the learned writings of them and their Successors, it hath been principally defended; *Cranmer, Ridley, Latimer, Hooper,* were all Bishops, *Coverdale* excercised Episcopall Jurisdiction. With what indignation doe all good Protestants see those blessed Men, stiled now in Print by a younge novice [marginal note: "*Two Books of Reformation.*"], *halting and time-serving Prelates,* and *common stales to countenance with their prostituted gravities every Politick fetch.* It was truely said by *Seneca,* that the most contemptible Persons ever have the loosest tongues."— [John Bramhall], *The Serpent Salve, or, a Remedie For the Biting of an Aspe,* [Dublin?], 1643, pp. 211-12.

5) 1644: "And whither such a Goverment as this ought to be embraced much lesse established among us (the sad effects whereof we have already experimentally felt, by the late dangerous increase of many *Anabaptisticall, Antinomian, Hereticall, Atheisticall opinions, as of the souls mortality divorce at pleasure, &c.* lately Broached, Preached, Printed in this famous City, which I hope Our grand Councell will speedily and carefully suppresse, and by our devisions betweene some of our commanders refusing to be *dependent* or subordinat one to another,) I referre to the judgement of all such who have any sparkes of love to God, Religion, their bleeding dying distracted native Country flaming in their brests, or any remainder of right reason residing in their braines."—William Prynne, *Twelve Considerable Serious Questions touching Church Government,* London (I.D. for Michael Sparke Sr.), 1644, p. 7.

6) 1644: "3. If any plead Conscience for the Lawfulnesse of *Polygamy;* (or for divorce for other causes then Christ and His Apostles mention; Of which a *wicked booke* is abroad and *uncensured,*

---

[4] Masson, II, 361 n., gives the latter part of this quotation. Bramhall seems to have found his quotations in Milton's tract rather than in Fuller (see above). The passage occurs near the end of the Bishop's (pp. xxviii+238) book, which, incidentally, Thomason did not collect. I quote from Bodleian 4° A. 89. Th. BS.

[5] Prynne's tract is a single sheet of eight pages. Thomason dated his copy September 16. Masson, III, 298-9, quotes liberally from Prynne, who, it will be observed, names neither Milton nor his divorce pamphlet. But Milton was offended by the inaccurate and unfair reference to his views, and replied in *Colasterion.* Another edition of *Twelve Questions* (F.L. for Sparke) bearing the same date contains more correct spelling and punctuation. Compare the title of Prynne's tract with that of the tract by John Goodwin, 1646 (no. 11).

[6] This comes near the end of the sermon (pp. vi+66), under the heading: "Instances to shew the Absurdity of an universall To[le]ration." The sermon was registered for publication November 7. Masson, III, 262-4, 298, quotes liberally from it; Todd, I, 41, was the first to find and quote the allusion.

though *deserving to be burnt,* whose *Author* hath been so *impudent* as to *set his Name* to it, and *dedicate it to your selves,*) or for Liberty to *marry incestuously,* will you grant a *Toleration* for all *this?*"—Herbert Palmer, *The Glasse of Gods Providence towards His Faithfull Ones. Held forth in a Sermon preached to the two Houses of Parliament, at Margarets Westminster, Aug. 13. 1644,* London (G.M. for Th. Underhill), 1644, p. 57.

7) 1644: *An Answer to a Book, Intituled, The Doctrine and Discipline of Divorce, or, A Plea for Ladies and Gentlewomen, and all other Maried Women against Divorce,* London (G.M. for William Lee), 1644.

8) 1645: "For they print not onely *Anabaptisme,* from whence they take their name; but many other most damnable doctrines, tending to carnall liberty, Familisme, and a *medley* and *hodg-podge* of all Religions. Witnesse the Book printed 1644. called *The Bloodie Tenet,* which the Author affirmeth he wrote in Milke; and if he did so, he hath put much *Rats-bane* into it . . . Witnesse a Tractate of Divorce, in which the bonds of marriage are let loose to inordinate lust, and putting away wives for many other causes besides that which our Saviour only approveth, namely, in case of Adultery. Witnesse a Pamphlet newly come forth, intituled, *Mans Mortality,* in which the soule is cast into an Endymion sleep, from the houre of death to the day of Judgement. Witnesse a bold Libell offered to hundreds, and to some at the doore of the house of Commons, called *The Vindication of the Royall Commission of King Jesus,* wherein . . ."—Daniel Featley, Καταβαπτισται καταπτυστοι. *The Dippers dipt. Or, the Anabaptists duck'd and plung'd Over Head and Eares, at a Disputation in Southwark,* London (for Nicholas Bourne and Richard Royston), 1645, pp. [xiii-xiv].

9-A) 1645: "They preach, print, and practise their hereticall opinions openly: for books, *vide* the bloody Tenet, witnesse a tractate of divorce in which the bonds are let loose to inordinate lust

---

[7] This pamphlet, registered October 31, licensed November 14, and dated by Thomason November 19, 1644, is reproduced on pp. 171-216 of the present volume. An introductory note follows on p. 270.

[8] This allusion comes in "The Epistle Dedicatory" of a long (pp. xx+228) attack on contemporary heresies. Milton's book is not mentioned when the topic of divorce is discussed in the text, e.g. p. 209; hence, one may assume that Dr. Featley heard of it fairly late. His book was registered December 17, 1644; the dedication is dated "From Prison" January 10, 1645; the volume was in Thomason's hands on or before February 7. Masson, III, 300-1, gives the above quotation.

[9] The reference to Milton's book in the Epistle Dedicatory of the first edition (registered March 5 and dated by Thomason May 8, 1645) is clearly an echo of Featley. Before

LIST OF PRINTED ALLUSIONS 75

. . ."—Ephraim Pagitt, *Heresiography: or, A description of the Heretickes and Sectaries of these latter times*, London (M. Okes for Robert Trot), 1645, sig. A3ᵛ.

9-B) 1645: "THese I terme Divorsers, that would be quit of their wives for slight occasions; and to maintaine this opinion, one hath published a Tractate of divorce, in which the bonds of marriage are let loose to inordinate lust, putting away wives for many other causes, besides that which our Saviour onely approveth; namely in case of adulterie, who groundeth his Error upon the words of God, *Gen.* 2. 18. *I will make him a helpe meet for him.* And therefore if she be not an helper, nor meet for him, he may put her away, saith this Author." —Pagitt, *Heresiography*, second edition, London (W. Wilson for John Marshall and Robert Trot), 1645, p. 142.

10) 1645: "Concerning Divorces, some of them goe farre beyond any of the *Brownists*, not to speak of Mr *Milton*, who in a large Treatise hath pleaded for a full liberty for any man to put away his wife, when ever hee pleaseth, without any fault in her at all, but for any dislike or dyspathy of humour; for I doe not know certainly whither this man professeth *Independency* (albeit all the Hereticks here, whereof ever I heard, avow themselves *Independents*); what ever therefore may be said of Mr *Milton* . . . [marginal note: "Mr *Milton* permits any man to put away his wife upon his meer pleasure, without fault and without the cognisance of any Iudge."]"—Robert Baillie, *A Dissuasive from the Errours Of the Time: Wherein the Tenets of the principall Sects, especially of the Independents, are drawn together in*

publishing his second edition, however, Pagitt may have seen Milton's pamphlet or the *Answer* to it, and so enlarged his reference, although he retained his original statement in the Epistle Dedicatory. In the second edition there is, indeed, a separate section entitled "Divorsers." The third edition, 1647, has an engraved title-page with a picture of a "DIVORSER" casting aside his wife, besides the Epistle Dedicatory allusion (A4ᵛ) and the section on Divorcers (p. 150). Among the additions in the third edition, the account of the Independents is enlarged, and on p. 87 we read: "Concerning Divorces, Mr. *Milton* permits a man to put away his wife upon his meere pleasure, without any fault in her, but for any dislike, or disparity of nature." In the fourth edition, 1647, "Miltons *divorse*" is indexed (wrongly), and the three allusions remain, pp. 86-7, 145-6. They are also present in the fifth edition, 1654, pp. 77 and 129, and in the sixth edition, 1661, pp. 100 and 233-4. Masson, III, 155, discusses without quoting the allusions to Milton in the third edition. Todd, I, 40, had noticed them in the fifth edition.

[10] The marginal note quoted above occurs also (with slight differences in spelling) in "The Contents" for Chapter 6, p. [xvii]. According to Thomason, the first edition appeared November 24, 1645; the second, January 22, 1646. There are only trivial spelling variants in the second edition. Baillie's *The Disswasive From The Errors of the Time*, London, 1655, is not a later edition but an entirely different book, containing no allusions to Milton. It is worth remarking that Baillie's comments are echoed by Pagitt in his third (1647) edition; see my note on Pagitt. Masson, III, 467, quotes the full passage. In accordance with his promise in the title, Baillie gives various quotations from Milton's *Doctrine and Discipline* (pp. 144-5), but these I have not reprinted.

one Map, for the most part, in the words of their own Authours, London (for Samuel Gellibrand), 1645, p. 116 (error for 112).

11) 1646: "I know it is objected, that many dangerous Bookes come out by my License, and that notwithstanding, by mine own acknowledgement, they are different from my judgement. To this I answer. First, The Books which meet with *harshest* censures, such as the *Bloudy Tenet*, the Treatise about *Divorce*, and others that have Affinitie with these, I have been so farre from licensing, that I have not so much as *seene* or *heard* of them, till after they have been commonly sold abroad; and how many such like I have refused to license, some *scores* can witnesse."—John Bachiler's address to the "Impartial Reader," prefixed to John Goodwin, *Twelve considerable serious Cautions, very necessary to be observed, in, and about a Reformation*, London (M.S. for Henry Overton), 1646.

12-A) 1646: "154. That 'tis lawfull for a man to put away his wife upon indisposition, unfitnesse or contrariety of minde arising from a cause in nature unchangeable; and for disproportion and deadnesse of spirit, or something distastefull and averse in the immutable bent of name; and man in regard of the freedome and eminency of his creation, is a law to himself in this matter, being head of the other sex, which was made for him, neither need he hear any judge therein above himself. [marginal note: "Vid. *Miltons doctrine of divorce*"]"—Thomas Edwards, *Gangraena: or a Catalogue and Discovery of many of the Errours, Heresies, Blasphemies and pernicious Practices of the Sectaries of this time*, London (for Ralph Smith), 1646, p. 34.

12-B) 1646: "There are two Gentlemen of the Inns of Court, civil and well disposed men, who out of novelty went to hear the women preach, and after Mistris *Attaway* the Lace-woman had finished her exercise, these two Gentlemen had some discourse with her, and among other passages she spake to them of Master *Milton* Doctrine of Divorce, and asked them what they thought of it, saying, it was a

---

[11] Bachiler's statement, which occurs on a page facing the title-page, is quoted in full by William Haller, *Tracts on Liberty*, I, 137-8. Thomason dated Goodwin's tract February 17. Masson missed this allusion.

[12-a] The quotation is from a "Catalogue of the Errours, Heresies, Blasphemies" in the First Part of *Gangraena*, dated by Thomason February 26; in the second edition of this, written about two months later, the allusion to Milton is unaltered except for slight changes in spelling. Masson, III, 468, gives the full quotation. Todd, I, 40, notes but does not quote it.

[12-b] The Second Part of *Gangraena*, dated by Thomason May 28, quickly followed the First Part and is a different book. The above quotation is from the second edition; in the third edition it is on pp. 10-11. Masson, III, 189-92, summarizes the story of Mrs. Attaway.

point to be considered of; and that she for her part would look more into it, for she had an unsanctified husband, that did not walk in the way of *Sion,* nor speak the language of *Canaan;* and how accordingly she hath practised it in running away with another womans husband, is now sufficiently known to Mr. *Goodwin* and Mr. *Saltmarsh* . . ."—Thomas Edwards, *Gangraena: the Second Part,* London, 1646, p. 9.

13) 1646?:   ⎧*Treatise*
               "M. Milton⎨*Vindication*
                          ⎩*Tetrachordon.*"
—John Wilkins, *Ecclesiastes, Or, A Discourse concerning the Gift of Preaching as it fals under the rules of Art,* London (M.F. for Samuel Gellibrand), 1647, p. 87.

?) 1647: *A Catalogue of the severall Sects and Opinions in England and other Nations. With a briefe rehearsall of their false and dangerous tenents,* London (by R.A.), 1647. s. sh. *

?) 1647: "20. That a man may lawfully put away his wife if she be not a meet helper."—*These Tradesmen are Preachers in and about the City of London, or A Discovery of the most dangerous and damnable tenets that have been spread within this few years: by many erroneous, heretical and mechanic spirits.* s. sh.†

14) 1648: "*That,* Indisposition, unfitnesse or contrariety of minde *(betwixt man and wife)* arising from a cause in nature unchangeable, hindring and ever likely to hinder the main benefits of conjugall society, which are solace and peace; are a great reason of

---

[13] I have not seen the first edition of this book (dated by Thomason October 10, 1646), and so I quote from the second edition. The allusion occurs on p. 119 of the third (1651) edition. In both it comes under a general heading of Divorce and Polygamy. On p. 181 of the fifth (1669) edition *"Mr. Milton"* is simply mentioned with Edm. Bunny and Dr. Hammond under this same heading. I am indebted to Professor Douglas Bush for this allusion.

* This single sheet, dated by Thomason January 19, contains an engraving representing members of the various sects. In addition to the Jesuit, Anabaptist, Arminian, Seeker, and Adamite, there is the Divorcer, portrayed by a man threatening his wife with a cane. There is some verse with the pictures, but no direct allusion to Milton or to his divorce pamphlets; hence the title has a dubious claim for inclusion here. Raymond, pp. 84-5, mentions the "caricature" and misquotes the title of the sheet. John Ashton, *Humour, Wit & Satire of the Seventeenth Century* (London, 1883, pp. 252-3), reproduces the engraving.

† Raymond, p. 84, notes this possible allusion to Milton's divorce heresy. Thomason dated the broadside April 26. There is no "Divorcer" on the engraved plate, which represents the mechanic arts only.

[14] More than fifty London ministers, all of them Presbyterians of the Sion College group, signed this attack on errors and heresies. Milton's is but one of twenty-two errors specifically and separately enumerated, and the last "That" of four under the heading of

Divorce, &c. [marginal note: "Doctrine and Discipline of divorce, by *I.M.* Lond. 1644 p 6. Peruse the whole Book."]"—*A Testimony to the Truth of Jesus Christ, and to Our Solemn League and Covenant; as also Against the Errours, Heresies and Blasphemies of these times, and the Toleration of them,* London (A.M. for Tho. Underhill), 1648, p. 19.

15) 1648: "In the booke called, *Little Nonsuch,* concerning Marriage. The very next of kin may joyne in Marriage by custome and command, for *Sarah* was *Abrahams* sister whom he took to wife. In the doctrine of divorce by *John Milton.* That unfitnesse or contrariety of minde betwixt man and wife, from a naturall cause which hindereth solace and peace are a great reason of divorce."—T.C., *A Glasse for the Times by which According to the Scriptures, you may clearly behold the true Ministers of Christ, how farre differing from false Teachers. With a briefe Collection of the Errors of our Times, and their Authors Names,* London (by Robert Ibbitson), 1648, p. 6.

16) 1649: "CASE II. *Whether marriage lawfully made may admit of any cause of divorce, save onely for the violation of the marriage bed by fornication or adultery.* Our Saviour hath so punctually decided the case in his divine Sermon upon the mount, that I cannot but wonder at the boldnesse of any man, who calls himselfe a Christian, that dares raise a question after so cleare and full a determination from the mouth of Truth it selfe. . . . Yet I finde this so evident an assertion checked by two sorts of adversaries; The one, certaine wild Novellists, who admit of very sleight causes of separation; the other, Romish Doctors, who plead for some other maine and important additions to this

---

"Errours touching Marriage and Divorce." Most of the attack in this section is against *Little Nonsuch,* 1646, which is cited four times. The *Testimony* is an argument against toleration, and many authors receive far more attention than Milton. John Goodwin, in his *Sion-Colledg Visited,* 1648, asserts "that my selfe only was the standing mark, at which the arrow of the *Testimonie* was shot; and that the rest were made to stand by only to give aime. They are brought in to partake of my condemnation; that so I might partake with them in their guilt and shame; or at least with such of them who being guilty, deserve shame" (p. 29). Goodwin does not mention Milton here by name. The *Testimony* was subscribed to "Decemb. 14 &c. 1647", and Thomason dated his printed copy January 18, 1648. Masson, III, 676-9, discusses the book in detail but does not quote the passage above.

[15] This 9-page tract is dated by Thomason July 29. Declares Mrs. Raymond, p. 84: "A pamphlet called *A Glass for the Times* mentions Miltonists as among the heretics who perplexed society in 1648"; and p. 101: "In *A Glass for the Times,* the author, 'A Friend of Truth,' dismissed Milton's doctrine of divorce as one so gross as not to require refutation." Compare Todd, I, 41, where the above allusion is noticed.

[16] The address to the reader is dated September 12, 1648; Thomason dated his copy April 9, 1649. In the second (1650) edition, the above quotation occurs on pp. 296-299. The third (1654) edition is entitled *Cases of Conscience Practically Resolved;* the allusion is on pp. 296-299. Masson, III, 62-3, gives most of the above quotation from the 1837 edition of Hall's *Works,* VII, 467. Todd, I, 40, noted the allusion.

liberty of divorce. I have heard too much of, & once saw, a licentious pamphlet throwne abroad in these lawlesse times, in the defence, and incouragement of Divorces (not to be sued out, that solemnity needed not, but) to be arbitrarily given by the disliking husband, to his displeasing and unquiet wife; upon this ground principally, that marriage was instituted for the help and comfort of man; where therefore the match proves such, as that the wife doth but pull downe a side, and by her innate peevishnesse, and either sullen, or pettish and froward disposition brings rather discomfort to her husband, the end of marriage being hereby frustrate, why should it not, saith he, be in the husbands power (after some unprevailing meanes of reclamation attempted) to procure his own peace, by casting off this clogge, and to provide for his owne peace and contentment in a fitter match? Woe is me, To what a passe is the world come that a Christian pretending to Reformation, should dare to tender so loose a project to the publique? I must seriously professe when I first did cast my eye upon the front of the booke, I supposed some great wit meant to try his skill in the maintenance of this so wild, and improbable a paradoxe; but ere I could have run over some of those too-well-penned pages, I found the author was in earnest, and meant seriously to contribute this peece of good counsaile in way of Reformation to the wise and seasonable care of superiours: I cannot but blush for our age, wherein so bold a motion hath been, amongst others, admitted to the light: what will all the Christian Churches through the world, to whose notice those lines shall come, thinke of our wofull degeneration in these deplored times, that so uncouth a designe should be set on foot amongst us?"—I[oseph] H[all], *Resolutions and Decisions of Divers Practicall Cases of Conscience in continuall Use amongst men,* London (M.F. for Nath. Butter, to be sold by H. Moseley, Abel Roper, & John Sweeting), 1649, pp. 388-392.

?) 1649: "Mr. Mabbott hath long desired severall members of the House and lately the Counsell of State to move the house that he might be discharged of licensing books for the future for the reasons following *viz.,* 1. Because many thousands of scandalous and malignant pamphlets have been published with his name thereunto as if he had licensed the same, though he never saw them, on purpose as he conceives to prejudice him in his reputation among the honest party of the nation. 2. Because that employment as he conceives is unjust and illegal as to the end of its first institution *viz.,* to stop the presse from publishing anything that might discover the corruption of church and State in the time of Popery Episcopacy and tyranny, the better to keep the people in ignorance and carry on their Popish, Factious, Traitorous and Tyrannical designs for the enslaving and destruction both of the bodies and souls of all the free people of this nation. 3. Because licensing is as great a monopoly as ever was in this nation in that all men's judgments reasons etc., are to be bound up in the licensers (as to Licensing) for if the author of any sheet, book, or treatise write not to please the fancie and come within the compass of the licensers judgment, then he is not to receive any stamp of authority for publishing thereof. 4. Because it is lawful in his judgment to print any book sheet etc., without licensing, so as the authors and printers do subscribe their names thereunto that so they may be liable to answer the contents thereof, and if they offend therein, then to be punished by such laws as are or shall be for those cases provided. A committee of the Councell of State, being satisfied with these and other reasons of Mr. Mabbott's concerning licensing, the Council of State report to the House upon which the House ordered this day that the said Mr. Mabbott should be discharged of licensing books for the future."—*The Kingdoms Faithfull and Impartiall Scout*, no. 16, May 25-June 1 [May 11-18?], 1649, p. 143.*

17) 1649: "[p. 47] Let me adde this from a late writer; that *from diligent search made into our ancient books of Law, it is affirmed, that the Peers and Barons of England had a legall right to judge the King: which was the cause most likely (for it could be no slight cause) that they were called his Peers, and Equalls.* [from Milton's *Tenure of Kings*, p. 23, but no marginal reference] . . . [p. 53] The Ministers were they who deposed the King: and consequently, who according to the common and known processe of Law and Justice in the Kingdom, exposed him both to that judiciary Trial, whereunto he was brought, as also to that Sentence, which passed upon him. For a King deposed, is no longer a King, but a Subject: . . . But this Doctrine (with a further explication, and proof of it) hath been lately taught them with Authority and Power, by another pen: the Sermon being in print, needs no repetition. [marginal note: "Tenure of Kings and

---

* Professor French kindly sent me this interesting quotation, which I have not yet had an opportunity to verify. Milton is not mentioned by name, but the possible allusions to *Areopagitica* justify, I think, the inclusion of the passage with a query. For more on Gilbert Mabbott see Masson, III, 432, and Birch's *Life of Milton* (1753), p. xxx. Birch gives the above quotation from *A Perfect Diurnall of Some Passages in Parliament*, May 21-28, 1649; but this I have not yet seen.

[17] Masson, IV, 95 and 106, does not quote from Goodwin's pamphlet—merely says that Goodwin quotes from Milton "several times with great respect." This is understatement. Goodwin manages altogether to devote more than four pages of text to Milton, alluding specifically to seventeen of Milton's forty-two pages. How much of Milton is indirectly in Goodwin's 156 pages it is difficult to say, but the *Tenure of Kings* was unquestionably a strong influence. When Goodwin quotes Milton, I do not always give the entire quotation, but try to give enough to enable anyone to find the passage. I have, moreover, supplied page references to the *Tenure* when Goodwin fails to do so. Milton's pamphlet was in Thomason's hands February 13, 1649; Goodwin's, May 30. The *Obstructours of Justice* was later called in by proclamation, along with two of Milton's books; see no. 84 following.

Magistrates, by *J.M. pag.* 29.30.&c."] ... [p. 71] For, not to insist upon that saying of one, who (upon good grounds I believe) is able to make it good against all gainsayers, *viz. That there is no Protestant Church from the first Waldenses of Lyons and Languedoc to this day, but have in a round made War against a Tyrant in defence of Religion and civil liberty, and maintain'd it lawfull.* [marginal note: "Tenure of Kings and Magistrates by *J.M. p.* 29."] ... [p. 73] Whereunto, if their [the Ministers] desire of a Reformation in their Judgements, (in case their miscarriage issued from hence) will so far serve them, and hold out, as to joyn the like perusall of a few pages (*viz.* 23. 24, 25, 26, 27.) in another book lately also published by *J.M.* intituled, *The tenure of Kings and Magistrates,* doubtlesse they will retract that ignoble and unclerklike assertion, wherein they affirm, that their inhumane Tenet, whereby they cannot but encourage Kings to turn Tyrants, to commit murthers, rapines, and all manner of abominations, that Tenet of theirs (I mean) wherein they deny unto Kings the help of that bridle for the ruling of their lusts, (more needfull for them, than for any other sort of men) *the fear of death* ... [pp. 78-80] There are some pieces published of late, where presidents of this kind [i.e. justified regicide], are to be seen as plentifull, as *silver,* or *Cedars* were in Jerusalem in the dayes of *Solomon* ... In one of these you may read, that when the *Romans,* their 'Empire decaying ... put them to death.' [marginal note: "Tenure of Kings and Magistrates by *J.M. pag.* 24."] The same Authour (not long after) reports from *Sleidan,* that 'in the year, 1546. the Duke of *Saxonie* ... but the power to do it.' [Milton, p. 26] He adds, that 'in the year 1559. the *Scotish* ... *or Queen is (in effect) deposed.*' [Milton, p. 26] 'And to let the world know' (saith my Authour in processe of discourse) 'that the whole Church ... if they saw cause, by right of ancient Laws *&c.*' [Milton, pp. 27-8] Concerning the State of *Holland,* the same Authour saith, that 'in the yeer 1681. in a generall Assembly ... chuse another in his stead.' [Milton, p. 28] Elsewhere in the same Discourse, having given a reason why Tyrants by a kind of naturall instinct both hate and fear none more than the true Church and Saints of God, inferrs thus: 'No marvail then if since ... had chosen in his room.' [Milton, pp. 22-3] (By the way he here bids us note, 'that the right of electing whom they pleas, is by the impartial testimony of an Emperour, in the people) for, said he, a just Prince ... before the Prerogative. And to prove ... had power to restrain them.' [Milton, p. 23] The fact of *Ehud* in killing *Eglon,* and so of *Jehu* in slaying *Jehoram,* the said Authour reconcileth with rules for standing practice [Milton, pp. 20-1]; with much more to this purpose, which I leave to the Readers perusal in the discourse it self. ... [Goodwin, pp. 94-5] He was not onely made (saith *J.M.*) obnoxious ... in the time of pestilence. Ministers of sedition ... we have enough experience, &c. [marginal note: "Tenure of Kings and Magistrates, *pag.* 35. 36."] The same Authour elsewhere chargeth these Ministers with oft *citing him* . . . *than ever Nero did*, with oft terming him *Agag*, &c. [marginal note: "*Ibidem pag.* 4. 5."] Not long after, to the same point, thus: *He who erewhile . . . though by themselves imprisoned.* [marginal note: "*Ibid. p.* 6."] . . . [p. 123] And (as one well observeth) the bloudy massacre at *Paris Anno* 1572 was the effect of that credulous peace, which the *French* Protestants made with *Charls* the ninth their King [marginal note: "Tenure of the Kings and Magistrates by *J.M.* p. 40."]; who likewise addeth, that 'the main visible cause . . . very year in *Naples.*' [Milton, p. 40] The same Authour likewise observeth (very pertinently to the point in hand) that '*David* . . . *not to hurt him.*' [Milton, p. 40]"—John Goodwin, Ὑβριστοδίκαι. *The Obstructours of Justice, or A Defence of the Honourable Sentence passed upon the late King, by the High Court of Justice,* London (for Henry Cripps and Lodowick Lloyd), 1649.

18) 1649: [an "eminently laudatory" reference to Milton's *Doctrine and Discipline of Divorce,* in Dr. John Hakluyt's *Metropolitan Nuncio,* no. 2, May 31-June 6, 1649.]

19) 1649: "There is lately come forth a Booke of *Iohn Meltons* (a Libertine that thinketh his Wife a Manacle, and his very Garters to be Shackles and Fetters to him: one that (after the Independent fashion) will be tied by no obligation to God or Man) wherein [marginal note: "184. *Meltons* Booke, *The tenure of Kings and Magistrates, &c.*"] he undertaketh to prove, *That it is lawfull for any that have power to call to account, Depose, and put to Death wicked Kings and Tyrants (after due conviction) if the ordinary Magistrate neglect it.* I hope then it is lawful to put to death wicked *Cromwells*, Councels of State; corrupt Factions in Parliament: for I know no prerogative that usurpation can bestow upon them. He likewise asserteth, *That those, who of late, so much blame Deposing, are the men that did it themselves,* (meaning the Presbyterians.) I shall invite some man of more leisure

---

[18] I take this reference, as yet unverified, from Raymond, pp. 123-4. She does not quote, and does not say in which number the allusion occurs. The British Museum has numbers one and three of this burlesque news-sheet (in which, by the way, any complimentary reference to Milton might be suspect), but the allusion does not occur in these. The Union Catalogue of the Library of Congress does not list the *Metropolitan Nuncio.* The Harvard Library has, however, number three (uncatalogued in September 1940).

[19] Masson, IV, 156, quotes only the first part of the first sentence; W. T. Allison quotes the entire passage which alludes directly to Milton, ed. *Tenure of Kings* (1911), pp. lii-liii. There were several editions of Walker's *History* in this same year, but the Milton allusion is practically identical in all. In Bodleian 4°Z.75. Jur., however, it is on pp. 196-197. Milton is not mentioned in the First Part of the *History,* 1648.

and abilities than my selfe to Answer these two Paradoxes: But shall first give him these cautions:

1. That for the Polemick part he turne all his Arguments into Syllogismes, and then he will find them to be all Fallacies, the froth of wit and fancy, not the Dictates of true and solid Reason.

2. That for the Historicall or narative part he would throughly examine them, and he will find few of them consonant to the plumb line of truth.

3. That he would consider that from the beginning of this Parliament there were three Parties or Factions in it:
   1. The *Royalists*.
   2. The *Presbyterians*.
   3. The *Independents*.

For though they were not then notorious by that name, yet the Persons confederated were then extant and active; being a complication of all *Antimonarchicall, Anarchicall heresies and schismes, Anabaptists, Brownists, Barrowists, Adamites, Familists, Libertines* of all sorts; the true Heyres and Successors of *Iohn of Leyden* and *Knipperdolling* in all their principles and practises united under the generall Title of *Independent:* and these were originally the men that by their close insinuations, solicitations and actings began, and carried on the Warre against the KING, with an intent (from the beginning) *to pull down Monarchy, and set up Anarchy,* notwithstanding the many *Declarations, Remonstrances,* abortive *Treaties, Protestations,* and *Covenants to the contrary;* which were Obligations (from time to time) extorted from them *by the Presbyterians,* although not strong enough to hold such subtile *Sampsons,* whose strengths to break such Wythes lay not in their Bushes of Hair, but in the Ambushes of their Hearts, wherein there alwaies lay hid some evasion, equivocation, or mentall reservation, which, like a back-dore, gave them leave to make an escape."—Theodorus Verax [Clement Walker], *Anarchia Anglicana: or, The History of Independency. The Second Part,* 1649, pp. 199-200.

20) 1649:   "Force can but in a Rape engage,
            'Tis Choice must make it Marriage.
            Hence a Conveyance they contrive,
            Which must on us their Cause derive:
            This must attaque, what holds out still,
            And is impregnable, the Will.
            This must enchant our conscious hands,

---

[20] The above quotation is from the poem, "The Return," spoken of in the title. This poem begins a new series of pagination, in which series the Milton allusion occurs on p. 3. Todd, I, 40, quotes this allusion, which was called to his attention by Thomas Park. *NED* gives 1806 as the earliest date for the word *Miltonist.*

> To slumber in like guilty bands,
> While like the froward Miltonist,
> We our old Nuptiall knot untwist:
> And with the hands, late faith did joyn,
> This Bill of plain Divorce now signe.
> Here their New Kingdom must commence,
> And Sinne conspire with Conscience."

—C[hristopher] W[ase], *Electra of Sophocles: presented to her Highnesse the Lady Elizabeth; With an Epilogue, Shewing the Parallell in two Poems, The Return, and The Restauration,* Hague (for Sam. Brown), 1649, E8^r.

21) 1650: ". . . it is the States policy to smother their sorrowes by a busle and pretence of setling Lawes and Courts for administration of Justice, in divers Cases: as of *Wills, Administrations, Legacies, Mariages* and *Divorces;* sure when such a Court is erected these *Regicides* will choose Mr. *Mylton* (who houlds forth the Doctrine of *Divorce,* and, like a State Champion, sham'd himselfe with handling his penne to oppose those Divine *Meditations* of our late King of happy memory) to bee Judge, and then bee sure the *Junctoes* Wills must bee obeyed."—*Mercurius Pragmaticus,* part 2, no. 39, January 22-29, 1649, p. [5].

22) 1650: ["In truth it is very hard to write good English: and few have attained its height, in this last frie of books, but Mr. Milton."—Charles Hotham, Fellow of Peter House, *An Introduction to the Teutonick Philosophie, Englished by D.F.,* London, 1650, preface.]

23) 1651: "From *Leyden* we had this accute representation of Affaires in *Holland,* of this 17. instant, *stilo novo.* SIr, our Citie affords little (though the seat of the Muses) worthy your knowledge, onely we wonder not a little you suffer our *Salmasius* to crow and cry *Victoria* so long without bidding him battaile: Are your Wits or your Cause barren, or why is the Pen and Presse so long bringing forth? But

---

[21] Masson, IV, 157, quotes the entire passage. This journal, formerly edited by Marchamont Needham, was openly "For King Charls II".

[22] I take this quotation, as yet unverified, from Todd, I, 145. The manuscript of this preface, with the allusion to Milton's style, is apparently B. M. Sloane MS 1325 f. 13; and this I have examined. See p. 59, n. 3, *supra*.

[23] The allusion to Milton's *Defensio Prima* at the close of the above quotation is an editorial comment on the preceding letter; it is dated "Jan. 27, 1651. *stilo novo.*" Masson, IV, 329, notices this, but does not give the complete quotation.

LIST OF PRINTED ALLUSIONS 85

leaving that ... Let the penner of this Epistle take notice, That a very victorious Reply to *Salmasius* is now in motion at the Presse."—*Mercurius Politicus*, no. 33, January 16-23, 1651, pp. 545-6.

24) 1651: Sir Henry Wotton, *Reliquiae Wottoniae. Or, a collection of lives, letters, poems; with characters of sundry personages.* London (Thomas Maxey for R. Marriot, G. Bedel, & T. Garthwait), 1651. [contains Wotton's letter to Milton of April 13, 1638, pp. 432-6]

25) 1651: "Wy sullen Vranckrijck nu voor een wijle tijts verlaten /en gaen over Zee nae Engelant: Alwaer tegens Claudius Salmasius sijn Verdediginge des Conungs Carolus de 1/aen Carolus de 2 toe-gewijt/een seer bondige en dappere Latijnsse Verantwoordinge voor't Parlement uytgekomen is/zijnde in de selve Tale diergelijcke in dese tijden niet te vinden/die van Politijcke saecken spreeckt: De Autheur is geweest eenen Johan Milton/Engelsman/eene der Secretarissen van den Raet van Staten binnen Londen/tot wiens Tractaet (als zijnde nu in Nederlantse/ Engelsse en Fransse Tale overgeset) wy den curieusen Leser heen wijsen."—*Hollandse Mercurius*, II (Februarius 1651), 16.

26) 1651: "I am thankfully glad of the promise *Politicus* gives us of *Salmasius* Answer, which we greedily expect, and *Salmasius* himself seems to desire it; *Goliah*-like, despising all his adversaries as so many Plgmies."—*Mercurius Politicus*, no. 37, February 13-20, 1651, p. 604.

---

[24] Wotton's letter to Milton was first printed by the latter in his *Poems*, 1645, and I have not reproduced it. In the first edition of the *Reliquiae* (dated by Thomason February 2, 1651), the letter is headed "To Master ...." The 1654 edition, pp. 394-7, heads it "To Mr. Milton"; the 1672 edition rearranges the letters, apparently with a view to chronological order, and the letter to Milton occurs pp. 342-4, undated but among letters of 1637.

[25] This journal calls itself *Hollandse* or *Hollantse* or *Hollandsche* or *Hollantze Mercurius*. It was published at Haerlem. The numbers for 1651 are paged continuously. The above quotation is printed entirely in black letter. Professor French called the passage to my attention. Following is a free translation: "We shall now leave France for a while and cross the sea to England, where there has appeared before Parliament a very concise and valiant answer to Claudius Salmasius' defence of Charles I, dedicated to Charles II. Such a political discussion is not to be found in these times in the same language. The author was one John Milton, Englishman, one of the secretaries of the Council of State in London; to which tract, now [being?] translated into Dutch, English, and French, we refer the curious reader."

[26] This allusion to Milton's *Defensio* comes at the close of a news-letter dated "*Hague* 16 Febr. *stilo loci*, 1651" and is an acknowledgment of the announcement made in *Mercurius Politicus* no. 33 (see above). Masson, IV, 329, quotes it.

27) 1651: "Now we hear in our *Academy*, and I was told at the Hague also, that your *Ambassadors* [i.e. St. John and Strickland] will bring with them, the Answer to *Salmasius;* I perceive by him [Salmasius], though he dreads no Antagonist, that he could wish it [i.e. his own book] to write again; for, it was never calculated for this change as is since faln out."—*Mercurius Politicus*, no. 39, February 27- March 6, 1651, p. 638.

28) 1651: "I hear *Salmasius* is not like to live to make any Reply to *Milton's* book, which here is very much applauded. It seems he is very ill in *Sweden*: that air doth not agree with his body."— *Mercurius Politicus*, no. 43, March 27-April 3, 1651, p. 697.

29) 1651: "*Miltoni Defensionem pro Populo Anglicano*, I got here lately and perused it with much satisfaction: To morrow, God willing, I send it to a Counsellor of the Elector of Brandenburg. The author (it seems) is a man of singular parts, acuteness and solidity. Some perhaps may finde fault with the personall jerks therein; but the least review of *Salmasius* will shew what tuned the *Eccho* to such a *Key*. I am sure if he lives yet, he will finde worke enough, and tough, to disentangle himself handsomly in the main."—*Mercurius Politicus*, no. 45, April 10-17, 1651, p. 722.

30) 1651: "SIR, The Bishop of *London-Derry* [John Bramhall] hath answered M. *Milton's* Book, called *Iconoclastes*, that was written in answer to the *King's Book*, called the *Pourtraiture of his Sacred Majesty in his Solitude and Sufferings*."—*Mercurius Politicus*, no. 48, May 1-7 [sic], 1651, p. 776.

31) 1651: "Mr. *Miltons* book hath been burnt at *Thoulose*, by an Arrest of that parliament: but the said Parliament, as you know, is under the Government of the Duke of *Orleans*, whose affec-

---

[27] The allusion to Milton's *Defensio* comes as a postscript to a news-letter dated "*Leyden* March 2. *new stile*." Masson, IV, 329, quotes it.

[28] A postscript to a letter from the Hague dated at the beginning March 31 but at the end March 30, 1651. Masson, IV, 330, quotes it. The passage proves that Thomason's date of April 6 for the *Defensio Prima* is late, since the book must have reached Holland before March 20 (English style).

[29] This allusion occurs in a letter from Amsterdam dated April 7 (new style). French, p. 248, gives the quotation.

[30] This allusion occurs in a letter from the Hague dated May 3, new style. Of this note French, p. 248, declares: it "reminds us that Milton was not the only person who failed to discover that Rowlands and not Bishop Bramhall was the author of *Pro Rege et Populo Anglicano Apologia*." But the allusion is more likely to the *Eikon Aklastos*, 1651, published anonymously, but actually written by Joseph Jane.

[31] This allusion follows two sentences of other news, dated from Paris July 5/June 25, 1637 [error for 1651]. Masson, IV, 330, quotes it.

tions are well known to you."—*Mercurius Politicus*, no. 56, June 27-July 3, 1651, p. 890 [error for 899].

32) 1651: "Salmasius is returning to Leyden from Sweden, he likes the Countrey there as bad as the Swedes like the French in that Court; he displeases those cholerick Bishops as much by his former Books against Episcopacy, as he pleaseth that Queen by his late defence of Monarchy: That Ladie loves French Learning and Medisance, but Des Chartes quickly died there, and M. Sanmase fearing the like fate and his crazie carkass, makes haste towards his Honorarious chair in our University: If he were clean out of it, I think he need not hope an new election the second time: but he thinks his Book forgotten now, and believes hee hath friends enough still to preserve his place and honour: hee tells his Confidents here, that he will vindicate his name and book from Milton's Reply. Which Book, we hear is burnt in Tholouse and Paris, for fear of making State-Heretiques. The truth is, that Doctrine begins to be studied and disputed more of late; and is pretty taking among such a people as they, who like Issacars Asse, sink under their burdens; and by this policy of the Court, in burning the Book, will make it a Martyr, whose ashes will be scattered far and wide, and the Cause and Book be more inquisitively desired."—*Mercurius Politicus*, no. 57, July 3-10, 1651, pp. 914-915.

33) 1651: "M. *Milton's* Book hath been burnt by the hands of the *common Executioner*, and with much more Solemnity than at *Tholous*. It is so farr liked and approved by the ingenuous sort of men, that all the Copies, sent hither out of the *Low-Countries* were long since dispersed, and it was designed here for the *Press;* whereof notice being taken, it is made *Treason* for any to print, vend, or have it in possession; so great a hatred is born to any piece that speaks liberty and Freedom to this miserable people."—*Mercurius Politicus*, no. 58, July 10-17, 1651, p [932].

34) 1651: "And therefore I wonder at that passage of his, (if it was his, which I doubt of) in that booke published under his name and called his Portraiture, . . . For the booke it selfe, it maintaines so many Contradictions unto those things manifested by his owne Letters under his owne hands unto the Queen, that I conceive the most part of

---
[32] This allusion occurs in a letter from Leyden dated July 1, new style. French, p. 249, gives the complete quotation.
[33] This allusion occurs in a letter from Paris dated July 19, new style. French, pp. 248-9, gives this quotation.
[34] Stern, III, 260, notes this allusion. Thomason dates Lilly's book August 6. I am grateful to Arthur A. Houghton, Jr., curator of rare books at the Library of Congress, for sending me the above quotation, which I have not yet verified.

it *Apocrypha;* the *Meditations* or *Psalmes* wholly were added by others; some loose Papers he had, I do well know, but they were nothing so well methodised, but rather Papers intended after for the Presse, or as it were a *Memoriall* or *Diary,* than such a well couched peece and to so little purpose. But it is answered by the learned *Milton.* He was seldome in the times of War, seen to be sorrowfull for the slaughter of his People or Soldiers, or indeed any thing else, whether by nature or custome his heart was hardened, I leave for others to judge."—William Lilly, *Monarchy or No Monarchy in England,* etc., London (for Humfrey Blunden), 1651, pp. 80-81.

35) 1651: "The reason why *Salmasius* left *Sweden* was, because *Milton's* book having laid him open so notoriously, he became thereby very much neglected, the Queen not having sent for him, nor seen him for the space of two moneths; so that perceiving a decay of her favor, he came himself and desired leave of departure, which was very readily granted, the Queen having at length understood, how impolitick it is for any Prince, to harbor so pernitious a *Parasite,* and Promoter of Tyrany."—*Mercurius Politicus,* no. 66, September 4-11, 1651, p. 1056.

36) 1651: [Joseph Jane], ΕΙΚΩΝ ΑΚΛΑΣΤΟΣ *The Image Vnbroaken. A Perspective of the Impudence, Falshood, Vanitie, and Prophannes, Published in a Libell entitled* ΕΙΚΟΝΟΚΛΑΣΤΗΣ *against* ΕΙΚΩΝ ΒΑΣΙΛΙΚΗ *Or the Pourtraicture of his Sacred Majestie in his solitudes and Sufferings.* 1651.

37) 1651: [John Rowland], *Pro Rege et Populo Anglicano Apologia contra Johannis Polypragmatici, (alias Miltoni Angli) Defensionem destructivam, Regis & Populi Anglicani.* Antverpiae (apud Hieronymum Verdussen), 1651.

38) 1652: "As to your desire to be informed whether Salmatius be returned from Sweden to our Town, you may be assured he is, for I have both seen and spoken with him here in Leyden, he made a long halt by reason of his gout and other infirmities in Denmark

---

[35] This is part of a letter from Delft dated September 8, new style. French, p. 249, gives the quotation.

[36] Jane's book was probably printed in England. In any case, there were enough unsold copies of it to be re-issued in London by John Garfield in 1660. See no. 89 below.

[37] This anonymous attack upon Milton was twice reprinted in 1652 by Verdussen. It was answered by John Phillips (see no. 45 below), and was acknowledged by Rowland in a *Supplementum,* 1653 (see no. 48).

[38] This letter is from Leyden, dated October 28, new style. French, p. 250, gives the complete quotation, and points out that the month of the letter, "October," is an obvious error for December.

at Sleswick. He travelled hence with his wife by land to Sweden, and back again. That Queen had sent for him by a Letter under her own hand, where being come to her, she sent to our States to have him dismist hence, to be preferd by her, and to live there: But he himself saith, they writ back word to her, there was but one sun, and but one Salmatius, therefore they would not spare him. She offerd him (he saith) a Titular honor, but he refused it, saying he could not serve two Masters, being sworn Titular Councellor to the King of France. The Queen made it appear she liked his Book for *M*onarchy well, and that besides Copper and Iron, other me als [*sic*] are found in Sweden. He came to Sweden, and saluted the King of Denmark in his way, who gave him a Chain of gold, and other Jewels for his Book, and for the fame of his Learning: that King also as well as the Queen of Sweden, being a great student and lover of Learning. Thus you see he hath gotten many Royal Benefactors: yet all this doth him no good, because Miltons Reply lies as a raw indigested gobbet upon his stomack; shortly now we shal see how far he holds himself bound to take notice of the said Reply."—*Mercurius Politicus*, no. 82, December 25-January 1, 1651/2, pp. 1316-1317.

39) 1652: "Our *Salmasius* bites his thumbs stiil in silence at *Leyden*, and gives out, that he scorns to give any Answer to *Milton;* but the truth is, I believe he knows not how to salve those wounds and scars that have been given him. *He* is now more haughty then ever, and takes himself (I think) for some great Emperor: There is no man so much a *Sot*, as he that is drunk with pride and ambition."—*Mercurius Politicus*, no. 84, January 8-15, 1652, p. 1344.

40) 1652: "But entring into the Body of the Book, and considering the choyse of the many Subjects whereof it treats, the whole contexture whereof hath already been sufficiently handled without mittens by a Gentleman of such abilities as gives place to none for his integrity, learning and judgment; . . ."—[Hamon L'Estrange?], *The Life and Reigne of King Charls, or, the Pseudo-Martyr discovered*, London (for W. Roybold), 1651, p. 179.

41) 1652: "Observations on Master Milton against Salmasius," in [Sir Robert Filmer's] *Observations concerning the Originall of Government, Upon Mr. Hobs Leviathan. Mr. Milton against*

---

[39] The above quotation is from the end of a section headed "From the *Hague*, January 12. *Stilo novo*." Masson, IV, 434, notes this allusion.

[40] Stern, III, 260, notices this allusion to Milton's *Eikonoklastes*. The Thomason catalogue da:rs this book January 29, 1652.

[41] Thomason dated his copy of this book February 18, and attributed it to Henry Hammond. Filmer's essay on Milton's *Defensio* and *Tenure of Kings* is reproduced on pp. 218-228 of the present volume. An introductory note follows on p. 278.

Salmasius. H. Grotius De Jure Belli. Mr. Huntons Treatise of Monarchy, London (for R. Royston), 1652, pp. 12-22.

42-A) 1652: [John Rowland], *Pro Rege et Populo Anglicano Apologia, contra Johannis Polypragmatici, (alias Miltoni Angli) Defensionem destructivam, Regis & Populi Anglicani*. Antverpiae (apud Hieronymum Verdussen), 1652. [191 pages].

42-B) [another edition, 122 pages].

43-A) 1652: [Peter du Moulin and Alexander Morus] *Regii Sanguinis Clamor ad Coelum Adversus Parricidas Anglicanos*. Hagae-Comitum (Ex Typographiâ Adriani Vlac.), 1652. [4°: pp. xvi+172]

43-B) 1652: *Regii Sanguinis Clamor ad Coelum Adversus Parricidas Anglicanos*. Hagae-Comitun [sic] (Ex Typographia Adriani Vlacq.), 1652. [12°: pp. xvi+148]

43-C) [another edition: 12°: pp. xxiv+190]

44) 1652: *Carolus I., Britanniarum Rex, a securi et calamo Miltonii vindicatus*. Dublin, 1652.

45-A) 1652: *Ioannis Philippi Angli Responsio ad Apologiam Anonymi cujusdam tenebrionis pro Rege & Populo Anglicano infantissimam*. Londini (Typis Du-Gardianis), 1652, pp. 112.

45-B) 1652: [another edition, in larger type, 262 pp.]

45-C) 1652: [another edition, Amsterdam, 70 pp.?]

---

[42] These are reprints of no. 37 above.
[43] There were at least three editions of the *Clamor* during 1652. No. 43-A is probably the first edition.
[44] Masson, IV, 436-7, discusses this scarce little book.
[45] The Thomason copy is dated December 24. See Masson, IV, 470-4, for a discussion of this work. Willems (*Les Elzevier*, Paris, 1880, no. 1671) mentions an edition of 69 pages by J. Jansson of Amsterdam, but this I have not seen. Phillips' book is an answer to no. 37 above, which he attributed to Bishop John Bramhall. In a letter to John Pierson, dated from Antwerp May 9/19, 1654, Bramhall wrote: "That lying abusive book was written by Milton himself, one who was sometime Bishop Chappell's pupil in Christ Church in Cambridge, but turned away by him, as he well deserved to have been both out of the University and out of the Society of men. If Salmasius his friends knew as much of him as I, they would make him go near to hang himself. But I desire not to wound the nation through his sides, yet I have written to him long since about it roundly. It seems he desires not to touch upon that subject. That silly book which he ascribed to me,

46) 1653: "Having gone thus far, I should soon be at an end of my gesses, were there not some *pretensions* of other men, who like not to have their *liberties* retrench'd, though by *Christ* himself, which may deserve to be a while considered. And the considering of them will be the most *ingrateful* part of this task; yet that which must be undergone, lest, having offered their *reasons* and *exceptions* against the *Doctrine* of the *Church*, and expresly of *Christ* himself, they be permitted to that dangerous *temptation*, of thinking themselves *successful* in the *attempt*, and so that prove to some men a more *perswasive* reason to *beleive* their *wishes*, then any yet hath been produced. The first open attempt that I remember that way, was made in a Discourse purposely on that *subject* [marginal note: "A Plea for Divorces."], and presented to the *Parliament*, at the beginning of these *licentious* times; and the *special* artifice made use of, was that, of bringing back *Christ* unto *Moses*, of interpreting the restraint laid on this matter in the *New Testament*, by *analogie* with the *Judaical permission* in the *Old*. . . ."—Henry Hammond, *A Letter of Resolution to six Quaeres, of Present Use in the Church of England*, London (J. Flesher for R. Royston), 1653, pp. 122-123.

?) 1653: "Q.8. *What are the opinions of the* Independents? . . . They permit divorces in slight cases."—Alexander Ross, ΠΑΝΣΕΒΕΙΑ: *Or, A View of All Religions in the World, From the Creation, to These Times*, London (for John Saywell), 1653, pp. 412-3.*

47) 1653: *Caspari Ziegleri Lipsienis Circa Regicidium Anglorum Exercitationes. Accedit Jacobi Schalleri Dissertatio ad Loca Quædam Miltoni.* Ludg. Batavorum (apud Johannem à Sambix), 1653.

---

was written by one John Rowland, who since hath replied upon him. I never read either of the first book, or of the Reply, in my life. . . . I answered whatever touched me in that pamphlet, of which there is not a true word." Bramhall, *Works*, Oxford, 1842, I, xciv.

[46] This 475-page book is dated November 1, 1652, in the catalogue of the Thomason tracts. There seems little doubt that Hammond has Milton's *Doctrine and Discipline of Divorce* in mind, but he mentions neither the author nor the tract by name. The quotation given above is followed by six and a half paragraphs, pp. 123-7, giving a general answer to Hammond's recollection of Milton's argument. The "allusion" is, therefore, so vague that I have not seen fit to quote in full. Hammond's chapter "Of Divorces," pp. 92-173, is significant in the history of Milton's reputation because, while there are only four and a half pages of vague rebuttal to Milton, forty-six and a half pages (pp. 127-173) are devoted to detailed rebuttal of Selden's *Uxor Hebraica* (1646).

* This possible allusion was called to my attention by Professor French. Thomason dated his copy of Ross' book June 7. On p. 400 we find: "They teach that a man may put away his Wife, though not for adultery; so taught the *Jews*." In the second edition of *Pansebeia* (1655), p. 376, we find: "there are amongst us *Divorcers*, who hold that men may put away their Wives upon small occasions."

48) 1653: John Rowland, *Polemica Sive Supplementum Ad Apologiam Anonymam pro Rege & populo Anglicano, adversus Jo: Miltoni Defensionem populi Anglicani. Et Irænica Sive Cantus Receptui Ad Christianos omnes. Per Io: Rowlandum Pastorem Anglicum.* 1653.

?) 1653: ". . . Hereticks and Schismaticks (seduced to *blind Obedience by their blind Leaders*) . . ."—William Prynne, *The Sword of Christian Magistracy supported,* London (R.I. for John Bellamy), 1653, p. 144.*

49) 1654: "There is also newly published, *A* second Defence, *Pro populo Anglicano,* by Mr. *John Milton,* in answer to a Book called *Regii Sanguinis clamor;* and are to be sold at the Rose and Crown in St *Pauls*-Church-yard."—*Mercurius Politicus,* no. 208, June 1-8, 1654.

50) 1654: *Joannis Miltoni Defensio Secunda Pro Populo Anglicano: Contra infamem Libellum anonymum, cujus Titulus, Regii sanguinis clamor adversus parricidas Anglicanos. Accessit Alexandri Mori Ecclesiastæ, Sacrarumque litterarum Professoris Fides Publica, Contra calumnias Ioannis Miltoni Scurræ.* Hagæ-Comitum (Ex Typographia Adriani Vlacq.), 1654.

51) 1655: *Alexandri Mori Ecclesiastæ & Sacrarum Litterarum Professoris Supplementum Fidei Publicæ, Contra Calumnias Ioannis Miltoni.* Hagæ-Comitum (Typis Adriani Vlacq.), 1655.

52) 1655: "But that opinion of a poor shallow-brain'd *puppy,* who upon any cause of disaffection, would have men to have a priviledg to change their Wives or repudiat them, deserves to be hiss'd at rather then confuted; for nothing can tend more to usher in all

---
[48] See nos. 37 and 45 above.
* This apparent allusion is quoted by Stern, who remarks, III, 283, "Die Stelle . . . könnte immerhin auf Milton gehen." See also III, 215, where the passage is also quoted. The same passage, however, occurs in the earlier (1647) edition of Prynne's pamphlet, p. 114; hence it was written before Milton's blindness.
[49] Thomason dated his copy of the *Defensio Secunda* May 30; the book was not registered at Stationers' Hall. From the imprint of the book we have known that Thomas Newcomb was the printer, but the above allusion tells us that one of the booksellers was George Thomason himself, whose address was the Rose and Crown (1643-66). His dating of the tract, therefore, is almost certainly accurate, and the above advertisement confirms it. French, p. 251, quotes this passage, but does not identify Thomason as the bookseller.
[52] This allusion does not occur in the 1645 or 1650 editions of Howell's *Epistolae;* volume IV was first printed in 1655 with its own title-page, signatures, and pagination. The apparent reference to Milton's divorce views is from letter no. 7, which is given no date. In later editions the letter (to Sir Edward Spencer, Knight) is dated *"London,* this

confusion and beggery throughout the world; Therfore that Wise-aker deserves of all other to wear a toting horn. In this Republic one man should be contented with one Wife, and he may have work enough to do with her:"—James Howell, *Epistolae Ho-Elianae*, London (for Humphrey Moseley), 1655, vol. IV, p. [19].

53) 1656: [an advertisement of Milton's *Poems*, in Thomas Blount's *Glossographia: or a Dictionary, Interpreting all such Hard Words*, etc., London (Tho. Newcomb for Humphrey Moseley and George Sawbridge), 1656, sig. a4^v]

54) 1656?: *Verax Prodromus in Delirium.* [Amsterdam? 1656?]

55) 1656: "Spadae cum esset, fallendi temporis caussa, protinus se accinxit confutando *Miltonio*, idque sine Libris, & sola adjutrice, memoria; cum esset ipse sibi Βιβλιοθήκη ἔμψυχος, & Muséum suum secum ferret. Jamque aliquot capita absolverat, cum commentationis filium abrumpere coëgit, solenne illi malum, Arthritis, quam & febricula comitabatur. Subinde tamen melius habens, biduo aut triduo ad relictum pensum per intervalla reversus est."—Antonius Clementius, *Claudii Salmasii, Viri Maximi, Epistolarum Liber Primus, Accedunt, De Laudibus et Vitaejusdem Prolegomena*, Lugduni Batavorum (Ex Typographia Adriani Wyngaerden), 1656, p. liii.

56) 1657: Jacobus Schaller, Erhardus Kiesser, and Christophorus Güntzer, *Dissertationis ad quaedam loca Miltoni pars prior et posterior, quas Adspirante Deo praeside Dn. Iacobo Schallero, SS. Theol. Doct. & Philos. Pract. Prof. Ord. h.t. Facult. Phil. Decano.*

---

24. of Jan." (no year). In both the 1678 and 1688 editions the allusion occurs on p. 442. Masson, III, 62, quotes the first part of the allusion from the 1754 edition, and conjectures that it gives Howell's impression about 1643-44. But Howell speaks of "this Republic" and, a moment later, of the Commonwealth; the date is probably, therefore, after 1650. The Thomason copy of *A Fourth Volume of Familiar Letters* is dated June 11. Todd, I, 40, also noted the allusion.

[53] Thomason dated his copy of this book July 23. I have the above reference from Professor French. My own copy of the 1656 *Glossographia* does not contain the advertisement, and it has not occurred in any other copies which I have examined. Professor French assures me, however, that it is a genuine reference, and I gratefully include it. A second edition of Blount's dictionary appeared in 1661, but contained no allusion to Milton.

[54] This is an invective against Milton's Cromwellian letter of August 1656, no. 75 in the "Columbia" edition, XIII, 236-7. The letter is reprinted on pp. 16-18 of the pamphlet, where it is there called *Literae Cromwellii ad Unitarum Provinciarum Ordines.* I take this reference from the "Columbia" edition, XIII, 598. Compare Raymond, p. 320.

[55] Masson, IV, 537-8, translates this passage.

[56] There is a copy of this book in the library of Christ's College, Cambridge. It consists of a reprint of Schaller's *Dissertatio* of 1653 (see no. 47 above), here called *Exercitatio*, followed by five sets of laudatory verses and the *Dissertatio* of Güntzer.

Solenniter defenderunt Erhardus Kiesser et Christophorus Güntzer. Argentorati (typis Friderici Spoor), 1657.

57) 1657: Josua Poole, *The English Parnassus: or, a Helpe to English Poesie. Containing a Collection Of all Rhyming Monosyllables, The choicest Epithets, and Phrases.* London (for Tho. Johnson), 1657, p. 42 *et passim.*

58) 1658: "[sig. P^v]—Mr *Milton.* Of Reformation. 4°.
—Of Episcopacy against Bp Vsher and Bp *Hall.* 4°.
—Reasons of Church Government. 4°.
—An Apology for *Smectymnuus.* 4°.
—Against *Salmatius:* Latin. 4°. And the same in *Folio.* ΕΙΚΟΝΟΚΛΑ´ΣΤΗΣ in answer to Σ'ΚΩ'Ν ΒΑΣΙΛΙΚΗ; The portraiture of his sacred Majesty in his solitudes and sufferings. 4°.
—The Doctrine and Discipline of Divorce, restored to the good of both sexes, from the bondage of the Canon Law, to the true meaning of the Scripture in the Law and Gospel compared. 4°.
—[sig. Ee4^v] Mr *Milton's* Poems with a mask before the Earl of *Bridgwater.* 12°."
—William London, *A Catalogue of the most Vendible Books in England,* London, 1658.

59) 1658: "[*index*] Joannis Miltoni Angli pro Populo Anglicano Defensio contra Claudii Anonymi, alias Salmasii Defensionem Regiam. Editio correctior & auctior, ab Autore denuo recognita."
—*Mercurius Politicus,* no. 443, November 18-25, 1658, p. 29.

Kiesser evidently undertook to defend, not a dissertation of his own, but the old one of Schaller. Masson, unable to find the whole work, discusses the B.M. copy of the *pars posterior* by Güntzer, V, 402-4. According to a MS note in the B.M. copy, Güntzer defended his dissertation on September 17, 1657, at Strasburg.

[57] "Miltons Poems" is listed among "The Books principally made use of in the compiling of this Work," pp. 41-2. It would be interesting to know the exact extent to which Poole used Milton. Poole's book was reprinted in 1677; the allusion to Milton here is on p. 34 of this edition. *The English Parnassus* is a posthumous publication. See above p. 23.

[58] Thomason dated his copy of the *Catalogue* September 25, 1658. In London's list of Milton's pamphlets most of the items are starred, indicating that they were printed before 1655. Under Mr. Gott (p. 30) London noted: "Novae Solymae, lib. Sex." Samuel Gott's book was attributed to Milton by W. Begley in an interesting edition of *Nova Solyma* (2 vols., London, 1902), but he had overlooked London's identification of the true author. Note that London omits *Animadversions,* 1641, but identifies Milton as the author of three pamphlets published anonymously.

[59] French, p. 252, notes but does not quote this advertisement. I am grateful to Mr. Victor Scholderer for sending me the quotation from the Thomason copy of *Mercurius Politicus,* which had been removed to the National Library of Wales for greater safety (September 1940).

?) 1658: "... the *King* was much inclining also to call one [a Parliament], which his candid and ingenious consideration of necessity grounded upon such Reasons, as himself expresseth in his most admired Treatise, his excellent Book EIKON BASILIKH, (which we hereafter shall have several occasions in some Particulars to mention) it being *the Portraiture of his Sacred Majesty in his Solitudes and Sufferings*, with his spiritual *Meditations* upon each *Chapter* and *Occasion*, written no doubt from the truth of a troubled Soul, and indisputable to be of his own compiling. And although an industrious malignant Pen hath laboured to wrest that honour from his Sacred memory, he cannot fix it in likelihood upon any other person in the World, the majesty and manner of the style onely his, and unimitable by any other."—William Sanderson, *A Compleat History of the Life and Raigne of King Charles from His Cradle to his Grave*, London (for H. Moseley, R. Tomlins, & Geo. Sawbridge), 1658, p. 324.*

60) 1659: "A Treatise of, Civil Power in Ecclesiastical Causes; shewing that it is not lawful for any power on *E*arth to compel in matters of Religion. Written by Mr *Milton*. Sold in *Pauls-Churchyard, Fleetstreet*, and *Westminster-Hall*, &c."—*Mercurius Politicus*, no. 554, February 10-17, 1659, p. 237.

61) 1659: "*Advertisements of Books newly Printed and Published.* [*index*] A Treatise of Civil Power in Ecclesiastical Causes; shewing that it is not lawful for any Power on Earth to compel in matters of Religion. By *J.M.* Sold at several Book-sellers shops in *Pauls* Churchyard, the *Old Exchange*, and at *Westminster*."—*Publick Intelligencer*, no. 174 (April 25-May 2, 1659), p. 397.

62) 1659: "The old Gunpowder Traitors only plotted, but never actually effected the blowing up of the King, Parliament, and House of Lords ... But our new *Salt-peter-men*, have with an high strong hand fully executed, accomplished whatever they designed;

---

* This passage was called to my attention by Professor French. I have questioned its right to inclusion in this list because the "industrious malignant Pen" could refer to the author of *Eikon Alethine* as well as to Milton.

[60] French, p. 252, notes but does not quote this advertisement, which reproduces the title-page of Milton's pamphlet except for the author's name and the imprint. The title-page reads: "*The author* J.M. London, Printed by *Tho. Newcomb, Anno* 1659." Milton, however, signed his preface in full.

[61] Milton's pamphlet is the first of the books listed. Mrs. Raymond, p. 198, noted this advertisement, which simply reproduces the title of Milton's pamphlet except for the imprint. The *Treatise of Civil Power* was registered February 16, and printed by Thomas Newcomb.

[62] Dated by Thomason May 13, 1659. The 20-page tract seems to have been missed by Masson and others.

and because they miscarried not in it, like them, but by Gods justice
upon them, us, our King, Lords, Parliament for all our crying sins,
have prospered in this *Fœlix Scelus*, and brought their *wicked devices
to pass;* they glory in it, as the *Highest Act of Justice*, the 𝕭𝖊𝖘𝖙 𝖔𝖋
𝕮𝖆𝖚𝖘𝖊𝖘, *the Greatest Mercy and Deliverance that ever befel* the English
Nation [marginal note: "See their Declaration of 17 March, 1648. &
May 6. 1659. John Godwins Obstructors of Justice, Cooks & Brad-
shawes Speeches, John Miltons Answer to Salmatius, and sundry other
printed Pamphlets."]"—William Prynne, *The Re-publicans and others
spurious Good Old Cause, briefly and truly Anatomized*, [London],
1659, p. 10.

63) 1659: "Themselves in divers of their printed *Declarations,
Knacks,* and their Instruments in sundry Books, (as *John
Goodwin, Markham, Needham, Melton,* and others,) justified, maintained, the very highest, worst, treasonablest, execrablest, of all Popish
and Jesuitical, Unchristian tenents, practises, Treasons, as the *murder-
ing of Christian Protestant Kings*, (under the notion of Tyrants) *the
blowing up of Parliaments, the subverting of Kingdoms, the altering of
all setled Laws, Governments, the forcible usurpation of others Crowns,
Honors, Officers, Estates, without Right or Title, by force, murder,
treachery, the breach of, dispensation with, absolution from all sacred
Oaths, Leagues, Covenants, Promises, Contracts, rebellion, against all
lawfull Superiours,* and the open Violation of the 5, 6, 8, 9 & 10. moral
Commands of God himself, under the pretences of publick *Justice,
Necessity, Self-preservation, Reformation, Religion, publick good,
safety, advancement of the Gospel and Kingdom of Iesus Christ, re-
payed with their own ejection."*—William Prynne, *A true and perfect
Narrative of What was done, spoken by and between Mr. Prynne, the
old and newly Forcibly late secluded Members, the Army Officers, and
those now sitting*, [London], 1659, p. 50.

64) 1659: "The other Objection is, that there being now no opposition
made to the Government of his Highness, that the people
following their callings, and trafficque, at home and abroad, making
use of the laws, & appealing to his Highnes courts of justice: That all
this argues the peoples tacit consent to the Government; and that there-

---

[63] This diatribe is dated by Prynne May 18, 1659. The tract, 102 closely printed
pages, seems to have been missed by Masson and others. There are three copies of it in
the Bodleian Library.

[64] This allusion was noted by Stern, III, 275. *Killing No Murder* first appeared in
1657; the above quotation is from the later edition, dated by Thomason June 9, 1659.
The inflammatory pamphlet by "Allen" is usually attributed to Edward Sexby and Silas
Titus. Two editions of *Traicté Politiqu., Composé par William Allen Anglois* appeared
dated "Lugduni, 1658"; they are translations of *Killing No Murder*, possibly by J. Car-

fore now tis to be reputed lawful, and the peoples obedience voluntary. To the first I answer with learned *Milton* that if God commanded these things, 'tis a sign they were lawful and are commendable. But secondly, as I observed in the Relations of the examples themselves; Neither *Sampson* nor *Samuel* alledged any other cause or reason for what they did, but retaliation, and the apparent justice of the actions themselves." —William Allen [pseud.], *Killing, No Murder: With Some Additions Briefly Discourst in Three Questions*, etc., London, 1659, p. [11].

65) 1659: "43. *Pro populo Anglicano.* Proving that Kings had many Evills, because the *Kings Evill* was so often cured." —[John Birkenhead], *Paul's Church-Yard. Libri Theologici, Politici, Historici, Nundinis Paulnis (unà cum Templo) prostant venales. Iuxta seriem Alphabeti Democratici. Done into English for the Assembly of Divines*, [London, 1659].

66) 1659: "Considerations touching the likeliest means to remove Hirelings out of the Church, wherein is also discours'd of Tithes, Church-fees, Church-Revenues, and whether any maintenance of Ministers can be settled by Law . The Author *J.M.*"—*Mercurius Politicus*, no. 585, September 1-8, 1659, p. 713.

67) 1659: "Considerations touching the likeliest means to remove Hirelings out of the Church: Wherein is also discours'd of Tithes, Church-Fees Church Revenues; and whether any maintenance of Ministers can be settled by Law. The Author *J.M.* Sold by *L. Chapman* at the *Crown* in Popes head Alley."—*Mercurius Politicus*, no. 591, October 13-20, 1659, p. [809].

68) 1659: "Yea, that *Christianity* it self in the primitive times did neither want able *pastours*, nor was so disquieted with *politically complying* opinions, curiosities, &c, untill *Constantine* began

---

pentier de Marigny, and the Milton allusion occurs on p. 72 of one, p. 127 of the other. In the 1689 reprint of the English version, the Milton allusion occurs on p. 19. The context of the allusion is obscure from the above quotation. "Allen" proposes three questions: (1) is Cromwell a tyrant; (2) is it lawful to kill him; and (3) if it is lawful, is it profitable or noxious to the Commonwealth? The Milton allusion comes in answer to two hypothetical objections to the second "question."

[65] This political satire is dated by Thomason July 6. The apparent allusion to Milton's *Defensio* is no. 43 under "Classis III": "*Historians and Philosophers.*"

[66] French, p. 252, notes but does not quote this advertisement, which reproduces the title-page of Milton's pamphlet except for the imprint. Compare no. 67 below.

[67] This advertisement, unlike no. 66 above, names the bookseller of Milton's pamphlet; he is named in the imprint of the pamphlet itself. French, p 252, notes but does not quote the advertisement.

[68] This book, which was dated by Thomason November 8, was called to my attention by Professor J. M. French. It is a revised version of a little 45-page pamphlet of the

to enrich the Churches, at what time a voice was heard from Heaven, *This day poyson hath been shed in the Church,* and of which act of his *Dantes* the famous *Italian* poet in his 19. *Canto* of *Inferno* singeth thus, as the excellent Mr. *J. Milton* doth render it in English blank verse
>*Ah* Constantine, *of how much ill was cause*
>*Not thy conversion, but those rich demeans*
>*That the first wealthy* Pope *received of thee.*"

Henry Stubbe, *A Light Shining out of Darknes,* etc., London, 1659, pp. 174-175.

69) 1659: "His Justice was as blind as his friend *Milton,*
>Who slandered the *Kings Book* with an ill tongue."

—*A Guild-Hall Elegie, upon the Funerals of that Infernal Saint Iohn Bradshaw, president of the High Court of Iustice,* 1659.

70) 1660: "The ready and easie way to establish a free Commonwealth, and the excellence thereof compared with the inconveniences and dangers of readmitting Kingship in this Nation. The Author *J.M.* Wherein by reason of the Printers haste, the Errata not coming in time, it is desired [t]hat the following faults may be amended. Page 9. line 32. for the *Areopa*[*g*]*us,* read of *Areopagus.* P. 10. l. 3 for full Senate, true Senate, l. 4 for s[i]ts, is the whole Aristocracy, l. 7. for Provincial States, States of every City, p. 17. l. 29. for cite, citie, l. 30. for left, [f]elt. Sold by *Livewell Chapman* at the Crown in Popes head Alley."—*Mercurius Politicus,* no. 610, March 1-8, 1660, p. 1151.

71) 1660: [Roger L'Estrange], *Be Merry and Wise; or, A Seasonable Word to the Nation,* etc., [London], 1660. [For the allusion to Milton see the first quotation under L'Estrange's *Apology,* no. 81 below. Thomason dated the earlier tract March 13, 1660.]

72) 1660: "But *John Milton* is their Goos-quill Champion, who had need of *A Help meet* to establish any thing, for he has a Ramshead, and is good only at Batteries, an old Heretick both in Religion

---

same name, which had appeared earlier in 1659 and contains no allusion to Milton. Milton's translation from Dante's *Inferno,* XIX, 115-7, had appeared in his *Of Reformation,* 1641.

[69] Thomason dated this single sheet November 9. Mrs. Raymond quoted the above allusion, p. 202.

[70] French, p. 252, notes but does not quote this advertisement. Thomason dated his copy of Milton's pamphlet March 3.

[72] Masson, V, 658-9, quotes the entire passage. Thomason dated this eight-page pamphlet March 17, 1660. The allusion to Milton is part of a vulgarly humorous attack on the Rump. Milton's *Ready and Easy Way,* which is referred to, had appeared on or before March 3.

and Manners, that by his will would shake off his Governours as he doth his Wives, foure in a Fourtnight, the Sun-beams of his scandalous papers against the late Kings book, is the Parent that begot his late new Commonwealth, and because he like a Parasite as he is, by flattering the then tyrannical power, hath run himself into the bryers, the man will be angry if the rest of the Nation will not bear him company, and suffer themselves to be decoyed into the same condition; he is so much an enemy to usual practices, that I believe when he is condemned to travel to *Tyburn* in a Cart, he will petition for the favour to be the first man that ever was driven thither in a *Wheel-barrow;* and now *John* you must stand close and draw in your Elbows, that *Needham* the Commonwealths Didapper may have room to stand by you . . . "— *The Character of the Rump*, London, 1660, pp. 2-3.

?) 1660: "From the *Doctrine,* and *Discipline* of now and anon;
  Preserve *us,* & our *wives:* . . .
From *Bradshaws* presumption, and from *Hoyle's Despaires*
From Rotten Members; blind Guides; Preaching Aldermen . . .
Libera nos, Domine."
—*A Free-Parliament-Letany*, 1660.*

73) 1660: "*XXII.* Whether *I.M.* his ready and easie way to establish a Common-wealth without re-admitting of Kingship (which *Tho. Newcomb* mentions in his advertisements and paraphrastical book of *Thursday* the 8th. instant) be not borrowed in copy from the States of *Holland,* or whether such a fool as the Author deserve not to be sent to Bridewell for pretending so much good to his Country and dare not shew his name to his Libell? *XXIII.* Whether his new frame of a Common-wealth without re-admitting of Kingship, together with that fool *Harringtons,* ought not to be sent to *terra incognita* or, Sir *Th. Moors* Utopia, together with the Authors themselves to frame a free State there. *XXIV.* Whether any ingenious person can choose but laugh at these fools assertions and pretence of maintaining such a rediculous thing as a free State, since in 12 years time we have found by experience, the Nation never was more Quiet, then when governed

---

* These lines from the fourth and last (eighteenth) stanzas of a verse satire published on a single sheet were noted by Mrs. Raymond, pp. 84 and 210. Thomason dated his copy March 17. The lines may not refer to Milton at all: the marginal note on the phrase "Doctrine and Discipline" is "Sedgewick," and "blind guide" was an epithet frequently used throughout the period. The verses were to be sung "To the tune of *An old Souldier of the Queenes.*"

[73] This eight-page pamphlet, which seems to have been missed by Masson, is dated by Thomason March 24, 1659/60. Note that Collinne appears not to have recognized Milton's initials. I have not seen the Newcomb advertisement of Milton's *Ready and Easy Way*. Raymond, pp. 210-11, mangles the above quotation.

by a single person?"—William Collinne, *The Spirit of the Phanatiques Dissected and The solemne League and Covenant solemnly discussed in 30 Queries*, [London] (for F. Wallis), 1660, pp. [7-8].

74) 1660: *The Censure of the Rota Upon Mr Miltons Book, Entituled, The Ready and Easie way to Establish A Free Common-wealth*. London [a facetious imprint], 1660.

75) 1660: G[ilbert] S[heldon?]. *The Dignity of Kingship Asserted: in answer to Mr. Milton's Ready and Easie Way to establish a Free Commonwealth*. London (E.C. for H. Seile and W. Palmer), 1660.

76) 1660: "[pp. 2-3] SOme two dayes since, came to my view, a *Bold, Sharp Pamphlet,* call'd PLAIN ENGLISH—directed to the GENERAL, *and his* OFFICERS, &c. —— It is a *Piece,* drawn by no *Fool,* and it deserves a serious *Answer.* — By the *Design;* —the *Subject;* —*Malice,* and the *stile;* I should suspect it for a *Blot* of the same *Pen* that wrote ICONOCLASTES. *It runs foule;* — *tends to Tumult;* —and, not content, Barely to *Applaud the Murther of the King,* the excrable *Author of it vomits upon his Ashes; with a Pedantique, and Envenom'd scorn, pursuing still his sacred Memory.* Betwixt *Him, and his Brother Rabshakeh,* I think a man may venture to divide the glory of it; It relishes the mixture of their *united faculties,* and *wickednesse.* As yet, 'tis true; the *Hand* is somewhat *Doubtfull* to us; but the *Drift,—Certain*: . . . [p. 5] Say, —*MILTON; NEDHAM; either,* or *both,* of you, (or whosoever else)—Say; where this *Worthy Person* [i.e. General Monk], ever mixt with you?" —[Roger L'Estrange], *Treason Arraigned, In Answer to Plain English,* London [for H. Brome], 1660.

---

[74] This satiric reply to Milton, dated on the title-page March 26 and dated by Thomason March 30, is reproduced on pp. 229-244 of the present volume. An introductory note follows, p. 280.

[75] This book was corrected in print by the author March 29 (see its *errata*) and registered March 31. Hence, the book must have appeared earlier than Masson (V, 691) and the Thomason Catalogue assume. There are copies in the Harvard and Huntington Libraries.

[76] This pamphlet was acknowledged and reprinted by L'Estrange on pp. 114-145 of his *Apology*; see no. 81 below. Masson, V, 665-6, quotes the entire passage. Thomason dated *Treason Arraigned* April 3, 1660. On p. 22 (error for 30) of the pamphlet, Milton is listed with many other *"Rebellious Devils"*. L'Estrange also wrote *Double Your Guards* (an answer to *An Alarum to the Armies*), dated by Thomason April 5, in which he does not mention Milton by name but says (p. 3): "I suppose they [the two pamphlets] are *Twinns; the issue* of the *same Brayne* . . . " Thus Milton is suspected of writing, not only *Plain English,* but also *An Alarum*.

LIST OF PRINTED ALLUSIONS

77) 1660: [Roger L'Estrange], *No Blinde Guides, In Answer To a seditious Pamphlet of J. Milton's, intituled Brief Notes upon a late Sermon*, etc., London (for Henry Broome), 1660.

78) 1660: "This 𝕰𝖞𝖊-𝕾𝖆𝖑𝖛𝖊, Gentlemen, which our *pretending Oculist* presents you with, is a medicine of the same Composition, which (by general report) strook *Milton* 𝕭𝖑𝖎𝖓𝖉: and 'tis his Interest that You should be so too."—[Roger L'Estrange], *Physician Cure thy Self: or, an Answer To a Seditious Pamphlet, Entitled Eye-Salve*, London (for H.B.), 1660, p. 2.

79) 1660: "But who appears here with the *Curtain drawn?*
What *Milton!* are you come to see the sight?
Oh *Image-breaker!* poor Knave! had he sawn
That which the fame of, made him crye out-right.
    He'ad taken counsel of *Achitophell,*
    Swung himself weary, and so gone to Hell.
This is a sure Divorce, and the best way,
Seek Sir no further, now the trick is found,
To part a sullen Knave from's Wife, that day,
He doth repent his Choyce, stab'd, hang'd or drown'd,
    Will make all sure, and further good will bring,
    The wretch will rail no more against his *King.*
—G.S., *Britains Triumph, for her Imparallel'd Deliverance*, London (for W. Palmer), 1660, p. 15.

80) 1660: "*Crom.* . . . Prethee, What will become of my Wife and Family. *Pet.* I professe Sir, I cannot tell certainly; but if I may guesse by the proportion and *Analogy* of *Lex Talionis*, they will not be left worth a Groat: For you know, that you and they did what you could to reduce the late Kings Family to the greatest exigences and extremities, that you could possibly imagine, or invent in all the world; and you endeavoured to bring upon them, and all the Nobility and Gentry of the three Nations, all the Indignities and Disgraces, that *Milton*, and *Nedham*, with the help of *Jack Hall*, and the Devill to

---

[77] This reply to Milton, dated April 20 on the title-page and April 25 by Thomason, is reproduced on pp. 245-260 of the present volume. An introductory note follows on p. 284.
[78] This tract is dated April 23, 1660 on its title-page. It was reissued along with *No Blinde Guides* as a part of L'Estrange's *Apology*; see no. 81 below.
[79] Thomason dated this poem May 14. The dedication is signed by G. S., and the colophon reads: "*Sic lusit Poemate fausto, ad Calendas Maij*, 1660. G. S." I have quoted stanzas 57 and 58 above. Todd, I, 40, quotes them in full. Raymond, p. 224, produces a metrical mismarriage of G. S. and Christopher Wase by confusing Todd's footnote with his text.

boot, could designe or contrive: And what then can you expect should be done with them?" —*A Third Conference between O. Cromwell and Hugh Peters in Saint James's Park,* London (Tho. Mabb), 1660, p. 8.

?) 1660: " . . . One allows plurality, or community of Wives; another allows a man to divorce that wife he hath upon sleight occasions, and to take another: . . . " —Joseph Hall, *The Shaking of the Olive-Tree,* London (J. Cadwell for J. Crooke), 1660, p. 161.*

81) 1660: "[p. 86] *In* fine, let the *General, the Secluded Members, and the Honest Souldjers, live Long, Happily,* and *Beloved;* and let the *Rest* take their *Fortune. I* could only wish his *Excellency* had been a little civiller to Mr. *Milton;* for, just as he had finished his *Modell of a Common-Wealth,* directing in these very Terms, the *Choyce;* —𝔪𝔢𝔫 𝔫𝔬𝔱 𝔞𝔡𝔡𝔦𝔠𝔱𝔢𝔡 𝔱𝔬 𝔞 𝔖𝔦𝔫𝔤𝔩𝔢 𝔓𝔢𝔯𝔰𝔬𝔫, 𝔬𝔯 𝔥𝔬𝔲𝔰𝔢 𝔬𝔣 𝔏𝔬𝔯𝔡𝔰, 𝔞𝔫𝔡 𝔱𝔥𝔢 𝔚𝔬𝔯𝔨 𝔦𝔰 𝔡𝔬𝔫𝔢. *In* come the *Secluded Members,* and *spoyle his Project.* To this *admirable discovery,* he subjoynes a *sutable Proposition* in favour of the *late sitting Members,* and This is it, having premised the *Abilities* and *Honesty, desirable in Ministers of State,* he recommends the *Rumpers* to us as so *Qualified;* advises us to quit that fond *Opinion of successive Parliament;* and suffer the Persons then in Power, *to perpetuate themselves under the name of a Grand or Generall Counsell,* and to rule *us,* and our *Heirs* for ever. *It* were great pitty these Gentlemen should lose their longings: . . . [p. 113] UPon the neck of this [i.e. *A Letter Intercepted,* answered by L'Estrange's *Sir Politique Uncased, or a Sober Answer*], came out Two sharper Pamphlets; written, (as I am of late Enformed) by a Renegado Parson; but as then, I took them to be either *Nedham's,* or *Miltons,* (a Couple of *Currs* of the same *Pack*) They were *Printed* by *Livewell Chapman,* and a *Proclamation* from the *Counsell* was issued out against him for it, to

---

[80] Mrs. Raymond, pp. 224-5, describes this allusion in one sentence but does not quote. Thomason dated his copy of the satire May 17.
* Todd, I, 40, noted this possible allusion. The quotation is from Hall's "The Mourner in Sion." Thomason dated his copy of the book June 1.
[81] Masson, VI, 326 n. 2, gives part of the above quotations. Thomason's copy of L'Estrange's *Apology* is dated June 6. The pamphlet is a detailed account of the author's activities up to the time of the Restoration. Pages 5-38 were deleted at the last minute (see the author's explanation in his preface), and unsold copies of *No Blinde Guides* and *Physician Cure thy Self* were included as part of the pamphlet. The above quotation from p. 86 is, of course, ironic in tone; it appeared first in L'Estrange's *Be Merry and Wise,* which Thomason dates March 13, 1660. The quotation from p. 157 prefaces the re-issue of *No Blinde Guides* and *Physician Cure thy Self,* both of which had appeared more than a month earlier. The quotation from p. 113 refers to *Plain English,* to which L'Estrange replied with *Treason Arraigned* (reprinted pp. 114-145), and *An Alarum to the Armies,* to which he replied with *Double Your Guards* (reprinted pp. 145-156).

which he never appeared. . . . [p. 157] the heart of the Design was almost broken: and yet they would not leave their Pamphleting. Particularly *Milton* put forth a bawling piece against Dr. *Griffith* and somebody else another scurrilous Libel, entituled, *EYE-SALVE:* I did not think it much material to reply upon these, the people being already convinc'd of the Right; but however, being excited to it by a private Friend, I return'd these following *Answers."* —Roger L'Estrange, *L'Estrange His Apology: with A Short View, of some Late and Remarkable Transactions, Leading to the happy Settlement of these Nations,* etc. London (for Henry Brome), 1660.

82) 1660: "51. Mr. *Milton* in answer to *Salmasius* gives the whole glory of this Heroick action (as he call'd it) to the English Parliament; And indeed it was properly their act originally, the Judges did but represent them; acted by their Commission, who in this are inexcusable also, that they took a Commission, and put it in execution against their undoubted King, which involved them alike in the guilt of perjury and Treason, being equally sworn to his Allegiance, and by this act (however Commissionated) they were questionless murtherers." —George Starkey, *Royal and other Innocent Bloud crying aloud to Heaven for due vengeance,* London (A. Warren for Daniel White), 1660, p. 18.

83) 1660: "3. Milton *that writ two Books against the Kings, and* Salmasius *his Defence of Kings, struck totally blind, he being not much above* 40. *years old."* —*The Picture of the Good Old Cause drawn to the Life In the Effigies of Master Prais-God Barebone, with Several Examples of Gods Judgements on some Eminent Engagers against Kingly Government,* London, 1660.

84) 1660: By the King. *A Proclamation, For calling in, and suppressing of two Books written by John Milton; the one Intituled, Johannis Miltoni Angli pro Populo Anglicano Defensio,*

---

[82] The Thomason copy of this pamphlet is dated July 13. Starkey addresses himself to Parliament. Raymond, p. 227, notices the allusion but does not quote. There is a copy of this scarce pamphlet in the New York Public Library.

[83] Masson, VI, 179 n., has a very full account of this single sheet, which was dated by Thomason July 14, 1660. Milton is the third of seven "Examples" of God's judgment, the others being Dorislaus, Anthony Ascham, Hoyle, Sir Gregory Norton, Lockyer, and Colonel Venn.

[84] This proclamation is dated from Whitehall August 13, 1660. There were at least three different issues of it printed more or less simultaneously; one of them erroneously makes it appear that Goodwin's book was written in defence of King Charles. Masson, VI, 181-2, quotes the text of the proclamation, but not the heading given above. Mrs. Raymond reproduces one of the issues (facing p. 226); three are reproduced in facsimile in the *Catalogue of Works by or relating to John Milton* by Maggs Bros. Ltd. in January 1936.

contra Claudii Anonymi, aliàs Salmasii, Defensionem Regiam; and the other in answer to a Book Intituled, The Pourtraicture of his Sacred Majesty in his Solitude and Sufferings. And also a third Book Intituled, The Obstructors of Justice, written by John Goodwin. London, 1660.

85) 1660: "*On Munday,* August 13. Several proclamations were given by his Majesty, *Against fighting of Duels; For calling in and suppressing books of* John Milton *and* John Godwin; *and for publishing a former Proclamation of the 30rh of* May, *entituled, a Proclamation against Vicious, Debauch't and Profane Persons.* . . . The Reader is desired to take notice, That in some printed Copies of the ensuing Proclamation, these words, relating to the Title of *John Goodwins* Book, *viz.* [*THE TRAITEROUS SENTENCE AGAINST*] were by mistake omitted; and that the Proclamation truly printed, is as followeth: . . . " —*Mercurius Publicus,* August 9-16, 1660.

86) 1660: "*Wherein is set down, the Acts of all those*
   In Pluto's *Black Court, that guarded* Nolls *Nose,*
   As Harrison, Hewson, *and* Cook *that curst Pigg,*
   With Cobbet, Vain, Scot *and* Nurse Haslerigg.
   And next those Black Chaplains that preach'd up Nolls *Nose,*
   Goodwin, Milton, *and* Peters *i'th close* . . . "
—Collonel Baker, *The Blazing-Star, or, Nolls Nose. Newly Revived, and taken out of his Tomb,* London (for "Theodorus Microcosmus"), 1660, p. [i].

87) 1660: [reprint of the King's Proclamation of August 13]—*The Parliamentary Intelligencer,* no. 34, August 13-20, 1660, pp. 538-540.

?) 1660: [a reference to the sect of Divorcers, in *A Breife Description or Character of the Religion and Manners of the Phanatiques in generall,* London, 1660, p. 33.]*

---

[85] The proclamation itself follows in this, the English edition of the *Mercurius Publicus.* The "Scotch edition" of the same journal for August 15-22 contains both the above quotations and the proclamation itself, with only slight variants. Raymond, p. 323, has a confused account of the two journals.

[86] The above quotation occurs on the title-page of this eight-page verse satire, which Thomason dated August 17. On p. 5 the line containing Milton's name is repeated:
   "Noll wants his old Chaplains were fit for his Nose,
      Goodwin, and *Milton* and *Peters* ith close;
   And *Stirry* that saw him so high intercede,
      At Heavens right hand for all Saints in their need."
Stern, IV, 8 and 195, notes this allusion.

[87] Raymond, p. 323, mentions a reprint in *The Publick* [sic] *Intelligencer* for this date. See also nos. 84-85 above.

* This reference, which I have not yet been able to verify, is noted by Todd, I, 40. Thomason dated his copy of the tract September 10.

88-A) 1660: *Ad Ioannem Miltonum Responsio, Opus Posthumum, Claudii Salmasii.* Divione (typis Philiberti Chavance, typographi Regii), 1660.

88-B) 1660: *Claudii Salmasii ad Johannem Miltonum Responsio, Opus Posthumum.* Londini (typis Tho. Roycroft; impensis Jo. Martin, Ja. Allestry, & Tho. Dicas), 1660.

89) 1660: [Joseph Jane], *Salmasius his Dissection and Confutation of the Diabolical Rebel Milton in his impious Doctrines of Falsehood.* London (J. Garfield), 1660.

90) 1660: "Nec suis unquam parasitis indiguit fanaticum istud genus hominum, qui exitiali facundiâ armati semper in procinctu stant, & quà jubenter [lubenter?] linguas venales flectunt, eorum turpissima crimina ut virtutes collaudant, aliorum omnium dotes dente Satyrico perfoduint [perfodunt?], et in Deum ipsum, si Senatus perduellis mandaverit, profanæ eloquentiæ arietes admovere non erubescunt. . . . Regicidium commendant posteris ut Heroïci facinoris exemplum singulare; Eversionem Ecclesiæ, extirpationem regni, regiique sanguinis, inter facta fortissima numerant. . . . Qui fructum cum semente conferre vellet & messem ex mellitis eorum globulis in nostra horrea

---

[88] The dedication to Charles II is dated "Divione, *Calend. Septemb. MDCLX.*" The book was registered in London September 19, not (as Masson says, VI, 203) September 29.

[89] A copy of this book, which Masson was unable to find, is now in the library of Christ's College, Cambridge. The title is fraudulently misleading, for the book is merely a re-issue of Jane's *Eikon Aklastos* of 1651, with a new title-page and a publisher's preface. Masson, VI, 213, is probably correct in his conjecture that the new title-page was an attempt to represent the unsold copies of an answer to *Eikonoklastes* as an English translation of the posthumous *Responsio* of Salmasius. If so, the above book doubtless appeared very late in 1660.

[90] These interesting excerpts from the preface to the *History of the Council of Florence* were very kindly sent me by Professor French; I have not yet had an opportunity to verify the quotations. Although there is no direct reference to Milton, Creyghton clearly has the Milton-Salmasius controversy in mind. Following is a free translation of the above passages: "Never has this fanatic group of people lacked parasites who stand always in readiness, armed with devastating eloquence; and whenever they wag their venal tongues, they praise their most heinous crimes as virtues, pierce with the tooth of satire what is outstanding in others, and do not blush to use the battering rams of their vile oratory even against God himself, if the hostile Parliament so ordains. . . . They commend regicide to generations to come as the prototype of the Heroic Deed; they count the subversion of the Church and the extinction of kingship and royalty among the actions of greatest gallantry. . . . Whoever wishes to compare the fruit with the seed, and to weigh the harvest sprung from their sugar-coated pills and carried into our granaries, may consider it better to return to that crude but honest stammering, in Latin, of our fathers, and to bray with the Golden Ass of Apuleius, than to stroll after *their* fashion in the gardens of Marcus Tullius and Titus Livius, and make fraudulent promises. . . . If by chance a person writes anything favorable about kings, they grow angry, gnash their teeth, rave, and go the limit of their noisome oratory, so that in no king whatsoever might be found one shred of decency, simply because they themselves have been thundering so indecently against the inviolable heads of all kings."

importatam ponderare, satius multo judicaret, ad rudem illam, sed honestam Latinae Orationis balbutiem cum nostris patribus, rudere cum aureo Asino Ampulei revertere, quam sic in Marci Tulli, ac Titi Livii viridariis expatiari, pollucibiliter [pollicibiliter?] mentiri. . . . Tum de Regibus si quis forte fortuna encomiasticè scripserit, succensent, frendunt, debacchantur, & in omne latus obstreperam volvunt facundiam, ne quis Rex pro pio habeatur, quando ipsi in omnium Regum sacrosancta capita tam impii detonuerunt." —Sylvester Sgouropolos, *Vera historia unionis non verae inter Graecos et Latinos, sive Concilii Florentini exactissima narratio Graece scripta per Sylvestrum Sguropulum. Transtulit in sermonem Latinum notasque adjecit Robertus Creyghton*, Hagae-Comitis (Ex typographia A. Vlacq.), 1660, sig. [c] *recto* and *verso*.

?) 1660: "*Sir,* Besides the natural *Antipathy* of my *Genius* to Controversies, I have been of late so *divorced* from my self and my own thoughts, by the motion of an higher wheel than my own occasions, that I am altogether discouraged to give you any account of this piece, upon so *transient* a view, that I fear I shall give you as ill an account of *it*, as he did of *Venice to King James*, that told him, He knew nothing of it, for he *rode post* through it: Yet, to satisfie your command, against all these discouragements, I shall adventure a few hasty lines to your more setled judgment. Sir, did not the *Authors* worth out-poize those petty exceptions that might be taken in advantage, as the scarce sense of the *title*, and some other inconsiderate expressions in the *whole*, that seem to clash one against another, I shall onely commend to your consideration these few thoughts. The Proverb is common (wherein wit and experience club, to say much in a little) *That marriages are made on Earth, but matches are made in Heaven.* . . . And having laid down this for a *ground*, I shall adventure this *Superstructure*, that it is not in the power of a man to *dis-joyn* himself from the companion which providence hath *joyned* him to, in so indissoluble a link of amitie, that one member is not more truly a part of a mans body than his *Wife;* and therefore he ought rather to *undergoe* with patience what God hath ordained him, perhaps for other reasons than he can understand, than to *forgoe* it with wilfulnesse. . . . To come as near therefore as I can, to comply with your Author, I shall lay down this *Position*, that it is altogether unlawful for a man or wife to divorce, *If both parties be not equally agreeing to it, and if either of them marry again.* . . . This farther, I must confess, there are some natures so *Hetrogenious*, that the streightest, and most gordion knot of Wedlock is not able to twist, of which the *Epigrammatist* speaks my mind better than I can my self:

> *Non amo te Sabide, nec possum dicere quare,*
> *Hoc tantum possum dicere, non amo te.*

Take the English, is the words of a Gentleman to his wife.

> *I love thee not* Nel,
> *But why, I can't tell:*
> *But this I can tell,*
> *I love thee not* Nel.

So that I must confesse I cannot but afford them my pitie, that are thus joyned in you know whose phrase, like a *Spread-Eagle,* with *one body, but two heads:* But whether this *division* ought to make a *Divorce,* I had rather subscribe to *your* judgment than tell you *my own,* who am
Sir, wholly at your dispose,
T.F."

—Thomas Forde, *Fænestra in Pectore, Or, Familiar Letters,* London (R. and W. Leybourn for William Grantham), 1660, pp. 103-106.*

91) 1661: "Ein ümgekaufter Milton / durch eine vergälte miltze gestochen / durfte seine verwegene zaunkönigs-feder gegen die hochfliegende adlers-feder [des Salmasius] schwingen / seiner fleisch-lüsternen Befehlgeber fleischliche / ja teuflische taht / durch einen fleischlichen / ja teuflischen aberwitz / zu rechtfärtigen. Aber die edele adlers-feder hat dannoch das feld und den sieg behalten."— Filip von Zesen, *Die verschmähete doch wieder erhöhete Majestaht: das ist Karls des zweiten königs von Engelland,* Amsterdam, 1661, pp. 185-6.

92) 1662: "Likewise how wonderfully was Mr. *Iohn Milton* [punished], who writ the seditious Antimonarchical Book against the King, in answer to Learned *Salmasius,* strucken blind soon after, and could never since by any art, or skill, either recover his sight, or preserve his Books from being burned by the hands of the common Hang-man."—I[ohn] T[aylor?], *The Traytors Perspective-glass. Or Sundry Examples of Gods just judgments executed upon many Eminent Regicides, who were either Fomentors of the late Bloody Wars against the King, or had a hand in his Death,* London, 1662, pp. 21-22.

---

* This possible allusion to Milton's tractate of divorce was noted by Todd, I, 41. The letter is to "Mr. T. P.," not (as Todd has it) T. C. Forde's translation of Martial's epigram is an interesting prototype of the better known "I do not like thee, Dr. Fell."

[91] This allusion is noted by Stern, III, 83 and 265, where most of the above quotation is given.

[92] Opposite the title-page there is a list of "such Persons as are mentioned in the following Treatise," but Milton's name is not included. Raymond, p. 240, notes this allusion, and gives part of the quotation.

93) 1662: "[p. 483] Cæterum Vir ille [John Durie], cui profectò pectus sapit, singulis fermè diebus cum Parlamentariis convivit; mihiq̀; sermonis communicatio de novæ Reip. statu cum illo solet esse creberrima. Hujusdem strenuus Defensor, *Miltonus*, libenter se in sermonem dat, pura ejus elocutio est, & scriptio tersissima. De antiquis Anglorum Theologis, horumq̀; in S. Scripturæ libros commentariis (ipsam eruditionem testor) sanè doctissimis, durius saltem, si non iniquius judicare judicium, omninò is mihi videbatur. . . . [p. 491] *Jo. Milton*, celebris ille Populi Anglicani defensor, olim & *Areopagitica* consignavit: *A Speech for the liberty of unlicenc'd printing, to the Parlament of Engeland*, i. Sermonem pro libertate sine licentia imprimendi libros, ad Parlamentum Angliæ; contra hujus constitutionem, qua non nisi cum licentia approbatos imprimere permissum erat. Percuriosus Scriptor iste jam pridem hodiernam libertatem, hoc est, A.C. 1644. in Areopagiticis suis cogitasse, mihi videtur." —*G. Richteri, J.C., ejusque familiarum, Epistolae selectiores ed. J.G. Richter*, Norimbergae, 1662.

94) 1662: "The Character of this deceased Statesman, (with whose Principles those two sayings carry little harmony) I shall exhibit to you in a paper of Verses, composed by a learned Gentleman, and sent him, *July* 3. 1652." —[George Sikes], *The Life and Death of Sir Henry Vane, Kt.*, 1662, p. 93.

95) 1663: "To better also his condition as to his Kingdoms, came forth several defences of his Authority in several Treatises, especially that of *Salmasius*, called *The Royal Defence* (which one *Milton*, since stricken with blindness cavilled at, who wrote also against that incomparable Book and Remains of King *Charles* the Martyr, about this time produced to light, though endeavoured by all means to be suppresst, called *Eikon Basilike*, in an impudent and blasphemous Libel, called *Iconoclastes*, since deservedly burnt by the Common Exe-

---

[93] Masson, IV, 350-2, translates generously from Christopher Arnold's letter to George Richter dated "*Londini, a.d.* 7. *Aug. A.S. MDC LI*." He does not, however, notice the early allusion to *Areopagitica*. The complete letter occupies pp. 482-94 of Richter's collection, and is a detailed account of personalities and books in learned and official England of 1651.
[94] These words, with their hidden allusion to Milton, introduce the first printing of Milton's sonnet to Vane. See Masson, IV, 442 n. Vane was executed June 14, 1662. I have a copy of the *Life* which was presented to Sarah Calvert by Frances, Lady Vane, and which is dated September 5, 1662.
[95] This is "The Second Impression [i.e. edition] greatly enlarged." There is no allusion to Milton in the first edition, 1662. The passage quoted above is the same in the second issue of the second edition, 1664, and also in the 1676 edition (p. 236), which contains additions by J.P. and has a marginal note on the Milton-Salmasius affair. The *imprimatur* to the 1663 edition is dated March 21. Masson, VI, 636 n., quotes only phrases from the ertire quotation.

cutioner) doth justly challenge to be here registred. Thus He triumpht by the Pen . . . " —I[ames] H[eath], *A Brief Chronicle Of the Late Intestine Warr in the Three Kingdoms of England, Scotland & Ireland with The Intervening Affairs of Treaties, and other Occurrences relating thereunto,* London (J. Best for William Lee), 1663, p. 435.

96) 1663: "*The Tenure of Kings and Magistrates* . . . Proving that it is Lawful for any who have the Power, to call to Account a Tyrant, or wicked King, and after due Conviction to depose, or put him to Death, if the ordinary Magistrate have Neglected, or Deny'd to doe it." —Roger L'Estrange, *Considerations and Proposals In Order to the Regulation of the Press: Together with Diverse Instances of Treasonous, and Seditious Pamphlets, Proving the Necessity thereof,* London (by A.C.), 1663, p. 19.

97) 1669: "ACCIDENCE commenc'd Grammar, supply'd with sufficient Rules, for the use of such (younger or elder) as are desirous, without more trouble than needs, to attain the Latine Tongue; the Elder sort especially with little teaching and their own industry. The Author, *John Milton*. In Twelves. Price, bound, 8d. Printed for *John Starkey* at the Miter in *Fleet street*, near Temple Bar."—*Mercurius Librarius*, no. 4, London, 1669.

98) 1669: "Joannes Miltonius præter alia quæ scripsit Elegantissima tum Anglicè tum Latinè, nuper publici juris fecit *Paradisum amissum* Poema quod sive sublimitatem Argumenti, sive Leporem simul & Majestatem Styli, sive sublimitatem Inventionis, sive similitudines & descriptiones quam maxime Naturales respiciamus, vere

---

[96] This short pamphlet is dated May 28 in the *imprimatur*, June 3 in the imprint. Shortly after publishing it, L'Estrange was appointed (August 1663) Surveyor of the Imprimery. Masson, VI, 480, noted the allusion but did not quote the passage given above. The Milton title illustrates, in L'Estrange's list of "Instances of Pamphlets containing Treasonous and Seditious Positions" (begins p. 17), the particular error that "The Power of the King is but Fiduciary; and the Duty of the Subjects but Conditional."

[97] This number of *Mercurius Librarius* was published in Trinity Term 1669, and licensed June 28. I have taken the above quotation from Edward Arber's transcript of *The Term Catalogues*, I, 14.

[98] William Godwin, on p. 145 of his *Lives of Edward and John Philips* (London, 1815), quotes the above passage from the 1669 edition of John Buchler's *Phrasium Poeticarum Thesaurus*, of which Phillips' *Tractatulus* was a part. Masson, VI, 636 n., relies on Godwin without having seen the book, but offers a slightly different translation of the Latin. I have been unable to find a 1669 edition of Buchler, and so quote from the 1679 edition. The passage is evidently identical except for punctuation. In the 1679 edition, Phillips' contributions begin on p. 375 of the *Thesaurus* but are given a separate title-page, as above. The *Thesaurus* was advertised in the *Term Catalogues* for Easter 1670, priced 2s. 6d., and printed for George Sawbridge.

Heroicum, ni fallor, audiet, Plurium enim suffragiis qui non nesciunt judicare censetur perfectionem hujus generis Poematis assecutum esse." —Edward Phillips, "Compendiosa Enumeratio Poetarum, &c.," in *Tractatulus de Carmine Dramatico Poetarum Veterum,* Londini (Typis T. Newcomb), 1679, p. 399.

99) 1670: "I am not I'le assure you, any of those occasional Writers, that missing preferment in the University, can presently write you their new ways of Education; or being a little tormented with an ill chosen Wife, set forth the Doctrine of Divorce to be truly Evangelical: The cause of these few sheets was honest and innocent, and as free from all passion, as any design." —[John Eachard], *The Grounds & Occasions of the Contempt of the Clergy and Religion Enquired into. In a Letter written to R.L.,* London (W. Godbid for N. Brooke), 1670, pp. [ii-iii].

100) 1670: "[F8ʳ] Duabus istis rationibus adductus Religionem & Ecclesiam mihi vindicandas esse duxi, quod solutâ potissimùm oratione pleniùs exequi conatus sum Gallicâ Diatribâ justi voluminis & libello cui titulus est *Clamor Regii sanguinis ad Cœlum,* in cujus calce *Oden* ad *Salmasium,* & *Iambum* ad *Miltonum* apposueram, quæ cum aliis ejusdem argumenti versibus hîc etiam exhibeo. . . . [Book III, pp. 141-2] *Epistolam quam Iambo in* Miltonum *Author subjunxerat, per operarum nostrarum festinantiam prætermissam, hîc exhibemus; ad paginam 36 Libelli secundi referendam.* In quod periculum me conjecerit prima hujus carminis cum *Clamore Regii sanguinis* editio, publicâ notitiâ dignum haud existimarem, nisi divini præsidii miraculum quo servatus sum incolumis, communi bonorum admiratione & summi Liberatoris laude dignissimum esset. Schedas meas ad Magnum *Salmasium* miseram qui eas eruditissimi Viri *Alexandri Mori* curæ commendavit; *Morus* Typographo tradidit, eisque Epistolam ad Regem sub Typographi nomine præfixit, oppidò eloquentissimam & bonæ frugis plenissimam. Istud *Mori* circa operas Typographicas studium, cùm

---

[99] This allusion occurs in the Preface, which lacks pagination. Mrs. Raymond, p. 269, noted and misquoted it. Eachard's pamphlet, which provoked several immediate replies, has been many times reprinted. The author was a Cambridge graduate, but not of Milton's college. Todd, I, 42, was the first to note and quote the allusion, which was called to his attention by Octavius Gilchrist.

[100] This collection of verses in three books contains, in the second book ("Ecclesiae Gemitus," pp. 36-42), the poem, "In impurissimum Nebulonem Joannem Miltonum, Parricidarum & Parricidii Advocatum," which had originally formed part of *Regii Sanguinis Clamor* (see no. 43); and this I have not reprinted. Masson, V, 219-21, translates the second passage above. The second and third books of the *Parerga* have separate title-pages, both dated 1669, and separate pagination, although the signatures are continuous. Du Moulin's book was advertised in the Michaelmas Term *Catalogue,* 1670, and again in Easter Term of 1671.

LIST OF PRINTED ALLUSIONS

Miltono per Regicidarum in *Hollandia* coryceos innotuisset, pro comperto habuit *Miltonus Clamoris* authorem esse *Morum:* Unde ille *Miltoni* (sub titulo *Defensionis secundæ pro populo Anglicano*) virulentissimus in *Morum* libellus, cui insuper inimicos in *Hollandia* creavit; Erant enim tunc temporis Anglicani Tyranni extra sua pomœria maximè formidati. Spectabam interea tacitus, nec sine lento risu, fœtum meum ad alienas fores expositum; & cœcum atque furiosum *Miltonum* Andabatarum more pugnantem & ἀερομαχόμενον à quo feriretur & quem contra feriret ignatum. At *Morus,* tantæ invidiæ impar, in Regia causa frigere cœpit, & *Clamoris* Authorem *Miltono* indicavit. Enimvero in sua ad *Miltoni* maledicta responsione, duos adhibuit testes, præcipuæ apud perduelles fidei, qui Authorem probè nôssent, & rogati possent revelare. Unde sanè mihi & capiti meo certissimum impendebat exitium. At magnus ille justitiæ vindex, cui & hanc operam & hoc caput libens devoveram, per *Miltoni* superbiam salutem meam asseruit; ut ejus sapientiæ solemne est ex malis bona, ex tenebris lucem elicere. *Miltonus* enim qui plenis caninæ eloquentiæ velis in *Morum* invectus fuerat, quique id ferme unicum *Defensionis secundæ* suæ fecerat argumentum, ut *Mori* vitam atque famam laceraret; adduci nunquam potuit ut se tam crassè hallucinatum esse fateretur. Scilicet metuens nè cæcitati ejus populus illuderet, eúmque compararent Grammaticorum pueri Catulo illi cæco apud *Juvenalem* qui piscem *Domitiano* donatum laudaturus
plurima dixit
In lævum conversus, at illi dextra jacebat Bellua.
Perseverante igitur *Miltono* totum illud periculosi in Regem amoris crimen *Moro* impingere, non poterant cæteri perduelles sine magna boni patroni sui injuria alium à *Moro* tanti criminis reum peragere. Cúmque *Miltonus* me salvum esse mallet quàm se ridiculum, hoc operæ meæ præmium tuli, ut *Miltonum* quem inclementiùs acceperam haberem patronum, & capitis mei sedulum ὑπερασπιστήν. Parce risu, Lector; & Deo Liberatori, Optimo, Maximo, & Sapientissimo, summas mecum gratias age."—Peter Du Moulin, *Petri Molinaei P.F.* ΠΑ´ΡΕΡΓΑ. *Poematum Libelli Tres,* Cambridge (John Hayes for John Creed), 1670.

101) 1670: "The History of *Britain,* that part especially now called *England,* from the first traditional beginning, continued to the Norman Conquest. Collected out of the Antientest and best

---

[101] This number of the *Catalogue* was published in Michaelmas Term 1670, and licensed November 22. I have taken the above quotations from Arber's transcript of *The Term Catalogues,* I, 56. Milton's *History* had appeared earlier in 1670, printed for James Allestry; when Allestry died during this year, Hickman became the publisher. *Paradise Regained* and *Samson Agonistes* were licensed July 2 and registered September 10, not (as Masson says, VI, 651) September 20. The title-page of the first edition, however, bears the date 1671.

Authors thereof, by *John Milton*. In Quarto. Price, bound, 6s. Printed for *Spencer Hickman* at the Rose in St. *Paul's* Churchyard. . . . PARADISE Regain'd. A Poem, in Four Books; to which is added, *Samson Agonistes*, a Dramatick Poem. The Author, *Jo. Milton*. In Octavo. Price, bound, 4s. Printed for *John Starkey* at the Mitre in *Fleet street.*"
—*A Catalogue of Books*, no. 3, London, 1670.

102) 1672: "*Joannis Miltoni* Angli, *Artis Logicæ Plenior Institutio, ad* Petri Rami *Methodum. concinnata.* Adjecta est *Praxis Analytica* et Petri Rami *Vita. Libris Duobus.* In Twelves. Price, bound, 2s."—*A Catalogue of Books*, no. 9, London, 1672.

103) 1673: "Come, you had all this out of the Answerer of *Salmasius*: and your way had been to have transcrib'd the whole side again just as it lay: For I see thou can'st not tell how to *apply* it."— *S'too him Bayes: Or Some Observations Upon the Humour of Writing Rehearsal's Transpros'd*, Oxford, 1673, p. 130.

104) 1673: ". . . he [Marvell] seems to have learned his *Accidence*, but not *Grammar*; he thinks that where-ever he meets with the Preposition *Ex*, the next Nown, though part of the same word, must always be the Ablative Case. But I am now quite tir'd with these petty Criticisms, so that for your farther satisfaction in the Grammatical part I refer, when you next see him, to blind *M*. who teaches School about *More-fields*."—*A Common-place-Book Out of the Rehearsal Transpros'd*, etc., London (for Henry Brome), 1673, pp. 35-6.

105) 1673: "*Johannis Miltoni,* Angli, *Artis Logicæ plenior Institutio ad* Petri Rami *methodum concinnata.* Adjecta est *Praxis Analytica et* Petri Rami *vita, Libris duobus.* In Twelves. Price, bound, 2s. Printed for *Robert Boulter* at the Turk's Head in *Cornhill.*"—*A Catalogue of Books*, no. 12, London, 1673.

---

[102] This number of the *Catalogue* was published in Easter Term 1672, and was licensed May 13. I have taken the above quotation from Arber's *Term Catalogues*, I, 105.

[103] This allusion seems to have been missed by Masson. The author of the 138-page book in which it occurs was possibly John Dryden (see the British Museum catalogue).

[104] Masson, VI, 704, mentions the fact that Milton is alluded to in this pamphlet, but does not give the quotation. The pamphlet was advertised in the Hilary Term *Catalogue* (see Arber, I, 128). The author may have been Roger L'Estrange.

[105] This number of the *Catalogue* was published in Hilary Term 1673, and was licensed February 7. I have taken the above quotation from Arber's *Term Catalogues*, I, 128. Boulter was the publisher of the second issue of the first edition; Spencer Hickman had published the first issue. See no. 102 above.

LIST OF PRINTED ALLUSIONS   113

106) 1673: "[p. 9] And thus much in consideration of the first Reason, that induc'd the Animadverter to call the writer of the Preface Mr. *Bayes,* because he hath no name: for which reason he might as well have cal'd him *Bayes Anonymus* in imitation of *Miltons* learned Bull (for that Bulls in *Latin* are *learned* ones, none will deny) who in his Answer to *Salmasius,* calls him *Claudius Anonymus.* . . . [p. 30] . . . methinks you might have so much studied the Readers diversion, and your own, as to have exercised your happy talent of *Rhyming,* in *Transversing* the Treatise of *Schism,* and for the Titles *dear sake* you might have made all the Verses rung *Ism* in their several changes. I dare assure you Sir, the work would have been more gratefully accepted than *Donns Poems* turn'd into *Dutch,* but what talk I of that, then *Prynnes Mount Orguil,* or *Milton's Paradise lost* in blank Verse. . . . [p. 32] 'Tis his scolding Common-place-book, which acquaints him with all the Moods and Figures of Railing; here he has all the terms of that Art which *Smectimnuus, Marchmont Needham, J. Milton,* or any other of the Professors ever thought of, for there is a certain form & Method in this as well as all other Arts . . . [pp. 41-3] . . . even timerous Minds are Couragious and bold enough to shape prodigious Forms and Images of Battels; & dark Souls may be illuminated with *bright* and shining thoughts. As, to seek no farther for an instance; the *blind* Author of *Paradise lost* (the odds betwixt a *Transproser* and a *Blank Verse Poet,* is not great) begins his third Book thus, groping for a beam of *Light.*

> *Hail, holy Light, Off-Spring of Heav'n first born,*
> *Or of th' Eternal Coeternal beam.*

And a little after,

> ————*thee I revisit safe,*
> *And feel thy Sov'raign vital Lamp; but thou*
> *Revisitst not these eyes, that rowl in vain*
> *To find thy piercing Ray, and find no dawn;*
> *So thick a drop Serene hath quencht their Orbs,*
> *Or dim suffusion veil'd.* ————

No doubt but the thoughts of this *Vital Lamp* lighted a *Christmas* Candle in his brain. What dark meaning he may have in calling this

---

[106] Masson, VI, 705-6, gives some but by no means all of the above quotations. Anthony à Wood calls Leigh the author of this 154-page reply to Andrew Marvell's *Rehearsal Transprosed,* part one, 1672. Marvell himself thought that it was Samuel Parker. Whoever the author, it is clear from the puns and allusions that he is aware of Marvell's authorship and of the Marvell-Milton friendship. He is also surprisingly familiar with Milton's published works; altogether he refers to ten pamphlets and *Paradise Lost.* Oddly enough, he does not seem to have noticed *Paradise Regained* or *Samson Agonistes;* the latter would have furnished him with neat illustrations of Milton's inconsistent stand on blank verse. This reply to Marvell was advertised in the Easter Term *Catalogue* (see Arber, I, 135), which indicates the London bookseller handling it.

thick drop Serene, I am not able to say; but for his *Eternal Coeternal,* besides the absurdity of his inventive Divinity, in making *Light* contemporary with it's Creator, that jingling in the middle of his Verse, is more notoriously ridiculous, because the *blind Bard* (as he tell us himself in his Apology for writing in blank Verse) studiously declin'd Rhyme as a *jingling sound of like endings.* Nay, what is more observable, it is the very same fault, which he was so quick-sighted, as to discover in this Verse of *Halls Toothless Satyrs.*

To teach each hollow Grove, and shrubby-Hill.

This, *teach each,* he has upbraided the Bishop with in his *Apology* for his *Animadversions on the Remonstrants Defence against Smectymnuus.* You see Sir, that I am improved too with reading the Poets, and though you may be better read in Bishop *Dav'nants Gondibert;* yet I think this *Schismatick* in *Poetry,* though *nonconformable* in point of Rhyme, as authentick ev'ry jot, as any *Bishop Laureat* of them all. . . . [p. 55] Every Age is not constellated for Heroes; such Prodigies are as rarely seen as a *New-star,* or a *Phœnix.* Once, perhaps in a Century of years, there may arise a *Martin-Mar-Prelate,* a *Milton,* or such a *Brave* as our present Author. Every day produces not such Wonders. Men, that mark out *Epocha's* are not born in many Revolutions. Time forms and perfects such as slowly, as teeming Elephants their young, and is deliver'd but of one at a Birth. . . . [p. 72] This Doctrine of *killing Kings in their own Defence,* you may safely vindicate as your own, it was never broacht before. And from such unquestionable Principles may we deduce your Account of the late War, p. 303. *Whether it were a War of Religion, or of Liberty, is not worth the labour to enquire. Which-soever was at the top, the other was at the bottom; but upon considering all, I think the cause was too good to have been fought for.* Which, if I understand not amiss, is nothing but *Iconoclastes* drawn in Little, and *Defensio Populi Anglicani* in Miniature. . . . [p. 98] That there is a Co-ordination of the three Estates, but this [opinion] is moderate; others go farther, and tell us the King is subordinate to the other two Estates *under whom* he governs: Nay, *Milton* holds, that the Legislative Power is in the Parliament exclusively, and the Executive only in the King. . . . [p. 110] Thus have you divested Princes of an *Unlimited and Uncoutroulable Power,* and given it to a more Imperious and Arbitrary Tyrant, Conscience. And because your Adversary had told you, that Princes have power to bind their Subjects to that Religion that they apprehend most advantagious to Publick Peace: to avoid this Rock, you split upon a worse, concurring rather with your *Dear Friend* Mr. *Milton:* who says, that the only true Religion if commanded by the Civil Magistrate, becomes Unchristian, Inhuman and Barbarous. . . . [p. 113] As to those Misfortunes which you observe, *page* 244, 245. befell some bold Princes that were too saucy with their Subjects, I shall only match them with some Historical Remarks in an ingenious Writer against Mr. *Milton,* concerning the Rise and Fall of Republicks, He tells us, 'That it was not the Tyranny of *Spain,* nor . . . [p. 126] It seems then in his *Accidence* (whether it be the same with *Miltons Accidence commenc'd Grammer,* I know not) it [i.e. J.O.] is *Hæc Jo,* a *Cow* both *He* and *She.* . . . [pp. 126-7] Which is almost as apposite a Description of an *Independent,* as his Friend Mr. *Milton* has given us of a *Bishop,* who in his *Apology for his Animadversions upon the Remonstrants Defence against Smectymnuus,* says, that *a Bishops foot that hath all his Toes maugre the Gout, and a linnen Sock over it, is the aptest Emblem of the Bishop himself; who being a Pluralist, under one Surplice which is also linnen* (and therefore so far like the Toe-Surplice, the *Sock*) *hides four Benefices besides the Metropolitan Toe.* So that when Arch-Bishop *Abbot* was suspended, we might say in Mr. *Miltons* style, his *Metropolitan Toe* was cut off. But since *Milton* is so great an Enemy to *great Toes* (however dignified or distinguisht, be they *Papal* or *Metropolitan*) we would fain know, whether his are all of a length, since the Leveller (it seems) affects a Parity even in Toes. Whether now his *Bishop* with a *Metropolitan Toe,* or our Authors *Congregational Man* with ten *Fingers* and long *Nails* upon all, be the fitter Monster to be shown, is hard to say. . . . [p. 128] But if *Milton's Sock* [see above] will not well endure a comparison with the *Surplice,* what think you of our Animadverter's joyning the *White-Surplices* and the *White-Aprons* in one period, *pag.* 195. (observe *John Milton,* they are both *Linnen* and both *White.*). . . . [p. 131] There is one Conceit behind which I had almost forgot, in his Discourse of the Liberty of Unlicens'd Printing *p.* 6. (which is little else but *Milton's Areopagitica* in short hand) . . . [p. 132] If you will have it in his Elegancy, I never saw a man in *so high a Salivation.* If in *Miltons* (I know he will be proud to *lick* up his *Spittle*) *He has invested himself withall the Rheume of the Town, that he might have sufficient to bespaul* the Clergy. But enough of these two loathsome Beasts, and their spitting and spauling. . . . [p. 133] As for his wonderful Gift in Rhyming, I could furnish him with many more of the *Isms* and *Nesses,* but that I should distast a *Blank Verse* Friend of his, who can by no means endure a Rhyme any where but in the middle of a Verse, therein following the laudable custom of the *Welsh Poets.* . . . [pp. 135-7]

> *O marvellous Fate. O Fate full of marvel;*
> *That* Nol's Latin *Pay two* Clerks *should deserve ill!*
> *Hiring a* Gelding *and* Milton *the* Stallion;
> *His* Latin *was gelt, and turn'd pure* Italian.

Certainly to see a *Stallion* leap a *Gelding,* (and this *leap't* fair, for he *leapt* over the *Geldings* head) was a more preposterous sight, or at least more *Italian,* then what you fancy of *Father Patrick's bestriding*

Doctor Patrick. Neither is it unlikely but some may say in defence of these Verses, that *Nol's Latin Clerks* were somewhat *Italianiz'd* in point of Art as well as Language, and for the proof of this refer those that are curious to a late Book call'd the *Rehearsal Transpros'd*, where p. 77. the Author or some body for him asks his Antagonist if the *Non-conformists must down with their Breeches as oft as he wants the prospect of a more pleasing* Nudity. And for his fellow Journey-man, they may direct the *Leaf-turners* to one of his books of *Divorce*, (for he has learnedly *parted Man and Wife* in no less then four Books) namely, his *Doctrine* and *Discipline*, where toward the bottom of the second *Page*, they may find somewhat which will hardly merit so cleanly an Expression as that of the *Moral Satyrist, words left betwixt the Sheets*. Not but that he has both *excus'd* and *hallow'd* his Obscenity elsewhere by pleading Scripture for it, as *pag*. 24, 25. *Of his Apology for his Animadversions upon the Remonstrants Defence against Smectymnuus.* And again in his *Areopagitica*, p. 13. for Religion and Morality forbid a Repetition. Such was the Liberty of his Unlicenc'd Printing, that the more modest *Aretine* were he alive in this Age, might be set to School again, to learn in his own Art of the *Blind School-master*. . . . [pp. 146-7] His Malicious and Disloyal Reflections on the late Kings Reign, traducing the Government of the best of Princes, and defaming his faithful Councellors in so foul a manner, as if he had at once made use of *Miltons* Pen, and *Gerbier's* Pencil. So black a Poyson has he suckt from the most virulent Pamphlets, as were impossible for any Mountebank but the Author of *Iconoclastes* to swallow, without the Cure of Antidotes. And certainly if that Libeller has not clubb'd with our Writer (as is with some reason suspected) we may safely say, there are many *Miltons* in this one Man."—[Richard Leigh?], *The Transproser Rehears'd: or the Fifth Act of Mr. Bayes's Play*, etc., Oxford [for Thomas Sawbridge in London], 1673.

107) 1673: "[p. 125] But fear not, you are I perceive concern'd (for what reason you your self best know, I know none) lest I should interpret it of the Rebellion of Subjects against their Prince. No, but (if it will do you any service) we will resign up this Text to the Long-Parliament side, and you know a friend of ours that has vindicated its true meaning against a learned Man abroad that indiscreetly and injudiciously enough objected it against the late Rebellion. . . . [p. 191] But to return; has not your beloved Press after all your fondness sold you a sweet bargain, and more than turn'd her tayl upon you? With

---

[107] Masson, VI, 704-5, quotes only the third of these three allusions to Milton in Parker's lengthy (536 pages) reply to Marvell. The ecclesiast speaks ironically of his "friendship" with Marvell in many places (e.g., pp. 18, 43, 81, 83, 105, 233, 527), but the above seem to be the only references to Parker's one-time mentor, Milton. The *Reproof* was advertised in the Easter Term *Catalogue* (see Arber, I, 134).

what zeal and courage have you asserted its Liberty from the bondage of *Imprimaturs* and the Inquisition of Prelates? What stiff and stubborn Homilies have you made to make it good that the suppression of a good Libel is *no less than Martyrdom, and if it extend to the whole Impression a kind of Massacre, whereof the Execution ends not in the slaying of an Elemental Life, but strikes at that ethereal and fifth essence, the breath of Reason it self, slays an Immortality rather than a Life?* [marginal note: "Areopag Pag. 4."] Such fustian bumbast as this past for stately wit and sence in that Age of politeness and reformation. . . . [p. 212] And what a lump of History have you here presented to Kings to terrifie them from making too bold, and being too sawcy with their people, *Pag.* 244, 5, 6? And if we take away some simpering phrases, and timorous introductions, your Collection will afford as good Precedents for Rebellion and King-killing, as any we meet with in the writings of *J.M.* in defence of the Rebellion and the Murther of the King."—[Samuel Parker], *A Reproof to the Rehearsal Transprosed, in A Discourse to its Authour*, London (for James Collins), 1673.

108) 1673: "Of true Religion, Heresie, Schism, Toleration; and what best means may be used against the growth and increase of Popery. The Author, *J. Milton*. In Quarto. Sold by *T. Sawbridge* in *Little Britain*."—*A Catalogue of Books*, no. 13, London, 1673.

109) 1673: "Poems, etc. upon several occasions. By Mr. *John Milton*. Both English and Latine, etc., composed at several times. With a small Tract of Education, to Mr. *Hartlib*. In Octavo. Price, bound, 2s. 6d. Printed for *Th. Dring* at the Blew Anchor, over against *Fetter lane*, in *Fleet street*."—*A Catalogue of Books*, no. 15, London, 1673.

110) 1673: "You do three times at least in your *Reproof*, and in your *Transproser Rehears'd* well nigh half the book thorow, run upon an Author *J.M.* which does not a little offend me. For why should

---

[108] This number of the *Catalogue* was published in Easter Term 1673, and was licensed May 6. I have taken the above quotation from Arber's *Term Catalogues*, I, 135. Milton's tract was published with only his initials on the title-page and with no bookseller's name in the imprint.

[109] This number of the *Catalogue* was published in Michaelmas Term 1673, and was licensed November 24. I have taken the above quotation from Arber's *Term Catalogues*, I, 151. The advertisement is for the second issue of this edition; Dring had changed his address during the year, and had caused the title-page of the *Poems* to be changed accordingly. See p. 49, n. 4, above.

[110] Masson, VI, 707-8, quotes the entire passage from Grosart's edition of Marvell. Todd, I, 103-4, quotes from the 1673 edition. The above passage occurs on pp. 339-42 of the second edition of *The Rehearsall Transpros'd: The Second Part*, 1674, and is identical

any other mans reputation suffer in a contest betwixt you and me? But it is because you resolved to suspect that he had an hand in my former book, wherein, whether you deceive your self or no, you deceive others extreamly. For by chance I had not seen him of two years before; but after I undertook writing, I did more carefully avoid either visiting or sending to him, least I should any way involve him in my consequences. And you might have understood, or I am sure your Friend the Author of the *Common Places* could have told you, (he too had a slash at *J.M.* upon my account) that had he took you in hand, you would have had cause to repent the occasion, and not escap'd so easily as you did under my *Transprosal*. But I take it moreover very ill that you should have so mean an opinion of me, as not to think me competent to write such a simple book as that without any assistance. It is a sign (however you upbraid me often as your old acquaintance) that you did not know me well, and that we had not much conversation together. But because in your 115. *p.* you are so particular *you know a friend of ours,* &c. intending that *J.M.* and his answer to *Salmasius,* I think it here seasonable to acquit my promise to you in giving the Reader a short trouble concerning my first acquaintance with you. *J.M.* was, and is, a man of great Learning and Sharpness of wit as any man. It was his misfortune, living in a tumultuous time, to be toss'd on the wrong side, and he writ *Flagrante bello* certain dangerous Treatises. His Books *of Divorce* I know not whether you may have use of; but those upon which you take him at advantage were of no other nature then that which I mentioned to you, writ by your own father; only with this difference, that your Fathers, which I have by me, was written with the same design, but with much less Wit or Judgment, for which there was no remedy: unless you will supply his Judgment with his High Court of Justice. At His Majesties happy Return, *J.M.* did partake, even as you your self did for all your huffing, of his Regal Clemency and has ever since expiated himself in a retired silence. It was after that, I well remember it, that being one day at his house, I there first met you and accidentally. Since that I have been scarce four or five times in your Company, but, whether it were my foresight or my good fortune, I never contracted any friendship or confidence with you. But then it was, when you, as I told you, wander'd up and down *Moor-fields* Astrologizing upon the duration of His Majesties Government, that you frequented *J.M.* incessantly and haunted his house day by day. What discourses you there used he is too generous to remember. But he never having in the least provoked you, for you to insult thus over his old age, to traduce him by your *Scaramuccios,* and in your own person, as a School-Master, who was born and hath lived much more ingenuously and Liberally then your self; to have done all this, and lay at last my simple book to his charge, without ever taking care to inform your self better, which you had so easie opportunity to do; nay, when you your self too have said, to my knowledge, that you saw no such great matter in it but that I might be the Author: it is inhumanely and inhospitably done, and will I hope be a warning to all others, as it is to me, to avoid (I will not say such a *Judas*,) but a man that creeps into all companies, to jeer, trepan, and betray them."—Andrew Marvell, *The Rehearsall Transpros'd: The Second Part*, London (for Nathaniel Ponder), 1673, pp. 377-80.

111) 1674: "*Joannis Miltonii* Angli *Epistolarum Familiarum liber unus.* Quibus accesserunt *Ejusdem jam olim in Collegio Adolescentis prolusiones quædam oratoriæ.* In Octavo. Printed for B. *Aylmer* at the Three Pidgeons in *Cornhill.*"—*A Catalogue of Books,* no. 17, London, 1674.

112) 1674: "*Paradise* Lost. A Poem, in Twelve Books; Revised and Augmented by the Author, *John Milton.* Price 3s."
—*A Catalogue of Books,* no. 18, London, 1674.

113) 1674: "Miltoni (Joan.) Poëmata, 8. Lond. 1645.
.... Defensio Populi Anglicani, 12. Amst. 1651.
.... eadem, 4. Lond. 1651.
.... Defensio pro se contra Alex. Morum, 8. ibid. 1655.
.... eadem, 12. Hagae Comitis, 1655.
.... Defensio secunda pro Populo Anglicano contra Alex. Morum, 8. Lond. 1654.
.... eadem, 12. Hagae-Comitis, 1654."
—*Catalogus Librorum Qui In Bibliopolio Danielis Elsevirii venales extant,* Amstelodami (Ex Officinâ Elseviriana), 1674, p. 121.

---

[111] This number of the *Catalogue* was published in Easter Term 1674, and was licensed May 26. I have taken the above quotation from Arber, I, 172.

[112] This number of the *Catalogue* was published in Trinity Term 1674, and was licensed July 6. I have taken the above quotation from Arber, I, 181.

[113] Todd, I, 223, noted the inclusion of the *Defensio Prima* and *Secunda* in this catalogue.

A MODEST CONFUTATION
OF
A Slanderous and Scurrilous LIBELL,
ENTITVLED,

ANIMADVERSIONS
VPON THE
REMONSTRANTS
DEFENSE
AGAINST
SMECTYMNUUS.

Κυλίω κατὰ τὸν ειδον. *Diog. apud Lucian. de Hist. confer.*

Printed in the yeer M.DC.XLII.

TO THE READER.

READER,

F thou haſt any generall or particular concernment in the affairs of theſe times, or but naturall curioſity, thou art acquainted with the late and hot bickerings between the Prelates and Smectymnuans: To make up the breaches of whoſe ſolemn Scenes, (it were too ominous to ſay Tragicall) there is thruſt forth upon the Stage, as alſo to take the eare of the leſſe intelligent, a ſcurrilous Mime, a perſonated, and (as himſelf thinks) a grim, lowring, bitter fool.

I have no further notice of him, than he hath been pleaſed, in his immodeſt and injurious Libell to give of himſelf: and therefore, as our induſtrious Criticks for want of clearer evidence concerning the life and manners of ſome revived Authours, muſt fetch his character from ſome ſcattered paſſages in his own writings. It ſeems he hath been initiated in the Arts by Jacke Seaton, and by Biſhop Downam confirmed a Logician: and as he ſayes his companions did, it is like hee ſpent his youth, in loytering, bezelling, and harlotting. Pag.10.

A 3 *Thus*

Pag.13.

Thus being grown to an Impoſtume in the breſt of the Vniverſity, he was at length vomited out thence into a Suburbe ſinke about London; *which, ſince his comming up, hath groaned under two ills,* Him, *and the* Plague. *Where his morning haunts are I wiſt not, but he that would finde him after dinner, muſt ſearch the* Play-Houſes, *or the* Bordelli, *for there I have traced him;* [among old Cloaks, falſe Beards, Tyres, Caſes, Periwigs, Modona Vizzards, night-walking-Cudgellers, and Salt Lotion.] *Many of late, ſince he was out of Wit and Cloaths, as* Stilpo *merrily jeered the poore Starveling* * Crates, *he is new cloathed in Serge, and confined to a Parlour; where he blaſphemes God and the King, as ordinarily as erewhile he drank Sack or ſwore. Hear him ſpeak:* [Our Liturgie runnes up and down like an Engliſh gallopping Nun, *Pag.* 16. While ſhee prankes her ſelfe in the weeds of Popiſh Maſſe, ſhe provokes the jelouſie of God, no otherwiſe than a Wife affecting Whoriſh attire, *Pag.* 22. Liturgie a bait for them (*Papiſts*) to bite at, *Pag.* 23. A Phariſaicall and vain-glorious project, *Ibid.* God hath taught them (*the People*) to deteſt your Liturgie and Prelacy, *Pag.* 24. Is Liturgie good or evill? Evill? *Pag.* 26. A * Meditation of yours obſerved at Lambeth from the Archiepiſcopall Kittens, *Pag.* 29. The Prelates would have Saint Pauls words * ramp one over another, *Pag.* 40. Let not thoſe wretched Fathers think they ſhall impoveriſh the Church of willing and able ſupply, though they keep back their ſordid ſperm, begotten in the luſtineſſe of their avarice, *Pag.* 57. Leſt thinking

---

Poſt prandia callirhoendo.
Perſ Sat. 1.
Pag. 8.

ὦ Κράτης, ſοκεῖς μοι χρείαν ἔχειν ἱματίω καινῶ, ὅπερ ἢν τῶ χιματίω La. *ert.lib.*2.*in vita* Stilpon.

Biſh. Halls Occaſ. Medit.

* In que vices ſubeunt, & luna teſte moventur. *Iuv. Sat.* 6.

thinking to offer them as a Present to God, they dish them out for the Divell, *Pag.*58. Your Confutation hath atchieved nothing against it, (*The Reply by* S M E C T Y M N U U S) left nothing upon it, but a foule taste of your Skillet foot; and a more perfect and distinguishable odour of your Socks than of your Night-cap, *Pag.*67.] *Christian, doest thou like these passages? or doth thy heart rise against such unseemly beastlinesse? Nay, but take heed:* [This is nothing disagreeing from Christian meeknesse, *Pag.*2. Not unauthorised from the Morall precept of *Solomon,* —— Nor from the example of Christ, and all his Followers, in all ages, *Ibid.*] *Horrid blasphemy! You that love Christ, and know this miscreant wretch, stone him to death, lest your selves smart for his impunity.*

This is my adversary; to *encounter whom at his own weapons* (*which he voluntarily chose* pag.4. *as* Goliah *his Sword and Spear, to defie the God and the Host of Israel*) *I am much too weak; and must despaire of victory, unlesse it may be gotten by the strength of a good cause, and a modest defense of it. I dare not say but there may be hid in my nature, as much venemous Atheisme and profanation as hath broken out at his lips;* (*Every one that is infected with the Sicknesse, hath not the Sores running upon him:*) *Of which should I be as lavish as he hath been, it might be said of us, that we encountred one the other like a* Toad *and a* Spider, *and each dyed of the others poyson: or whiles we would seem to fall out about some petty matters in Religion. we well enough agreed together to be eminently wicked. It is my Prayer to God, that all those*

and

and the like scandals, with which Hee hath, and I may grieve the Church, may be forgiven to him, and prevented in me: And that in his good time himselfe would undertake the Curing of his Churches wounds, which by the ignorance of some, and malice of others, are like to be but the worse for the Plaster.

Faerwell.

THE

THE PREFACE

§. I.

S apologeticall; and well may it be so. *Satisfaction to tender Consciences*, is that which we look for, and that which you ought to give; as having done violence through all your book to the person of an holy and religious Prelate, the eares of all good Christians within our Church, the established Laws of the Kingdom, the pretious and dear name of our common Master and Saviour Christ Jesus.

We must suppose you have *undertaken a religious cause*. that is your pretended subject; we shall examine the truth of it by and by; we must now look to your manner of handling it: a suspicious way you think; and so do I. Here we agree. Your defense is, *In such a cause, it is nothing disagreeing from Christian meeknesse, the morall precept of* Solomon, *the example of Christ.* What? to weary God and man, with lewd profanations, scurrilous jests, slanderous and reproachfull calumnies? What morall precept in *Solomon* countenances such language as this *[*Scum, Ladles, Kitchen-Physick, Brawn, Beef, Kickeshaw and Crambe-Prayers, Motley and patcht incoherences. With hey passe, repasse, and the mysticall men of Sturbridge: Your Barber leading in Balaams Asse. Christ and his Apostles, Capon and white-broath in the same leaf. Esaus red pottage, and a spur-galled Galloway. Bastards and Centaurs of spirituall fornications. A Christian Ministers Surplice, and an Egyptian Priests frock in the same suds: your Primero of piety, Cogging of Dice into heaven. Gleeking and Bacche-*

* *See more of the same botch-patch in the Epistle.*

B

Bacchanalia, and Flanks, and Briskets, &c.] Such language you should scarce hear from the mouths of canting beggars, at an heathen * altar; much lesse was it looked for in a treatise of controversall Theologie, as yours might have been thought, had you not thus prevented it. As for Christs example, which you blasphemously urge, surely that holy mouth was never so foul, but then when it was spit upon: Yet neither was that indignity so bad as this.

* δι μὲν ὖν τῷ γελοίῳ ὑπερβάλλοντες, βωμολόχος δοκοῦσιν εἶναι. *Arist. Eth. l. 4. c. 8.* Βωμολόχος *Latinis Scurra dicitur, sumtâ metaphorâ à mendicantibus, qui ad aras & templa Deûm sedebant & jacebant, & à sacrificantibus stipem mendicabant. Interea autem seipsos multis jocis & scommatis vexabant, & interdum praetereuntes conviciis prosequebantur. à* βωμὸς *ara, &* λέχομαι *jaceo seu accubo.* Vid. Mag. Com. n Eth. Arist.

Well, but what if the benefit of this kind of writing will make amends for the fault of it? Shall we do evill that good may come thereof? God forbid: not if the good which followed were far better than it is like to prove: for let us see, what does it promise? [*Even this vein of laughter, as I could produce out of grave Authors, hath oft times a strong and sinewy force in teaching* ——] doubtlesse you mean Atheism. For what else it can teach I am as far to seek, as you are of those grave Authors that defend it. I care not to know what your reading hath been; and mine own is confest small: Yet * One I have met withall, who (till you confute him with a graver) shall speak home to the purpose. *To leave all reverend compassion towards evils, all religious indignation towards faults, to turn Religion into a Comedy or Satyr, to rip up wounds with a laughing countenance, to intermixe Scripture and scurrility sometimes in one sentence, is a thing far from the devout reverence of a Christian, and scant beseeming the honest regard of a sober man.* Is this your *noble jealousie*, your *dear love* to the *souls* of weak Christians! this your *well-heated fervency!* for shame render not that holy fire of zeal, which burned as bright in our fore-fathers breasts, as it lyes dead in ours, any further suspected to the world; lest anon, men think it nothing but a name, an *ignis fatuus*, or the lying and false bragge of some vainglorious fools.

* Sir Fr. Bacon.

Τὸ φορτικὸν τοῦτο κὴ ὅσιον παρὰ τοῖς πολλοῖς ἀνθρώποις λαλόμενον κατάψευσμά ἐστιν ἀλαζόνων ἀνθρώπων κὴ σοφιςῶν *Vid. Mer. Casaub. in Praefat ad Med. Mar. Aur. Anton.*

Again,

Again, it muſt be beleeved, you have done this *not without a ſad and unwilling anger, not without many hazzards*: and therefoꝛe we muſt pardon your endevours! Who put you upon the task? who forced an unwilling, relenting man, to commit ſuch inſolencies? Little charity doth he deſerve, who will chooſe to ask forgiveneſſe, rather than not to * offend.

* Næ tu, Aule, nimium nugatores, cùm maluiſti culpam deprecari quàm culpâ carere: ——te oro, quis perpulit ut id committeres, quod priuſquam faceres, peteres uti ignoſceretur. *Cato apud Macrob. in Præfat. ad Saturn.*

§. II.

Not to tarry longer in your Preface; the intent of it was, as of other paſſages in your book, rather to maintain and defend libelling, than to give any pretended ſatisfaction: yet at the ſame time you condemn it too: condemn it on the Biſhops ſide, defend it on your own. If any of their party (for indeed thus the matter ſtands now) do chance to write, then their writings are *defaming* * *Invectives*; if any of yours, then it is *liberty of ſpeaking, permiſſion of free-writing: nothing more injurious, nothing more pinching, than the reſtraint of them to free-born ſpirits*, p. 8. For my own part, I diſlike them equally in both, unleſſe in you ſomewhat worſe, than in all that in this kinde have wrote before, becauſe you ſtand up to juſtifie it. That *Lyſimachus Nicanor*, which you inſtance in, (is but one, and truly to my remembrance I have ſeen no more; one of theirs to an hundred of yours is oddes:) I miſliked and cenſured as much as any that I have read. But what have *all* the Biſhops, on whom you ſo hotly charge it, to do with that? nay what *he*, in whoſe diſh you ſo enviouſly and maliciouſly lay it? no more than you had ſure with *Newes from Hell*, or the *Proteſtation proteſted*. Before I anſwer your Juſtification of theſe libels, I muſt tell you, you have wronged the noble ingenuity and fair memory of that wonder of our age, Sir *Francis Bacon*, whom you here bring in as a witneſſe againſt the Biſhops: He complains (you ſay) *of the Biſhops uneven hand over theſe kind of Pamphlets.* You ſay ſo: Hear him. [*And here I do much eſteem the wiſedome and religion of that Biſhop,*

Ask your Lyſimachus Nicanor what defaming invectives &c. p. 7.

Pag. 7.

which

which replyed to the first Pamphlet in this kinde; who remembred that a fool was to be answered, but not by beccmming like unto him; and considered the matter he handled, and not the person with whom he dealt.]

You will say perhaps, this was but one Bishop: Hear him again in the name of them all. [*I hope assuredly that my Lords of the Clergie have no intelligence with these other Libellours, but do altogether disallow, that their dealing should be thus defended: For though I observe in him many glozes, whereby the man would insinuate himself into their favour, yet I find too ordinary, that many pressing and fawning persons do misconjecture of men in authority; and many times* Veneri immolant suem, *they seek to gratifie them with that they most dislike.*] —[*For I have great reason to satisfie my self touching the judgment of my Lords the Bishops in this matter, by that which was written by one of them, whom I mentioned before with honour.*] Whom have you wronged most now? your Authour, your Reader, or the Bishops? Beleeve me, who ever you are, such collusion as this is unchristian.

I return to you again. *This permission of free-writing (so you are pleased to stile the most bitter and Atheisticall libels) were there no good else in it, yet at some time thus licenced, is such an unripping, &c.*

Let the good be what it will, I am sure it is the most unworthy way of procuring it that may be. What Generall, in whose brest there lived but one spark of noble valour, would first disarm the enemy, and then fight! The just arms that they have who defend a good cause, is innocence, integrity, and repute; which when they are deprived of, layes them open to such impotent nakednesse, as inevitably brings their ruine. [*These courses (* saith Master *Sandys) are base and beggarly, even when singlenesse of mind and truth do concurre with them, and far unworthy of an ingenuous and noble spirit, which soareth up to the highest and purest pathes of* Verity, *disdaining to stand raking in these puddles of obscœnity,&c.*] *When singlenesse of mind and verity concurre*; both which are wanting here in your cause: no *singlenesse of mind*, because these corruptions in manners are urged by you as arguments to disprove a clear and divine

Militum virtute non hostium imbecillite, potentia quæri debet. Themist. apud Iust. Spec. Europæ p. 94. Lond. 1632.

vine truth, (which Sir *Francis Bacon* will tell you, is as well now a policy of the Devils, as formerly pretended holinesse was to raise errors.) *No truth*, because though some corruptions, and those grievous ones, are confessed and lamented, yet not on his hand to whose person you lay them. Hear then my fore-cited Authour: [*But if to this basenesse of discoveries, other basenesse be also added; if malice prefer them, if sleight increase them, if falshood and slander taint them, then do they not onely abase men from the dignity of their nature, but even associate them with the foul enemy and calumniator thereof; whose name is the slanderous accuser of his brethren.* *Sandys Spec. Europ.*

The good that arises of these libels, (as the Florentine informs me) is, to incite the people to fury and tumult, to breed hatred, sidings, factions, ruine. [*And yet it is somewhat pinching among free-born spirits, if this liberty be denyed.*] Yea, *Some Citizens have served themselves of these calumnies, and made them steps and helps to their ambitious ends.* How? *By confirming the people in an ill opinion of them that do oppose, thereby to get their votes and partage.* And as it depresseth that scale wherein you put all the Prelates, so it raiseth that as much, wherein you put your selves. *The ripping up with exceeding severity the faults of higher callings, begetteth a great good opinion of integrity, of zeale and holinesse, to such constant reprovers of sin, as by likelihood would never be so much offended at that which is evill, were they not singularly good themselves.* And further (as you have used the matter, imputing personall faults to the government in generall, of which I shall say somewhat anon) *It gets you the opinion of wise men too*, that can see farther into Ecclesiasticall affairs, than either the Founders or Conservers of this established Polity. Thus much of libels in generall. I come now to yours. *Mach. discourses upon Livie, lib. 1. c. 8.*

Vide Hooker Eccl. Pol. in Præfat.

§. III.

Nor would I have done you the injury to have called it so, were it not too too manifest. For that which even you professedly disavow (private and personall spleen, p. 3. lin. 18.) is the greatest matter in your book; the other businesse

nesse being handled but by the by, or not at all: and where it is, in such a wretched, loathsome manner, as once I did almost doubt me, whether or no you did not jeer at both sides, at Religion, and God, and all. I shall first answer to those personall injuries, and then to the cause. Only first let me satisfie you concerning my engagements and dependencie, which perhaps you may possibly think might have wrought me to this vindication. I am free, as you, or any true subject may or need be: I have a fortune therefore good, because I am content with it: and therefore content with it, because it neither goes before, nor comes behind my merit. God hath given me a soul, eager in the search of truth; and affections so equally tempered, that they neither too hastily adhere to the truth, before it be fully examined, nor too lazily afterward. Such excesse fills the world with furious, hot-braind Hereticks, Schismaticks, &c. the defect, with cold speculative Atheists. I have alwayes resolved that neither person nor cause shall improper me, further than they are good; and so far it is my duty to give evidence.

ẟ. IV.

HE that shall weed a field of corn, bind the weeds up in sheaves, and present them at once to the eye of a stranger, that is ignorant how much good wheat the field bears, beside those weeds, may very well be deceived in censuring that field; especially if he which presents them hath put into the heap such weeds as came from elsewhere Thus it fares with men, when the evill actions of the best are picked and culled out from their virtues, and all presented in grosse together to the eye or ear of him who is otherwise ignorant of the persons whose vices or faults they are; what monsters do they seem! This and more have you done to our Prelate: This, in pinning upon his sleeve the faults of others: More, in that those which you pretend faults are indeed virtues. What hath the Remonstrant to answer for the * scorn that is by some thrown upon our Martyrs; while it is known to all, that will not be ignorant,

Foxian. Conf. ſſ. p. 14.

that

that he doth both honour their memories, and tread in their steps; and that he doth not, as they did, in an holy zeal sacrifice his blood to his God, is not that he is backward to it, but that it is not yet required at his hands. God is my witnesse, I do not, neither can I flatter him: He that so patiently hath offered up his fame, his civill life, to be torn by the teeth and phangs of calumny, how shall I think he will love his blood better than that? I know what it is that hath rendred many Martyrs and their stories so suspected as they are, to wary and uncredulous men: Sometime a * wrong cause; when Traytours shall engage God in a conspiracy, and then being detected and brought to execution, dye for it no lesse undauntedly than if it were for the dearest truth; unhappily priding themselves in that, for which they ought rather to have repented. What glory is it, if when ye are buffeted for your faults ye take it patiently? Sometimes the seeking their own deaths in a good cause, out of ambition of obtaining that honour, which those first times of the Church had set upon Martyrdome. Whence I should think it as discommendable for men to seek thus over-eagerly their own deaths, banishments, confiscations of goods, stigmatizings, as the Philosopher did the seeking of * preferments: Neither shall I ever esteem either their names or memories who shall thus gather sticks for their own severall piles; and as if God knew not what honour was fit for them, be their own Carvers: so may the same thorns which Christ wore as the *Crown of Humility*, be upon their heads the *Crown of Pride*. Otherwhiles the ignorant or malitious unfaithfulnesse of the Martyrologers, in transmitting to us those Church-stories, big-swoln with untrue Legends, as so many invincible arguments of the truth of that cause, which those Martyrs sealed with their blood. I have seen beyond sea what the Jesuites of our own nation have carped at Master *Fox* his History; which made me think, though I durst not say, that they injured them no lesse now than formerly: and if any one of ours shall do the like, I shall think he wisheth no better to the Protestant cause than they do.

Vide Donnes Pseudom.

1 Pet. 2, 20.

Τὸ αὐτὸν ἀξιοῦσθαι τὸν ἀξιωθησόμενον τῆς ἀρχῆς, ἐκ ἐρρωμένης ἐχεί. *Arist. Pol. 1. c. 7.*

§. V.

§. V.

AFter you have born the people in hand, that our Remonstrant hath defamed the old ones, it is an easie thing to perswade them that he hath made new. So you do; [*haled some into the Gehenna at Lambeth, strappado'd others with an oath ex officio* —] If that Court hath been illegall, either in the constitution of it, or in its proceedings, it is more than I know: but if so, the Remonstrant is as guiltlesse of such illegalities, as I am ignorant: And a fault committed there can no more prejudice *Him*, than the Divine right of Episcopacy. Though your *Bow-men* here were quick in the delivery of their arrows, yet they were wide of the mark.

Pag 12.

§. VI.

IF you missed before, now you will be sure to hit him. [*You love toothlesse Satyrs; Let me inform you, a toothlesse Satyre is as improper as a toothed sleek-stone, and as Bullish.*] I wonder you go no lower; perhaps his cradle might have yeelded you some worthy observation: It was reckoned amongst Saint *Augustines* faults, that in his infancy he did *morosius flere*. Such a note had not been amisse here; but *vixit* is enough for that; an happy time, that you cannot invent a slander to fixe upon. You begin therefore with his youth; the sport and leisure of his youth, even that must be raked up out of the dust, and cited to witnesse against him, as it were to disparage the holinesse of his Age and Calling. [*When my early sinnes are done away as a morning cloud, they shall never obscure or darken my setting Sun: God will never impute them to me, man may*] hath been the comfort of many a dying Saint, in the day of evill, when the iniquity of their heels have encompassed them; many, whose first years have been as famous for * debauchednesse, as their latter for devotion: whiles this *Remonstrant* no sooner came to be capable of the more violent impressions of sin, but his nature and it fell foul; and because he had overcome vices in himself,

Ger. Moringus in vita Sancti August.

Primam ætatis partem ne quæras, in cœno perdidit. &c. 7 lef. de S. Aug.

he

he took liberty to whip them in others. Which timely zeal, as it did not mis-become his youth, so can it not disparage his * Prelacy; no, not as Poesie, not as Satyr: The first you cannot condemn; and the latter I will maintain, against greater Criticks than you would dare boast to have been conversant with: only if I appeal to such, my fear is, I shall have no adversary.

*Non corrumpuntur in deterius quae aliquando etiam à malis, sed honesta manent, quae saepius à bonis fiunt. P in.l.5.ep.3: Arist. apolog. pro suis l.dictis.

To let passe therefore your simile of the *sleek-stone* (which shews that you can be as bold with a Prelate, as familiar with your Laundresse,) why, in the name of Philology, is a toothlesse Satyr improper? why Bullish?

Euge novam Satyram, Satyrum sine cornibus euge!
Monstra, novi monstri, hæc; & Satyri & Satyra!

The Authour himself furnished you with the exception: and had you had but so much life or quicknesse in your pallade, as to have tasted an Epigram, you might have understood he speaks there in the person of such carping Poetasters as you, and your now-despised Tribe, are: They say, they are Monsters; you, that they are Bulls: you mean, I suppose, Chymæra's; absurd and ridiculous compositions of words, inconsistible with sense. Let us therefore, if you will, take them in pieces, and see where the incongruity lyes. *Satyra* signified anciently any kind of miscellaneous writing, which we now term *Essayes*; whence *Varro* entituled many of his books of divers subjects, *Satyras suas*: Whence there was also a Law called metaphorically *Lex Satyra*, when by one and the same Vote, divers things were enacted. Last of all, it came to be restrained to such kind of writings, as contained the vices of the times, whether in verse or prose; more commonly now of later times in verse. *Dens* or *dentatus* you cannot think should come here into composition with a Satyre, in the primitive or proper signification of it, so as to make *Satyra dentata* as we say it of a child, after its teeth are grown, or before, that he hath teeth, or is toothlesse: we must seek then some other sense for it; where I finde teeth and horns to signifie strength, used to defense or injury.

Epig. ad suas Satyras.

Farrago libelli Iuv.Sat 1. lege cell. Moselianus ad Gell. l.1.c.17.

injury. Nothing is more familiar in Scripture, than *horn* for strength: ἤγειρα κέρας σωτηρίας, *He hath raised up an horn of salvation*: a strong salvation. So also for injurious strength, *fœnum habet in cornu* is a common Proverb. The word *Matth.* 10.16. which we translate *simple*, or *harmlesse*, is ἀκέραιοι, *ab* ἀ *&* κέρας *cornu*. Thus *Martial lib.*13.*ep.*91.

<small>Luk.1.69. Hebræis fami-liare est (Keren; id est cornu, pro vi & robore usurpare, sumpta metaphora ab animalibus cornupetis. *Beza ad loc.*</small>

> *Dente timentur apri, defendunt* cornua *tauros* ·
> *Imbelles damæ, nil nisi prædæ sumus.*

So *vinum edentulum* was used by the Ancients for small wines, such as we say in plain English, will do a man no hurt: *Vinum edentulum, hoc est nullarum virium, vel saltem perexiguarum. Salmuth.ex Gualth.Tit.*25.*p.*84. In the same sense *Horace* speaks of the effects of strong wines:

> *Tu spem reducis mentibus anxiis,*
> *Viresque,& addis* cornua *pauperi.*

makes a man bold or injurious: and in this sense (unlesse these Authours are improper, it is no *Bull* to say a toothlesse Satyr, *i.e.* an harmlesse Poem, that doth

> *Parcere personis, dicere de vitiis ;*

spare the person, but strike the vice: For such should a true Satyrist be,

> ——— *asper*
> Incolumi *gravitate*. *Horat.de Art.Poet.*

Satyræ incolumes are harmlesse (more elegantly) toothlesse Satyrs; in opposition to *Satyræ mordaces*, biting or toothed Satyrs; such as for their loose insolencies were by Law forbidden to the Ancients.

<small>* Qui ille Mutius? is qui damnavit eum qui carmine lusisset nomine expresso. L. *Dorleans Nov. Cogit. ad Cornel.Tacit.*</small>

> *Quid refert dictis ignoscat* * *Mutius annon?*

To

To which decorum our Authour professes himself to have had respect, *Virgidem.lib.3. in Prol.*

> *For look how far the Ancients Comedy*
> *Past former Satyres in her liberty,*
> *So far must mine yeeld unto them of old,*
> *'Tis better to be bad than to be bold.*

And Sir *David Lindsey* in his Satyr *in Prol.*

> Prudent peopill I pray yow all
> Take na man grief in speciall,
> For we sall speik in generall
> For pastime and for play:

> Thairfoir till all our rimis be rung, &c.

Though what was, and is denyed the stage, is got up into the Pulpit: much as the manner was with *Chaucers* Pardoner.

> Then woll I sting hem with my tonge smert
> In preaching, so that he shall not astert
> To been diffamed falsely, if that he
> Hath trespassed to my brethren or me:
> For though I tell not his proper name,
> Men shall weil know it is the same
> By signes or by other circumstances,
> Thus quite I folk that doth us displeasances,
> Thus put I out my venym under hiew
> Of holinesse, to semen holy and true.

As you have censured the Remonstrants Poesie, so in like manner you have justified a slip in the Smectymnuans Philology; I mean, so weakly, not so malitiously, they mistook a Bench for a Judge; or rather the place for the men: *Areopagi* for *Areopagitæ*; and you make it good: How? [*if in Pag. 6.* dealing with an outlandish name they thought it best not to screw the English mouth to an harsh forrain termination, they did no more than the elegantest Authours among the Greeks, Romans, Italians, &c.] Every Countrey, I know, takes and gives that leave in the use of forraign words, to fit them to their own easiest pronunciation and best liking: sometimes out of necessity, sometimes of choice and pleasure onely. The Greeks when they met with words terminated in any of these letters, ζ, λ, μ, because such terminations were unknown to them, usually changed them. As *Polybius* for Ἀφρικαλ writes Ἀφρικας. And *Suetonius* (as some will have it) tells us how the Romans used the old Germane word (ᵃ *Rutters*) which they still use to signifie horsemen in war. And so perhaps our English word (Peat) is but *Mattya* fashioned to our Dialect:

Dives & ex omni posita est extructa macello
Cœna tibi; sed te ᵇ *Mattya sola juvat.*
Mart. lib. 10. Ep. 59.

So the Italian *Inciostro* from the Latine word ᶜ *Encaustum*, as likewise our English word (Inke.)

Encaustes ᵈ *Phaeton tabula tibi pictus in hac est,*
Quid tibi vis, dypyron qui Phaetonta facis?
Mart. lib. 4. Epig. 47.

[*Our learned* Chaucer *did not sticke to doe so.*] True.

——— There was a King
That hyght Ceys, and had a wyfe,
The beste tha myght beare lyfe,
And this Queene hyght Alcione.   Fol. 267.

Semiramus, Candace and Hercules,
Byblys, Dido, Lysbe and Piramus.
Fol. 275.

---

c. 19.
ᵃ Nam parum abfuit cuin à Bructero quodam occideretur. Suet. in T b. Some readings for Brutero have Rutero: Torrentius his manuscript hath Rutero.

ᵇ Mattyæ seu mactæ sunt bellaria, Græcis πήμματα, τραγήμματα, omne mensæ secundæ genus.

ᶜ Ex purpurâ atramenti genus conficiebatur, quod Encaustum nominabatur: hoc soli Imperatores privi giis & literis subscribendis utebantur. —unde & Inchiostro postea derivatum credo. Guido Pancirollus rerum memorab it. Encaust. p 10.

ᵈ ἐγκαύσαι λέγονται οἱ ζωγράφοι οἱ διαγράφοντες τοὺς τείχους. ab ἐγκαύω uro. Lege Cl. Salmas. in Flav. Vopisc. p. 393.

(13)

Be like the pytte of Pegace
Under Pernasse where the Poets slept. (Fol. 30r.

What is all this to the purpose? *Chaucer* hath mollifyed *Ceyx for Ceyx,* a termination, *ξ quod valet ut in ς:* he hath not metamorphosed the name of a place into the name of a man: or if he had, it were one of those *faults which ought to be forgiven* (not imitated) *in so reverend antiquity.* The old Latines wrote *im* for *eum, joure* for *jure, nox* and *noctu* for *nocte, diequinte* for *die quinto:* Would you do so now ? Yes, yes, any thing, rather than acknowledge the least errour: For either you are as dis-ingenuous in matters of Grammar as of Religion; in both, purposing therefore to maintain a thing, because you have said it; or else perhaps you have a designe to innovate as well upon our language as upon our Church-government. If you be remembred, you set *Afranius* in *Lucian* to laugh at the Bishops; to return you an innocent jest, I will set *Demonax* upon you. This *Demonax* asked one a question, who answered him in old obsolete affected words; *Prethee fellow* (saith he) *where are thy wits? I ask thee a question now, and thou answerest* 400 *years ago.* I ask in the sixteenth of King *Charls,* and you answer in the first of King *John.* For your *Aula & Olla,* that you say is the same in old Latine, I could clap you on the shoulder with a Greek Proverb as old, πολλάκι κỳ μωρὸς ἀνὴρ ἐπιταίριον, *Children and Fools, &c.*

Sir Ph. Sidney Defense of Poesy.

Ἐπὶ γὰρ ἐρωτηθέντι ὑπ' αὐτᾶ λόγον τινά, ϗ ὑπερατ]ικῶς ἀποκριθέντι ἐγὼ μὲν σε ἔφη. ὦ ἐταῖρε, νῦν ἠρώτησα, σὺ δὲ μοι ὡς ἐπ' Ἀγαμέμνονις ἀποκρίνη. Luc. Demonax.

Senex avarus vix sibi credens Euclio,
Domi suæ defossam multis cum opibus
Aulam invenit.   Plaut. Aulular.

But for your application of it in plain English [*Aula* and *Hall*] I must tell you it was an observation as unchristian & slanderous in that particular, as in the generall [a] superstitious. [a] *Omina quædam occultiora sumpta sunt ex rebus, locis, nominibus, vestibus. Vide Isa. Pont. in Collection. ad Macrobium. Ex nominibus, Roma quasi ῥώμη sive ῥώμη, robur. Roma, n n Romula, ne male ominaretur diminutivum. Ne mihi damnum in Epidamno duas. Plaut. in Men. ch. omen, non à loci aliquâ incommoditate, sed à nomine tantùm. Item, Si te cicem, Lucridem fore confido &c. in Persa. Vnde à diis plerunque auspicata nomina: A Iove, Diocles, Diogenes, Diomedes: A Iunone, Heraclides, Heraclitus; A Sole, Heleus, Heliodorus, &c. Hugo Grotius in Februis ad Mart. Capell. Satyricon.*

§. VII.

§. VII.

NExt you impugne his Logick: The Remonstrant had said,

> Da- *Civill Polity in generall notion is variable and arbitrary*; you subsume, *But*
> ri- *The Polity of our Kingdome is Civill Polity:*
> Ergo,
> i. *The Polity of our Kingdome is variable*, &c.

And thereupon you cry, *Treason!* and want of *Logick!* In the first you are uncharitable; in the last, irrationall, only guilty of that failing which you impute to the Remonstrant. For look upon your syllogism; there is in the major proposition, *fallacia ad plures interrogationes*: For either we ask, what is possible only; or what is possible and lawfull. The Remonstrant answers; It is possible Civill Polity may vary; or, It is in the generall notion left of God to a various administration; subject to divers forms, Monarchy, Aristocracy, Democracy. You answer; It may be lawfully done at any time, or by any what ever undertakers: For so much is inferred in your conclusion.

> *Civill Polity is at any time, or by any undertakers variable and subject to a lawfull alteration:*
> *But the Polity of England, &c* Ergo,
> *It is at any time, by any undertakers, &c.*

This makes the Treason, this you must and do inferre, or else you charge him with Treason unjustly. In this sense, *as lawfull*, and, *at any time*, and, *by any undertakers*, the Remonstrant denyes the particular to be inferred upon his generall. But in his own he grants it, *viz*. That it is *possible*, subject to a condition of variation, though it be Treason against the highest Majesty of heaven, whose substitute the King is, in him or them who do attempt a change. And in this saying

he

he sayes no more, than all Statesmen of the generall, and Sir *Francis Bacon* of our particular, had said before him. [*All civill governments are restrained from God unto the generall grounds of justice and manners, but the Policies and forms of them are left free;*] free, and to the arbitrement of a people, met together and consenting by the secret impression and instinct of God, ζῆν εὐδαιμόνως καὶ καλῶς, *Arist. lib. 3. Pol. cap. 6.* to take what form of government they please: which being setled according to the generall rules of justice, and particular rules of the best advancement of publike good, is so immediately ratified by God, by his infusion of soveraignty into him or them, who by the joint consent of all is advanced to the helm; as also (to us Christians) by laying so many injunctions upon the people, to obey and honour all those in authority, not for wrath, but for conscience sake; that it is a sinne of the highest degree, onely but in thought to meditate an alteration.

Considerations touching the Church of England.

Rom. 3. 5.

The Apostles distinction, διὰ τὴν ὀργὴν, καὶ διὰ τὴν συνείδησιν, shewes us what is the Kings *hold*, and what is our *duty*. The Kings hold is divine; he hath a *deputed soveraignty*, which works upon the conscience, either willing or refusing to submit, in just lawfull and indifferent things: our duty is, in these things, willingly to obey: and in case of substraction of our obedience, to know that he hath τὴν ὀργὴν, a compulsory power, without which God had put the sword into his hands in vain; that is, made him like a *George* on horse-back, with his hand and sword lift up, but not able to strike.

In this point I suppose both they that labour for and against Episcopacy, do agree jointly.

§. VIII.

ENvie is a make-bate, alwayes doing ill offices: if it cannot compasse its own ends one way, it will another. You, not having any thing to accuse the Remonstrant to the King, do it to the Parliament. [*Gladly you say, we beleeve you, as gladly as your faction wished for the assembling of this Parliament.*

Pag. 6.

Parliament. — *Whether this reflect not with a contumely upon the Parliament.*—] Let the theef or murderer dread the Judge; Let fear dwell where it ought, in guilty bosomes. Doubtlesse the Remonstrant, and those which you esteem his faction, are as glad of, and wish as well to this Honourable Assembly, as you and yours do. It is not the Parliament they make head against, but you and your furious complices, who between soft flattery towards some of that House, and rough violence to others (witnesse your Libels against so many of them, as their consciences made Vote contrary to some proceedings) are like to over-turn all. They know, and so do I, That the Sunne looks not upon a braver, nobler Convocation, than is that of King, Peeres, and Commons; whose equall Justice, and wise moderation, shall eternally triumph, in that they have hitherto deserved to do, what the sowre exorbitancies on one hand, and eager solicitations on the other, not permitting them to consult with reason, would have prompted them to: who know how to ponder wise and grave [a] sentences, not from the number, but the worth of them that propound them. Among whom, even the youngest and unskilfullest may stand a pattern and example to future times, teaching State-Novices, rather to inform their judgments to the good of the next Assembly, than to use them to the [b] prejudice of this present. The gravest and most experienced, to be what they are thought, and to deserve all that praise, with which the people [c] load them. So to satisfie their desires as they are just, not as they are [d] vehement: considering that the multitude crave only out of the sense of evils; of which so long they will have a sense, as they are willing to obey. All conspiring unanimously, so to advance the pure Religion of our dearest Saviour, that it be not dispirited

[a] Numerantur sententiæ, non ponderantur: nihil est tam inæquale, quàm æqualitas ip a: nam cum sit impar prudentia, par omnium jus est. *Plin, l.3. ep:ist.12.*
[b] Rudes nos & imperitos reducta libertas deprehendit, cujus dulcedine accensi, cogimur quædam facere antequam nosse. *Idem l.8.ep.14.*
[c] Senatus, humanum genus reverendus, Orbis terræ consilium, Asylum mundi, Fidei m & altum reipublicæ pectus. *Vide Filesacum l.3. select. T. t. Senatus Ven.Sen.§.4,5,&c.*
[d] Non considerandum est quid vir optimus in præsent â velit, sed quid semper sit probaturus. *Plin.lib.1.ep.7.* Sunt quæ non dare, sed negare, beneficium est. Poscit æger frigidam, iratus ferrum, &c. exorari in perniciem rogantium, sæva est bonitas, *Sen. de Benef.*

on one hand by gaudy ceremonious Formalists; nor lost on the other amids a Crowd of sullen and ignorant Sectaries: and after that (to which it is an honour for him to submit) the divine soveraignty and royall Immunities of our most Gratious Master.

§. IX.

WE must go higher yet, and if we *will*, may beleeve the Remonstrant to be [*a notorious enemy to truth*, pag. 2. *a false Prophet*, pag. 3. *a belly-god, proud and covetous*, pag. 5 *squeezed to a wretched, cold, and hollow-hearted confession of some Prelaticall ryots*, pag. 15. *whose understanding nothing will cure but Kitchin-physick*, pag. 17. *a Laodicean*, pag. 24. *a dissembling Joab*, pag. 28 *a dawber with untempered morter*, pag. 62.] Good God! thou that hast promised to direct the steps of the humble, and to be with those that are of a meek heart, instruct me how to chuse some other path to walk in towards my Eternity; for this my soul hates! Let me for ever be shut out of that heaven, that is the reward of such black calumny, such malitious and divellish slanders! And, O you my dear brethren, who are disaffected towards the Prelate, look upon and give evidence to the man! How is he an enemy to the truth, unlesse the Gospel of Christ be a lye! How is he a false Prophet, unlesse your selves who professe the same faith be impostors? View well that heap of age and reverence, and say whether that clear and healthfull constitution, those fresh cheeks and quick eyes, that round tongue, agile hand, nimble invention, stay'd delivery, quiet calm and happy bosome, be the effects of threescore yeers surfeits and * gluttony. What time could he steal to bestow upon Mammon, the God of this world, who hath given us so large an account of his idlest ᵃ minutes? whose whole life hath been nothing but a laborious search after humane and divine truths, which having pickt out, (as that little miracle of nature doth honey) from weeds and flowers, he did not improper to himself, but liberally dealt *runique vigor integer, inde agile & vividum corpus, solaque ex senectute prudentia*. Pl. n. lb 3. epist 1. ᵃ *Occasionall Medit.*

* Apponitur cœna non minus nitida quàm frugi, suâ delectatur, nn nascitur; inde illi post 77 annum, aurium oculorum &c.

them

^b Non sibi, sed them to the ^b good of the publike; his toyl being impleaoreri bibunt. santed to himself, in that he loved the work he went about;
Quint. decl. 13. and accepted of the world, because they knew he dished out
Apes paupe. is. nothing to them, but what he tasted of himself; penned nothing but what first he practised. How could he be lazie and idle, whose volumes are so many, whose preaching so frequent, whose studies so early and late; so that it is onely questionable whether his lips did drink in more grace than they distilled? I commend not, but vindicate. Must he be
See Shepherds therefore luke warm, because his zeal burns not as hot as
sincere Convert. hell? must his conscience be therefore cauterized and seared,
Ch. ista Mode. because he brands not every Christian out of the Church of
L. Ex. 15. p. 70. England with the marks of reprobation? writes not the dreadful doom of God in the forehead of all Popishly given, in France, Spain, Italy, Germany? Sends not all Russian, Abassine, Grecian, Armenian, Ethiopick Churches, which all the day have flown different wayes, and laboriously cull'd (with the Bee) such sweets as they could light upon, in the evening swarming to hell; or presently sets not fire on their hives? Alas! how long hath this been the doctrine of the Church of England? and I cannot yet, beleeve it. Shall I ever think, with that foolish Anchorite, that the Sun shines no where but into my Cell? Or can I not enough enjoy and blesse God for the warmth of his great light, unlesse I confidently affirm, that at no time, in no measure it shines beyond our Tropick. Let who will confine the mercies of God in Christ to so narrow limits; I dare not.

Pag. 18. Brethren, hath he forsaken the faith, that is so far an enemy to the Pope, as the Pope is an enemy to Christ? Is it come to this now, that he must be bid *part* from the rest of his brethren, that holds not Episcopacie to be Antichristian; All forms of Prayers and Liturgies to be quenching of the Spirit, evill (*quatenus ipsum*;) An equality of Ministers, living upon niggard contributions; demolishing of Churches and all kind of Sacriledge lawfull? That calls not the royall, noble, and devout munificence of our Ancestors, who received, cherished, and transmitted our Religion to us, the price of their damnation? Doth that good Spirit of God dwell

no

no where but in dry or marifhy conftitutions? Will Grace mixe with nothing but aduft choler, or lowring morofe peevifhneffe? Cannot Grace and Nature confift? When we deny our felves, muft we deny humanity? Doth Gods Spirit now infpire Chriftians, as the Devill did his Priefts of old, by putting them out of their wits? Is converfion nothing but a turning about to this mans opinion, or that mans novelties? a flavifh imitation of fome forraigne Church abroad, or doting upon fome great Mafters at home? Why elfe cannot a fober, modeft, humble, orthodox Prelate go for a Chriftian among us? Why are we weary of him, if we be not fo of our Religion? him, who had been as holy, wife, learned, temperate, bountifull, fincere a Proteftant, as any this day in our Church, had he but been of your opinion in matters of difcipline? How almoft a Saint, how altogether a Devill? No preaching, no care of the peace of the Church, no learned Volumes writ, no hofpitality, no poor fed, no holineffe of life, no Church, no falvation, but in the Presbytery? Worthy you of your chains and fagots, O ye Martyrs, that commended this government unto us; perifh and rot the memories of thofe famous Affemblies, that confirmed it, and bound us to the maintenance of fuperftition and Antichriftianifme! And now that I finde them fo ungratefull to the dead, it leffens my wonder, though not their impiety, that they are fo to the living. Away with thofe cheap as numerous leaves, that image forth to us his ravifhed and devout thoughts; away with the clear and bright mirrour of a difpaffioned foul, a rectified underftanding, a liberall and Chriftian charity; with that fweet and heavenly *eloquence that prepares a way for the

*Vellem mihi, etfi non qualis in Marco Tullio fuit, aliquam tamen proximam eloquentiæ contingere facultatem. *Lactan.l.3.div.Inft c 1.* Veritas licet poffit fine eloquentia defendi, tamen claritate & nitore fermonis illuftranda eft, ut potentius in animos influat. *Idem.* Quid igitur? annon adfuit Paulo fua δεινότης? certè adfuit, quanta nulli unquam obtigit; fed cœleftis, non humana. *Beza ad 1.Cor.1.17.* — ἢ τοῖς μὲν ἐπιεικέσιν ἀρετῆς ὅπλον, τοῖς δὲ μοχθηροτέροις κέντρον κακίας γίνεται. *Naz.1.in Iul.* — ἣν οἱ πολλοὶ χριστιανῶν διαπτύουσιν, ὡς ἐπίβουλον ἢ σφαλεράν ἢ Θεοῦ πόρρω βάλλουσαν, κακῶς εἰδότες. *Idem Orat. 20.in funere Bafil.*

D 2

Spirit

Spirit of God; that opens our eares, the gates of our soules, that the King of glory may enter in, and dwell there; that awakens our understandings to arise and be ready to entertain that λόγον ἔμφυτον, the engrafted Word, which is able to save our souls; yea and away with it from the earth, lest it upbraid to future ages, the tyrannous malice and affected barbarisms of these present times. Blind men! that will not see our own good; that shut our eyes, and then complain that we want the Sunne! If you will not look upon his works, which testifie of him, ask his great Master, or his noble retinue at Court, whether this confession of the riots and disorders of Courts, Officers, Palaces, City, Countrey, were now squeezed from him? Whether it came not then from his lips as freely as now? Whether his reproofs seemed cold, wretched, or heartlesse? Or if there lurked hidden evils which he saw not, or those which he saw were not reformed, why doth he suffer as a countenancer, as a contriver? It was a word fell from the boldest and most undaunted spirit that Rome ever saw, * *I would, but the times would not.* Zeal must have discretion as well as knowledge. He that pressed too hard upon the enemy and lost himself, was in the old discipline of warre accounted as infamous as he that fled. He that regulates his actions by a good conscience, rather than popular fame, however they hear abroad, findes ever the content and reward of them at home.

*'Animus mihi certè nunquam defuit, tempora defuerunt, *ul* 4. Phil p. No i prosequi, non fugere.

But in good earnest, What should he do to please you? what way, besides abjuring his Prelacy, or being as wicked as you would make him, is there left for him to content you? If he write controversies, then he is a Swash-buckler against the Pope; then he careers with speare in rest, and thunders upon the steel cap of *Bellarmine*: If he preaches, then he sermonizes and dawbes with untempered mortar: If he contemplates or meditates, then he playes with Lambeth Kittens: If at Court, he is crowding for preferment, or accusing the people to the King: If at home, he is a belly-God, &c. O the love, and charity, and reverence of these times, to so holy, so deserving a Bishop! May ye stay for such another glorious light of the Church, till ye can deserve

serve him! and never enjoy the benefit of this, till ye have made him amends for these injuries! *Had former times shewne him, or forraigne Churches nourished him, he that is now your scorn had been your wonder: Happy had that man been that could have dressed a Sermon in his grave and waighty Sentences, or his Study with his Picture: only now we wanton at the full brest, and because we are at spring-head, rather puddle the clear stream with our foot, than slake our thirst. Froward spite, that makes us therefore hate, because we cannot love enough; therefore revile, because we cannot sufficiently praise. But go on, revile, slander, belye holy men; your selves can give us the best and truest character of what ye are: Neither in this point would I ever have condemned ye, had I not heard it from your own mouths. And you, Reverend Sir, stand up; the disadvantage of your old age, your spent and decayed strength, that would naturally shrink under such pressures, makes but Grace more eminent in you: We can never better see how the foundation bears the weight of the building, than when the props be removed. How can any one say, Lo this man leans to an arm of flesh, when he sees it withered? The *evill* dayes of a man are the *best* of a Christian: Now may *Grace* borrow her Masters Chariot, and triumph, saying, I have trod the Wine-presse alone, and of the people (feare, hope, boldnesse, glory) there was none with me. And to thee, O God, be the praise of this exercise of his Christian fortitude; it is thou that hast shewn (as the last and most glorious blaze of this dying light) That he that could deserve all praise, could suffer all injury.

* At si inter eos quos nunquam vidimus floruisset, non solum libros eius, verum etiam imagines conquireremus: ejusdem nunc honor præsentis & gratia quasi satietate languescit: at hoc pravum malignumque est, non admirari hominem admiratione dignissimum, quia videre, audire, alloqui, complecti, nec laudare tantum verum etiam amare contingit. *Plin. lib. 1. epist. 16.*

Eccl. 12.1.

Esa. 63.3.

§. X.

THe scraps and offall that remain of your Libell, concern Liturgie and Episcopacie; both which you have handled, as you esteem of them, unworthily and basely.

Forsooth

Forsooth you would give the world to know these two things; First, that you are no Bishop: Secondly, that you can pray *ex tempore*. Surely a man of strong parts, and a mortified ambition! It was thought of old, that the Philosophers did therefore contemn and speak ill of riches and pleasures and high places, because they were never born to them; as the Fox cursed the Grapes that were out of his reach. But we will not think so uncharitably of you; A rich Widow, or a Lecture, or both, contents you.

To the first you make way, by a long, tedious, theatricall, big-mouthed, astounding Prayer, put up in the name of the three Kingdomes; not so much either to please God, or benefit the weal-publike by it, as to intimate your owne good abilities to her that is your *rich hopes*.

Petit Gemellus nuptias Maronilla,
Et cupit, & instat, & Precatur.

Because you shall never say I am envious, and go about to disgrace you, I will give this testimony of your Oraisons, That there wanted but one petition to make them complete, which was, That God would forgive you the profanation of the rest of your book.

To the second you make way (a very compendious way in this age, if as honest as compendious) by flattery and rayling: at both which you are old excellent, or as your own expression is, *sufficiently tryed*. How you can performe the first hath been already heard; now let us heare the second. Speak out, the Parish is big. [*Our great Clerks think these men, because they have a Trade, as Christ himself and S. Paul had, cannot therefore attain to some measure of knowledge, and to a reason of their actions,* p. 13.] *As Christ had; Christ preached,* Ergo *Sam. How* may. Take heed friend, you border upon blasphemy. *Our great Clerks thinke, &c.* Truly, small Clerk, you know but little of those mens mindes: I will insure you they do not think so. But why should you plead this? Methinks it were much better for you, and more conducible to your ends if it were so: For could they not attain

tain to a reason of their actions, there were great hopes they would choose you to be their Minister. But I know not how unluckily you have spoyled your own market; if that be true which you elsewhere affirm of them [*That they are competent Judges of a Ministers abilities, as it wil, not be denyed that he may be the competent Judge of a neat picture or elegant Poem, that cannot limne the like,*] unlesse in your simile you recover your selfe and abuse them: For who ever accounted an ignorant Gull a sufficient and competent Judge of a terse Poeme?

——— Versus reprehendet inertes?
Culpabit duros? Incomptis allinet atrum
Transverso calamo signum? Ambitiosa recidet
Ornamenta? Parum claris lucem dare coget?
Arguet ambiguè dictum? Mutanda notabit?
Fiet Aristarchus? ———

All which is the office of a Critick. Who but you thinks an inspired Cobler may judge of *Apelles* his workmanship? διὰ τοῦτο Λυσίππ۞ Ἀπελλῶ εἰς τὰς γραφὰς εἰσῆγε, κὴ Λυσίππον Ἀπελλῆς, *Synes Epist.* 1. δοκεῖ ἢ κὴ γραφικὴ χρήσιμ۞ εἶ) πρὸς τὸ κρίνειν τὰ τῆς τεχνιτῶν ἔργα, Arist. Pol. 8. c. 3. *Ut de pictore, fictore, sculptore, nisi artifex judicare, ita nisi sapiens non potest perspicere sapientem,* Plin. lib 1. epist. 10. (These Authours testimonies, I hope Sir, may be considerable against your insolent affirmation.) Who but you, against the command of God himself, dare bring not the Congregation onely, but the very beasts of the people, within the borders of the Mount? Sober and wise Christians, I doubt not but they know where to stay; neither will they follow such Ringleaders as you, to their own destruction: Such men will acquit our great Clerks well enough, of any or all your pretended slanders; and besides tell you, (that though against all sense and reason they make them not Judges of their abilities, and against all antiquity and custome of the Church, above what ever is written or practised in Scripture, they receive not their ordination from them;) yet they

both

both encourage them in, and blesse God for their safe knowledge, and becomming actions. Go you then to your mutinous rabble, and if you can appease their furies, enthrone their sage wisedomes upon some stall or bench, and cite before them the Clerks of either University: those competent Judges, I guesse, will do like themselves, reject one as unsufficient (so as they the Horse which *Polygnotus* had exquisitely painted, damned the whole piece, because contrary to the nature of that beast, he had made him with hairs on his nether eye-lids,) onely for that he hath too little haire on his upper lip, or too much upon his fore-head; because he useth not to wear wrought night-caps, or mastick patches. In the mean while another (as the Good-wife in *Plutarch* judged of *Philopœmen*) shall be thought fitter to cleave blocks than divide a Text, because he hath a sowre or crabbed countenance; because either his learning is too much, or that little he hath lodges, as their Prentices do, in an ugly Garret: Whiles a third shall be deeply suspected of Arminianism, because he hath a squint-eye, or is of the Archbishops Colledge. Briefly all those glorious lights, and bright stars of eminence and lustre in either Horizon, shall be no better esteemed of, than *Tyro* in *Gellius* observes the *Hyades* were, which by his Clownish Ancestors were taken for so many sucking-pigs: and perhaps under that name shall be driven to Hogs-Norton to pipe upon the Organs (if they be yet standing.) But I leave these grave Censors, these *Areopagi*, if you will, to their own discretion; lest while I am busied in observing of theirs, I forfeit mine: and this Paragraph be taxed for that fault of your whole discourse, which in the easiest Censurers mouth is but *Levity* and *Digression*.

Fr. Iun̄us de Pict.vet.l.3

Ingenium Galbæ malè habitat.

ὑάδες Suculæ dictæ. A.Gell. l.13.c.9.

§. XI.

OF Liturgie first. Into which that distinction of Saint *Pauls* shall lead the way: *All things are lawfull, but all things are not expedient*. A thing in its own nature indifferent, and so lawfull, doth sometimes οὐρὰ ᾖ become inexpedient, and so unlawfull. By this rule we will examine the

1 Cor. 10.23. a Restringendum est τὸ χα. Sόλα a seas res de quibus agitur, sc. indiff.

the point in hand. For that set forms of Prayer are in themselves at least indifferent, the precept and practice of Christ confirms, and no man in his right wits ever denyed. [*Some set forms of Prayer, by some men, in some cases may be lawfully used.*] The question is therefore of the expediency, not of the lawfulnesse of such prayers, *viz.* Whether a set form of Prayers, this in particular to which the Church of England hath been, and is laudibly as piously accustomed, may συμφερόντως, expediently be used, and enjoyned by all to be used, in a nationall Church, as ours is.

Lord Viscount Say and Seal in his answer to the Archbishop.

To the clearing of which point, there are two things of necessity to be done:

1. *The conveniencies and inconveniencies of such prayers in the generall, must be weighed.*
2. *The blemishes with which this of ours in particular is charged must be examined*

According as we find which, for or against, our conclusion must be made.

1. It suits to, and agrees best with Gods own proceedings in the government of his Church. In which it hath pleased his divine wisdome so to order the matter, that (since all men are not alike capable of knowledge, nor have the same abilities,) his providence should as it were conform it self to this unequall condition of men: whence it is, he hath made choice of some to teach others, and pray for others; chose some to be Apostles, some Ministers, Pastors, Teachers; whereas had he not had respect to this, and purposed to go along with this weaknesse of mans nature, he could as well have infused abilities (I mean supernaturall) into the brest and brain of the most ignorant despicable member of the Church, sufficient without other teachings or helps, to have raised him to converse with God here, and possesse God hereafter, as ever he did into the ablest of the Apostles.

And now having thus ordered the matter; (for thus it is, was, and ever will be, let men dream never so long, torture and rack Scripture, to make it roare out an imaginary lying perfection) God looks that those some which he hath chose, endued, set apart to teaching and praying, and all other offices

fices of ministeriall function, as they are publike men, so should have a publike care of that Church wherein they are: So drive, as the Church may go like a flock together, a due respect had to the Lambs and Ewes big with young, to the weary, faint, and lame:

Hanc egram vix Tytere duco: which alwayes are the most considerable number.

Yea, come we to the Shepheards themselves: How many laborious, painfull, conscionable men are there, that if these helpes may not be allowed them, must either tempt God, fail in the performance of their duties, or give them quite up, as *not sufficient for these things?* And if it come to this once, how many souls, (every one, for ought we can say of this or that particular, being to God alike pretious,) will here be desperately, irrecoverably lost! For what help? will our Land afford enow such *ex tempore* men? no nor the much magnified Amsterdam, with Geneva and New-England to boot. *Hope* is a brave, heroick, sublimed Christian virtue, but it is of *things which make us not ashamed.*

2. Such Liturgies and set forms are most expedient, if we look to the nature of Prayers *(publike Prayers.)*

Prayer in it self considered, Is the proper act of the soul, of the will and understanding, and may be completely and perfectly offered up to God, without those subsidiary helps of invention, disposition, memory, language; these, when we speak of private Prayer, are but the vain pomp of it: when of publike, the necessary adjuncts.

I will pray with the Spirit, and I will pray with understanding, 1 *Cor.*14.15. This often mis-applyed Text is to be understood of publike Prayer, as you may see by comparing it with the second verse, *He that speaketh or prayeth in an unknown tongue, speaketh or prayeth not unto men, but unto God.* By *Spirit* is meant (not as our vain humourists would have it) an extemporall faculty of wording it, but that gift of the Spirit which Saint *Paul* mentions vers.5,6,&c. viz. the miraculous gift of tongues, or faculty of speaking divers languages: by understanding is meant the understanding of the people; for he that prayeth in an unknown tongue, prayeth

margin: 2 Cor.2.16.

ἐλπὶς οὐ καται- σχύνει. Rom. 5.5.

not

not unto men, that is, not to their understanding. That which I gather from hence is this; That those publike Prayers are most expedient to be used, which are most accommodated to the capacity of the people. Herein I know you will agree with me. I go on. But a set form is most accommodate, *Ergo*. This proposition is easily proved: I make it good thus.

1. The understanding is præ-acquainted with, and the subject otherwise difficult is thus made obvious and easie. 2. The matter is the same, not at the will, or passion, or ignorance, or negligence of him that prayeth to be varied: by reason of which, sometime the people cannot, sometime dare not go along with their Minister. 3. Though the language be not in it self unknown, yet the harshnesse of it in some, the length and tediousnesse of stile in others, the affected heighth of forced Allegories and Tropes, not to say the nonsense and ridiculously absurd variations of many pretenders to the faculty, renders it altogether as unintelligible, as it were Latine or Greek. If I were to make good this assertion by a particular instance, I would go no farther than your prayer you have given us, *pag* 26,37,38. which infinite of honest and simple Christians would no more know how to understand, than they would doe a Scene out of *Iohnsons Cataline*.

But what command in Scripture is there for it? Where is *conceived prayer* mentioned? what such virtue is there in the extemporall wording of a Prayer, that for the giving it such undoubted liberty we must run all these hazzards? The soul may be as much inflamed that prayes in a set form, as that which doth not: and that may be as cold that prayes *ex tempore*. Will you say, that every one that hath the gift, hath also affections answerable? you dare not. That then may be belyed, and we shall admire the spirit where it is not: what is this, but to warm our selves at a painted fire? For indeed it is not the volubility or roundnesse of tongue, that is the work of Gods Spirit primarily in him that hath this gift of Prayer, but the enkindling of the affections: I say primarily; for where the Spirit of Grace, which is as

fire

fire in the heart, findes such abilities, such naturall abilities, either actuall or potentiall, it doth catch hold of them, and make suell as it were of them, whereby the soul burns the more ardently: But where it finds them not, God never infuseth them, (this is meer Anabaptisme) otherwise no such abilities, no grace, no extemporall expressions, no Prayer. And this being thus, doth it make a Prayer ever the more acceptable to God, that it is extemporall? Doth it make a Prayer unacceptable, that it is not so? In truth, no: But this is it, there is more of the man in the extemporall Prayer, and that makes us doat so much upon it; as the fond mother commonly loves that child best, whose face is most like her, though perhaps of worst conditions. You cannot but know, that there are of the holiest men, and most able Ministers about London, and elsewhere, that both use our Liturgy, and accustome themselves to a set form of their own; wisely considering as I said before, that they are publike men, and are bound to do not what they could more to their own benefit, but what they must, to the peoples. Yea, those that do use extemporall expressions, I would ask them, how far they are from a set form: Is not yesterdayes, to dayes, to morrows, and every dayes Prayer alike, in the frame, œconomy, or disposition of the matter? Is not the matter the same? do they not preface, petition, conclude always alike? Not in the same words, you will say. Well, but S. *Paul* did so in all his Epistles in the very same words; and it is more than probable did so in all his Prayers. If there be new emergent occasions, do not those men insert into their own? doth not the Church insert into the Common-prayer book such petitions as are needfull for those occasions? Consider then in what things their Prayers come near yours, and yours come near theirs, and where's the difference? why is the world distracted about nothing? either you are exorbitant, or both may agree.

See Perkins cases of Consc. of set forms of Prayer.

3. Most expedient to attain the end such worship drives at; Order, Unity, Piety, and the best advancement of Gods glory: Whereas an unbounded liberty in extemporall and fanaticall Prayers, brings forth the quite contrary; disorder
dis-

dif-union of affections between man and man, impiety, atheism, and anarchy. *Ex ungue leonem.* What leud demeanours, what insolent and irreligious behaviours, both towards the Book of Common-prayers, and the men that use them, hath this lawless time shewn? now, while the laws are still in force that authorize them. The King and Parliament devoutly use them, religious people morning and evening frequent them; now some to spurn and tear them, others spit at them, you to call them superstitious, evill, a Crambe, a Kickshoe, an Hotch-potch, a Drench, &c. If this be not the highest degree of profanation, nothing is. Surely, if we do not repent for this, our posterity will; and besides that, blush when ever they shall be upbraided by such prodigiously Atheisticall Ancestors. But to proceed: What order can ever be expected? what uniformity looked for? what consent and harmony betwixt Church and Church, when every one shall differ in that which should make them truly one? a Communion of Saints, even their community of Prayers? How, while some are starved, shall others be pampered? and then what likenesse? Tell me not, that they that will shall use the Churches set forms; for either they will be wholly neglected, where others cannot be had, being so discountenanced, if left arbitrary; discountenanced, I say, by publike authority, & depraved, condemned, damned, by private persons; or else, whiles both are in use, it will nourish a continuall enmity betwixt the users of each. It is a requisite in the Church of Christ, that the particular Congregations which are the members of that mysticall body, be of one heart and one minde, especially in their Prayers to, and Praises of God; more especially in publike meetings, at publike deliverances, in publike dangers: how shall we be so, when we shall not know what one anothers hearts and mindes are? No, but the designe of your dear friend, the Authour of *The Protestation protested*, and some since him, is, to have the Church at length sifted and winnowed, and the grain laid apart by it self, that is your faction; and for the chaffe, all else, let them do or be what they will, it matters not. If the Kings State will maintain the faith of Christ, well

well and good, they shall have your fair leave : if not, they shall have your leave too; so you may enjoy your consciences you are indifferent. This is the *Common good* that is cryed up, though indeed the *Publike wo:* and thus you tread a fair way to it : you shall have the hold of the hearts of the people, the surest hold that may be, of their consciences, of all their religiousest actions, their Prayers, Supplications, &c. and the State shall have none of you : not command you to pray for the King, that (you say) is time spent in flattery; not for Bishops, they are Antichristian ; not for his subjects, that they may live godly and peaceable lives under him, they are *dogs, shut out of the gates of the new City, howling.*

Immortale odium, & nunquam sanabile vulnus
Ardet adhuc Ombos & Tentyra ——

What can the end of these proceedings be, but an irreconcileable distance between party and party; then jealousies, then provocations, then wars, then ruine! I doubt not, but if Christ had been pleased to have converted to his faith but one King and his whole State, and so to have ordered a nationall Church, and have given over to us that order as a pattern, surely it should not have been any such independent anarchicall Government as your platform is, nay will be if we can tell when; for as yet the Whelp is not licked into any fashion. You say that set forms of Prayers are quenching the Spirit; whether it be so or no, I am sure your Extemporall will set such a fire on your Spirits, that they will need quenching, or the whole Kingdome will burn with them. Weigh these circumstances, and you will see that there is an expediency of set forms in a nationall Church.

2. Of set forms some of ye will grant, but not of these that are. Your reason?

[*The form of your Liturgie is phantastick and superstitious, and the end sinister, the imposition violent,* pag. 2 .]

Phantastick ? Like enough they might think so, that saw or heard you read them ; *Sed male dum recitas, &c.* But then the fault was not in the Prayers, but your officiating. If
ever

ever you were present at a Synagogue in Amsterdam, and saw how the Jewes with voice and gesture read a Section of the Law, or one of *Davids* Psalmes, you might justly say the men were phantastick, yet the matter was good.

'But the Forme is so. Wherein I pray ? I suppose you mean the same thing, with those importunate triflers in Queen *Elizabeths* dayes, who were offended at the short cuts or shreddings, at the intermingling of praying and reading in it, in such manner, as if supplicants should use the same to a mortall Prince in proposing their suits, all the world would think them mad. If thus, the answer is, where you had the objection; I have turned down the leaf, pray save me the labour of transcribing, and look it your self: Onely the close is this; *Our case were miserable, if that wherewith we most endevour to please God, were in his sight so vile and despicable, as mens disdainfull speeches would make it.* Hooker Eccl. Pol.p.241.

Though you borrow your arrowes (your objections) from their quiver, yet what with being new feathered with the peoples discontents, perhaps flying with the wind; and lastly, their heads being poysoned with the gall of Aspes, they pierce deeper now than formerly: then our Prayers were but *ridiculous*, now *superstitious*. Were they alwayes so? Yes. Belike it was beyond the skill of those holy men to refine *a Scorpion into a Fish*, pag. 14. Where then was their errour in transmitting over this superstition to us ? Was it malice, or ignorance, or both ? that when we asked them *Bread*, would give us a *Stone*; when we asked a *Fish*, would give us a *Serpent* ? [*It bribed their judgements with worldly engagements*, pag. 16.] O the inconsiderateness of eager and headlong ambition ! that men, who but now were, some returned from banishment, others drawn out of prison, should in an instant be so turned about, that they would forfeit their Religion, their Wisedomes, their Credits, yea their Souls, in obtruding upon a Church superstitious and damnable Rules for Devotion ; and all this to

get

get a narrow incompetent Bishoprick. If they had minded preferment, why looked they not abroad, where sacriledge and misdevotion had not so streightned their walkes, nor demolished their goodly prospects, nor washed out their gilded titles? they could not have been worse there, if they were superstitious at home. I wonder not now to hear them so traduced by the Papists, when our selves doe thus uncharitably misreport them. *Martin Mar-prelate* (as Master *Sandys* can tell you) is in the disgrace of our Clergie cited by the Papists, as a grave unquestionable Authour: and what place your *Animadversions* may once have in the Vaticane, is yet dubious; though it be certain that those Spiders of Rome cannot have a fitter subject from whence to draw poyson. But is it certain they are superstitious now? Will your *Smectymnuans* affirm so much? Truly then they are as deeply concerned in it, as any of the rest of their brethren, who before the unhappy distaste of the late Convocation, could alike swallow so much Popery. However; where is the superstition? In this, this, or this Prayer, or any of the rest? If not in any of the parts, not in the whole. O but [*it symbolizeth with the Masse, and pranks it self in Popish weeds, and goes too garish upon holy-days*, p.22.] They have Anthems, and Organs, and Copes, and Surplices in the Church of Rome: True; and when all this is away, still they have Prayers: and if you will wholly abolish them because symbolicall, Antichrist will symbolize with ye ἐν τῷ συμβόλῳ, in his Creed in spite of your teeths, unlesse you mean to have no other but *The Christian Beleef concerning Bishops*. That soul that can soar aloft upon the strength of his own wings, or hath its flagging Pinions completely ymped with feathers from the *Dove*, the Spirit of God, shall little need such advantages as are these things which we speak of; (for advantages they are, and but advantages;) onely take you heed you do not, *Icarus*-like, over-dare, and give all the Christian world else leave to acknowledge and remedy as they may, their almost irremediable weaknesses. This outward State and glory (sayes my fore-cited Author)

Spec. Europ. p. 130.

being

being well disposed, doth ingender, quicken, encrease and nourish the inward reverence and respectfull devotion, due to so soveraign, so awfull a power: which, those whom the use thereof cannot perswade so, would easily by the want of it be caused to confesse.

Next, [*the end is sinister: a bait for Papists to bite at.*] Saving your scorn Sir, such baits are laid by his direction, that made his Apostles fishers of men. But what would that do? bring them to our Churches? Yes, and did: Alas, what was that you will say? I will tell you; It was a shame to such Recusant Protestants as you are, that will not only not bite, but not so much as nibble. But you have answered your self: It was [*a greedy desire of winning of Proselytes, by conforming to them unlawfully.*] I will confesse with you, that there was a greedy desire of winnning Proselytes, and is still; but no unlawfull meanes used, till you have proved that those things, with which our Church and the Church of Rome do symbolize, are either in their own nature, or due use, superstitious. If you know what is the meaning of that passionate entreaty of S. *Paul, Destroy not him with thy meat for whom Christ dyed:* or of that which he alledgeth as his own example; *To the weak became I as weak, that I might gain the weak; I am made all things to all men, that I might by all means save some:*] you would not call it, as you do, a vain-glorious and Pharisaicall project; unlesse you think that a Papist cannot have a tender conscience; or if he hath, that he ought not for his satisfaction to be yeelded unto in things indifferent. Neither is this *end* (a respect indeed it is, that was and is had in having such forms, though not the main and ultimate) frustrate if they do not come; for it keeps as many Protestants at Church now, as it did Papists at first (till they were upon other reasons diverted;) many of which by so unsufferable a scandall, would either abstain from the worship of God altogether, or go where they might have it nearest to their ancient manner.

Rom. 14.15

1 Cor. 9.22.

In the last place, you say the imposition is violent: you mean this in respect to your selves, who have resolved never but by force to submit to any thing, how just soever: otherwise I see not how you can possibly call it so, since the authority is lawfull and just; the thing in it self indifferent, and in the circumstances expedient,

F

pedient, the extent of the imposition no farther than as it may stand together with Prayers of our own framing, whether as private men or as publike. To conclude this Section, you and I might have bin far better busied in using those pious forms, than in thus disputing them either of the one side or the other.

§. XII.

Pag 19. I Was glad at my heart when I heard you cry out[*set the grave Councels upon their shelves, string them hard*] for from such your slighting of them, I conjectured your ignorance in that kind of learning to be, though not so ingenuously confessed, yet altogether as much and great as mine. And see, my conjecture proves true; where my fear was most, I finde least cause why to fear: you have shewn that Episcopacy, as it cannot be upheld but by well-grounded reason, and diligently searched antiquity, (the Scripture in this, as in a lesse materiall point, being lesse clear:) yet it may be beaten down both by the clubs of the base rabble, and the rude fist of your false Logick. For what is all your confutation of that holy Order, but insinuative and cheating inconsequences, or spitefull and malicious rayling; as if you intended so only to triumph over the cause, (as lately ye did over the person of a Prelate) by throwing dirt in his face? Though your bright and new-varnisht *Modona* vizard (under which you so hansomely play the hypocrite) have deceived the people, yet (*Non omnes fallis* --) others there be will know it to be but a vizard, especially when I shall have rendered it more ugly by scraping off the paint. In doing which I must follow you somewhat more close than formerly.

Animad. *It had been happy for this Land, if your Priests had been but onely wooden; all England knows they have been to this Iland not wood but wormwood, that have infected the third part of our waters, like that Apostate* &c pag. 53.

Confut. It is an unhappy, though necessary misery, that doth accompany the Church of Christ; that not only the people, but the guides of those people are subject to corruptions and depravations, as well in manners as doctrine: and it is yet a more unhappy misery, that those corruptions have a farther mischief, *viz.* that too too often advantage is taken by and upon them, to discountenance, yea to ruine many truths. As here; a Bishop is
incestu-

inceſtuous or beſtiall, ambitious, or tyrannicall, or hereticall, or pſeudodoxe, Therefore the Calling is Antichriſtian: One is ſo: therefore all are ſo. What could make rationall men ſwallow ſuch abſurdities, but offenſe taken at thoſe perſonall faults and miſdemeanours? confeſſe with you, that there is nothing more intolerable, more juſtly abominable in the eys of God and man, than a lewd, vicious, or lying Prophet; that there is nor higher nor lower among them, nor Prieſt nor Prelate, but ſome of them hath been and is ſo: What, ſhall we therfore have no more Miniſters? Is it the office, or the man, that bears this curſed fruit? you ſay the office. I ask of Prelacy only: why is it then that the inferiour Clergy is moſt faulty? how can they be ſo lewd, if no Prelates? or if lewd, why is not their order aboliſhed? Hath Prelacy ſome ill quality in it, that makes good men bad? why are not all the Prelates alike vicious? why are there ſo many good men amongſt them? Or look again; Were not they which have miſbehaved themſelves in that office, bad men before they were in it? or thoſe that were good before, did they not continue ſo? It is the man then, the ſinfull corrupt nature of man, that yeelds theſe bitter fruits, not Epiſcopacy.

Animad. *What ſhou'd I tell you how the Univerſities (that men look ſhould be fountains of learning and knowledge) have been poyſoned and choaked under your governance &c.*

Confut Fair and pure may thoſe living ſtreams ever flow, both *Iſis* and *Chame*! but who, I wis, hath troubled them? yea, who goes about to dry them up? if either they fail, or be pudled, you cannot blame Epiſcopacy for either. If ſome Biſhops be Arminians, and ſome Scholars at either Univerſity, that infection came from beyond ſea, though not in the ſame ſhip with your Presbytery. Was *Arminius* a Biſhop? ſurely no more than Mr *Calvin*: Why then ſhould that be objected to them or the cauſe? Or pray tell me, do you think if you have pulled down Epiſcopacy that thoſe opinions will dye? Alas, never till you can kill depraved and curious reaſon, which hath the ſtart of Grace in theſe two things; namely, that it is ſooner up at, and better cheriſhed and heartned in its operations than ſhe commonly is; it being as naturall to man to love the one, as to hate the other. What other choaking you ſhould mean, if not this, I can no
more

more conceive, than I can how it concerns the businesse in hand.

Animad. And if to be wooden be to be base, where could there be found among all the reformed Churches, nay in the Church of Rome it self, a baser broode of flattering or time-serving Priests? &c

Confut. To recriminate is so poor a way of justification, that I should think he wants all other excuses that flyes to that; therefore though you and your faction lye open no where more than on this part, I purposely spare you; yet so, as I will shew you the advantage I had you at. For observe me; What is that which you call flattery? standing up by the King. Is it not their duty? and yours too, were ye not so great Patrons of popularity? If the Kings Soveraignty be inviolable, may it not lawfully be published? may not a Minister dare preach it? yea, and if your Parlour Oratours have defamed, may not the Pulpit vindicate? There is difference, I hope, between a Libell clapt upon White-hall gates, and a Panygirick at *Pauls*: In my opinion those flatterers shall do very ill to be silent, till either their Prince be lesse vertuous, or you lesse malitious.

Animad. And as for your young Scholars, that petition for Bishopricks and Deanaries to encourage them in their Studies, and that many Gentlemen else will not put their sons to learning, &c. That which they alledge for their encouragement, should be cut away forthwith, as the very bait of pride and ambition, the very garbage that draws together all the fowls of prey, &c.

Confut. It is one of those young Scholars that asks your Eldership, whether there were not birds and beasts of prey, that did devour the flock, before ere the Church were so much beholding to the bounty of Princes and Nobles as now she is? Whether the Devill can allure never a Cobler from his *awl* and *last* under a fat Prebendary? Whether a Widows house be not as tempting as a Bishops Palace? or there be not of those degenerate sort of men, who will desire the Priesthood for a morsell of bread? If so, how are we, or shall we be then more safe than now? Poor soul! how envie and anger befools thee! Bethink your self better; are not Parsonages, Vicarages, and Lectures prey too? and do we not see halt and dumb too often possesse the former, and crazed men the latter? away with them then by any means. No, but away with those fowls and beasts rather, and

then

then that prey will be meat for honest and able Preachers; or I doubt not else but sacriledg Hook and his neighbour Gentlemen will make many a pleasant meal on it. But in good earnest Sir, for Bishopricks and Denaries, they are in too wise a Dispencers hands to be given to Vultures; had it been otherwise, perhaps yours and your fellows mouths ere this had been stopt.

   Anim *The heathen Philosophers thought, virtue was for its own sake inestimable, and the greatest gain of a Teacher to make a soul virtuous. Was morall virtue so lovely or so alluring, and heathen men so inamoured of her, as to teach and study her, with greatest neglect and contempt of worldly profit and advancement: and is Christian Piety so homely and unpleasant, and Christian men so cloyed with her, as that none will study and teach her but for lucre and preferment! O stale-grown Piety! O Gospel rated as cheap as thy Master!* &c. pag. 54.

   Confut. Now I see you know somewhat: and were I not assured that other passions distracted you, I could easily be enclined to think that this volley of expressions proceeded from a love of *goodnesse:* indeed so much the more easily inclined, by how much I would fain have it so. For were there no guile in them, as I do continually nourish such thoughts, so would I never desire to have them better cloathed: if at any time a floud of eloquence becomes us, it is when we expresse such a love, or such an indignation! But it is one thing that you say, and another thing that you prove: the means is often times rested and taken up in stead of the end; therefore the means is not the means; or therfore the means cannot be looked at as the means: illogicall and absurd! A Philosopher loves virtue; and a Christian loves him that is the fountain of that virtue; What then? The Philosopher, you say, loved virtue for it self; So doth a Christian love God much more. But he did it with neglect of others things, wealth, honours, &c. He came then so much short of his own Philosophicall perfection: They that stood a begging in the streets, might (if it had pleased them) have been as *liberall* as their best Masters; And that Philosopher that flung his gold into the sea, might have been perhaps lesse an Infidell, if he had provided for himself and his family with it; I am sure might have been more magnificent. But that offends you, that our Church should use the same means

F 3   to

to entice men to the pure service of God, that were used to tempt our Saviour to the service of the Devill. Those means were neither in themselves, nor as enticements, any way dangerous; but so far as they were tendered by him, from whom it was a sin to receive them; to him, who could make no use of them; for such an end, as it had been a sin to accept them. Otherwise how could God entice the children of Israel with the promise of Canaan; or *Solomon*, with riches and honours and all kind of abundance? But these *desires mixe.* As subordinate they may: The holy Ghost witnesseth ot *Moses*, that he had an eye to the reward; I ask whether in that *Moses* sinned: yea, God himself hearteneth on the Church of Smyrna, *Be thou faithfull unto the death, and I will give thee a Crown of life. Du Moulin*, whose Tractates you would seem to be acquainted with) in a discourse *Of the love of God*, tells us, the most imperfect and incomplete degree of this love is, to love God for the good we receive from him: Thus children (saith he) say Grace, that they may go to break-fast. Indeed a childish love. The perfectest is, to love him and nothing else; a love onely the glorified Saints are capable of: betwixt which two he placeth a third, a mixed love; which is, when we love God with other things; yet so, as that we love those things for Gods sake; that is, as helps and furtherances of our own piety and his glory. Either you wilfully oversee much truth, or are very ignorant.

Heb.11:29

Rev.2:10.

Animad. *A true Pastor of Christs sending hath this especiall marke, that for greatest labours and greatest merits in the Church, he requires either nothing, if he could so subsist; or a very common and reasonable supply of humane necessaries. We cannot do better therefore than to leave this care of ours to God; he can easily send Labourers into his harvest.* —— *He can stir up rich fathers to bestow exquisite education upon their children, and so dedicate them to the service of the Gospel, he can make the sons of Nobles his Ministers*, &c pag. 56. Animad. No man doubts of what God can do; but we may well doubt he will not do what we would have him, while we are thus froward and unthankfull; while we are under persecution, poor, wretched, and despicable, fed but from hand to mouth, (as we say) whiles God leads his Church through a desart or wildernesse: If we expect our drink to drop

out

out of a flint, or from the shivers of a barren and dry rock; if we spread our table to a miracle, or every morning and evening look out for a Raven to feed us, it becomes our condition, and therefore God answers our expectation: but if when he hath brought his Church into a land that flows with milk and honey; when he hath made *Kings our nursing Fathers, and Queens our nursing Mothers,* we will then over-look all that bounty, and say God can do thus and thus, *can raise out of these stones children unto Abraham,* and bring up those children to his own work, at his own miraculous expences; this is but to tempt his providence. God can do this and more, but his wayes are his own. He can rain Manna into our mouths, as well as dew upon the earth. Shall we be angry, because we have our Corn at the second hand? he could have sent us into the world with our cloaths on; is it not as well that he sets the worm to the wheel to spin it for us? doth he not shew a work of providence in preparing both for us, as well as in giving them to us? so no doubt he could have immediately from himself supplyed the necessities of his Ministers; is it not as well that he doth it by others? doth he not make a virtue out of what we have, in their hands through which it passeth? is it not liberality, is it not munificence in them that give it? why should we envie good men their piety? or are these virtues out of date, were they only ceremoniall? hath God impropriated all the riches of the earth for the use of the Lay men only? are not Clergy-men members of the body of Christ, why should not each member thrive alike? if these must be poor and naked, so let the rest be; and though there be in this but little wisdome, yet will there be some indifferency. *Vide Hooker in præfat. Eccl. Pol.*

But you will say, It is too much, and ill placed: Any thing is so that is ill used: Single out the man, and if you can make better use of it than he, I wish you had the preferment. But for Church livings in generall, a judicious Surveyor once said, (and I dare say they have not been much bettered since) that they were insufficient for the Church-men: and that all the Parliaments since 27. *H.* 8. who gave away Impropriations from the Church, seemed to him to stand in some sort obnoxious and obliged to God in conscience to do somewhat for the Church (he did not mean to rob it) to reduce the patrimony thereof to a competency. *Becons consid.*

Animad,

Animad. *Can a man thus employed (in preaching, &c.) finde himself discontented or dishonoured, for want of admittance to have a pragmaticall vote at Sessions, --- or be discouraged though men call him not Lord : --- would he tugge for a Barony, to sit and vote in Parliament ?* pag. 57.

Confut. Yes marry, what else ? That man that was and could have still been content without those honours, will be very loath now to let them go ; yet not so much that he loves the honours or means that accompany them, as that he would not have his countrey made guilty of so shamefull a depriving him of them. Why should sacriledge and injustice triumph over Gods cause, whiles he hath tongue or pen to defend it ? yea, why should he or any the rest of that sacred function forsake their *Great Master* in it ? Me thinks if all other arguments failed, it were sufficient proof of the goodnesse of it, that it hath him to be its *Defender* that is *Defender of the Faith:* A Prince, who if for nothing else, will therefore keep the *munificence* of his Predecessors inviolate, that he may teach succeeding ages a *reverence* to his *Own:* which indeed is so much the more estimable, in that it is exercised in so perverse an age of the world, as is so far from giving it its just value, that it scarce allows it * *pardonable.* Alas! what an heap of disorder and ruines had this Church even now been, had not God sent it *So Gracious a Governour !* But if, notwithstanding what divine and humane lawes, what the King and all Good men vote to the contrary, such a desolation must come; may the curse which hath alwayes been wont to accompany such *Desperate Robbery*, be to this land turned into a blessing; and may it never fall any whit below that *Happinesse*, which in Gods extraordinary supply of *New Means* is and may be *Imagined.*

* As for the Kings gift, regall bounty may be excusable in giving. p. 59.

FINIS.

TO preserve the strength of the Mariage-bond and the Honour of that estate, against those sad breaches and dangerous abuses of it, which common discontents (on this side Adultery) are likely to make in unstaied mindes and men given to change, by taking in or grounding themselves upon the opinion answered, and with good reason confuted in this Treatise, I have approved the printing and publishing of it.

Novemb. 14 1644. JOSEPH CARYL.

Errata.

IN pag. 1. line 17. read *aut* for *and*, p. 2. l. 29. r. *Kens case* for *Keras case*, p. 9. l. 9. r *to* for *as*, p. 12. l. 24. leave out *naturall* in the first place, p. 14. l. ult, r. *Obligee* for *Obligor*.

An Answer to a Book, Intituled,
THE
Doctrine and Discipline
OF
DIVORCE,
OR,
A Plea for Ladies and Gentlewomen,
and all other Maried Women
against Divorce.

Wherein,
Both Sexes are vindicated from all bonadge of Canon
Law, and other mistakes whatsoever: And the unsound Principles of the Author are examined and fully confuted by
authority of Holy Scripture, the Laws of this Land,
and sound Reason.

Concil. Anglic. Anno 670. Can. 10.
Nullus conjugem propriam nisi (ut sanctum Evangelium docet,) fornicationis causa relinquat.

LONDON,
Printed by *G. M.* for *William Lee* at the Turks-Head in Fleet-street, next to the Miter Taverne. 1644.

An Answer to a Book, intituled, *The Doctrine and Discipline of Divorce restored to the good of both Sexes from the bondage of the Canon Law.*

Or our more orderly proceeding in this question of Divorce, *viz.* whether a man may divorce or put away his Wife for indisposition, unfitnesse, or contrariety of minde, we will do these three things.

1. Shew what the Doctrine or discipline of Divorce is.

2. Give some reasons why a man may not put away his wife for indisposition, unfitnesse, or contrariety of minde, although manifested in much sharpnesse.

3. We will answer the Arguments and Scriptures, which are brought by the Author of the Book, intituled, *The Doctrine and Discipline of Divorce*, to prove that a divorce may lawfully be for contrariety of minds, &c.

Concerning the first thing, what Divorce is, or the Doctrine and discipline of it.

The word Divorce comes from the Latine word *divortium*, which comes *a divertendo aut divortendo*, to intimate that by divorce a woman is separated, divided, or turned aside from her husband: the Greek is αποπομπε ex αποπεμπω, *i.e. repudio, rectius αποτασιος, dicitur quod ab απο, i.e. ab & ιςημι, i.e. sto, quasi dicas abscessio.* The Hebrew word is *Cherithuth* from *Charath*, which signifies a cutting off, dismembring, or separating, or *foedus icere*;

B   but

An Answer to a Book, intituled,

but *Cherithuth* is ܟܪܝܬܘܬ ܐܬܪܘܬܐ, properly a Bill of divorce or parting. Thus concerning the word.

Now concerning the divorce it selfe, to shew what it is, we must consider it under a twofold notion.

First, as it hath been practised by the Jewes according as they thought directed by *Moses*'s Law, and so Divorce was a free and a voluntary act of the Husband, made known by writing, whereby he did dismisse and for ever put away his Wife, and give her leave to marry to another man: To this purpose some of the Hebrew Rabbines have set down the form of the Bill of Divorce used amongst the Jewes: in effect thus.

I such an one (setting down his name, the day and year) do voluntarily, with the willingnesse of my soule without constraint, dismisse, leave, and put away, thou, even thou, (naming her name) which hast been my wife heretofore, but now I dismisse thee, that thou maist be free, and be married to whom thou wilt: And this is unto thee a writing of divorce, according to the law of Moses, Witnesse *R.* and *T.*

The Jewes require to make a lawfull divorce, that the man must put her away willingly, that it must be by writing, that he must put her quite out of his possession, that she be truly named in the deed of divorce, and that the deed of divorce be given to her either by himself or his Deputy before witnesse.

Thus of Divorce as practised by the Jewes in relation to *Moses*'s Law.

In the second place we will consider of it as practised by the lawes of England.

And so Divorce is a sentence pronounced by an Ecclesiasticall Judge, whereby a man and woman formerly married, are separated or parted. Cook *lib.* 7. *Kent case.*

This Divorce is twofold. 1. There is a divorce *a vinculo matrimonii* from the very bond of matrimony it selfe. 2. There is a divorce *tantùm à mensa & thoro*, from bed and board only.

Concerning the first kinde of divorce from the very bond of matrimony it self: the cause of this divorce must precede or go before mariage: amongst which are,

1. *Causa precontractus*, because the parties or one of them was contracted to another before: and so if a man marry one precontracted and have issue, its the fathers childe till divorce for precontract,

contract, and then is it *nullius filius*, a Bastard. *Cook lib. 6. 66. Dier 105.*

2. There is a divorce *à vinculo matrimonii, causa frigiditatis, vel causa impotentiæ,* for cause of impotency to mariage duties: yet if after a man be divorced for impotency, and take another wife and have children by her, these shall not be Bastards, because a man may be *habilis & inhabilis diversis temporibus,* able and unable at divers times. *Cook lib. 5. 93. Dier fol. 178.*

3. There is a divorce *à vinculo matrimonii, causa minoris ætatis vel impubertatis,* because they are within age at the time of mariage: and so if two be maried *infra annos nubiles,* and after full age are divorced for the same, the woman may bring an Assise against the man, for land given her in frank-mariage, *Lib. Ass. 19. An. plac. 2.* which proves the divorce is from the very bond of matrimony. Besides these there are divers other causes of divorce *à vinculo matrimonii,* as *causa affinitatis & causa consanguinitatis,* by reason of affinity and consanguinity or kindred, *Cook com. Littleton.*

So *causa professionis,* and *termino paschæ* 30 *Edw. 1. coram Rege,* there *William de Chadworths* case, how that he was divorced from his Wife, because he carnally knew the Daughter of his Wife before he maried her mother: these are causes of divorce from the very bond of matrimony allowed on by the Common law; concerning which the Civill or Canon law makes some distinctions and additions. So in the case of divorce *causa impotentiæ vel frigiditatis,* for impotency to mariage duties, Although *Justinian* (as some think discreetly) did will, that there should be three yeares triall of the disability: yet here the Canon law expects present proofe: yet some think this cause doth not dissolve from the very bond of matrimony, except the impotency or impediment can be proved to be before mariage, and not to fall out after: So of impotency the same they say, *Ut per ea matrimonium nunquam extitisse judicitur.* And concerning mariage of kindred in the line ascendant or discendant, it is counted so detestable, that *Bartel* sayes, they suffer confiscation of goods and deserve exile.

The Civill and Canon law allow of divorce after a long time absence of either party, but they certainly agree not of the time of absence. So *Cod. lib. 5. tit. 1. leg. 2. const. sponsa post biennium,*

&c. allowed to marry after two years absence, but *tit.* 27. after three years, *leg.* 27. after four years. Others say the Civill law requires five years absence.

In *Confil. Lateran.* part. 50. *cap.* 23. There is an example of a Decree, upon a woman complaining her husband had been gone ten yeares, and it was commanded the parents of the husband should send for him home, and he in a long time came not; upon which the Bishop did pronounce a sentence of divorce, and gave the woman leave to marry, and the sentence was allowed of by the whole Councell.

So the Canon law decrees *causa* 28. *queft.* 1. *cap.* 4. That if the wife refuse to dwell with her Christian husband, he may without any fault leave her.

Thus of the first kinde of divorce from the bond of matrimony it self, and this makes the children Bastards and bereaves the woman of her dower.

Secondly, there is a divorce *à mensa & thoro*, from bed and board only, and this is for some cause subsequent or during mariage, and not before mariage, as for adultery committed. Yet this being subsequent to the mariage, the bond of mariage by the law is not dissolved, but the freehold continues, the wife shall be indowed, and the children are mulier, and not Bastards.

Concerning the justnesse or conveniency of all these lawes in every thing, whether they will stand *in foro conscientiae* its not needfull now to dispute: our end being only a little to open the law of Divorce, that we may see what it is. And so now we leave this first thing what Divorce is, and the doctrine and discipline thereof, and come to the second thing.

2 Thing And that is to prove that whatsoever other causes of Divorce may be allowed of, yet that disagreement of minde or disposition between husband and wife, yea though it shewes it selfe in much sharpnesse each to other, is not by the law of God allowed of for a just cause of divorce, neither ought to be allowed of by the lawes of man.

For the proof of this second thing propounded to be handled, to prove that Husbands and Wives ought not to be divorced for contrariety or unfitnesse of mindes or dispositions, although it should be manifested by much harsh cariage each to other, I shall as briefly as I can demonstrate the same. Where

The Doctrine and Discipline of Divorce.

Where the Scripture commands a thing to be done, it appoints *1 Arg.*
when, how, and for what it shall be done: as in the case of
death: when any one is by the law to dye, it sets down for what
cause and fact: and so excommunication it teacheth when and
for what. But now concerning Divorce for disagreement or
contrariety of disposition, in regard there is between all maried
people some contrariety or disagreement of mindes: and the
Scriptures speak nothing to direct to what a measure of disagreement or contrariety it must grow to, before it shall be lawfull
to divorce or part: therefore I conclude the Scripture allowes
not of any divorce at all for disagreement, &c.

If it be not lawfull for a Husband to put away an Infidell wife *2 Arg.*
who acknowledges not Christ, in case she be content to dwell
with him: Then may not a man put away his wife for disagreement of mindes only: but the first is true, *ergo* the latter.

For the first part of the Argument the Apostle saith, 1 *Cor.*7.
13. *If any brother hath a wife who is an Infidell, if she be content to dwell with him, let him not put her away.*

And for the second part, that if a man may not put away his
wife who is an Infidell, much lesse may he put his wife away
for disagreement of disposition, this seems clear: because difference in religion in its own nature, breeds as great a dislike and
disagreement and greater than any naturall disagreement of disposition, constitution, or complexion whatsoever. Christ speaking of this difference, even between them of the nearest relation,
saith, *The father shall be against the sonne, and the sonne against the father*, even to persecute with extremity: And that *the Disciples should be hated of all for Christs sake*: and yet I never heard of any
that was hated of every man for his contrariety of naturall disposition.

So that if disagreement in religion be a greater cause of hatred
and variance then disagreement of naturall dispositions and constitutions; and yet a man may not put away his wife for that
disagreement, then much lesse for this.

The third Argument shall be from *Deut.* 22. 13, 14, 15, &c. *3 Arg.*
There if a man shall take a Wife and hate her, and raise an ill report upon her, to the end that he might be rid of her: and if the
report be found true she shall be stoned to death; but if it be not
found

An Answer to a Book, intituled,

found true he shall not put her away all the dayes of his life : here although a man hates his Wife, so that he seeks by false reports to scandalize her, even to danger of her life, yet is not he permitted to put her away all the dayes of his life; and yet how great the disagreement of minde and disposition must of necessity be between such a man and his wife who so did hate her, let any man judge.

4. *Arg.* If every Christian ought to beare the burthens and infirmities of another Christian, to whom he is not bound by any civill relation; much more is he to bear the burthen and infirmities of his Wife who is so neerly bound to him: but the first is true, *Gal.* 6.1. *Ergo* the latter. But he that for infirmities or contrariety of minde, or the like, puts away his wife, doth not bear with her infirmities, and therefore he breaks the law of Christ.

5. *Arg.* If the Husband ought to love his Wife, as Christ doth his Church, then ought not a man to put away his Wife for weaknesse of nature, contrariety, or indisposition of minde. But the first is true. *Ergo* the latter.

For the first part, the words of *Paul Ephes.* 5.29. *Husbands love your wives as Christ doth his Church.*

If any shall say, Similitudes hold not in every thing, and therefore *Paul* may not mean a man should love his Wife in perpetuity as Christ doth his Church, but for the sincerity, so long as she continues his wife.

Answ. Paul specifies wherein they should expresse their loves like to Christ, at least implicitely: that is, by passing by and healing the faults and infirmities of their Wives, as Christ gave himself, &c. that he might wash his Church, &c. And for the second part of the Argument its clear, because such love as is there required ought to hide and passe by faults, disagreement of minde, contrariety of disposition, &c.

6. *Arg.* The sixth Argument is from the expresse words of Christ, *Matth.* 5.32. where he being a preaching to his Disciples concerning the true sense of *Moses*'s law (as it seemes) and of some addition thereto by his own Evangelicall precepts: he precisely tels them: *That whosoever puts away his wife except it were for πορνεια, scortatio, adultery, he commits adultery:* so that whether you make it a true interpretation of *Moses*'s law against the

glosses

glosses of others, or take it as a new precept belonging to the law of the Gospell, yet will it be an impregnable proofe against all effeminate and childish divorces, for disagreement and contrariety of mindes.

If any shall say, if Chrifts words hold univerfally and except no caufe but adultery: then all other caufes, as frigidity, mariage within degrees forbidden by *Moses*, &c. are no caufes of divorce no more then contrariety of minde.   *Object.*

Chrifts fpeech holds univerfally according as he intended it, namely, to condemne all fuch grounds of divorce as were groundlefly practifed amongft the Iewes, for every caufe which they thought fufficient, and yet no wayes checks the law which forbids mariage within the degrees of affinity or confanguinity, or forbids other caufe which makes mariage void *ipfo facto*; or by due proofes may make void the mariage. If there be any other objections againft this place, we fhall refer them to what will afterwards be faid in explication of this text, and of *Deut.* 24. 1.   *Anfw.*

The feventh Argument is: If the Husband and Wife be by the Ordinance of God one flefh, then may they not feparate or be feparated from one another, except it be for fome caufe which either in it felfe or by confequence may juftly be thought to be a juft caufe of diffolving the union of being one flefh. But the firft is true, *Ergo*, alfo the latter.   *7 Arg.*

For the firft part, that the Husband and Wife are one flefh, *Paul* confirmes it, *Ephef.* 5 and Chrift himfelfe *Matth.* 19.

And for the fecond part of the Argument as it depends upon the former, *viz.* if they be one flefh, then they ought not to feparate or be feparated. Its the Argument of Chrift himfelfe againft the Pharifees, why divorce ought not to be for light caufes, but for adultery only; becaufe faith he, *they are no more two but one flefh*, therefore, *whomsoever God hath joyned together, let no man put afunder.*

Only as I intimated, fuch other caufes may be allowed of as diffolves this union of being one flefh, either directly, or by confequence.

But fure contrariety of difpofition and unfitneffe of minde can be no fuch thing as makes the Husband and Wife (being once by mariage one flefh) to be two againe.

In

8 Arg.

In the next place I conceive something may be gathered to this purpose from the words of *Paul*, 1 *Cor*. 7. when speaking of mariage, he tels them, *such should have troubles in the flesh*, and not that freedome to serve God which the unmaried had: yet he concludes, he spared them, and would not forbid them for that cause to marry.

Now if troubles in the flesh comming by mariage which hinder the cheerfull service of God, be not a just cause to forbeare mariage: Then it would seem that to persons that are already maried and bound to each other by the union of one flesh, by covenant, by love, by the bonds of Christianity, although through the peevishnesse or ill dispositions of their natures, their troubles should increase to multitudes above what is ordinarie betwixt maried persons, yet ought they not to part and to marrie to others, because some sort and measure of troubles and discontent in mariage are inavoidable; and therefore where one is by mariage bound by so many bonds, he ought not to break the bonds to ease himself of disquietnesse and trouble which is inseparably incident to mariage, though not in that degree as he now lies under, and is subject to.

Yet am I not over confident of this Argument, but that with some colour of reason it may be evaded.

9 Arg.

In the next place, if the Husband ought to love his Wife as himself, then may he not for discontent or disagreement put her away, no more then for some discontent or disquietnesse in himselfe, he may separate his soule from his body. But the first is true. *Ephes*. 5. *ult*. *Ergo* the latter.

10 Arg.

Lastly, we may fetch an Argument from the inconveniencies that would follow if divorce were suffered, for this disagreement of disposition and unfitnesse of minde, as for example, it would be an occasion to the corrupt heart of man without any just cause at all, meerely for to satisfie his lust, to pretend causes of divorce when there is none; and to make quarrels and live discontentedly with his Wife, to the end he might have a pretence for to put her away: who sees not, how many thousauds of lustfull and libidinous men would be parting from their Wives every week and marying others: and upon this, who should keep the children of these divorcers which somtimes they would leave in

their

their Wives bellies? how shall they come by their Portions, of whom, or where? and how shall the Wife be endowed of her Husbands estate? Nay, commonly, to what reproach would the woman be left to, as being one left who was not fit for any ones company? and so who would venture upon her againe. And so by this means through her just cause of discouragement, she would probably hazard her self upon some dishonest and disgracefull course, with a hundred more the like inconveniencies, even to the overturning and overthrowing of all humane society, which would inevitably follow if this loose Doctrine of Divorce were once established by law.

To these Arguments we might adde the consent of Antiquity, who in this follow the direction and doctrine of Christ.

As *Concil. Tolet.* 12. *Can.* 8. *Preceptum Domini est, ut excepta causa fornicationis, uxor a viro dimitti non debeat. &c.* Its the command of the Lord, the Wife should not be put away but for fornication. So *Cod. lib.* 3. *tit.* 38. *leg.* 11. *const. Quis ferat, &c.* who can endure that Children from Parents, and Wives from Husbands should be separate?

So *Concil. Anglic.* 670. *Can.* 10. No man may put away his Wife, except as the Gospell teacheth for fornication. It is true, some of the Imperiall lawes allow Homicide, Sacriledge, Robbery, Manstealing, &c. for causes of divorce. *Cod. lib.* 5. *tit.* 17. *leg.* 8. but the Canon law decrees otherwise.

Divers other authorities might be alledged as to this point rightly agreeing, as *Greg. causa* 29. *quest.* 7. *cap.* 19. So *Zach. causa* 29. *quest.* 2. *cap.* 2. So *Iustin Martyr Apol. pro Christianis sub initio. Tertullian* agrees *lib. de Monogamia.* As also the Confession of Saxony *Artic.* 18. Especially is *Erasmus* most cleare in this, in his Paraphrase upon the New Testament: And for our own Writers it is endlesse to name them being so numerous.

Thus have we briefly passed over the two first things propounded to be handled.

In the third and last place we come to answer the Book intituled, *The Doctrine and Discpline of Divorce,* which maintains the contrary, to what hath been here asserted, to answer which was the main thing intended in this Discourse.

So without any Preamble or Answer to the Introduction to

C   this

An Answer to a Book, intituled,

this following Discours, we will presently come to the main Pillar upon which his whole Book is built, which is laid downe in these words.

Position.   *That undisposition, unfitnesse, or contrariety of minde, arising from a cause in nature unchangeable, hindring and ever likely to hinder the main benefits of conjugall society, which are solace and peace, is a greater reason of divorce then naturall frigidity, especially if there be no children, and it be with consent.*

This being that which all his insuing discourse is brought to prove, we shall first consider of the position it self, and then come to answer his reasons brought to defend the same.

This his Position or Ground-work as we conceive, may be divided into these four entire Propositions or Conclusions.

1. That there is in some men and women a disposition, unfitnesse, or contrariety of minde, arising from a cause unchangeable in nature.

2. That such a contrariety of disposition hinders the main benefit of mariage or conjugall society.

3. That solace and peace are the main and chiefe ends of mariage or conjugall society.

4. That such a contrariety of minde or disposition is a greater cause of divorce then naturall frigidity.

1. Answ.   To the first we answer, that there is no such disposition in nature as is unchangeable, so teacheth Philosophy: That by the carefull use of diet and the help of Physick, there is no disposition or constitution but may be altered, if not altogether, yet in a great measure. And as Philosophy teacheth so, that it may be; so Naturall History teacheth, that sometime there is a change even in the naturall disposition, if not wholly, yet in part.

2. Answ.   Suppose there were some disposition in nature altogether unchangeable, yet the Scripture teacheth, That by the grace of the Gospel, the Lionish dispositions shall so be changed that they shall be fit for the society of milder natures; and if so, it will follow, that if the disagreeing dispositions of a man & his Wife are from their own corruption, and for want of the grace of the Gospell, that they may not for this be separate the one from the other: for it is a rule in all lawes both Divine and just Humane lawes, that no man shall take advantage of his own corruption,

to

The Doctrine and Discipline of Divorce.

to release himself from such bonds as God and Nature hath knit him in. So that here, unchangablenesse of a corrupt disposition proceeding from a mans or womans own fault and corruption, will never be allowed for a just ground, for any man to seek a Divorce from his Wife, or the Wife from the Husband, but rather a Divorce or parting with their own corruption, which is the cause of all discord and disagreement.

2. To the second Position, that such a contrariety of disposition will hinder the maine ends and benefits of mariage or conjugall society.

We answer:

1 Answ. That if by contrarietie of minde is meant diversities of constitutions, then is it untrue: for the soft words and cariage of the patient man or woman, will so farre prevaile with the cholerick or sullen disposition of the other party, not only to a submission to the main conjugall and mariage duties, but even to ordinarie converse, as experience declareth, and *Salomon* teacheth, namely, that *soft words pacifie wrath*, which in effect is the same we speak.

2 Answ. If by contrarietie of minde or disposition he will mean some unheard of thing, which God and Nature hath planted on purpose in such a man and woman who afterwards shall marry, who shall hate one another with that mutuall antypathie as a man doth a Toad or Poyson; and this is not at all for any ill qualities that either sees in each other, but because they will hate each the other, as creatures between whom in nature cannot be any agreement. If he can finde such an example in the World, let him send his Book to them for to take the benefit of it.

3 Answ. If by your contrariety of disposition, you mean a sordid filthy sullen disposition, or other crabbed qualitie, kindled in each against the other after mariage, and increased by each mutuall provocation; this is not naturall: no contrarietie in Nature, but a sinfull and corrupt aberration from Gods law and their owne duties, which they are bound to purge away and to amend; and so not being naturall or of nature, but corruption wilfully nourished, if this should hinder in any the main benefits of mariage, yet doth it make nothing to your purpose.

3. To your third Proposition, That solace and peace are the main benefits of conjugall society.

Answ.

We Answer.

That this is very true in a right sense. But that solace and peace which is contrary to discord and variance (in which sense you seem to take it) is not the main end of mariage or conjugall society, is very plain and apparent: nor yet the solace and content in the gifts of the minde of one another only, for then would it have been every wayes as much, yea more content and solace to *Adam*; and so consequently to every man, to have had another man made to him of his Rib instead of *Eve*: this is apparent by experience, which shews, that man ordinarily exceeds woman in naturall gifts of minde, and in delectablenesse of converse; upon which we suppose it may be plainly concluded, that the solace and meetnesse of a helper to *Adam* which is spoken of, was not that which you seem to speak of as contrary to discord only, but is a solace and a meetnesse made up chiefly as of different Sexes, consisting of Male and Female.

4 *Prop.*

To your fourth thing, that contrariety of disposition is a greater cause of divorce then naturall frigidity.

We Answer.

1 *Answ.*

Contrariety of disposition or constitution is no cause at all of divorce (as shall be afterwards shewed in the Answer to your Arguments) or if it were a cause, yet not greater then naturall frigidity, as will appear. For,

1. Contrariety of minde or disposition, may easier, or at the least as easie in nature be taken away and cured, as naturall frigidity or coldnesse.

2. But secondly, to prove that contrarietie of disposition is not so great a cause of naturall divorce as naturall frigidity, I argue thus.

If contrariety of minde or disposition be not so great a cause to have maried persons to burning in lust towards others, as naturall frigidity is, in the one maried partie, to leave the other to burn in lust to others, then is it not so great a cause of divorce as naturall frigiditie is. But the first is true, *Ergo* the latter.

For the first part of this Argument its apparent, for contrariety of dispositions is no cause of burning in lust towards others; because notwithstanding that, they may, and we see usually doe performe mariage duties each to other. But on the other side

where

where naturall frigidity or coldness bears sway, *i.e.* an impotency to mariage duties, there the other partie is, as to burning in lust, as if they were not maried at all, or very little better, and for want of conjugall duties by their yoke-fellow, and an impotencie to the same, they are in a great measure as likey to burne in lust towards others as unmaried persons are; which such as have only a contrariety of minde or disposition properly so called are not likely so subject to.

As for the second part of the Argument, that if contrariety of mindes be not so great a cause of burning in lust as naturall frigidity, that then it is not so great a cause of divorce as naturall frigidity. This appears from what was said before, namely, because by the naturall frigidity of the one, the other is in its manner, as to mariage or mariage duties, as if they had no yoke-fellow, and so if the mariage it selfe be not void *ipso facto*, yet all law and reason must yeild, that for the reason before cited he ought rather to be relieved by leaving his impotent yokefellow, then the other by leaving his or her wrangling yoke-fellow.

So much for to shew the error of your position, upon which all your following discourse is, or ought to be grounded.

Now to your reasons which are to prove contrariety of disposition a just cause of divorce; where we are to take notice, that you in your reasons go not about to prove your Position as you have laid it down, but only that contrarietie of minde is a just cause of divorce betweene maried persons, not taking notice whether it be unchangeable in nature, or whether it be a greater cause of divorce then naturall frigidity, or whether there be children between them, or consent, as he hath exprest himself in his Position.

We shall endeavour to trace you in the Roade you goe, only we shal be driven to contract or shorten your arguments for brevity sake.

But before we come to your particular Arguments, the Reader is to take notice of one thing, namely, that all his Arguments, to prove a man may put away his wife for disagreement of minde or disposition, except it be his Argument from *Deu.* 24.1. they prove as effectually, that the Wife may sue a Divorce from her Husband upon the same grounds.

C 3 *Your*

1 Arg.

Your first proofe is the institution of mariage Gen. 2. *to make woman a meet help for man, because it was not good that man should be alone: whence you collect that a happy conversation by preventing lonelinesse, was the chiefest and noblest end of mariage; and in case this end cannot be found in mariage, there may be reliefe by parting.*

Answ.

We answer and tell you againe, that it is a happie or a pleasant conversation, made up by creating them male and female, and not simply as *Eve* was a fit conversing soule for *Adam*, as you afterward expresse it, for then would it have been more pleasant and beneficiall to *Adam* to have had another man created, then a woman.

2. What will follow upon this if it should be granted? will it follow, think you, that because the end of mariage is, that woman should bee a meet helpe to man, therefore if shee prove not so meet as is expected, he may then put her away and take another: I hope no: Such kind of reasoning deserves no answer at all. But now to his second Argument.

2 Arg.

His second Argument is, *From the violence and cruelty which is in forcing the continuance of those maried persons together, whom God and nature in the gentlest ends of mariage never joyned.*

Answ.

As for the phrase of the gentlest ends of mariage, its too abstruse and of no use, except it be as you think to please the Reader with a neet phrase.

And for the maine of your Argument, you take too much for granted: for though the case may be so, that some persons are joyned together in mariage neither by God nor Nature, viz. not allowing of it; yet that for disagreement of dispositions or contrariettie of mindes the mariage should be void, wee deny; for voide it must needs be, if it be neither of God nor Nature. Now where a thing is void *ipso facto*, there needs no legall proceeding to make it void. For clearing of this I hope you remember this distinction in our law, that some things are void, and some voidable by due processe of law. For example, if *John a Stiles* should enter into a bond of an hundred pound to *John a Nokes* with condition annexed, that if the Obligor did kill a third person before such a day, then the Obligation should be void. This Obligation being with a condition against law, is void by the very making of it, and the Obligor needs not

to

The Doctrine and Discipline of Divorce.

to sue the Obliged in Chancery, to compell him to free him of the penaltie, because void in it self.

On the other side, some things are voidable, *i.e.* to be made void by the partie himself by Processe of law; as if *Titus* within the age of twenty one years makes a feoffement, levies a fine, or suffers a recovery of land to *Sempronius*, this is not simply void, but voidable: so that *Titus* when he comes to age, if the conveyance were by feoffement, he may remedie it by his Writ of *Dum fuit infra ætatem*, if it were by fine or recovery reverse them by error, because within age at the time. To apply it to your case, if men and women of disagreeing dispositions being joyned in mariage, the mariage is void, being neither of God nor Nature, then there needs no Divorce or legall proceeding to part them, and then it is nothing to the Title of your Book, being *The Doctrine and Discipline of Divorce*, which you pretend to handle, briefly when you have proved, that such men and women who are maried, and are of contrary dispositions or mindes, that their mariage is void, or not of God nor Nature, we will grant you the whole controversie, in the mean time it is too great a begging of the question.

In your prosecution of this Section, you are pleased to faine an Objection, *That the disposition ought to be knowne before mariage.*

You are pleased to answer, *That a discreet man being wary in this, yet may be mistaken*; for say you, *the sobrest and best governed men are least practised in these things.*

But how so? if sobrest and best governed I hope they are the better able to judge of the disposition and cariage of a Maid or Widow: But go on. You say, *who knows not that the bashfull muteneße of a Virgin may oft times hide all the unlivelineße and naturall sloth, which is really unfit f'r conversation.*

Some are bashfull and mute indeed: but what of that? you *Answ.* speak of triall of them whether they are fit for conversation or no: if you would once tell what you mean by conversation, I doubt there is none so modest but you may make tryall of that: If you mean fit for discourse, and flexible to your desires, to go abroad or stay at home, &c. I know nothing of any modesty to hinder you, the tryall of these things before mariage, if you have so much time.

You

You adde, *That there is not that freenesse of accesse granted or presumed, as sufficeth to a perfect discerning till it be too late.*

Sir we beleeve you fain things to your self, to make good your Arguments. Kings and Princes indeed usually have little accesse to their Queeen or Princesse before mariage; but for lower degrees, sure so much accesse is granted, without any immodestie to discerne what you speak of.

You further go on, and say, *That though they who have lived most loosely, prove most successefull in their matches, because their wilde affections unsetling at will have been as so many divorces to them to teach them experience: When as the sober man honouring the appearance of modesty, and hoping well of every sociall vertue under that veile, may easily chance to meet, if not with a body impenetrable, yet often with a minde to all other due conversation inaccessible.*

Answ. Modest men seldome deal with any, who as they are not of bodies impenetrable, so neither are they to all due conversation inaccessible. It is true, if every man were of your breeding and capacitie, there were some colour for this plea; for we believe you count no woman to due conversation accessible, as to you, except she can speak Hebrew, Greek, Latine, & French, and dispute against the Canon law as well as you, or at least be able to hold discourse with you. But other Gentlemen of good qualitie are content with meaner and fewer endowments, as you know well enough.

Very true it is, that it is not amisse, for men of the best capacities, learning, and breeding, that they should match with those of the best wits, qualitie, and breeding, and leave the duller Virgins for the simpler sort; there is enough to own them, and ordinarily they fall to their shares, and that it is not alwayes so, you have no need to attribute it to modestie, that men doe not try their Sweet-hearts wits before they have them: you know that may be done with modesty enough, although to try whether their bodies are impenitrable (as you call it) savours of the contrary.

Well, but you goe on to make up this your second Argument from the diverse evils that would follow if Divorce should not be suffered for contrarietie and disagreement of mindes.

The

The first you say, *Is an imputation upon God and his law, of dispensing with open and common adultery among his own people; which, say you, the rankest politician would think it shame and dis-worship, that his lawes should countenance any such thing. But the shewing how this comes to passe, you say you will reserve to another place.*

We answer you, that we think this the fittest place for this *Answ.* Controversie, seeing you have named it here, and therefore shall free the law of God from any such imputation, and clear that here which you after bring from *Moses*, permitting divorce, and the sence of Christ in the Gospell.

Only first we shall speak to your phrase and manner of speaking, and then to the matter of it.

Your phrase is, *That such an imputation as would be cast upon the Law of God by this means, the rankest Politician would think it shame and dis-worship that his lawes should be charged with any such thing.*

Is this the fine language that your Book is commended for: Good your worship look a little upon your Rhetorick in this one piece, shall I say of nonsense: however I am sure it is contrary to all lawes and customes of speaking. *Rankest Politician.* Wonderfull!

What a Boarish Adjective you joyne with a Politician. Politician is a title worthie of honour and respect, and why you should so disgrace it with this homely language, I cannot imagine; except it be, because Polititians ordinarily differ from you in this your opinion. For although its likely some Polititians sometimes at a time of need are content to make use of others then their own wives, yet to be divorced from their own upon a little contrariety of mindes or dispositions, Polititians will not easily agree to it.

But to go on, *The rankest Politician would think it shame his laws, &c.* His lawes; strange! Where were you bread? Sir, What are the lawes of your Common-wealth made only by one Polititian? sure that same is a barren Countrey of Noble and Learned men. And if it be not barbarous, yet is it a very harsh phrase, to call the lawes made in any Common-wealth, the lawes of the Polititians, much more of one only Polititian.

But peradventure you mean the King, and the lawes may be called his, you think.

D   If

If you do mean him, its no usuall phrase to call him Polititian without farther addition: or if it were, you know its no good sense in your own countrey, for I beleeve you are not to heare of, *Qui vulgus elegerit*: And if you meane of some other Countrey, write your Book in their language, for the English will but deride such language as this is.

Againe, *He would think it shame and dis-worship*, (say you) to what, say I? to his lawes: strange Philosophy! Are lawes now capable of shame and blushing? Speak a little plainer if you have any such point to broach.

But, peradventure you meane, the Polititian would think it shame and dis-worship. Well, but upon whom do you mean he thinks this shame and dis-worship will light? for you shew us not whether the Polititian would think this shame to redound to the lawes themselves, or to himself, or to a third person or thing, pray let's know the next time.

But againe, why shame and dis-worship? Do the lawes or the Polititian that makes them, use to be worshipped in your Common-wealth? Well, we leave the Gentleman of that worshipfull countrey, who looks for Good your Worship at every word, and *Utinam* they are not too worshipfull to be W.

Thus from your phrase we passe on to the matter, which should be put in here for the proofe of this first evill: namely, that denying of divorce for cause of contrarietie of minde and disposition, will cast an imputation upon the law of God, of dispensing and conniving with common and open adultery amongst his own people.

Well, how do you prove this? For the proofe of this we must be driven to bring in your Text of *Deut.* 24.1. which as you say, *permits, nay, is a Wise and pious law, that such who did not love their Wives for some displeasing naturall quality or unfitnesse in her, he should write her a Bill of Divorce*: so you speak *pag.* 26. compared with pag. 10. Now how this imputation will come to fall upon the law of God, I believe you mean thus. That for a man to divorce his Wife unjustly and to marrie another, is adultery: But the law of God allowes divorce unjustly, except disagreement of minde, or unpleasant naturall qualitie be a cause. *Ergo.*

In plaine tearms you mean God by *Moses* suffered men to put
away

The Doctrine and Discipline of Divorce.

away their wives, if they found not love and favour in their eies; by reason of some unpleasing natural qualitie, (for so you are pleased to reade the Text of *Deut.* 24.1.) Now you infer, if *Moses* allowed this, and yet indeed it was not a just cause of divorce, then did God by *Moses*'s law tolerate adulterie, in that it tolerated a man or woman to marrie to another, whilest they were not lawfully parted from their first Husbands or Wives.

To take off this great Scare-crow and the maine Pillar which he trusts in to hold up his whole Book, or most part of it: it will be necessarie a little to consider of this Text of *Deut.* 24. 1. whether it doth indeed speak any such thing or no. Our English Translation hath it, If a man shall take a Wife and lie with her, and she finde not grace in his eyes because of some uncleannesse, let him write her a Bill of Divorce. So that it is for some uncleannesse, and not for some displeasing qualitie that is in her. According to our English: the French Bible agrees, *Pourtannt que il a trouue quelque laide tache in elle*, because he hath found in her some foule, unhonest, or abominable reproach, spot, or infamy; for so signifies *laide tache*. *Ieromes* Translation hath it, *Propter aliquam fœditatem*, filthinesse or shamefull thing. *Iunius* and *Tremelius* agrees. *Answ.*

A Translation according to the Septuagint printed at *Basil* hath it, *Quoniam invenit in ea fœdam*, the Septuagint reads it ὅυερ ἐν αὐτῆ ἄγχμον πρᾶγμα, the Substantive *pragma*, is used, *Acts* 5.4. to signifie *res*; and 1 *Cor.* 6.1. *negotium*, businesse: *Iames* 3.16. *opus* or work: and the Adjective is used by *Paul* 1 *Cor.* 12.23. for *indecorus*, shamefull, dishonest, or unbeseeming: so signifying that they understood this place of *Deut.* 24. 1. to be meant of some shamefull or dishonest thing. So they which translate by the Septuagint have it, *rem turpem*, filthy thing. In the Hebrew it is *Gneruath Dabhar*, the very same words which are used *Deut.* 23. 14. The Lord thy God walketh in thy Camp to deliver thee, therefore shall thy Campe be holy, that he see no *Gneruath Dabhar* in thee: that is, no uncleannesse or uncleane thing, as is apparant by the foregoing Verses: so here, if she finde not favour in her Husbands eyes because of some *Gneruath Dabhar*, some uncleannesse or uncleane thing. The Hebrewes themselves expound this Text, to be understood of a woman of evill condi-

tion,

An Answer to a Book, intituled,

tion, who is not modest according to the honest Daughters of Israel. So that here seems to be no ground for your understanding the Text to speak of any unpleasing naturall quality, when as indeed it speaks of uncleannesse: so that as we conceive, the maine Pillar of your Book is not able to hold up it self, much lesse will it serve for a prop to hold up the rest of your discourse.

Object. But it may be demanded, what manner of uncleannesse this Text speaketh of; for it seems it cannot be meant of adulterie: for Christ speaking (as it seems) with a relation to this Text, *Matth* 19. saith, *Moses* indeed suffered you to put away your Wives, &c. But I say unto you, whosoever shall put away his Wife except it be for fornication, commits adulterie; so that which *Moses* suffered to put away Wives for, was another cause then what Christ here speaks of, namely, fornication, which could not be that which *Moses* suffered putting away for, seeing Christ opposeth putting away for fornication to putting away by *Moses's* law.

Answ. To this we answer, that though it be little materiall to our point in hand, what uncleannesse this Text *Deut.* 24. 1. speaks of; whether it be a legall, ceremoniall, or a morall uncleannesse: for it sufficeth to our purpose, if it be not some unpleasing naturall qualitie, as this author hath affirmed: Yet we shall humbly propose to the judicious and learned with their favour, and under correction, what uncleannesse this Text of *Deut.* 24. speaks of.

Not proposing it as a sense infallible, but one which may be something probable.

And that is, that this Text *Deut.* 24. 1. speaks of an uncleannesse committed before mariage, which we usually call by the name of fornication; the same uncleannesse which is spoken of *Deut.* 22. 13, 14, 15, &c. Where it is said, *If a man take a wife and lye with her, and hate her, and shall say, I took this woman to wife, and when I came in unto her I found her not a maide*; and the Text goes on, and shewes what shall be done in this case

This Text is doubtlesse to be understood of a man who takes a Wife and findes she hath committed follie before mariage, which we ordinarily call by the name of fornication. The same kinde of uncleannesse (under correction) may be here meant: that when a man marries a Wife and findes her not a Maide, but defiled,

filed, and to be uncleane by fornication committed before mariage.

Against this sense of the place we conceive there may be two strong objections made which we shall endeavour to answer, and so leave it to the consideration of the Reader.

The first Objection may be from that Text *Deut.* 22.12,13, &c. where the direction is there, that if it be found according to the complaint of her Husband, that she was not a Maide but defiled, that she should be stoned to death, and not be put away by Divorce; by the same reason, if this Text of *Deut.* 24.1. speaks of that uncleannesse, she ought to be stoned to death, and not suffered to escape by Divorce.

1 *Object.*

To this we answer two things.

First that there was a twofold uncleannesse or defilement of Virgins by the law; the one was, when she consented not to the uncleannesse or defilement, but it was committed upon her by force, and this in the Maide did not deserve death, as is shewed *Deut.* 22.26.

1 *Answ.*

Secondly, there was a defilement with the consent of the Maide, and this seems to be distinguished by the law to be of two qualities.

1. The first was, when a man by intising words should tempt and intice a Maid to lye with her, and she upon his promises and inticements yeilded to it, but presently after the fact did discover it to her father or kindred, to compell the same man to marrie her: and of this kind it seems is spoken of *Exod.* 22.16. In this case the man was compellable to marry her, and so she was not in this case to be punished with death.

Secondly, there was another distinction of this defiling of a Virgin, *viz.* When the Maide consented to commit folly with any privately, and so as it proceeded from her whorish spirit principally, with a meer desire to commit filthinesse, as a comman Strumpet or Whore, and concealed this; so that the partie by her concealment could not be compelled to marrie her: and after, this defiled Virgin takes another man to Husband, and he findes her not a Maid, but to have committed follie in her fathers house, and never declared it, to the end the man who committed follie with her might be compelled to marrie: this (under favour)

D 3

vour) is that which *Deut.*22.12,13,14, &c. was to be punished with death, and a Divorce not to serve the turn.

But then for the uncleannesse, *Deut.*24.1. which a man found in his Wife, it might very well be, that a man ignorantly took such a woman to wife, as either had been ravished by force (as in the first sense) and so was defiled, or that had been defiled by the inticement of some man, of which fact she had made knowne to her father, to the end to compell him to marry her who defiled her, and her father upon knowledge of it utterly refused to give her to him to Wife, as *Exodus* 22.17. and she after marries another who findes her defiled or uncleane is displeased therewith, so that she findes no favour in his eyes, he may not in this case prosecute her to the death, as in *Cap.* 22. but only divorce her, as *Cap.*24.1. & 2.

But secondly we answer, that in case it should be the same uncleannesse and defilement with that *Deut.* 22. 11,12, &c. then we say it was left by the law to the choice of the man to prosecute her to death, as *Cap.* 22. or to Divorce her, as *Cap.* 24. And though I know this will sound very harsh and irreconcileable at the best: yet (under favour I conceive) I may as easily reconcile these two places thus together, as Christs speech, *Matthew* 5. 32. can be reconciled to the law of adultery. For as I conceive, there is no man but will confesse that at that time when Christ spoke, the law of putting to death for adulterie was in force; and yet you see, *Matthew* 5. 32. he sayes not, he that prosecutes not his Wife to the death for being an Adulteresse, is guiltie: but whosoever puts away his Wife, except for fornication, he commits adulterie.

Now if there had been an absolute necessitie in the man to prosecute his Wife to death for adulterie, I suppose Christ would never have mentioned Divorce, for that which must of necessity have death. So it may seem it was left to the mercy of the Husband. The same I say to the reconciling the command of putting to death the defiled Virgin, *Deut.*22. and divorcing her, *Cap.*24.

It

The Doctrine and Discipline of Divorce.

It may further by objected, that it cannot be the same uncleannesse meant here which in *Chapter* 22. because there direction is given for a triall of the charge of uncleannesse laid to her, but not so here: and if upon triall there it be found a false charge he may not put her away all the dayes of his life.   *Object.*

To this we answer two things.

First it will not follow, but that the same triall ought to be in the 24 *Chapter* as in the 22. although not mentioned, yet to be understood; as well as the fathers dissent to the mariage of his Daughter to one who hath defiled her be not mentioned, *Deut.* 22.29. yet is to be understood as well as it is *Exod.* 22.17. where it is mentioned.   1 *Answ.*

But suppose the same triall be not to be understood in the 24 *Chapter* as in the 22. yet will it not follow but that it may bee the same uncleannesse: (onely differing in the consent of the Maide, &c.) for though it be the same uncleannesse, yet doth there not need that examination and tryall where onely a divorce is intended, as where death is intended.   2 *Answ.*

But there seemes to be another great Objection against this sense of the word Uncleannesse, that it cannot be meant of fornication before mariage; because Christ speaking with relation to this Text, as it seemes, understood it otherwise then of fornication, as appeares by his conclusion, that whosoever should put away their Wives except for fornication, &c. So that it would seeme plaine CHRIST understood not this Text to bee meant of fornication, for he seemes to blame this putting away founded upon this Text, and yet allowes divorce for fornication.   *Object.*

For answer to this briefly, wee conceive the words fornication and adultery are used in the New Testament, if not reciprocally, yet at the least promiscuously: and that that by fornication is many times meant more then uncleannesse committed betweene unmaried persons: as 1 *Corinthians* 5.1. there the word fornication is used and applyed to incest: And in 1 *Corinthians* 10.7. Neither let us   *Answ.*

be

be fornicators, &c. being applyed to the Israelite *Numb.* 25 who lay it is said, with the woman of *Midian*, which seems to be no Maid, for the title Woman is seldome applyed to them: So 1 *Cor.* 6 he that commits fornication sins against his own bodie, is doubtlesse to be understood of adulterie as well as of uncleannesse between single persons, if it be not solely meant of adultery.

So then our answer is, that the word fornication is often used for adulterie, after mariage: and we conceive Christ intended it so, when he saith, *Whosoever shall put away his Wife, except for fornication, &c.* that is, for adultery, or defiling his mariage bed; and so Christ speaks not of the same uncleannesse *Moses* doth, although *Moses*'s should be meant of fornication.

Thus you have our first answer to this your place of *Deut.* 24. 1. that it is meant of uncleannesse, as the Originall and other languages reads it: and though we are not over confident of the kinde of uncleannesse whether it be fornication before mariage, as we have shewed, or some naturall, legall, or sinfull uncleannesse, it much matters not: this we only propose to the Readers consideration, upon triall to reject it, or receive it as he findes it upon examination.

But in case this answer fails; we have two other answers to your place of *Deut.* 24. 1. only two Objections remain.

Object. 1. That Christ findes fault with this Divorce grounded upon *Moses*'s law, and shewes it was not so from the beginning, nor ought not to be so now: which proves the divorce for uncleannesse *Deut.* 24. 1. cannot be understood of fornication, or uncleannesse committed before mariage, for that was alwayes allowed of from the beginning as a just cause of divorce, and so seems to be now.

Answ. To this we only answer; that when either of these two are proved, we shall willingly let fall that interpretation; in the mean time we leave it to the considerate Reader.

Object. 2. But it may be further objected, that whatsoever it was that *Moses* allowed of Divorce for, whether for fornication before mariage, as is said before, or for some unpleasing naturall quality, as our Author would have it; yet the imputation of dispensing with common adultery is not taken away, in case it was not a just

The Doctrine and Discipline of Divorce.

just cause of divorce. For answer to this we come to our second answer to this place of *Deut.* 24.1.

In the second place we answer to *Deut.* 24.1. in case your reading should be found good to be of a displeasing naturall qualitie, and that they did unjustly put away by this law their wives: then we answer, this place of *Moses* permits no divorce at all; but was only a law made in favour of the woman who was unjustly put away, and a sufferer: in this case *Moses* provides, that though a woman should be wrongfully & by force be put away, yet he would by this law compell the Husband to give her a Bill of divorce, which should be a token to her father and her friends that it was the act of her husband to dismisse and put her away, and not her voluntary act: for which, had it been voluntary on her part, she would have been judged a Whore and a wandering Vagrant, and so would scarcely have been received into her fathers house: so that *Moses* may seem here not to give any law of divorce; but rather a law to compell such of the Jewes, who in their cruelty, and from the hardnesse of their hearts would unjustly and by force put away their wives, to make them a writing of divorce and to give it her, which should be a testimony for the woman after she departed, that she wandered not as a Whore or a Vagrant of her own minde from the company of her Husband, but it was his fact by force to put her away.

Answ

For the proofe of this sence of the place we conceive three things make to this purpose.

1. Because I finde no law of divorce allowing men to put away their wives before this law, (if in case this should be found to be such a law) and yet I finde divorce practised by the Jewes, therefore *Levit.* 21.14 it is commanded to the Priest, that he should not marry a Widow, or a woman that was divorced, which implies there were some women divorced. Now if divorce was practised and no law allowing it, I have reason to think this place of *Deut.* 24.1. is a law to remedie the extremity of their unlawfull divorces, by compelling them to make a Bill in favour of the woman that was put away, and not a law either commanding or allowing the divorce it selfe.

2. It seemes to appear from the connexion of the words, hee shall give her a Bill of divorce, that when she is departed out of
his

E

his house she may become the Wife of another man; so that the Bill seems meerly to be made for her benefit.

3. The Text here allowes the woman to marry againe, she being the suffering partie and unjustly put away; but he being the offending, it speaks nothing of allowing him to marrie againe; so it seems the provision of the Bill of Divorce was for her benefit only.

Object. Against this the words of Christ will be objected, *Math.* 19. and *Mark* 10. to the Pharisees, when they had asked, if a man might put away his Wife for every cause, *Matth.* 19. 3. Christ answers, That *God at the beginning made them Male and Female, and that a man shall forsake Father and Mother and cleave unto his Wife*: the Pharisees upon this, ask Christ, why *Moses* did command to give a writing of Divorce, and to put her away; then Christ answers, *Moses, because of the hardnesse of your hearts suffered you to put away your Wives, but from the beginning it was not so*. So that some may say, Christ here seems to affirme not only the Bill of Divorce to be of *Moses*, but even the Divorce it self.

Answ. It appears not to be so, but rather that Christ answers the Pharisees according to their opinion of *Moses* law, and he grants them that in some sort *Moses* might be said to suffer men to put away their Wives, because he commanded the Bill to be made in favour of the woman, the suffering party: but saith Christ, *from the beginning it was not so*, that men should put away their Wives as the Jewes did, neither was this Bill then invented: and this may seem to be the substance of Christs words.

3 *Answ.* We answer to your Text *Deut.* 24. 1. in the third place, that if the other two satisfie not, then may that be a good positive law made by *Moses*, during the time of the Jewish politie or government, properly called Mosaicall: yet now Christ under the New Testament hath abolished that law to all his followers. To this purpose that of Christ *Matth.* 5. 31, 32. *It was said unto of old, that whosoever shall put away his Wife, let him give her a bill of divorce*: then Christ addes, *But I say unto you, Whosoever shall put away his Wife except it be for cause of fornication, causeth her to commit adultery, and whosoevr shall marry her that is divorced committeth adultery.* This place of our Saviour concerning divorce may seem not to be to the end to reforme the false glosses

of

of the Pharisees concerning divorce, (as it is usually thought) but rather to shew the law of the Gospell to require more mutuall love and passing by injuries then the law: As who should say, under *Moses*, where there was many duties required; and yet through the darknesse of the dispensation of heavenly things, there was little grace and power to performe what was required, then the law of Divorce did mercifully bear with the infirmities of people; and during the time of this dispensation, this law of Divorce was a good positive law: But now whosoever will be my follower and professe himself to have received the plenteous grace of the Gospell, he must be so farre from using hardship or unkindnesse to his Wife, or others to whom he is neerly bound, that he must not revenge wrong done from strangers & enemies, but pray for them, and blesse them; he must be so farre from turning his Wife out of doores for her ill cariage, yea although it should proceed to cursing and persecuting him, that he must use all mildnesse, and love, and godly means to reforme her; compare this with *verse* 43, 44. and indeed with all the latter part of the Chapter, and you will finde the drift of Christ, to give as it were new inlargements of lawes under the Gospell, requiring more spiritualnes in observation, then the Mosaical government.

This interpretation I cannot conceive to be either contrary to the scope of Christ in this Chapter, which principally is, to shew that he came not to destroy the law but to fulfill it: nor is it contrary to any other sound and wholesome Doctrine laid downe in Scripture, neither opens any gap to any to throw away *Moses*'s law, as not at all pertaining to us. I think there is none that thinks, but that there were given by *Moses*, not only ceremoniall Precepts, but even judiciall, to the Jewes, which for us to observe under the Gospell, would be so farre from piety, that it would be sinfull; and I know nothing why this law of Divorce may not be one.

Only one word to your corrupt and wicked glosse upon our Saviours words, *Matth*. 19. and *Mark* 10. where he tels the Pharisees, that whosoever should put away his Wife, except for fornication, he did commit adultery; you to put off the matter, as if Christs speech was never intended to forbid a Divorce, for your indisposition, unfitnesse, or contrariety of minde, but was only

An Answer to a Book, intituled,

only as you say, *That Christ here did only deale like a wise Physitian administring one excesse against another to bring us to a perfect meane, and that where the Pharisees were strict, there Christ seemes to be remisse; and where they were too remisse he saw it needfull to seeme most severe: In one place,* say you, *he censures an unchaste look to be adultery already committed, and at another time he passeth over actuall adultery with lesse reproofe then for an unchaste look: So here,* say you, *he may be thought to give this rigid sentence against Divorce, not to cut off all remedy to a good man who consumes with a disconsolate matrimony, but to lay a bridle upon the bold abuser of these overweening Rabbies, &c.*

Answ. To this we answer, that this your glosse is not only intolerable abuse of Scripture, but smels very strongly of little lesse then blasphemie against Christ himself.

For what is it else, to say Christ was here most severe, where the Pharisees were most remisse, and that here he administred one excesse against another, &c. For though it should be found that Christ sometimes, to check the pride and hypocrisie of the Pharisies, should by his not affording them an answer seem remisse, where they were too severe, and so on the contrary. Yet that Christ should positively lay down a resolution, as one of his Precepts under the Gospell without any exception; and this his Precept to be an excesse to reduce the Pharisies to a mean, is too bold and dangerous an assertion for any man to venture upon.

And for your examples which you cite where Christ was one time remisse, and another time more severe against a lesse sinne, they are both utterly false; for in the one place Christ doth not say, that an unchaste look is adultery, but he that upon looking on a woman doth lust after her, he hath committed adultery in his heart, so that it is not the looking on her, but the lusting after her which is adultery, and that but of the heart neither: truely I finde not here an excesse, or too much severity in Christ, but fearfull audacity in you.

And for your other example of the woman taken in adultery, where he was more remisse, and gave her not so sharpe a reproof as here for an unchaste look; this is as false, for he bids her *goe away and sinne no more least a worse thing* then death by stoning *came to her*; and I hope this is severer then Christ speaks of the unchaste look, as you call it.

But

But to answer to what you chiefly intend, you are to know, Christ *Matthew* 19. doth not direct his speech concerning Divorce, as an excesse against the Pharisies tempting question only, but as a firme stable resolution of the Gospell: to clear this consider but two things.

1 That Christ before this time had given the same resolution to his Disciples *Matth.* 5. 32. where he spake principally to his Disciples, as appeares *Verse* 1. And therefore it cannot be intended that Christ spake it to represse the pride and false glosses of the Pharisies only.

2 And secondly its apparant that Christ did intend otherwise then you say to contradict the Pharisees, for if he had only told them, that he which puts away his Wife except for fornication, committed adultery, this had been enough to have contradicted them: but he addes, that whosoever shall marry her who is put away otherwise, he commits adultery: And so I conclude, Christ intended this speech to his Disciples, as a direction binding all Christians under the Gospell; and gave it not as an expressive resolution to represse and cresse the pride and false glosses of the Pharisies.

Now for the rest of your stuffe which fils many Pages about the sense of *Moses Deut.* 24. 1. and of Christ *Matth.* 19. and the opinions of other men upon the same, of which, some you approve, and some you confute, we conceive it needlesse to trace you, as thinking we have given you the true sense of *Moses* and Christ alreadie, to which we referre the triall of all which you are pleased to speak upon the same.

In briefe the summe of our answer to this place of *Deut.* 24. 1. for the lawfulnesse of putting away a mans Wife for some displeasing naturall qualitie, is, that first, that it speaks of Divorce for uncleannesse, and not for disagreement: or secondly, if it doth, it allowes not of the Divorce, but appoints the Bill in favour of the woman: or thirdly, if it allowes both, yet now is it altered by Christ under the Gospell.

If any shall think these answers to fall foul upon each other, we easily grant it, and say its usuall in this kinde; and besides we write not as Prophets but as men: and if any of the answers be to the point, and overthrow that which we conceived to be an error, its sufficient.

An Answer to a Book, intituled,

Your second evill which you say would follow, if Divorce were not lawfull for displeasing naturall qualities, &c. is, *That the Law and the Gospell would be subject to more then one contradiction, but to shew this you deferre it to another place.*

Answer. We shall take it here, and tell you, its no contradiction at all, that *Moses* should allow a Divorce and Christ deny it, if it could be proved: For there is a twofold contradiction (as you know well enough;) one is, when the Gospell shall blame the Law for tolerating things contrary to it self, that one time it made a thing lawfull, at another time unlawfull; this is the contradiction you must speak of if you speak to the purpose, that the Gospel shall blame or contradict *Moses*'s law, for maintaining contrarie things in it self.

Then secondly, there is a contradiction of the Gospell to the Law; that the Gospel counts some things under its dispensation to be altogether unlawfull to be done, which the Law allowed as lawfull and pious in the time of its dispensation: this kind of contradiction we grant there is betweene the Law and Gospel many times, but is nothing to your purpose at all: for example, Circumcision was a dutie of weight; now its a hainous crime: so Sacrifices, Offerings, Washings, and a hundred the like, and yet the Gospel blames not the Law for these things in the time of its dispensation: no more will it follow in case of Divorce, if it should be allowed then and denied now, except you can shew the first kinde of contradiction.

Your third evill which you say would follow if Divorce should be denied to such as are of contrariety of dispositions is, *That hereby the supreame dictate of Charity, would bee many wayes violated and neglected.* But how is this done? You say, *we know Paul saith, it is better to marry then to burne:* tis true, *Paul* doth say so: what will follow of that? Is *Pauls* positive resolution become the supreame dictate of Charitie? else how followes it, the supreame dictate of Charitie is violated by denying Divorce on your grounds, because *Paul* saith *it is better to marry then to burne:* remember your self well, sure you think all Gospel you speak.

Well, what would you inferre from *Pauls* words, *it is better to marry then to burne?*

You say, *That mariage was given us a remedy of that trouble.* So say

The Doctrine and Discipline of Divorce.

say we; but yet not properly that ordination of mariage first in Paradise, for then was no such burning.

Well, go on; we ask you what this burning in lust is which *Paul* means: you are pleased to answer, *That, certainly not the meer motion of carnall lust, not the meer goade of a sensitive desire,* God doth not principally take care for such cattell.

Answ. Truly you are apt to speake very high language: but what would follow if *Paul* should take care, not for the neurishment, but for the suppressing of a meer motion of carnall lust? Sure no evill.

Well, but we will have your advice positively, as well as negatively, what the Apostle means, when he sayes *it is better to marry then to burne.*

You say, *It is that desire which God put in Adam in Paradise, before he knew the sinne of incontinency: it was that desire, Which God saw it was not good that man should be left alone, to burne in a longing to put off solitarinesse, by uniting another body, but not without a fit sense to his in the cheerfull society of wedlock.*

Answ. We pray you seriously to retract this sentence, and openly to confesse you were asleepe when you writ it.

We desire any indifferent man but to consider the scope of the Apostle in that Chapter of 1 *Cor.* 7. and to tell us if your exposition of these words, *it is better to marry then to burne,* be not such a meer trifling and abusing the Scripture as seldome is met with. This must needs be a just Paraphrase upon *Pauls* words if your exposition were sound.

I *Paul* am a Batchelour, and I never met with any fit and meet conversing soule, to fit my desire, to discourse and converse with me as I had when I was in *Adam*; but I speake to you Virgins and Widowes, although it be thus with me, yet it were good if you could remaine solitary without any fit conversing soule to discourse with you: but if you cannot live altogether alone all the dayes of your life (however I shift for my selfe) yet doe you marrie, *viz.* get some fit conversing soules, such an one as *Adam* thought of when he was alone in the Garden, and no bodie created but he. For it is better for you seeing you cannot live alwaies alone, to have some such fit conversing soule, to drive away the time with, then to pine away like a Dove in a Wildernesse,

where

where there is none to beare her company. This is the effect of your exposition of *Paul*, when he saith, *it is better to marry then to burne*: the relating of which your exposition is enough to confute it and make it lighter then vanitie it self.

So we passe to your third Argument, the effect whereof seems to be this.

3 *Arg.* *That the not allowing of divorce in case of contrariety of mindes and dispositions in maried persons, will be a ground or occasion of their desire after other persons, besides their own Wives; because when a man findes no contentment at home he is apt to looke for the same abroad.*

Answ. We answer you, what if he do look abroad, so long as it is but to meet with a fit conversing soule, provided he meddles not with her bodie, let him recreate himself, its lawfull enough: tis your own doctrine, A fit conversing soule for man is the noblest end of mariage: Therefore I think we may without danger, let a mans reines loose to accomodate himself so, if his Wife hath not such a fit conversing soule as she should have, only let him remember to come home to her at night. If you should say, that you meane want of content at home will cause a man to lust unlawfully after the bodies of other mens Wives.

Answ. Wee answer you there is no congruitie in that sense with the rest of your Book: for according to your own Doctrine we may reason thus: That desire which is not satisfied at home by a mans own Wife, will break out towards other mens Wives; but the desire which is to be satisfied by a mans owne Wife is, that she be a fit conversing soule: *Ergo*, the not finding a mans Wife a fit conversing soule, will not endanger or stir up any other desires but to converse with the soules of other mens Wives; and this we allow you to do and keep your own still.

But enough of this: only we desire the next time you write, to tell us the meaning of this fit conversing soule. We have heard that Angels converse with one another as they are Spirits; but for Husbands and Wives, though they ought not to love in word only, but in deed and in truth with the affections of the heart, yet we know no conversing with one another, but what is by words or actions.

Well you goe on and talk in this Section, *Of a man meeting instead of a sweet co-partner of pleasant society, it often happens, that young*

The Doctrine and Discipline of Divorce.

young men, who have put their chiefe content in a contented mariage, yet they meet with an Image of earth and fleame.

We confesse this is something a sad case: but yet I believe you speak but hyperbolically (as they use to say) for VVomen are usually more then earth and fleame, they have many times spirit enough to weare the Breeches, if they meet not with a rare Wit to order them. I wonder you should use such phrases; I know, nor heare of any Maids or VVomen that are all earth and fleame, much lesse Images of earth and fleame: If there be any such, yet you need take no thought for them, there are enough dull enough to own them; & for your self or any other who desire them, there are spirited Dames enough, who are something besides meere Images of earth and fleame. *Answ.*

Your fourth Argument is, *Because mariage is a Covenant, whose very being consists not in a forced cohabitation or a counterfeit performance of duties, but in unfeined love and peace.* 4 *Arg*

It is true, but how prove you by this, that if there be not found this peace and joy between maried persons, there may then be a Divorce: for where the chiefe end of a thing is not alwayes attained in its ful measure, yet will it not be lawfull to seek a separation from it. Will you argue, that because *Heman Psal.* 88. found not that peace and solace which is the main end of communion with God, that therefore he might break off that communion. Or how think you; suppose you should covenant with a man at *Hackney,* that he should dwell in your house at Aldersgatestreet, & you in requital would dwel in his house at *Hackney* for a time; I doubt not but your main end in this your Covenant was your own solace, peace, and refreshing. Well, but suppose when you come there, the *Cavaliers* or other Souldiers should trouble you, and should be quartered there; who peradventure if they did not quite put you out, yet would lie in your most pleasant Chamber best scituate for your solace and refreshing; and divers other waies would annoy you; by meanes whereof you could not enjoy that pleasure and delight which you intended in your Covenant, when you changed houses with the other. Think you in this case it would be lawfull or accepted on by the other partie if now you should come to him and say; Sir, I covenanted for your house at *Hackney* for my own refreshing, comfort, and solace, *Answ.*

F but

An Answer to a Book, intituled,

but I am disturbed of it, I do not enjoy the end of my Covenant, give me my own house again, and go you live there. He would tel you, and so he might justly, stay Sir, take your own fortune, a bargain is a bargain, you must even stand to it. In the same case I suppose, though it be the end of mariage, that love and peace should be maintained; yet if it fall out otherwise they must be content.

But let us see your proofes to the contrarie: and that is say you, in such a case, where we finde not that content in mariage which was the end of it, but on the contrary vexation: *Paul* himselfe speaking of Mariage and Divorce, determines therein, that God hath called us to peace and not to bondage.

Answ. Well, we will examine what *Paul* makes for you, the place 1 *Cor.*7. (though you seem loath to quote the place) where the Apostle speaks to Men and Women, who were Christians and had Infidels to their Husbands or Wives: And he tels them if any believer had a Wife who is an Infidell and yet she was content to dwell with him, that he should not put her away, &c. And then when he hath given the reason of it in the next Verse, he after tels them, that notwithstanding if in such a case the Infidell Husband or Wife will not dwell with their Christian Husband or Wife, but that they will depart and go away to live in some other place; a believer, saith *Paul*, is not in subjection in this case, but God hath called us to peace. Now what an argument will this be, if a Christian Husband hath an Infidell to his Wife, who out of spight and hatred to religion and to her Husband, and will depart and divorce her self, in such a case the Husband is not bound to follow her wandring about, to keep her company whether she resorts, on purpose from his companie. *Ergo*, will it follow that when a man dislikes his Wife, and she peradventure willing to live with him, yet he may by force a-against her will put her away: the truth is, this place makes quite against you as hath been shewed. But besides, you mistake the very Gramaticall sense, when you will bring in these words, God hath called us to peace, as a reason why the believing Husband may suffer his Wife being an Infidell to depart: for they rather seeme to be an Introduction to what he speaks after, how knowest thou O man whether thou shalt not save thy Wife, &c. As much as if he should say, though I tell you in the case before cited,

The Doctrine and Discipline of Divorce.

cited, a believer is not in subjection to his Wife, where there seems no means availeable with her to procure her cohabitation; yet sayes *Paul* I must tell you, God hath chiefly called us to peace, that is, he rather expects that as we are to follow peace with all men whatsoever, so especially with our Husbands and Wives, and to keep company and cohabitation together: and the Apostle saies in effect, I will give you a good reason for this; For how knowest thou O man, but that thou by dwelling and conversing with thy Wife, thou maist convert her and save her. So that it seems you are quite mistaken, in alledging this Text for your opinion.

Well, but have you any other Scriptures to prove this? Yes, say you,, *For God himselfe commands by his law more then once, and by his Prophet Malachy, as Calvin and the best Interpreters reade, that he who hates his Wife let him divorce her, that is, say you, he who cannot love and delight in his Wife.*

Answ. We desire you to shew out of your new Scripture (if any such you have) where God in his Law commands, and that more then once, that he who hateth his Wife, should put her away; shew it but one time and we will yeild you the whole controversie: If you meane *Deut.* 24. 1. that is but one place, and we have given you an answer to it.

And as for *Malachy*, although it be true, that some translations do reade it so, as *Jerome* and some Margents: yet why you should call these the best Interpreters of this Text, I know no reason, but because they agree with your opinion, which you dream to be the best. The last of our English Translations which other men count the best, hath it otherwise, *Mal.* 2. 16. and it saies, *for the Lord God of Israel saith, that he hateth putting away.* In the Hebrew it is, *Ci sane shallach, amar Iehovah Elohe Israel:* which if your learning can make any other then a reason of what God had spoken before, you may peradventure make this place speak something for you. The truth is, this your reading is quite contrarie to the scope of the place; for God by his Prophet *Malachy* in the former verses vehemently complaines against the Jewes for dealing treacherously with the Wives of their youths: Now how this was, although it be not so plain, yet it seems probable it was, by having of other lovers, and growing wearie of

F 2 their

their own, and so a pretending some fault in them, to the end to put them away: Well saith God in the 16 *Verse*, *The Lord God of Israel hateth this treachery of yours in seeking other lovers and being weary of your own wives put them away*. But on the other side, if your reading should be admitted, what a preposterous sense would here be; as if God should say, Oh you deceitfull Jewes, you treacherously deal with your own Wives, I pray let me heare no more of this treacherie; but this I command you, if you would faine be rid of them, do but hate them and then put them away, and then you are at libertie: And so God to prevent treacherie against mens wives, should command the greatest treacherie that can be devised.

In the prosecution of this reason you are pleased to say, *It is a lesse breach of wedlock to part with quiet consent betimes, then still to prophane that mystery of joy with a polluting sadnesse.*

Answ. Mysterie of joy, what language is this? is mariage now a Sacrament signifying joy? this I never heard of before: the Papists indeed make it a Sacrament, but not of joy, and yet I doubt they can say more for their opinion then you for yours.

But how a lesse breach of wedlock? is not wedlock quite broke by your divorce, though it should be with consent: but I am sure it is not quite broke by living sad and pensive lives; and yet their duties are to amend their faults which are the occasion of the sad living, and not to be separated from one anothers persons.

And whereas you say, *It is not the outward continuance of mariage which keeps the covenant of mariage whole, but whosoever doth most according to peace and love, whether in mariage or divorce, he breaks mariage least.*

Answ. We answer: this is a wilde, mad, and frantick divinitie, just like to the opinions of the Maids of Algate: Oh say they, we live in Christ, and Christ doth all for us; we are Christed with Christ and Godded with God, and at the same time we sin here, we joyned to Christ do justice in him, for our life is hid with God in Christ. So you, what, tell you of bearing the infirmities of your Wife, and so fulfill the law of Christ, and of giving honour to her as the weaker vessell: why you can do this when you have put her away, you do all in love and peace, you keep these

Commandements

Commandements well enough. Fie, fie, blush for shame, and publish no more of this loose Divinitie. But I would ask you a question or two.

1 Quest. May a man keep and maintaine that love which is required between maried persons towards her who was his Wife, but now is divorced from him. If not, why say you in effect, if there be but peace and love mariage is kept well enough, either by continuing in mariage or by divorce. If he may maintain that love to her that is divorced, this is just fast and loose, marry and hate, divorce and love: I will hate her now she is my Wife, but love her when my Concubine: So, so, you teach us good courteous Doctrine.

2 Quest. I ask you, whether mariage may continue after Divorce, if not, why say you in effect, that the mariage covenant is better kept by Divorce, so there be but love and peace, then by continuance in the sad companie of mariage. I grant according to the lawes of the kingdome there is a Divorce only *a mensa & thoro*, yet I believe they hardly allow that manifestation of love to each other which the covenant of mariage requires.

But let us see, have you any Scripture for this your new Gospell: yes, enough, say you, often repeated: yea, what is, that? The words of *Paul* forsooth, *Love only is the fulfilling of every commandement*.

Answ. You must remember you put in the word only, and so adde to the Scripture. But well it is true, the Scripture doth say, *love is the fulfilling of the law*, and so by consequence of every Commandement: but how this will make for your purpose I cannot yet possibly see. Sure I am *Paul* never intended to be a Patron of all injustice and injurie to be committed, under a fained pretence of keeping the same Commandements they broke, by a secret unknown love in their hearts. Its true indeed, he that doth unfeinedly love his Neighbour, he will honour his Parents, not commit murther, nor by adulterie defile his Neighbours Wife, nor steale his goods; this is *Pauls* Doctrine. But *Paul* never taught, that a man might despise his Parents, murther, steale, and commit adulterie, and yet with a pretence of the grace of love earnestly burning in his heart, say he hath kept all the Commandements: No more doth he suffer a man to hate and put away his

his Wife with strife and variance, and tell him by the love and peace he had in his heart towards her, he had kept the Command of mariage unpoluted. *Pauls* intent in urging us so often with the dutie of love is, to put us in minde not to content our selves with the bare performance of duties to our Neighbour, without Christian love to their persons, he sayes 1 *Cor.* 13. 2. *If I give all my goods to the poore, and yet have no love, it profiteth not,* &c. But he never intended men should gape altogether upon this generall precept of love, and stick there, for *Paul* knew that would deceive thousands: therefore in the same place he descends to particulars, and thinks it not enough to bid them to love one another, but he bids to pay tribute to whom tribute belongs, and so keep the fifth Commandement: that they should owe nothing to man, and so keep the eight Commandement: *To walk honestly as in the day time, not in chambring and wantonnesse,* and so break the seventh Commandement; not in strife and envying, and so break the sixth Commandement: (this I speak according to the ordinary received opinion of ranking duties under each commandement, though I could never yet see how these duties can so well be brought in as being required in the 10 Commandements in a proper sense so to speak: its fit every Scripture should have its own weight and authority.) But to our purpose; as *Paul* is thus particular with the Romans, notwithstanding his generall precept of love; so if you will here bring in that love which is commanded between Husband and Wife, *Paul* means you shall expresse it, by covering or passing by a multitude of her faults, and by seeking to heale her errours; and by your meek, wise, and godly conversation towards her, labour to win her to God, and your self, and not most inhumanely hate her and put her away, and still say, you keepe the command of love. Thus of your fourth Argument.

5 *Arg.* The effect of your fifth Argument is, *That as the Priests of old were not to be long in sorrow, to the end they might execute their Priesthood rightly: So Christians now being Priests to God, dedicate to his service, they ought not by trouble and vexation of a disagreeing Wife to be hindred from serving God, but rather by divorce put her away, and so procure liberty to serve God.*

Answ. This Argument is far fetched, yet is it not good for Ladies, nor

nor scarce deserves any answer: but we tell you, most things concerning the priests were typicall, do you shew this to be the morall of this under the Gospel, that men might put away their Wives if they were cause of continuall heavinesse to them: how think you? might not many poor men by the same reason, who are by the providence of God compelled to labour, and so are hindred much from the cheerfull serving God in the things of his worship, which others have libertie in: may they not lawfully now leave their honest labour and fall to plunder or steal one hour or two in a day, and serve God cheerefully the rest? Why not, as well as when a man is by the providence of God maried to a yoke-fellow, which is in divers things cause of grief and vexation to him, therefore he may now break all bonds of law and providence, and under a pretence of serving God chearfully, he may unchristianly thrust his Wife out of dores with a bare Bill of Divorce in her hand to seek her living. For the rest of our discourse in this Division concerning divorce from Hereticks, we shall passe it over as nothing to our purpose, and so passe to your sixth Argument, the effect of which is.

That mariage which nature it selfe teacheth to be unlawfull, may be destroyed or dissolved by divorce. But the mariage of persons of contrary mindes & dispositions, nature teacheth to be unlawfull. Ergo, 6 *Arg.*

For the present we agree to the proposition, that such mariages as Nature it self teacheth to be unlawfull, may be dissolved by divorce. *Answ.*

But for the second part, that Nature teacheth such mariages to be unlawfull, as are made betwixt persons who are of a contrarie minde or disposition, this we utterly denie: and look for your proofs to the contrarie.

Well, you want not proofs, for you say, *Moses teacheth the Iewes that they should not sow their Vineyards with divers seeds, nor plough with an Oxe and an Asse together.*

Ho brave stuffe! but goe on; *Moses* teacheth so indeed: but how will you make this last to fit your shooe?

This you will do well enough, but how? *By following the example of Pauls reasoning,* say yoy. Well, lets see whether *Paul* or you are the best Logician. *Paul* reasons; doth God take care for Oxen and Asses how ill they yoke together, or is it spoke altogether

ther for our sake? for our sakes doubtlesse: thus you would have *Paul* to reason for you: but the truth is, *Paul* doth reason thus, but it is in another case, the place is, 1 *Cor.* 9. *Paul* reasons thus; we that bestow our labour in preaching the Gospel, ought to be maintained thereby: and he proves it by familiar examples, that every one ought to be maintained by that which he takes paines in: as the Wayfaring man by travelling, the Vinedresser by planting, the Shepheard by looking to his flock; all these eat the fruit of their labour; and to put it out of doubt, *Paul* cites the Law of *Moses*, proving that not only Men, but even Beasts ought to eat the fruits of their labour, for it saith, *Thou shalt not muzle the mouth of the Oxe which treads out the corne*. Well, *Paul* goes on in his reasoning, lest any idle pated fellow should answer and say; *Paul*, what makes this for you, I hope you are no Oxe, neither do you tread out the corne. No, sayes *Paul*, that's true; but the force of my Argument is this, That God by *Moses* did not only intend in that speech, that Oxen should be fed, but it was with reference to other cases among the rest even for us Ministers of the Gospel, that we should not take pains in the Gospel, but should also be maintained thereby, as well as Oxen and other mean Callings are maintained by their labour: lo this is *Pauls* reasoning, and it is impregnable Logick: let's see how yours agrees. *Moses* tels the Jewes they should not plough with an Oxe and an Asse together, nor sow their field with divers seeds; *Ergo*, there being some other sense in this then meerly to take care for Oxen, &c. it will follow from hence, *that it is a foule incongruity and a great violence to the reverent secret of Nature, to force a mixture of mindes that cannot unite, and to sow the furrow of mans nativitie with seed of two incoherent and incombining dispositions*. Is this your reasoning like *Pauls*, as you promised: sure *Paul* would be ashamed to reason thus.

For although we believe there may be some typicall signification of that of *Moses*, yet that it should be yours is ridiculous. But you say, *Paul* 2 *Cor.* 6. alludes to that of *Moses*, and applies it to mis-yoking in mariage, as say you *by the Greek word is evident*.

To this we answer; that it may be likely both by the Greek word and English also, that *Paul* alludes to that in *Deuteronomy*. Yet that he applies it to mariage with Infidels you cannot prove,

but

but rather to all needleſſe converſation, but eſpecially of companying with them in their ſervice of Idols.

But ſuppoſe he did applie it to mariage with Infidels, and forbad it; yet you ſee after mariage is perfected and conſummated, he will by no meanes allow of a Divorce if the Wife be but ſo much as content to live with her Husband, as was ſhewed upon 1 *Cor*. 7. And ſo this no waies makes for your purpoſe.

Now for that reverent expreſſion of yours, *That it is a foule incongruity, and a great violence to the reverent ſecret of Nature, to force a mixture of mindes which cannot unite, and to ſow the furrow of mans nativitie with the ſeed of two incoherent and incombining diſpoſitions.*

This Court complement, ſo neatly and modeſtly dreſt, I believe deſerves the pains of the beſt Ladie at Court to learn it. For anſwer to it being but a complement, for your forcing of a mixture of mindes that cannot unite; I know no bodie by force or fair means intends any ſuch mixture in mariage: mindes are not capable of mixing but only agreeing and uniting; indeed you talk much of fit converſing ſoules, whether you mean by mixture or otherwiſe, it matters not, the language is too ſublime and Angelicall for mortall creatures to comprehend it. And for your other phraſe of *a great violence to the reverent ſecret of nature by ſowing the furrow of mans nativitie, with the ſeed of two incoherent and incombining diſpoſitions.*

Anſw

This frothie diſcourſe, were it not ſugred over with a little neat language, would appear ſo immeritous and undeſerving, ſo contrary to all humane learning, yea, truth and common experience it ſelf, that all that reade it muſt needs count it worthie to be burnt by the Hangman.

For who ever thought before you, that the reverent ſecret of Nature, or the furrow of mans nativitie (ſo there was lawfull mariage preceded) might not be ſowed by the ſeeds of ſuch as are of different or uncombining diſpoſition, if any ſuch there be, without violence or foul incongruitie? If any think otherwiſe as you it ſeems doe; give advice that a Petition may be drawn, to have a Committee in every Countie of the Kingdome who ſhall carefully ſee to, and ſeverely reſtraine the mariage of any two Men or Maids who differ in conſtitution, complexion, hair,

G countenance,

An Answer to a Book, intituled,

countenance, or in disposition, left this reverent secret of Nature be defiled and violated.

7 Arg. Your seventh Argument is, *The Canon law and Divines allow a Divorce where one of the parties conspires the death of the other: but sometimes through disagreement of dispositions, by a sad pensivenesse the life of one of the parties at least, is brought into danger*, Ergo it seems a divorce ought in the latter case to be tolerated.

To this I answer three things.

1 Answ. 1. For the opinion of the Canon law, the whole bodie of it is not of your minde, for *Nichol. 1. de matrim. Can. 6.* is contrarie, *quicquid mulier contra te cogitaverit, non est excepta causa fornicationis rejicienda.* Whatsoever thy Wife conspires or plots against thee, there is no other cause of putting her away but fornication.

2 Answ. The case is not the like, betwixt the conspiring of one partie to kill the other, and your case: for where the one partie conspires to take away the life of the other, and the conspiration continues, there the offender doth implicitely at least act a Divorce; and though it should be true, that the partie grieved may in this case sue a Divorce, yet will it not follow in your case, that because a man may seek divorce from her who seeks his life, to the end to save his life, which Nature teacheth: therefore for disagreement of disposition, causing sadnesse, and wherein they are both actors, if not equals, there the Husband may will, she nill she, put her away; this is just a taking advantage of our own faults and corruptions, to release us from our duties.

3 Answ. But thirdly it would seem that there is no such cause meerly in Nature properly so called, that may cause such griefe as is destructive to the life: and if the cause be not in Nature, but in corruption, in pride, haughtinesse, sullennesse, &c. let them amend their faults, represse their pride and sullennesse, or else let them if they think best, die of the sullen disease, let them try who will pittie them.

8 Arg. The effect of your eighth Argument is this:
Those who are destitute of all mariage gifts, but only fitnesse of body, they have no calling to marry, and consequently if maried ought to be divorced: but such some are, Ergo,

Answ. Briefly to this simple Argument, quite besides that which ought to be the scope of your Book, for what is here to contrariety

riety of dispositions, now it is a disabilitie to all maried duties: This wavering & shaking in your opinion is not fit to be answered: for if it be a Lunatick *non compos mentis*, without any wit, a naturall Foole, which cannot count the daies in the week, or tell twenty, or measure a yard of cloath; you need not to inveigh against them, and you can seldome shew such an example: if Guardians doe sometime marrie such let the Lawyers alone with it, they know how to relieve the suffering partie well enough.

9 *Arg.* *Mariage is a humane society, and so ought to have the consent of the minde; but if the minde cannot enjoy that in mariage which it may reasonably desire, it is no humane society. Ergo.*

Answ. The consent of the minde ought to be had in mariage, or else it will hardly become a humane societie: but that after mariage the mindes of the Husband and Wife must in all things agree, or else the mariage becomes no humane societie, is a new principle unheard of till now, and so I leave it. As for the discourse of *Deut.* 24. 1. and Christs exposition to the Pharisees, we have spoken of it in answer to your second Argument.

Now a word to your last Argument and so farewell.

10 *Arg.* *Every law is made for some good, which good may be attained unto without a greater inconvenience: but such is not the law that prohibits Divorce for disagreements of mindes and dispositions: Ergo, it is not a just law.*

Answ. We denie this your Argument, and say, that there are many laws which are made for good, and yet that good is not attainable through the defaults of the partie, but a greater inconvenience followes, and yet are indeed still just lawes.

I will give you two or three instances in our lawes of England. It is the righteous and just law of England, that every one shall peaceably enjoy his estate in lands or otherwise, according to the goodnesse and latitude of his title: and I hope none will denie this to be a just law: yet see by the default of the partie how this may be evaded, and he fall into great inconvenience.

And so if a man having fee-simple in lands, and yet will take a lease from another of the same lands, this shall be an Estoppell to him in an Assise to recover his own land. *ter. leg. estop.*

So if a Daughter *mulier* will sue liverie of lands with her sister who is a Bastard, she shall not avoid it after by saying her sister was a Bastard not *mulier*.

So if a man had a rent, liberties, Common, &c. by prescription, and after takes a grant of the same from the King by Patent, that shall determine this prescription. 32 *H. 8. Bro. tit. Estop.* 200.

So 37 *H. 8. Bro. Estop.* 218. If two joyn-tenants are, which hold of the King *in capite*, and the one release to the other in fee, and after both respite homage in the Exchequer, the other hath by this gained his moitie againe against the other, without any valuable considerations, by the default of the other.

So it is a just law in England, that no man shall be unjustly charged or taxed contrarie to the right, and what he is bound to doe.

Yet a man by his own fault may charge himselfe, or doe such things as the law will compell him to be charged, where before he was free.

For example. If a Towneship or a Corporation are bound to repaire or maintaine a Causey or a Bridge, and a private man where he is not bound will repaire this Bridge or Causey, time beyond the memorie of man, he shall then be compelled to repaire it for ever by the Law, and at the first he was compellable.

The end of citing these cases is to shew you the weaknesse of your reason against the law of England which prohibits Divorce, for your pretended contrarietie of minde. For though it should be granted this law of prohibition of Divorce, the end of it could not be attained without a greater inconvenience: yet this inconvenience comming, arising and growing from the fault of the parties, and not from the Law; this Law of prohibiting Divorce shall remain (maugre the malice of all opposers) a just and a righteous law.

FINIS.

OBSERVATIONS
ON
Master *MILTON*
against SALMASIUS.

I.

Mong the many Printed Books, and severall Discourses touching the Right of *Kings*, and the Liberty of the *People*, I cannot finde that as yet the first and chief point is agreed upon, or indeed so much as once Disputed. The word *King* and the word *People* are familiar, one would think every simple man could tell what they signified; but upon examination it will be found, that the learnedst cannot agree of their meaning.

Ask *Salmasius* what a King is, and he will teach us that *a King is he who hath the Supreme power of the Kingdome, and is accountable to none but God, and may do what he please, and is free from the Laws.* This definition *J. M.* abominates as being the definition of a Tyrant: And I should be of his minde, if he would have vouchsafed us a better, or any other definition at all, that would tell us how any King can have a Supreme Power, without being freed from humane Laws: To finde fault with it, without producing any other, is to leave us in the dark: But though Mr. *M.* brings us neither Definition nor Description of a King, yet we may pick out of several passages of him, something like a definition, if we lay them together. He teacheth us that *power was therefore given to a King by the people, that he might see by the authority to him committed, that nothing be done against Law: and that he keeps our Laws, and not impose upon us his own: Therefore there*

is

Observations *on Mr.* Milton *against* Salmasius.   13

is no regal power but in the Courts of the Kingdome, and by them, pag. 155.

And again he affirmeth, *the King cannot Imprison, Fine or punish any man, except he be first cited into some Court; where not the King, but the usual Judges give Sentence*, pag. 168. and before we are told, *not the King, but the Authority of Parliament doth set up and take away all Courts*, pag. 167.

Lo here the description of a King, He *is one to whom the People give power, to see that nothing be done against Law:* and yet he saith there is *no regal power but in the Courts of Justice and by them, where not the King, but the usual Judges give Sentence.* This description not only strips the King of all power whatsoever, but puts him in a condition below the meanest of his Subjects.

Thus much may shew, that all men are not agreed what a King is. Next, what the word *People* means is not agreed upon: ask *Aristotle* what the People is, & he will not allow any power to be in any but in free Citizens. If we demand who be free Citizens? that he cannot resolve us, for he confesseth that *he that is a free Citizen in one City, is not so in another City.* And he is of opinion that *no artificer should be a free Citizen, or have voice in a well ordered Commonwealth*; he accounts a *Democratie* (which word signifies the Government of the people) *to be a Corrupted sort of Government*; he thinks *many men by nature born to be Servants, and not fit to govern as any part of the people.* Thus doth *Aristotle* curtal the people, and can give us no certain rule to know who be the people: Come to our Modern Polititians, and ask them who the people is, though they talk big of the people, yet they take up, and are content with a *few Representors* (as they call them) *of the whole people*; a point *Aristotle* was to seek in, neither are these Representors stood upon to be the whole people, but the *major part of these Representors must be reckoned for the whole people*; nay *J. M.* will not allow the major part of the Representors to be the people, but the *sounder and better part only* of them, & in right down terms he tells us *to determine who is a Tyrant, he leaves to Magistrates, at least to the uprighter sort of them and of the people, though in number less by many, to judge as they finde cause.* If the *sounder, the better, and the uprighter* part have the power of the people, how shall we know, or who shall judge who they be?

P. 126
P. 7.

C 2

II.

One Text is urged by Mr. *Milton*, for the peoples power: Deut. 17. 14. *When thou art come into the Land which thy Lord thy God giveth thee, and shalt say, I will set a King over me, like as all the Nations about me.* It is said, by the tenure of Kings *these words confirm us that the right of choosing, yea of changing their own Government, is by the Grant of God himself in the people:* But can the foretelling or forewarning of the *Israelites* of a wanton and wicked desire of theirs, which God Himself condemned, be made an argument that God gave or granted them a right to do such a wicked thing? or can the narration and reproving of a future fact be a donation and approving of a present right, or the permission of a sin be made a commission for the doing of it? the Author in his Book against *Salmasius*, falls from making God the Donor or Grantor, that he cites him onely for a Witness, *Teste ipso Deo penes populos arbitrium semper fuisse, vel ea, quæ placeret forma reipub. utendi, vel hanc in aliam mutandi; de Hebræis hoc diserte dicit Deus: de reliquis non abnuit.*

That here in this Text *God himself being witness, there was alwayes a power in the people, either to use what form of Government they pleased, or of changing it into another: God saith this expresly of the* Hebrews, *and denies it not of others.* Can any man finde that God in this Text expresly saith, that there was alwayes a right in the People, to use what form of Government they please? The Text not warranting this right of the People, the foundation of the defence of the People is quite taken away; there being no other grant or proof of it pretended.

2. Where it is said that *the Israelites desired a King, though then under another form of Government*; in the next line but one it is confessed they had a King at the time when they desired a King which was God himself, and his Viceroy *Samuel*, and so saith God, *They have not rejected thee; but they have rejected me that I should not reign over them:* yet in the next verse God saith, *as they have forsaken me, so do they also unto thee.* Here is no shew of any other form of Government but Monarchy: God by the mediation of *Samuel* reigned, who made his Sons Judges over *Israel*;

Israel; when one man constitutes Judges, we may call him a King; or if the having of Judges do alter the Government, then the Government of every Kingdome is altered from Monarchy, where Judges are appointed by Kings: it is now reckoned one of the duties of Kings to judge by their Judges onely.

Where it is said, *He shal not multiply to himself horses, nor wives nor Riches, that he might understand that he had no power over others, who could decree nothing of himself, extra legem*, if it had said *contra legem Dei*, it had been true, but if it meant *extra legem humanam*, it is false.

4. If there had been any right given to the People, it seems it was to the Elders onely; for it is said it was the Elders of *Israel* gathered together, petitioned for a King, it is not said it was all the People, nor that the People did choose the Elders, who were the Fathers and Heads of Families authorized by the Judges.

5. Where it is said, *I will set a King over me like as all the Nations about me*. To set a *King*, is, not to choose a King, but by some solemn publick act of Coronation, or otherwise to acknowledge their allegiance to the King chosen; It is said, thou shalt *set him King whom the Lord thy God shall choose*. The Elders did not desire to choose a King like other Nations, but they say, *now make us a King to judge us like all the Nations*.

III.

As for *Davids* Covenant with the Elders when he was annointed, it was not to observe any Laws or Conditions made by the People, for ought appears; but to keep Gods Laws and serve him, and to seek the good of the People, as they were to protect him.

6. The *Reubenites* and *Gadites* promise their obedience, not according to their Laws or Conditions agreed upon, but in these words, *All that thou commandest us we will do, and whithersoever thou sendst us we wil go, as we harkned to* Moses *in all things, so wil we harken unto thee: only the Lord thy God be with thee as he was with* Moses. Where is there any condition of any humane Law expressed? Though the rebellious Tribes offered Conditions to *Rehoboam*: where can we find that *for like conditions not performed,*

ed, *all Israel deposed Samuel*? I wonder Mr. *M.* should say this, when within a few lines after he professeth that *Samuel had Governed them uprightly.*

IV.

Jus Regni is much stumbled at, and the definition of a King, which saith *His power is supreme in the Kingdome, and he is accountable to none but to God, and that he may do what he please, and is not bound by Laws*: it is said if this definition be good, no man is or ever was, who may be said to be a Tyrant, for *when he hath violated all divine and humane Laws, neverthelefs he is a King, and guiltlefs jure Regio.* To this may be answered, That the definition confesseth he is accountable to God, and therefore not guiltless if he violate Divine Laws: Humane Laws must not be shuffled in with Divine, they are not of the same authority: if humane Laws binde a King, it is impossible for him to have supreme power amongst men. If any man can finde us out such a kinde of Government, wherein the supreme power can be, without being freed from humane Laws, they should first teach us that; but if all sorts of popular Government that can be invented, cannot be one minute, without an Arbitrary power, freed from all humane Laws: what reason can be given why a royal Government should not have the like freedom? if it be tyranny for one man to govern arbitrarily, why should it not be farre greater tyranny for a multitude of men to govern without being accountable or bound by Laws? It would be further enquired how it is possible for any Government at all to be in the World without an arbitrary power; it is not power except it be arbitrary: a legislative power cannot be without being absolved from humane Laws, it cannot be shewed how a King can have any power at all but an arbitrary power. We are taught, that *power was therefore given to a King by the People, that he might see by the authority to him committed, that nothing be done against Law, and that he keep our Laws, and not impose upon us his own:* therefore there is no royal Power, but in the Courts of the Kingdome, and by them p.155. and again it is said, *the King cannot imprison, fine or punish any man except he be first cited into some Court, where not the King but the usual Judges give sentence,* p.168.

P.14.

p.168. and before we are told *not the* King, *but the Authority of* Parliament *doth set up and take away all Courts,* p.167.

Lo here we have Mr. *Miltons* perfect definition of a King. He is one to whom the People gave *power to see that nothing be done against Law, and that he keep our Laws, and not impose his own.* Whereas all other men have the faculty of seeing by nature, the King onely hath it by the gift of the People, other power he hath none; he may see the Judges keep the Laws if they will; he cannot compel them, for he may not imprison, fine, nor punish any man, the Courts of Justice may, and they are set up and put down by the Parliament: yet in this very definition of a King, we may spy an arbitrary power in the King, for he may wink if he will: and no other power doth this description of a King give, but onely a power to see: whereas it is said *Aristotle doth mention an absolute Kingdome, for no other cause, but to shew how absurd, unjust and most tyrannical it is*: There is no such thing said by *Aristotle,* but the contrary, where he saith, that *a King according to Law makes no sort of Government*; and after he had reckoned up five sorts of Kings, he concludes that there were in a manner but two sorts, the *Lacedemonian* King, and the absolute King; whereof the first was but as a General in an Army, and therefore no King at all, and then fixes and rests upon the *absolute King, who ruleth according to his own will.*

V.

If it be demanded what is meant by this word *People?* 1. Sometimes it is *populus universus,* and then every childe must have his consent asked, which is impossible. 2. Sometimes it is *pars major,* and sometimes it is *pars potior & sanior*; How the major part, where all are alike free, can binde the minor part, is not yet proved.

But it seems the major part will not carry it, nor be allowed, except they be the *better part and the sounder part.* We are told, *the sounder part implored the help of the Army, when it saw it self and the Commonwealth betrayed*; and that *the Souldiers judged better then the Great Councell, and by Arms saved the Commonwealth, which the Great Councell had almost damned by their Votes,* p.7.

Here we see what the *People* is; to wit, *the sounder part, of which the Army is the judge*: thus upon the matter the Souldiers are the People: which being so, we may discern where the liberty of the People lieth, which we are taught to consist *all for the most part in the power of the Peoples choosing what form of Government they please*. A miserable liberty, which is onely to choose to whom we will give our liberty, which we may not keep. See more concerning the People, in a Book entituled *The Anarchy*, p 8 9,10,11,12,13,14.

VI.

We are taught that *a Father and a King are things most divers. The Father begets us, But not the King; but we create the King: Nature gives a Father to the People, the People give themselves a King: If the Father kill his Son he loseth his life, why should not the King also?* p.34.

Ans. Father and King are not so divers; it is confessed that at first they were all one, for there is confessed *Paternum imperium & hæreditarium*, p.141. and this fatherly empire as it was of it self *hereditary*; so it was *alienable* by the Parent, and *seizable* by an usurper as other goods are: and thus every King that now is hath a Paternal Empire, either by Inheritance, or by Translation or Usurpation, so a Father and a King may be all one.

A Father may dye for the murther of his Son, where there is a superior Father to them both, or the right of such a supreme Father; but where there are onely Father and Sons, no Sons can question the Father for the death of their brother: the reason why a King cannot be punished, is not because he is excepted from punishment, or doth not deserve it, but because there is no superior to judge him, but God onely, to whom he is reserved.

VII.

It is said thus, *He that takes away from the People the power of choosing for themselves what form of Government they please, he doth take away that wherein all civil liberty almost consists*, p.65. If almost all liberty be in choosing of the kinde of Government, the

the people have but a poor bargain of it, who cannot exercise their liberty, but in chopping and changing their Government, & have liberty onely to give away their liberty, then which there is not a greater mischief, as being the cause of endless Sedition.

VIII.

If there be any Statute in our Law, by which thou canst find that Tyrannical power is given to a King, that Statute being contrary to Gods will, to nature and reason, understand that by that general and primary law of ours, that Statute to be repealed and not of force with us, p. 153. Here if any man may be judge, what Law is contrary to Gods will, or to nature, or to reason, it will soon bring in confusion : Most men that offend, if they be to be punished or fined, will think that Statute that gives all Fines and Forfeitures to a King, to be a Tyrannical Law; thus most Statutes would be judged void, and all our forefathers taken for fools or madmen, to make all our Laws to give all penalties to the King.

IX.

The sin of the children of *Israel* did lie, not in desiring a King, but in desiring such a King, like as the Nations round about had ; they distrusted God Almighty that governed them by the Monarchical power of *Samuel*, in time of oppression, when God provided a Judge for them; but they desired a perpetual and an hereditary King, that they might never want : in desiring a King they could not sin, for it was but desiring what they enjoyed by Gods special Providence.

X.

Men are perswaded that in the making of a Covenant, something is to be performed on both parts by mutual stipulation, which is not alwayes true : for we finde God made a *Covenant with* Noah *and his seed, with all the fowl and the cattel, not to destroy the earth any more by a flood.* This Covenant was to be kept on Gods part, neither *Noah*, nor the fowl, nor the cattel, were to perform any thing by this Covenant. On the other side, *Gen* 17. 9, 10. God covenants with *Abraham*, saying, *Thou shalt keep my Covenant——every male child among you shall be circumcised.* Here it is called Gods Covenant, though it be to be performed onely by *Abraham*; so a Covenant may be called the Kings Covenant, becauſe it is made to him, and yet to be performed onely by the people. So alſo, 2 *Kin.* 11. 17. *Jehoiada made a Covenant between the Lord and the King and the people, that they ſhould be the Lords people.* Between the *King* alſo *and the People,* which might well be, that the people ſhould be the Kings ſervants: and not for the Kings covenanting to keep any Humane Laws, for it is not likely the King ſhould either Covenant, or take any Oath to the people when he was but ſeven years of age, and that never any King of *Iſrael* took a Coronation Oath that can be ſhewed: when *Jehoiada* ſhewed the King to the Rulers in the houſe of the Lord, he took an Oath of the People: he did not article with them, but, ſaith the next verſe, *Commanded them to keep a watch of the Kings houſe, and that they ſhould compaſs the King round about, every man with his weapon in his hand, and he that cometh within the ranges, let him be ſlain.*

XI.

To the Text, *Where the word of a King is, there is power, and who may ſay to him, What doſt thou?* J. M. gives this anſwer, *It is apparent enough that the Preacher in this place gives precepts to every private man, not to the great Sanedrin, nor to the Senate:* —— *ſhall not the Nobles, ſhall not all the other Magiſtrates, ſhall not the whole People dare to mutter, ſo oft as the King pleaſeth to dote?* We muſt here note, that the great Councel, and all other Magiſtrates or Nobles, or the whole People compared to the King, are all but private men, if they derive their power from him: they are Magiſtrates under him and out of his preſence, for when he is in place, they are but ſo many private men. *J. M.* asks, *Who ſwears to a King, unleſs the King on the other ſide be ſworn to keep Gods Laws, and the Laws of the Country?* We finde that the Rulers of *Iſrael* took an Oath at the Coronation of *Jehoaſh*: But we finde no Oath taken by that King, no not ſo much as to Gods Laws, much leſs to the Laws of the Countrey.

XII.

A Tyrant is he who regarding neither Law, nor the Common Good, reigns onely for himſelf and his faction, p. 19. in his defence

he

he expresseth himself thus, *He is a Tyrant who looks after onely his own, and not his peoples profit*, Eth.l.10.p.189.

1. If it be Tyranny not to regard the Law, then all Courts of Equity, and pardons for any offences must be taken away: there are far more sutes for relief against the Laws, then there be for the observation of the Laws: there can be no such Tyranny in the world as the Law, if there were no equity to abate the rigor of it. *Summum jus* is *Summa injuria*, if the penalties and forfeitures of all Laws should still be exacted by all Kings, it would be found that greatest Tyranny would be for a King to govern according to Law, the Fines, Penalties and Forfeitures of all Laws are due to the Supreme Power onely, and were they duly paid, they would far exceed the Taxes in all places. It is the chief happiness of a Kingdome, and their chief Liberty, not to be governed by the Laws onely.

2. *Not to regard the Common Good, but to reign onely for himself*, is the supposition of an impossibility in the judgement of *Aristotle*, who teacheth us, that *the despotical power cannot be preserved, except the Servant or he in subjection be also preserved*. The truth of this strongly proves, That it is in nature impossible to have a form of Government that can be for the destruction of a people, as Tyranny is supposed; if we will allow people to be governed, we must grant they must in the first place be preserved, or else they cannot be governed.

Kings have been and may be vitious men, and the Government of one, not so good as the Government of another; yet it doth not follow that the form of Government is or can be in its own nature ill, because the Governour is so: it is Anarchy or want of Government, that can totally destroy a Nation. We cannot finde any such Government as Tyranny mentioned or named in Scripture, or any word in the Hebrew Tongue to express it. After such time as the Cities of *Greece* practised to shake off Monarchy, then and not till then (which was after *Homers* time) the name of Tyrant was taken up for a word of disgrace, for such men as by craft or force wrested the power of a City from a multitude, to one man onely; and not for the *exercising*, but for the ill *obtaining* of the Government: but now every man that is but thought to govern ill, or to be an ill man, is presently termed a

Tyrant, and so judged by his Subjects. Few remember the prohibition, *Exod.22.28. Thou shalt not revile the Gods, nor curse the Ruler of thy people*: and fewer understand the reason of it. Though we may not one judge another, yet we may speak evil or revile one another, in that which hath been lawfully judged, and upon a Tryal wherein they have been heard and condemned: this is not to judge, but onely to relate the judgement of the Ruler. To speak evil or to revile a Supreme Judge, cannot be without judging him who hath no Superior on earth to judge him, and in that regard must alwayes be presumed innocent, though never so ill, if he cannot lawfully be heard.

I.M. That will have it Tyranny in a King not to regard the Laws, doth himself give as little regard to them as any man, where he reckons that *contesting for Priviledges, Customs, Forms, and that old entanglement of Iniquity, their gibrish Laws, are the badges of ancient Slavery,* Tenure, pag. 3. *a disputing Presidents, Forms and Circumstances,* pag. 5.

I.M. is also of opinion, that *If at any time our Fore-fathers out of baseness have lost any thing of their right, that ought not hurt us, they might if they would promise Slavery for themselves, for us certainly they could not, who have alwayes the same right to free our selves, that they had to give themselves to any man in slavery.* This Doctrine well practised, layeth all open to constant Anarchy.

Lastly, if any desire to know what the liberty of the People is which *I.M.* pleads for, he resolves us, saying, that *he that takes away from the people, the right of choosing what form of Government they please, takes away truly that in which all liberty doth almost consist.* It is well said by *I.M.* that all liberty doth almost consist in choosing their form of Government, for there is another liberty exercised by the people, which he mentions not; which is the liberty of the peoples choosing their Religion; every man may be of any Religion, or of no Religion; *Greece* and *Rome* have been as famous for *Polytheisme,* or multitudes of gods, as of Governors, and imagining Aristocraty and Democracy in Heaven, as on Earth.

OBSER-

The Censure of the
R O T A
Upon Mr MILTONS Book,

ENTITULED,

The Ready and Easie way to Establish

A Free Common-wealth.

Die Lunæ 26. Martij, 1660.

Ordered by the Rota, that M. Harrington *be desired to draw up a Narrative of this dayes proceeding upon* Mr. Miltons Book, called, The Ready and Easie way, &c. *And to cause the same to be forthwith Printed and Published, and a Copy thereof to be sent to* Mr. Milton.

Trundle Wheeler, Clerk
to the *ROTA*.

LONDON,

Printed by *Paul Giddy*, Printer to the *Rota*, at the sign of the Windmill in *Turne-againe Lane*.
1 6 6 0.

The Censure of the
ROTA
Upon Mr. *Milton*'s Book,

ENTITULED,

A Ready and Easie way to Establish a Free COMMON-WEALTH.

SIR,

I Am commanded by this ingenious Convention of the *Rota*, to give you an account of some Reflections that they have lately made upon a Treatise of yours, which you call, *The ready and easie way to establish a Free Commonwealth*; in which I must first bespeak your pardon, for being forced to say something, not onely against mine own sense, but the Interesse which both you and I carry on; for it is enjoyn'd me to acquaint you with all that was said, although I take as little pleasure to repeat it, as you will do to hear it. For whereas it is our usuall custom to dispute every thing, how plain or obscure soever, by knocking Argument against Argument, and tilting at one another with our heads (as Rams fight) untill we are out of breath, and then refer it to our wooden Oracle the *Box*; and seldom any thing, how slight soever, hath appear'd, without some Patron or other to defend it. I must confesse, I never saw Bowling-stones run so unluckily against any Boy, when his hand has been out, as the Ballots did against you, when any thing was put to the question, from the beginning of your Book to the end.

for

for it was no sooner read over, but a Gentleman of your acquaintance said, he wish'd for your own sake, as well as the Cause you contend for, that you had given your Book no name (like an Anabaptist's child) untill it had come to years of discretion, or else that you had got some friend to be Gossip, that has a luckier hand at giving Titles to Books than you have: For it is observ'd, you have always been very unfortunate that way, as if it were fatall to you to prefix Bulls and Nonsense to the very fronts of your learned Works, as when you call *Salmasius, Claudius Anonymus*, in the very Title of that admired piece, which you writ to confute his Wife and his Maid. As also in that other learned Labor of yours, which you style *Tetrachordon*, that is to say, a Fiddle with four strings; but, as you render it, a Four-fold Cord, with which you undertake (worse then Captain *Ottor*, and *Cuthbert* the Barber) not to bind, but (most ridiculously) to unty Matrimony. But in this Book, he said, you were more insufferable; for you do not onely style your Declamation, *The ready and easie way*, as if it were the best or onely way, to the disparagement of this most ingenuous Assembly, who are confident, they have propos'd others much more considerable; but do very indiscreetly profess in the same place, to compare the Excellencies of a Common-wealth with the inconveniences and dangers of Kingship; this, he said, was foul play, and worse Logick: For, as all conveniences in this world carry their inconveniences with them, to compare the Best of one thing with that Worst of another, is a very unequall way of comparison. He had observ'd, that Comparisons were commonly made on the wrong side, and so was this of yours, by your owne confession. To this, another added, He wondred you did not give over writing, since you have always done it to little or no purpose; for though you have scribled your eyes out, your works have never been printed but for the Company of Chandlers and Tobacco-men, who are your Stationers, and the onely men that vend your Labors. He said, that he himself repriev'd the *Whole Defence of the People of England* for a groat, that was sentenced to vile *Mundungus*, and had suffer'd inevitably (but for him) though it cost you

much

(5)

much Oyle and Labor, and the *Rump* 300 l. a year, to whose service it was more properly intended; although in the close, you pronounce them to be as very Rascalls as *Salmasius*, and all the Christian world calls them, if ever they suffered any of their fellow-Members to invade the Government (as *O. Cromwell* and others have since done) and confesse your self fool'd and mistaken, and all you have written to be false, howsoever you give your self the second lye in writing for them again. After this, a grave Gentleman of the long Roab, said, You had broken the heads of all the Sages of the Law, and plaid false in the very first word of your Treatise. For the Parliament of *England* (as you call the *Rump*) never consisted of a pack'd Party of one House, that by fraud and covin had disseaz'd the major part of their Fellows, and forfeited their own right, by abetting the ejectment of the whole House of Peers, and the greater part of their own (which was always understood to be the whole House) with whom they had but a joynt Right. That they had been severall times justly dissolv'd by the Army, from whom they really deriv'd their Authority; and the generall Voices of the People, in whom they had declar'd the supream Power to reside; and their own confession upon Record in their Journall-Book. But this, he said, you stole from Patriot *Whitlock*, who began his Declaration for a Free State with the same words; and he wondred you would filch and pilfer Nonsense and Fallasies, that have such plentifull store of your own grouth. Yet this was as true as that which follows, *That a great number of the faithfullest of the People assisted them in throwing off Kingship*; for they were a very sleight number in respect of the whole, and none of the faithfullest that forswore themselves, to maintain and defend that which they judg'd dangerous, and resolv'd to abolish. And therefore they turn'd Regall Bondage (as you word it) into a Free Common-wealth, no more justly and magnanimously, than other Knights of the Post do their feats, by plain down-right perjury. And the Nation had little reason to trust such men with their Liberty or Propriety, that had no right to their own ears, but, among the rest of

their

their Cheats, had defrauded the very Pillory of its due. This being put to the Ballot was immediately carried on in the Affirmative, without a dissenting Pellet. When presently a Gentleman, that hath been some years beyond-Seas, said, He wonder'd you would say any thing so false and ridiculous, as that this Common-wealth was the terrour and admiration of *France* it self; for if that were true, the Cardinall and Councell were very imprudent to become the chief Promoters of it, and strive by all means to uphold that, which they judg'd to be dangerous to themselves, and for the Interesse of a Nation, which they hate and fear so much as they do us; for if this Free State be so terrible to them, they have been very unwise in assisting it to keep out the King all this while; especially if they saw the people of *Paris* and *Burdeaux* disposed (as you say) to imitate us, which appears very strange; for by their history, any man would judge we had catch'd the disease of them. As for our actions abroad, (which you brag of) he said, he never heard of any where he was, untill *O. Cromwel* reduc'd us to an absolute Monarchy under the name of a Free state; and then we beat the Potent and flourishing Republique of the *United Provinces*. But for our actions at home, he had heard abroad, that they savoured much of *Goth* and *Vandal* barbarism, if pulling down of Churches, and demolishing the noblest Monuments in the Land, both Publick and Privat, (beside Religion and all Laws, Human and Divine) may amount to so much. And yet, he said, he granted what you affirm, That they were not unbecomming the rising of a glorious Common-wealth, for such are usually founded in Faction, Sedition, Rebellion, Rapine, and Murther. And how much soever you admire the Romans, ——*ab infami gen em deducis Asylo*, if you remember, they were at first but a Refuge for Thieves and Murtherers. In all *Asia*, *Africa*, and the New World, there is no such thing as a Republick, nor ever was; but onely that of *Carthage*, and some paltry Greek Colonies upon the skirts of *Asia minor*; and for one Common-wealth there have been a hundred Kingdoms in the world, which argues, they should be the more

agreeable

agreeable to Mankind. He added, Commonly Republicks arise from unworthy causes, not fit to be mention'd in History; and that he had heard many Persons of Honor in *Flanders* affirm, That it was not the Tyranny of *Spain*, nor the cruelty of Duke *D' Alva*, nor the blood of their Nobility, nor Religion, nor Liberty, that made the Dutch cast off their obedience to their Prince; but one penny Excise laid upon a pound of Butter, that made them implacably declare for a Common-wealth. That the *Venetians* were banish'd into a Free State by *Atila*, and their glorious Liberty was at first no other, then he may be said to have that is turn'd out of his house. That the *Romans* were Cookolded into their Freedom, and the *Pisans* Trepand into theirs by *Charls* the eighth. That as Common-wealths sprung from base Originalls, so they have ruin'd upon as slight occasions. That the same *Pisans*, after they had spent all they had upon a Freak of Liberty, were sold (like Cattle) by *Lewis* the 12th. The *Venetians* Hector'd, and almost ruin'd by *Maximilian* the first, a poor Prince, for refusing to lend him mony, as they were not long before by *Francesco Sforza* about a Bastard. The *Florentines* utterly enslav'd for spoyling an Embossador's Speech, and disparaging *Petro de' Medici*'s fine Livereys. The *Genoeses* ─────── But as he was going on, he was interrupted by a Gentleman that came in and told us, that Sir *Arthur Hazlerig*, the *Brutus* of our Republique, was in danger to be torn in pieces (like a *Shrovetuesday* Bawd) by the Boys in *Westminster-Hall*; and if he had not shewn himself as able a Foot-man as he that cudgell'd him, he had gone the way of Doctor *Lamb* infallibly. This set all the company a laughing, and made the Traveller forget what he was saying. After a little pause, a learned Gentleman of this Society stood up, and said, He could not but take notice of one absurdity in your Discourse, and that is, where you speak of Liberty gloriously fough for, and Kingly Thraldome abjur'd by the people, &c. for if by liberty, you mean Common-wealth, (as you do) There was never any such thing, as either the one, or the other: unlesse yon will state the Quarrell at the end of the Warre, which is very senseleffe, and directly contrary to all Oaths and Engagements:

ments : or can prove that Hanging, Drawing, and Quartering of some of the People, and selling others as Slaves, for taking up Arms in all parts of the Nation for the *King*, are abjurations of his Authority; and he wonder'd, you could be so weak, or impudent to play foul in matters of Fact, of which there are so many thousands witnesses to disprove you. But he was of opinion, that you did not believe your selfe, nor those reasons you give in defence of Commonwealth, but that you are sway'd by something else, as either by a Stork-like Fate, (as a modern Protector-Poet calls it, because that Foul is observ'd to live no where but in Common-wealths) or because, you have unadvisedly scribled your selfe obnoxious, or else you fear such admirable eloquence as yours, would be thrown away under a Monarchy, (as it would be) though of admirable use in a Popular Government, where Orators carry all the Rabble before them: For who knows to how Cheap a rate this goodly Eloquence of yours, (if well manadg'd) might bring the price of Sprats, as no wiser Orators then your selfe have done heretofore, in the petty factions, Greek Republiques, whom you chiefly imitate; for all your Politiques are derived from the works of Declamers, with which sort of Writers, the Ancient Common-wealths had the fortune to abound, who left many things behind them in favour, or flattery of the Governments they liv'd under, and disparagement of others, to whom they were in opposition, of whom we can affirm nothing certain, but that they were partiall, and never meant to give a true account of things, but to make them finer or worse then they really are; Of which men, one of their owne Common-wealth Poets, gives a just Character, by sorting them among the worst of men.

  ——Ἱερόδουλοι, ῥήτορες,
  Καὶ συκοφάνται, ᾗ ποιηταὶ——

  All which you have out-gone, (according to your Talent) in their severall wayes, for you have done your feeble endeavour to Rob the Church, of the little which the Rapine of the most sacrilegious Persons hath left, in your learned

                 work

work against Tithes; You have slandered the Dead, worse then envy it selfe, and thrown your dirty out-rage, on the memory of a Murther'd Prince, as if the Hangman were but your Usher. These have been the attempts of your stiffe formall Eloquence, which you arme accordingly, with any thing that lies in your way, right, or wrong, not onely begging, but stealing questions, and taking every thing for granted, that will serve your turn; For you are not a-sham'd to rob *O. Cromwell* himselfe, and make use of his Canting with signall Assistances from Heaven, and answering Condescensions: The most impious Mahometan Doctrine, that ever was vented among Christians, and such as will serve as well to justifie any prosperous villany amongst men. He said, when God punishes a Nation for sin, The Executioners of his Judgments, are commonly but Malefactors reprieved, as they are usually among men; For when he punish'd the Israelites for Idolatry, he made use of greater Idolaters then themselves: And when he afflicts a people for their disobedience, to a just Government, and fantastique longing after imaginary Liberty, it is with infallible Slavery, for their deliverers alwaies prove their Tyrants. This the Romans found true, for they had no sooner banish'd their Kings, but they were in few years glad to banish themselves, from the Tyranny and oppression of their Patriots, the Assertors of their Liberty, and that very Contest furnish'd their Free-State with Sedition, and Civill War for 500 years, and never ended, untill they were reduc'd to an absolute Tyranny, under the power of that faction, that took upon it to vindicate their Liberty; He added, that he could not but smile at one thing you sayd, and that is, That King and Bishops will encroach upon our Consciences, untill we are forc'd to spend over again all that we have spent, and fight over again all that we have fought, &c. For if you did not look very like a Cunning man, no body would believe you, nor trust your predictions of the future, that give so ill an account of things past. But he held you very unwise to blab any such thing, For that party you call, *We have gain'd so abundantly much more then they have spent, that they desire nothing more, then to fight over the same fights*

B

fights again, at the same rate; and if you could but make your words good, he would undertake, they should be the first men that should set Bishops about your Consciences; for how vile soever you make the Blood of faithfull English men, they have made such good markets of it, that they would be glad at any time to broach the whole Nation at the same price, and affor'd the treasure of Miraculous deliverances, (as you call it) into the Bargin. This he added, was easier to be understood then your Brand of *Gentilesm*, upon King-ship, for which you rest Scripture most unmercifully, to prove, that though Christ said, His Kingdome was not of this world, yet his Common-wealth is. For if, the Text which you quote, The Kings of the Gentiles exercise Lordship over them, and they that exercise authority over them, are called Benefactors: But it shall not be so among you, &c. be to be understood of Civill Government, (and to infer Common-wealth (as you will have it right or wrong) and not to be meant of his spirituall Reigne, of which he was then speaking, and expressely calls so; You must prove that he erected a Republique of his Apostles, and that notwithstanding the Scripture, every where calls his Government the Kingdome of Heaven, it ought to be Corrected, and Rendred the Common-wealth of Heaven, or rather the Common-wealth of this World; and yet the Text, does as well prove Benefactors heathenish as Kings, for if our Saviour had meant to brand Kingship with any evill Character, He would never have styld himselfe King of the Jewes, King of Heaven, King of Righteousnesse, &c. as he frequently do's, but no where a State-holder, or Keeper of the Liberties.

To this, a young Gentleman made answer, that your writings are best interpreted by themselves, and that he remembred in that Book, wherein you fight with the King's Picture, you call Sir *Phillip Sydnes*, Princess *Pamela*, who was born and bred of Christian Parents in *England*; A Heathen woman, and therefore, he thought that by Heathonish, you meant English, and that in calling Kingship, Heathenish, you inferd, it was the only proper and naturall Government of the English Nation, as it hath been proved in all Ages.

To

(11)

To which another objected, that such a sense was quite Contrary to your purpose, to which he immediately repli'd; That it was no new thing, with you to write that, which is as well against us for your purpose: after much debate, they agreed to put it to the Ballot, and the young Gentleman carried it without any Contradiction. That done, a Gentleman of good credit here, taking occasion from the former discourse, said, you had shown your selfe as able a Divine, as a Statesman; For you had made as politique provision for spirituall, as civill Liberty in those pious and Orthodox, (though seeming absurd and Contradictory) grounds you have laid down in order thereunto, which being rightly interpreted, do say, or by consequence inferre thus much. That the Church of Christ ought to have no Head upon Earth, but the Monster of many heads, the multitude, who are the onely supream Judges of all matters that concern him; a Priviledge they claim'd, when he was upon Earth, when they took upon them to condemn him, and cri'd Crucifige: That all Christian Lawes and Ordinances have a Co-ercive power, to see themselves put in Execution, and yet they ought to be subject to every Man's will and humor, (which you call his best light) and no man to them but in his own sense. That the Scripture onely ought to interpret it selfe, (just as it can read it selfe) and every man is to take the interpretation in such a sense, as best suites with his owne capacity, or his occasions; That every man may do what he pleases in matters of Religion, but onely those that are in Authority, who ought not to meddle in such matters, as being of so different a nature from their Cognizance, (or any other) that if it be their will to Command the onely true Religion to be observ'd, it presently becomes inchristian inhuman, and Barbarous. That no man can serve God, nor save his owne Soul, but in a Common-wealth, in this certainty, you go after your owne invention, for no man ever heard it before: But if it should be true, it is a sad thing to think, what is become of the Apostles themselves, and all the Saints in the Primitive times, when there was never a Christian Common-wealth in the World? That any man may turn away his Wife, and take another as oft as

B 2 he

he pleases, as you have most learnedly prov'd upon the Fiddle, and practic'd in your Life and Conversation, for which you have atchieved the honour to be Styld the Founder of a Sect. All this you call Liberty of Conscience, and Christian Liberty, which you conclude no Government is more inclinable, not onely to favour, but protect, then a Free Common-wealth. In this, (he said) you say right; For it is notorious enough, that since we have been but call'd a Common-wealth, such pious Doctrines as these, have been so wonderfully propagated, that *England* does now abound with new Christians, no lesse then *Spain* did of late years, and of the same mungrell breed; all which agree in nothing, but the extripation of Christian Religion, and subversion of Government, to which your Discipline does naturally conduce. For certainly, the most ready and easie way to root out Religion, is to render it contemptible, and ridiculous, which cannot be sooner done then by giving Licence, and encouragement to all manner of Frenzies, that pretend to new discoveries in matters of Faith, these will quickly make it become a sport and mockery to the People, untill it be utterly extinct; And this, some of the Church of *Rome* found true, who give a greater check to the growth of Reformation, by cloathing some of the new professers in Fools Coats, and exposing them to the derision of the multitude, then by persecuting, and putting thousands to death. And this is the way you goe which will never fail you, as long as there are Fooles and mad men to carry on the work. And with this if you could but introduce the wholsome Cannons of the Councill of *Munster* it would make an admirable Model for the Ecclesiasticall part of the Republique, if it were not for one unlucky Circumstance, and that is that *Knipper Dolling* Proclaimed *John* of *Leyden* King, and not State-holder. This (he said) was an unhappy mistake and no lesse out of your way then that of the Fift *Monarchy* Men, who would have been admirable for your purpose if they had but dream't of a fift Free-State.

By this time they began to grow weary of your perpetuall falshoods and mistakes, and a Worthy Knight of this
Assem-

Assembly stood up and said that if we meant to examin all the particular fallacies and flawes in your writing we should never have done, he would therefore (with leave) deliver his judgement upon the whole, which in briefe was thus. That it is all windy foppery from the beginning to the end, written to the eleuation of that Rabble and meant to cheat the Ignorant. That you fight alwayes with the flat of your hand like a Retorician, and never Contract the Logicall fist. That you trade altogether in universals the Region of Deceits and falacie, but never come so near particulars, as to let us know which among diuerse things of the same kind you would be at. For you admire Commonwealths in generall, and cry down Kingship as much at large, without any regard to the particular Constitutions which onely make either the one or the other good or bad, vainly supposing all slavery to be in the Gouernment of a single Person, and nothing but liberty in that of many, which is so false that some Kingdomes have had the most perfect form of Common wealths as ours had, and some Republiques haue proved the greatest Tirannies, as all have done at one time or other. For many if they combine have more Latitude to abuse power then a single Person, and lesse sence of shame, conscience, or honour to restrain them, for what is wickedly done by many is own'd by none, where no Man knowes upon whom in particular to fix it. And this we have found true by experience in your Patriots and Assertors (as you call hem) for no one person could ever have done halfe the mischief they have done, nor outliv'd the infamy they have suffered without any sence of shame. Beside this, as all your politiques reach but the outside and circumstances of things and never touch at realties, so you are very solicitous about weeds as if they were charmes, or had more in them then what they signifie: For no Conjurer's Devill is more concerned in a spell, then you are in a meer word, but never regard the things which it serves to expresse. For you believe liberty is safer under an Arbitrary unlimited power by vertue of the name Commonwealth, then under any other Government how just or restrain'd soever if it be but cal'd Kingship. And therefore very prudently you

would

would have the Name Parliament abolished, because it signifies a Parly of our Commons with their Norman Kings. But in this you are too severe a *Draco* to punish one word for holding correspondence with another, when all the liberty you talk so much of consists in nothing else but meer words. For though you bragge much of the Peoples Manageing their own affaires, you allow them no more share of that in your *Utopia* (as you have ordered it) then only to set up their thrpates and Baul (instead of every three yeares, which they might have done before) once in an Age, or oftner, as an old Member drops away, and anew one is to succed, not for his merit or knowledge in State affaires, but because he is able to bring the greatest and most deep mouth'd Pack of the Rabble into the field; a more wise and equall way (in your opinion) of choosing Counsellors, then any King is capable of. But he added, you had done worst of all, where you are most like your self, and that is in that false and malitious asperfion of Popish & Spanish Councels which you cast on the present King. For it is well known to all the world, he hath prefer'd his Conscience before three Crowns, and patiently endured to live so many years in exile, rather then change his Religion; which if he would have done, or been mov'd with such Councels, he might long since have procured all the Forces of the Catholique world upon us, whereas it cannot be denied of his greatest opposers, That they are so jealous of their ill-gotten Purchases bought with their Crimes, that rather be in danger of loosing a Pigge, they would (with the *Gergesens*) desire Christ to depart out of their Coasts. After this said, he mov'd the Assembly that I might be desired to deliver my judgment upon the Book, as he and others had done, which being immediatlypast; I knew not (though unwilling) how to avoyd it; and therefore I told them as briefly as I could, That that which I disliked most in your Treatise was, That there is not one word of the ballance of Propriety, nor the *Agrarian*, nor *Rotation* in it, from the beginning to the end: without which (together with a Lord *Archon*) I thought I had sufficiently demonstrated, not only in my writings but publique exercises in t'at Coffee-house, that there is no possible foundation of a Free

Common-

Commonwealth. To the first and second of these (that is the Ballance and the *Agrarian*) you made no objection, and therefore I should not need to make any answer. But for the third (I mean *Rotation*) which you implicitly reject in your designe to perpetuate the present Members, I shall only adde this to what I have already said and written on that subject, That a Common-wealth is like a great Top, that must be kept up by being whipt round, and held in perpetuall circulation; for if you discontinue the *Rotation*, and suffer the Senate to settle, and stand still, down it falls immediatly. And if you had studied this poynt as carefully as I have done, you could not but know, there is no such way under Heaven of disposing the Vicissitudes of Command and Obedience, and of distributing equall Right and Liberty among all men, as this of Wheeling, by which (as *Chauser* writes) a single Fart hath been equally divided among a whole Covent of Friers, and every one hath had his just share of the favour. I told then, I could not but be sorry to find so learned a man so ignorant in the nature of Government, as to make disproportionate Parallels of Councills as you do, where you compare the Senate of *Rome* with the Grand Councell of *Venice*, between which there is no Analogy at all: for the Senate of *Rome* was never the supream Power of the People, as the Grand Councill of *Venice* is, but meerly a Councill of State. But I wondred most of all at what politique Crack in any mans Scull the imagination could enter of securing Libery under an Oligarchy, Seized of the Government for tearm of life, which was never yet seen in the world. The Metropolitan of all Common wealthes the *Roman* did but once adventure to trust its whole Power and Authority in the hands of one Councill; and that but for two yeares, and yet they had like to have lost their Liberty for ever; whereas they had frequently in all ages left it wholy in the power of a single Person, and found it so far from danger or inconvenience, that the only Refuge they had in their greatest extremity was, to create a Dictator. But I could not but laugh (as they all had done) at the pleasantnesse of your fancy who suppose our noble Patriots, when they are in-

—vested

vested for tearm of life, will serve their Country at their own charge: This (I said) was very improbable, unlesse you meant as they do, that all we have is their own, and that to prey and devour is to serve, in which they have appeared so able and industrious, as if they had been made to no other purpose, but, like *Lobsters*, were all Clawes and Belly. For though many laugh at me for accounting 300000l. in wooden ware toward the erecting of a Free-State (in my *Oceana*) but a trifle to the whole Nation,) because I am most certain that these little Pills the Ballots are the only Physick that can keep the Body Politique soluble, and not suffer the humors to settle) I'le undertake that if the present Members had but a lease of the Government during life (notwithstanding whatsoever impeachment of Waste) they would raise more out of it to themselves in one year, then that amounts to; beside the charge we must be at in maintaining of gaurds to keep the boys of them, and before halfe the term be expired, they would have it untenantable. To conclude, I told them, you had made good your title in a contrary sence; For you have really proposed the most ready and easie way to establish downright slavery upon the Nation that can possibly be contrived, which will clearly appear to any Man that doe's but understand this plain Truth, That wheresoever the Power of Proposing and Debating, together with the Power of Ratifying, and Enacting Lawes, is entrusted in the hands of any one Person, or any one Councill (as you would have it) That Government is inevitable Arbitrary and Tyrannicall, because they may make whatsoever they please lawfull or unlawfull. And that Tyranny hath the advantage of all other that hath Law and Liberty among the Instruments of Servitude.

J. H.

NO Blinde Guides,

In ANSWER

To a seditious Pamphlet of
J. MILTON's,

INTITULED

Brief Notes upon a late Sermon Titl'd, the fear of God and the King; Preach'd, and since Publish'd, By Matthew Griffith, D.D. *And Chaplain to the late* KING, *&c.*

Addressed to the Author.

If the Blinde lead the Blinde, Both shall fall into the Ditch.

LONDON,

Printed for *Henry Broome* April 20. 1660.

NO Blinde Guides, &c.

Mr. Milton,

Although in your *Life,* and *Doctrine,* you have *Resolved one* great *Question*; by *evidencing* that *Devils may indue Humane shapes*; and proving your *self,* even to your own *Wife,* an *Incubus*: you have yet *Started Another*; and that is, whether *you* are not of *That* Regiment, *which carried the Herd of Swine headlong into the Sea: and moved the People to beseech Jesus to depart out of their coasts.* (*This* may be very well imagined, from your suitable practises *Here*) Is it possible to read your *Proposals of the benefits of a Free-State,* without Reflecting upon your Tutours —— *All this will I give thee, if thou wilt fall down, and worship me?* Come, come Sir, lay the Devil aside; do not proceed with so much *malice,* and against *Knowledge*: —— Act like a *Man*; —— that a good Christian may not be affraid to pray for you.

Was it not *You*, that scribled a Justification of the *Murther* of the *King,* against *Salmasius*: and made it *good* too, Thus? *That murther was an Action meritorious, compared with your superiour wickedness.* 'Tis *There,* (as I remember) that you *Common place* your self into *Set ferms* of *Rayling,* two Pages thick: and lest, your Infamy should not extend it self enough, within the Course and Usage of your *Mother tongue,* the *Thing* is Dress'd up in a *Travailing*

ling Garb, and *Language*: to blast the English Nation to the Universe; and to give every man a Horrour for *Mankind*, when he Considers, *You are of the Race*. In This, you are above all *Others*; but in your ICONOCLASTES, you exceed your *self*.

There, not content to see that Sacred Head divided from the *Body*; your piercing Malice enters into the private Agonies of his struggling *Soul*; with a Blasphemous Insolence, invading the Prerogative of God himself :.(Omniscience) and by Deductions most *Unchristian*, and *Illogical*, aspersing his *Last Pieties*, (the almost certain *Inspirations* of the *Holy Spirit*) with *Juggle*, and *Prevarication*. Nor are the *Words* ill fitted to the *Matter*. The Bold *Design* being suited with a conform *Irreverence* of *Language*. (but I do not love to Rake long in a Puddle.)

To take a view in particular of all your Factious Labours, would cost more time, than I am willing to afford them. Wherefore I shall stride over all the *rest*, and pass directly to your *Brief Notes upon a Late* SERMON, Titl'd,

The Fear of God and the King.

Preach'd, and since Publish'd by MATTHEW GRIFFITH D. D. *and Chaplain to the late* KING, &c.

ANy man that can but *Read* your *Title*, may *understand* your *Drift* & that you Charge the *Royal Interest*, & *Party* thorough the *Doctour*'s sides. I am not *bold* enough to be his *Champion*, in all particulars; nor yet so *Rude*, as to take an Office most properly to him Belonging, out of his Hand: Let him acquit *himself*, in what concerns the *Divine*; and I'll adventure upon the most material parts of the *Rest*. (but with this Profession, that I have no design in exposing *your* Mistakes, saving to hinder them from becoming the *Peoples*.)

Your

Your *Entrance* is a little *Peremptory*, and *Magisterial*, methinks (but that shall be allowed you) 'please you, wee'll see how *Pertinent* it is, and *Rational*.

I Affirmd in the Preface of a late discourse, Entitl'd, *The ready way to establish a free Commonwealth, and the dangers of readmitting Kingship in this Nation*, that *the humor of returning to our old bondage, was instilld of late by some deceivers*; and to make good, that what I then affirmd, was not without just ground, one of those deceivers I present here to the people; and if I prove him not such, I refuse not to be so accounted in his stead.

TO the *First*: give me leave to mind you, that you make an *Observation* of things *Past*, amount to a *foretelling* of what's to come. This *Sermon* was not Preach'd, when *that Humor* you mention, was *Instill'd*. Next; You'll as hardly satisfie the *people*, that you your self, are *no Deceiver*, as prove the *Doctor* one of those you *meant*. And thus I'll Instance; KINGSHIP, is *your old Bondage*; RUMPSHIP, *ours*: (Forgive the Term) *You* were *Then*, Past the *One*: we are now (God be thanked) past the *Other*: and should be as loth to Return, as *You*. Yet you are Tampering to *delude* the *People*, and to withdraw them from a *Peaceable*, and *Rational expectancy* of *good*, into a *mutinous*, and *hopeless attempt* of *mischief*.

By *your own Rule* now, who are the *Deceivers* : *We*, that will *not Return to our old Bondage*; or *you*, that would *perswade* us to't ?

Your next Paragraph talks of *Purgatives, Myrrhe, Aloes*, &c. It may be an Apothecaries Bill, for ought I know, and I have no skill in Physique.

As little shall I concern my self in your unmannerly descant upon the *Epistle*, which is the Business of your *Second* Page. The *Third*, conteins your *Gloss* upon the *Text*, and that I shall examine.

The Text.

PROV. 24. 21. *My son, fear God and the King, and meddle not with them that be seditious, or desirous of change*, &c.

Letting

Letting pass matters not in controversie, I come to the main drift of your Sermon, *the King*; which word here is either to signifie any supreme Magistrate, or else your latter object of fear is not universal, belongs not at all to many parts of Christendom, that have no King; and in particular, not to us. That we have no King since the putting down of Kingship in this Commonwealth, is manifest by this last Parlament, who to the time of thir dissolving not only made no address at all to any King, but summond this next to come by the Writ formerly appointed of a free Commonwealth, without restitution or the least mention of any Kingly right or power; which could not be, if there were at present any King of *England*. The main part therefore of your Sermon, if it mean a King in the usual sense, is either impertinent and absurd, exhorting your auditory to fear that which is not; or if King here be, as it is, understood for any supreme Magistrate, by your own exhortation they are in the first place not to *meddle* with you, as being your self most of all the *seditious* meant here, and the *desirous of change*, in stirring them up to *fear* a *King*, whom the present Government takes no notice of.

NOt to contend about the *Large*, or *Limited* Sense of the word KING: since 'tis agreed upon, at all hands, to signify *Supreme Authority*; and, where a *Single Person governs*, to denote the *Monarch*. The issue rests upon this Point: *Is* there, or *is there not* at present, any King of *England*? You say, *No*; I'm of another mind: Compare our Reasons.

You Argue; *First, the Putting down of Kingship*; and *then*, —— the Tacit *confirmation* of that *Act*, by the last *Session*: who *without any Address to any King, or Restitution of any Kingly Right, summoned the next to come by the Writ formerly Appointed of a Free Commonwealth*.

To your Assumption, that *Kingship was put down*; I cannot subscribe, till I am better satisfied, *by what Authority*: for no *Form of Government can be altered, but by consent of all the Parties to it*. In short, the late *King* was *Destroy'd*, *Kingship Abolish'd*, the *House of Lords Disauthoris'd*, and at least 7. parts of 8. of the *Commons Members secluded* —— *by the same Power*.

Come to your *Inference* now; *That*, halts of all four, *There was*

was no King, because they did not mention him: you are a little bold methinks, to lay your *Brat* at the *Parliament Door*: and Father your opinions upon *them*, that in the case, would not declare their *own*.

Reasons of *State*, of *Honour*, and *Convenience*, might very fairly move them to suspend. Suppose they thought it *Prudence* to refer all to the next Convention, without so much as a Debate; whether a *King* or *No*: and upon this point of extreme necessity (the Nation running headlong, into another War without the Interpose of a new Representative) rather dispence with something of Informality in the Writs, than otherwise to hazzard the main Issue of the Publique weal. If all this be not yet enough, I hope the re-minding the *Nation* of the COVENANT; and their *own* refusal of the Oath of ABJURATION, will content you.

Your 4th Page, runs away in some mistakes concerning *Gideon*; — (a Person, *Call'd* and set apart by God himself; guided by Divine *Inspirations*; and Acting without Partnership, the work he was employ'd upon)

A little further, you deny the King, *the Power of life and death*; urging [*Page 4*.] *that tis against the declared Judgements of our Parliaments, nay of our Laws*; which *reserve to themselves only the power of life and death, &c.*

I'LL not deny, but a Parliament is above the King: (That is : The King is greater in Conjunction with his two *Houses*, than by *Himself*) but still this weakens not the force of my assertion; which is; that Kings must necessarily have that power: *without it*, they're no Kings (and 'tis the same thing in all Governments whatsoever, 'tis one of the Prerogatives Inseparable from supreme Authority) But since you urge *the Declar'd Judgements of our Parliaments*, in favour of your opinion, I should be glad to see them.

Now for the Laws; 'tis true; they Pronounce Life, or Death; but the King's left at Liberty to Take, or to Remit the forfeiture, at pleasure. Enough is said of this.

If

If I were bent to *Cavil*; your 5th. Page would afford matter abundantly, where you extravagate upon the word *Anointed*: but That is more Peculiarly the *Doctor's* Businesse, and I refer you to him. So are your slips, [*Page 6.*] but *Those*, I cannot passe without a marque: For *There*, you shew your *Teeth*. (I might have said, your *Eares* to boot)

But how will you confirm one wrested Scripture with another: 1 *Sam.* 8, 7. *They have not rejected thee, but m:* : grosly misapplying these words, which were not spoken to any who had *resisted or rejected* a King, but to them who much against the will of God had sought a King, and rejected a Commonwealth, wherein they might have liv'd happily under the Reign of God only, their King. Let the words interpret themselves: *v.6,7. But the thing displeased Samuel, when they said, give us a King to judge us. And Samuel prayed unto the Lord. And the Lord said unto Samuel, harken unto the voice of the people in all that they say unto thee ; for they have not rejected thee, but they have rejected me, that I should not reign over them* Hence you conclude, *so indissoluble is the Conjunction of God and the King*. O notorious abuse of Scripture! when as you should have concluded, So unwilling was God to give them a King, So wide was the disjunction of God from a King.

Mr. *Milton*, when your hand was *In*, another verse methinks should not have over-charg'd you : and 'tis the very next too. *As they have ever done (*sayes God to Samuel *) since I brought them out of Egypt, even unto this Day, (and have forsaken me, and served other Gods) even so doe they unto thee.* This, would have given you light to read the *Rest* by ; and (possible) have done *you* the *same* service, which you pretend to doe the *Doctour*. (But none so Blind as they that will not see) especially, had you but taken in likewise the verse next Antecedent to your Quotation, which speaks the *motive* to their such *Desires*; as the other does fairly imply the *Reason* of Gods *Disapproval* of them, 'twas a hard misse, and an industrious one (I fear) to scape the 5, and 8, verses, without the which, the 6 and 7, (which you make use of) have no intelligible Coherence. *Make us a King*, (say they) *to Judge us like the* NATIONS *v.* 5. and after That, *v.* 8. God charges them with inclinations to *Idolatry*; so that the inference is open; They had a hankering after the *Gods* of the Nations, as well as the *Kingship*; and *That* moved the All-seeing wisdome, (that knew their hearts) to tell *Samuel*, saying, *they have not Rejected Thee, but Mee*: a Speech applyable to their *Disobedience*, rather, than to their *Proposition: God* is rejected, in the rejection of his *Ministers.* —— This is a stubborn Text Sir, and will not mould as you would have it.

Had not they against the will of God, sought a KING, *and rejected a Common-wealth*, you tell us, *that they might have liv'd* HAPPILY *under the reign of God onely their King*. (Indeed you have the best intelligence) —— I beseech you how doe you know this? whom God *loves*, he *chastens*: and *persecution*, in *this* world, is the Portion of the Saints. It's true; their obedience to God *here*, would certainly have rendred them Happy *hereafter*; but *this* is not the Happinesse you drive at. Look back now upon the 3. *verse* of the same Chapter; and there you'll find some Reason to apprehend the contrary. For *Samuel* being Old, and having made his sonnes *Judges* over *Israel*; the Text sayes, that *his sonnes walked not in his wayes, but turn'd aside after Lucre, and took Rewards, and perverted Judgement, &c.* now, if from *hence*, you can perswade your self into a good opinion of a Popular Government, I cannot blame your stickling for the *Rump*; But that this *mis-rule* should please *God*, your modesty I hope will not pretend to offer. You'll say however, that the *Popular form* did; I'll not contend about it; Did not the *Regall* too, as much in *David*; a *King* of God's particular *choice*, and a *man* after his Own Heart? So that you gain little by the odds of a *Free-state* in ballance against *Monarchy*. In one word: The *Saviour* of the *world* was a KING, and a *King* of *Jewes*.

Grant, or *Denie* at pleasure, I have you in a Net Why would you meddle with a Chapter, that you were sure would burn your fingers? There's no Relief you see, against Authority.

B   'Tis

'Tis well you stopp'd short of that *Lex Regni* which *Samuel* opens to the People; (beginning at the 11. *verse* of the same *Chapter*;) from whence, lyes *no* Appeal. Truly, your insincerity in this Section, is more exposed, than I could wish it.

Under the Reign of God onely their King you say. This expression, doubtfully implies you a Millenary Doe you then, really expect to *see* Christ, Reigning upon Earth, even with *those very eyes* you *Lost* (as 'tis reported) *with staring too long, and too sawcily upon the Portraiture of his Vicegerent, to breake the* Image, as your Impudence Phrases it? (It is generally indeed believed, you never wept them out for this *Losse*.)

In my Passage from hence, to your *Frog-morall* : I cannot but remember you that there was a *Plague* of Frogs as well as a *Fable*. Frogs that crept into the *Kings Chambers, and into the Houses of his Servants, &c.* ──── Now to your *Fable*.

Nor are you happier in the relating or the moralizing your Fable. The *frogs* (being once a free Nation saith the Fable) *petitioned Jupiter for a King* : *he tumbl'd amongst them a log. They found it insensible* : *they petioned then for a King that should be active* : *he sent them a Crane* (a Stork saith the fable) *which straight fell to pecking them up*. This you apply to the reproof of them who desire change : whereas indeed the true moral shews rather the folly of those, who being free seek a King; which for the most part either as a log lies heavie on his Subjects, without doing ought worthie of his dignitie and the charge to maintain him, or as a Stork is ever pecking them up and devouring them.

Mr. *Milton*, (to agree with you as far as possible) if *One Log* be so *Intollerable*, for the *Burthen*; or *One Stork*, for the *Cruelty*, and *Greedinesse* what do you think of 40. *Storks*, and every *Stork* a Log in his belly?

What do you think of a Grand, *Arbitrary* & Perpetual Counsel; and no more Parliaments? (according to your Gratious Proposition, [*Page* 8.] of your *Free and easie way*, &c.) And, in regard that *in a free Commonwealth*, they who are greatest, are Perpetual

Servants

Servants, and Drudges to the publique, at their own cost and Charges, neglect their own Affairs; yet are not Elevated above their Brethren, Live soberly in their Families, wa k the Streets as other men; may be spoken to freely, familiarly, friendly, without Adoration, [*Page* 4.] What do you think of the Rump Parliaments Perpetuating it self, *under the name of That grand Counsel ?* [*Page* 10.] *the Government being in so many* Faithfull, *and* Experienced *hands, next under God, so Able; especially Filling up their number, as they intend, and abundantly sufficient so happily to govern us:* [P. 11, &c.] Alas, these very Gentlemen are *Pigeons,* not a *Stork* among them, do not deceive your self Sir; you're one of those they have Fed: of the same *Plume,* and *Kind,* ask but the honest party of the Nation, and they shall tell you, that *Tom. Scot,* and his *Associate Patriots,* can *Peck,* as well as *Bill.*

Now we have *Play'd,* let's to our *Book* again, and be a little *Earnest.*

You charge the Doctor, in your 8. *Page,* for saying,

That by our Fundamental Laws, the King is the highest power, Page 40. If we must hear mooting and Law-lectures from the Pulpit, what shame is it for a Dr. of Divinitie, not first to consider, that no law can t *fundamental,* but that which is grounded on the light of nature or right reason, commonly call'd *moral Law*: which no form of Government was ever counted; but arbitrarie, and at all times in the choice of every free people, or their representers. This choice of Government is so essential to their freedom, that longer then they have it, they are not free. In this Land not only the late *K*ing and his posteritie, but Kingship it self hath been abrogated by a law; which involves with as good reason the posterity of a *K*ing forfeited to the people, as that Law heretofore of Treason against the King, attainted the Children with the Father.

M Ethinks you might have spar'd your Criticism upon the word *Fundamental,* being a *Term,* that *Usage* hath authorized; were nothing more in't: and soberly, I do not find but it may stand a nicer Test, than perhaps you'll impose upon it.

No Law (you say) *can be Fundamental but that which is grounded in the Light of Nature, or right reason,* — *which no* FORM *of Government was ever counted, &c.* — So that tho' GOVERN-MENT it *self* directs to *Fundamentals*: yet the *Specification* of it, into such or such a FORM, does not. You are Queint, Sir: shew me *Government* without a *Form*, further than in *Notion*; and only *Notional* must be the *Laws* too that *support* it. *Obedience* to *Superiors*, is a Moral *Fundamental*: and where, to *One*, or *More*, vested with *unconditionate Dominion*, (I mean, as to the Power of Revocation) we once Contract a *Duty*; as the *Person*, and *Authority* are *Inseverable*, so is the *Obligation Indispensable*, which by a *Fundamentall Law* is become due; as well to the *King himself*, as unto *Kingship*. I shall be tedious, if I unty all your knots.

The Choice you say is Arbitrary; so 'tis in *Mariage*, that is, till we have pass'd away our *Freedom*. (but you are for *Divorce*, I see, as well of *Governours*, as *Wives*) Your next now is a shrewd one, (is it your *own* I pray'e?) *This choice of Government* (you tell us) *is so essential to the Peoples Freedoms, that longer then they have it, they're not free.* In truth, you're in the Right. Is any *People Free*, where there is any Government? This is somewhat worse, than the Doctors FUNDAMENTALL. FREEDOME and GOVERNMENT (in *Politiques*) *Contra-Distinguish* one another. (have a care of this argument; for if the People are *Free* to *Chuse*, they'll never Chuse any of your Friends again)

But if the *King*, his *Posterity*; nay, and *Kingship it self, have been abrogated by a Law*; That's another matter.

By what *Law* I beseech you? By the Law of a little *Faction*, that dares not put their heads upon a Tryal by the Establish'd Law of the Land? (your next shift is wretched)

If that no Law must be held good, but what passes in FULL *Parliament, then surely, in exactnesse of Legality no Member must be missing, &c.* ——

I Answer you, that it is not the *Actual sitting of All*, but the *Liberty of All to Sit*: not the *Fullnesse* of the *House*, but the *Freedom*

dom of the *Members*. It is one thing; a Law that's made in the *Absence* of many of the Members, that might have been Present, if they would; (and are possibly fined for *non-attendance*) and another thing; the Vote of a *tenth Part* of That Body, which it *self entire*, is but the *third Part* of the *Legislative Power*: This *Remnant* too by force of *Armes* violently secluding the *Rest*.

But you have no Conscience with you. *Kingship Abolished* will not do your work it seems.

You suppose it never was establish'd by any certain Law in this Land, nor possibly could be: for how could our forefathers bind us to any certain form of Government, more then we can bind our posteritie? If a people be put to war with their King for his misgovernment, and overcome him, the power is then undoubtedly in their own hands how they will be govern'd. The war was granted *just* by the King himself at the beginning of his last Treatie; and still maintained to be so by this last Parliament, as appears by the qualifications prescrib'd to the Members of this next ensuing, That none shall be elected, who have born arms against the Parliament since 1641 If the war were *just*, the Conquest was also just by the Law of Nations And he who was the chief enemie, in all right ceased to be the King, especially after captivitie, by the deciding verdit of war; and royaltie with all her Laws and pretentions, yet remains in the victors power, together with the choice of our future Government.

IF *Kingship* was never established, what was I beseech you? had we *no Government*?

Nor *could it be*, you say: Alas then for *your ready, and easie way to* ESTABLISH a FREE COMMONWEALTH, what will become then of YOUR STANDING COUNCIL? *If no certain form of Government can bind our posterity* (as you affirm) Then is it free at any time for the People to *Assemble*, and *Tumult*, under the colour of a new *Choyce*.

Your *next* for altering the *Form* of *Government* upon a Quarrel rell onely in point of *male-administration* : I think that cleers it felf.

You fay that *the Warre was granted juft by the King himfelf, &c.* and (a while after) *if the War were juft, fo was the Conqueft alfo, by the Laws of Nations*; —— *and that the victors, are free to chufe, a Future Government.*

What would you give that I'd difpute the *Originall* of the *Quarrell* with you ? Come, we'il not differ about the *Kings Concefsions* : Take it for granted, that the *Warre* was *juft* : That is, *The Warre was Juft to fuch intents*, and *with fuch limits, as were the evident, and declar'd fcope, and Bounds of it*. The *Reafons*, and the *Tendency* thereof, me-thinks they fhould know beft that *Levied*, and were *Parties* in it, and for *That*, take but one paffage of above a Hundred, to the fame purpofe.

"We are (fay they) fo far from altering the Fundamentall Con-"ftitution, and Government of this Kingdom, by King, Lords, and "Commons (*that we have onely defired, that with the confent of the* "*King, fuch Powers may be fettled in the Two Houfes, &c.* —— A Declaration bears date *Ap.* 17. 1646. and is entitled —— A Declaration of their true intentions, concerning the Antient Government of the Nation, *&c.*

Now if the *Profpect* of the *War* was *bounded*; in *Reafon*, and in *Honour*, the Conqueft ought to be fo likewife. Efpecially, where onely, *extreme necefsity* was pleaded to make it appear *warrantable*; and where the *difpute* was Lawfull Liberty, and Safety; not Dominion.

Again; 'twas not againft the *King*, the *warre* was *raifed*, therefore the *Conqueft* cannot in Reafon Reach him. His Honour, Safety and Support, the *two Houfes Vowed* and *Covenanted to maintain*.

Further; thofe *Things* that you call *Victors*, may, by the fame Pretence, claim to a Conqueft over the *Lords*, and their *Fellow-Members*, whom they Forcibly caft out; as well as over the *King*, and his *Pretenfions*.

Laftly;

Lastly; if *Victory* gives *Title*, your *Masters* are gone too.

You fall now into a vein of *weighing Governments*: (your old Trade; and the very *Coffee-Boyes* have got the knack on't almost as well as you.) As you order the Scales, the *Common-wealth* goes *Down* most usually, but now your great Civility gives *Us* the Better on't. FREE-COMMMON-WEALTHS (as you will have it) *have been ever counted fittest, for* CIVILL, VIRTUOUS, *and Industrious* Nations, *&c.* believe *me* then, That Form's not Fit for *you*, and your *Adherents*.

MONARCHY, *Fittest*(as you hold it forth) *to curb* DEGENERATE, CORRUPT, IDLE, PROUD, LUXURIOUS *People*; *This*, does your businesse then.

Upon necessity yet at last, I find, a *Single Person* you'l vouchsafe to entertain; provided, *such a one as ha's best aided the People*, and *best merited against Tyranny.* (That's your *Caution*) this must be one of those that turn'd the *Rump* out: for never was a more meritorious Service to the Nation.

Your next Page is a very Angry one. You'll have the *Parliament Ride the King*, you say, as well as *Bridle* him; and you'il perswade the People that there's *Law* for't too. The Question's triviall; to cut it short: *Rumps* are no Parliaments. But if they be so Sacred, as you argue them; how bold are you, that durst propose the finall *Abrogation*, and *extinction* of them! (As in your *Ready way* you have, *in* Terminis, so often done.)

In the next place; If as you idlely seem to imagine, all our *Kings* are created *by Parliament, or Conquest.* What becomes of that *Maxime, Rex non moritur?* and why doe you swear Allegeance to *Him* and his *Heirs* positively, if there be any *uncertainty* of his being admitted to the Crown? [*In short, his* Birth *entitles him to the Soveraignty.*] I doe not delight my self in these contests, but I am willing to lay open your little Tricks to the People.

You urge next his *Coronation-Oath*, but Deceitfully, you make him by his Oath, accomptable to Act, (in Effect) according to
the

the *Judgement* of the *People*, but he swears to Govern according to his *own* (neither does this suppose him at Liberty to Rule according to his *Will.*)

Once more; You say, That the *Kings* principall *Oath* was to maintein those *Laws* which the *People* SHOULD chuse. (*Consuetudines quas Vulgus Elegerit*) Reconcile *Consuetudines* (referring necessarily to what is *Past*) to *Elegerit*, in the Future *Tense*, and I have done.

FINIS.

NOTES

on the foregoing pamphlets

NOTES ON *A MODEST CONFUTATION*

The story of the Smectymnuan controversy has been told many times, but a reminder in the form of a bibliographical and chronological table may be welcomed. Following are the most important dates and facts, with special reference to Milton:

1639	Aug.	(?)	Milton returns from his Italian journey.
1640	Feb.	10	Joseph Hall's *Episcopacie by Divine Right* (1640) registered for publication.
	Nov.	3	Beginning of the Long Parliament.
1641	Jan.	13	Hall's *An Humble Remonstrance to the High Court of Parliament, by A dutifull Sonne of the Church* (1640) registered for publication; published Jan. 26-29.
	Feb.	(?)	[Robert Blair?], *An Anti-Remonstrance to the late Humble Remonstrance* (1641) published.
	Mar.	1	Archbishop Laud imprisoned in the Tower.
	Mar.	20	Smectymnuus, *An Answer to a Book Entituled, An Humble Remonstrance* (1641) registered for publication.
	Apr.	12	Hall's *A Defence of the Humble Remonstrance, Against the frivolous and false exceptions of Smectymnuus* (1641) registered for publication, at least two editions published.
	....		Abraham Scultetus, *The Determination of the Question, Concerning the Divine Right of Episcopacy* (1641): actually a reprint of the last dozen pages of Hall's *Defence* (see above), plus a reissue of *The Judgment of the Learned Divine, D. Abrahamus Scultetus.*
	May	12	Petitions of the two Universities in favor of Deans and Chapters.
	May		Milton's *Of Reformation* (1641) published anonymously, probably between May 12 and May 31.
	May	21	James Ussher's *The Iudgement of Doctor Rainoldes touching the Originall of Episcopacy* (1641) registered for publication.

1641	June		"Peloni Almoni," *A Compendious Discourse, Proving Episcopacy to be of Apostolicall, and Consequently of Divine Institution* (1641); preface dated May 31.
	....		Milton's *Of Prelatical Episcopacy* (1641).
	June	26	Smectymnuus, *A Vindication of the Answer to the Humble Remonstrance* (1641) registered for publication.
	July	28	Hall's *A Short Answer to the Tedious Vindication of Smectymnuus* (1641) registered for publication.
	....		Milton's *Animadversions upon The Remonstrants Defence against Smectymnuus* (1641) published.
	Sep.	9	Parliament in recess until Oct. 20.
			Certain Briefe Treatises, Written by Diverse Learned Men, concerning the ancient and Moderne government of the Church (Oxford, 1641).
	Dec.	9	John Milton aged thirty-three.
	Dec.	30	The bishops arrested and imprisoned.
1642	....		Milton's *Reason of Church Government* (1641) published.
	Feb.	(?)	H[enry] P[eacham], *A Paradox, In The Praise of a Dunce, To Smectymnuus* (1642).
	....		*A Modest Confutation of A Slanderous and Scurrilous Libell, Entituled, Animadversions upon the Remonstrants Defense against Smectymnuus* (1642).
	....		Milton's *An Apology Against a Pamphlet call'd A Modest Confutation* (1642).
	June	(?)	Milton marries Mary Powell.
1646	Mar.	10	John Saltmarsh's *Groanes for Liberty presented from the Presbyterian ... Brethren ... in some Treatises called Smectymnuus* (1646) published; licensed Feb. 27.
1651	Oct.	21	Hamon L'Estrange's *Smectymnuo-Mastix: or, Short Animadversions Upon Smectymnuus Their Answer, and Vindication of that Answer, to The Humble Remonstrance* (1651) published.

1652	Apr.	15	Rights in Hall's *Episcopacy by Divine Right, Humble Remonstrance, Defence of Humble Remonstrance,* and *Short Answer to Smectymnuus* transferred from Nathaniel Butter to John Grismond.
1654	Feb.	1	*Jus Divinum Ministerii Evangelici, or the Divine Right of the Gospel-Ministry* (1654) registered; published on or before Feb. 7 by the Provincial Assembly of London.
			Smectymnuus Redivivus. Being An Answer to a Book, entituled, An Humble Remonstrance (1654).
			Milton's *An Apology for Smectymnuus, with the Reason of Church-Government* (no date): a reissue of unsold copies of the 1642 tracts.
			Smectymnuus, *A Vindication of the Answer to the Humble Remonstrance* (no date): a reissue of the 1641 tract.
1660	Aug.	16	*Smectymnuus Redivivus* (1660) registered for publication.

The strange word, SMECTYMNUUS, was coined from the initials of five Puritan divines who in 1641 joined forces against Episcopacy: Stephen Marshall, Edmund Calamy, Thomas Young, Matthew Newcomen, and William [double-U] Spurstow. Young, who had been Milton's tutor, was the oldest of the five and, by a contemporary account, the ring-leader. He was no doubt chiefly responsible for the poet's connection with the group. On the other hand, Milton may very well have been acquainted with several of these men before 1641. Newcomen, who was a year or so younger than he, had been a student at St. John's College, Cambridge (1626-1633), while Milton had been a student at Christ's. Newcomen had since married the sister of Calamy's first wife. Spurstow, only a few years older than Milton, had been a student (1623-1630) and then a fellow (1630-1637) at Emmanuel College, Cambridge. Marshall and Calamy[1] were also Cambridge men, but their residence at the University was before

---

[1] The parish register of St. Thomas the Apostle, London (Harleian Society, vol. VI, 1881), contains the baptismal and burial dates of Calamy's family for a considerable period. Edmund Calamy himself was baptised February 24, 1600.

Milton's time. Three of the Smectymnuans—Marshall, Calamy, and Newcomen—had the further connection of having lived and preached in Essex at some period of their lives (and Milton, we might recall, had relatives living in Essex). All five of them were nominated to the Westminster Assembly on the original summons of June 12, 1643. To complete their strange, eventful history: Marshall and Young both died in the month of November, 1655; Calamy and Spurstow both died in the year 1666. Newcomen, the youngest, died at Leyden in 1669.

With his *Animadversions* of mid-summer 1641, Milton aligned himself directly with the Smectymnuans in a satiric attack on Bishop Hall's *Defence of the Humble Remonstrance*. His pamphlet quoted verbatim many of Hall's statements and heaped ridicule on them. It was his first attempt at flippancy and wholesale sarcasm, and, though somewhat heavy-handed, it was effective. Hall, who had announced his intention of abandoning the controversy (in his *Short Answer*, probably published about the same time that Milton's *Animadversions* appeared), must have been annoyed at this unexpected and unusual attack. Milton's tract, incidentally, survives only in its author's expurgated version, about 1700 words having been deleted after the manuscript was set up in type. The missing portion was devoted to sections VI-XII of Hall's *Defence*, pages 54-91, but any reconstruction of the contents would be pure conjecture.

A Modest Confutation of Milton's *Animadversions* appeared in 1642, probably after March 25.[2] It was not registered, and its imprint read, simply: "Printed in the yeer M.DC.XLII." The anonymous author gives few clues to his identity. He calls himself a "young Scholar," one "free, as you, or any true subject may or need be," whose reading, modestly, "is confest small." Milton was manifestly puzzled about the authorship of this attack. In his rebuttal, *An Apology*, he expressed his "suspicion that in setting forth this pamplet the Remonstrant [Bishop Hall] was not unconsulted with"; again, "this confutation was not made without some assistance or

---

[2] Most printers and booksellers still observed the Old Style of dating. Hall's *Humble Remonstrance*, for example, was dated 1640 although it appeared late in January 1640/41. All of Hall's publishing in this period was by Nathaniel Butter, who may have handled the *Modest Confutation*.

advice of the Remonstrant"; but throughout the *Apology* he usually distinguished between his opponent and "his owne friend," the Bishop. When Milton made a vigorous assault on Hall's satires, he said: "let the Remonstrant thank the folly of this confuter, who could not let a private word passe, but he must make all this blaze of it." In one passage in his *Apology*, however, Milton came near to offering a specific identification: "if they be not one person, or as I am told, Father and Son." This statement makes us notice a later charge: "How well dost thou now appeare to be a Chip of the old block"! But there is nothing more to help.

On this, and apparently only this evidence, Masson states positively that the writer was mainly Bishop Hall, but that parts may have been written by his son, Robert Hall. Why *this* son in preference to the others, it is a little difficult to see. And why the pamphlet should be laid mainly at the door of a Bishop who was in prison, who had washed his hands of the controversy, and whom Milton himself does not chiefly blame, it is still harder to understand. Milton had merely *heard* that it was a father-son collaboration. He would certainly have preferred to address himself to the father; and if he had placed much credence in the gossip, he would probably have ignored the "lozel Bachelour of Art," the "matriculated confutant," whom he chooses to rebuke, and would have devoted his attention to the more influential enemy. In the light of the few facts which we possess, we must conclude that, although the author may have been one of Hall's sons, his identity remains a secret.

On the other hand, Milton is probably correct in his personal "suspicion" that Hall assisted or advised in the composition. Milton was a keen judge of style; he points out various stylistic mannerisms of the Remonstrant, and even absolves him of complicity in one particular section. Moreover, it would be only natural for Hall to pass judgment on this defence of himself, just as Milton later corrected his own nephew's reply to an anonymous attack on the *Defensio Prima*. There is one curious passage in the *Modest Confutation* where, perhaps, Hall's hand betrays itself. Throughout the Smectymnuan controversy runs a quaint quarrel over the misuse of a word: in the first Smectymnuan tract there was a reference to the

Areopagi, which, as Hall was quick to point out, was "the name of the place, not of the men." Smectymnuus tried to defend its collective scholarship; Milton came to their aid in his *Animadversions;* but Hall merely laughed and repeated his correction. In the *Modest Confutation* the subject was revived, and Milton's explanations were criticized as obsolete. Said the confuter (page 13): "I ask in the sixteenth of King *Charls,* and you answer in the first of King *John.*" Now the sixteenth year of King Charles' reign ended March 26, 1641. Bishop Hall may have been writing his *Defence of the Humble Remonstrance* (where the blunder is first exposed) "in the sixteenth of King *Charls,*" but the present confuter is writing in a later year. The point is a small one, but it may have its significance.

The author of *A Modest Confutation* knows little or nothing about Milton, although Milton was "credibly inform'd he did inquire." After his scurrilously humorous attempt to "fetch his character from some scattered passages in his own writings," the confutant shows that he is unaware of Milton's two earlier pamphlets and the signed *Reason of Church Government,* and that he thinks he is dealing with a "small Clerk" who might be eager for a lectureship. The much-discussed reference to Milton's seeking "a rich Widow" was probably a blind thrust, although it may have been an indirect hit at Stephen Marshall, who had, in fact, married a rich widow. Masson believed that the references to Downam and Seton prove that Milton had been identified as a Cambridge graduate; but Milton had several times mentioned Downam in his *Animadversions,* and Seton is merely an obvious allusion to the remarks on logic on page ten of that pamphlet. "Such carping Poetasters as you, and your now-despised Tribe," exclaims the confuter of Milton, and Masson thought that this showed "he knew of Milton's pretensions to poetry"; but the context makes it plain that the epithet is a hit in the dark. Milton's *Animadversions* had been published anonymously, and the author of *A Modest Confutation* announced in his preface that he had "no further notice of him, than he hath been pleased . . . to give of himself." His "character" of Milton is, therefore, a mixture of pure invention and satiric inference, with some possible aid from rumor. Since Bishop Hall could surely have obtained information about his opponent if he had wished, the ignorance of Milton's personal history and the wild guesses about his character displayed in the *Confutation* are not without significance. Either Milton was not considered important enough to have his personality figure in the controversy, or, as he himself declared, they did inquire but found "small comfort from the intelligence" received.

It would be interesting to know whether the manner of the *Animadversions* was Milton's own idea, or whether it was suggested to him by the Smectymnuans, who were not in a position to attack Bishop Hall with jests. At least two of the Smectymnuans, Spurstow and Newcomen, had been students at Cambridge when Milton delivered his Vacation Exercise speech; and there are some interesting parallels between the style of the *Sixth Prolusion* and the style of *Animadversions*. More to the point: just as Milton had formerly interjected lengthy explanations of his unaccustomed language in the Vacation Exercise, so in his *Apology* of 1642 he defended in detail his flippant rebuttal of Hall. The *Modest Confutation* had accused him of "beastlinesse," of "lewd profanations" and "scurrilous jests"; and this charge, more than the obviously absurd inference of "his character from some scattered passages," prompted him to reply. Let anyone who considers the *Apology* a humorless and unnecessary defence, consider Milton's strict views of decorum in speech and composition. He was gradually evolving a style for controversy, and he needed to rationalize it completely—and publicly. His own conscience was clear, but he really felt that he owed his readers an explanation.

The inferential "character" drawn by the writer of the *Confutation* contained one or two chance remarks that caused Milton some concern. On the basis of page thirteen of the *Animadversions*, he pretended to believe that Milton had "spent his youth, in loytering, bezelling, and harlotting." This was patently absurd, but, to round it off, the confutant concluded: "Thus being grown to an Impostume in the brest of the Vniversity, he was at length vomited out thence into a Suburbe sinke about *London*." By "vomited out" the satirist probably meant nothing more than "graduated," but to Milton, who had actually been punished with rustication, the words were a slap in the face which demanded a rebuttal of some sort. Furthermore, in 1642 he was actually living in a suburb (that is, outside the city walls) of London, and although the neighborhood was quite respectable (in the same precinct lived Sir Thomas Cecil, Alexander Gill, Justinian Povey, and other reputable persons), the confutant appeared to be defaming it specifically.

A glance at *A Modest Confutation* reveals a writer fond of "marginal stuffings" of a learned (not to say pedantic) variety, and Milton several times in his *Apology* ridicules this practice. Oddly enough, Smectymnuus had been more guilty of this "affectation" (if such it is) than Bishop Hall, although Hall, like the author of the *Confutation*, was "not yet content with the wonted room of his margent, but he must cut out large docks and creeks into his text to unlade the foolish frigate of his unseasonable autorities."

The reply to Milton's *Animadversions* is not without significance in the history of the poet's contemporary fame, for, besides giving him his first taste of controversy, it served to accentuate an already sensitive concern for reputation. It suggests, moreover, that although Milton was not personally known to many people and had not yet established himself as a writer, he had developed enough nuisance value to draw a rebuttal. The initials "I.M." were not included in SMECTYMNUUS, and the Remonstrant did not himself answer the animadversions upon his *Defence*, but the force of Milton's style and scholarship had nevertheless made itself felt in one of the more important controversies of the period.

The foregoing text of the *Modest Confutation* reproduces a copy of the first (and only) edition from my own collection. The pamphlet has never before been reprinted.

NOTES ON *AN ANSWER*

Because the bibliography of Milton's *The Doctrine and Discipline of Divorce* has long been in a state of confusion, some attempt to clarify it may prove welcome. The first edition contains neither the author's name nor his initials, and the imprint reads: "LONDON, Printed by *T.P.* and *M.S.* In Goldsmiths Alley. 1643." On the title-page of his own copy Thomason noted: "written by J: Milton", and, in the imprint,

"Aug: 1st". The collation of the book is: 4°: A¹, B-G⁴, H¹; pp. ii+50. Of the two printers, Thomas Paine and Matthew Simmons, and of the circumstances in which the pamphlet was published, I have written in "Milton, Rothwell, and Simmons," *The Library*, XVIII (June 1937), 89-103. The first edition, a rather scarce little book, exhibits no striking bibliographical peculiarities.

For some reason it has been customary to speak of *two* editions of *The Doctrine and Discipline*, and of the second edition as existing in various states. Thus, in the *Milton Tercentenary* Catalogue of books exhibited at Christ's College in 1908, four states were recognized; and the recent *Columbia Milton* (1931) announced a fifth "variant of second edition (now listed for the first time)." Actually, there are *four* editions of *The Doctrine and Discipline*, representing a variety of "states" or issues. Failure to recognize this fact has apparently been due to two causes: first, no one has taken the trouble to look closely at more than a couple of copies of any "state"; and second, the terminology employed has been ambiguous. To a bibliographer the term "edition" means "the whole number of copies of a book printed at any time or times from one setting-up of type"; and the term "issue" means "some special form of the book in which, for the most part, the original printed sheets are used but which differs from the earlier or normal form by . . . some difference in arrangement." Seventeenth century printing practices were such that different copies of any given edition may exhibit a number of minor variants, sometimes of such quantity or nature as to constitute a true separate issue.

The second edition of *The Doctrine & Discipline of Divorce* is a longer book than its predecessor. It contains the author's initials on its title-page, and its imprint reads: "*LONDON*, Imprinted in the yeare 1644." Its collation is: 4°: A-L⁴, M¹; pp. viii+82. Signature G2 is a cancel, with a stub usually visible; and pages 43-44 are misnumbered 45-46 as a result. Some copies may survive with G2 in an uncancelled state, but I have never seen one; such a copy, with pages 43-44 numbered correctly, would be a true "first issue," and *might* contain interesting textual variants. Manuscript corrections occur in many copies on pages v, vi, 15, 38, 65, and 73. There are numerous minor variants, but a few so striking that they almost constitute separate issues. For example, page 33 may be misprinted, running over into the text of page 34. In such copies the catchword is "CHAP." instead of "were" (Bodleian Radcliffe e.40(12) and N. Y. Public Library). In some copies pages 70 and 72 are misnumbered 76 and 70, with minor textual variants in signatures F, G, and H, although such copies may or may not contain the misprinted page 33 mentioned above (for example, Bodleian 4°I.4.Th., Pamph. 63, and 4°F.56.Th., and B.M. 117.i.59, do not).

The third edition of *The Doctrine & Discipline* is a fairly accurate reprinting of the second edition, very similar in appearance although the book has been newly set up in type. It is to be distinguished from another edition of the same year (1645) by its ruled border on the title-page. A close examination of the second and third editions reveals a good many differences. For example, although the 1644 title-page has been carefully imitated, there are some variants: *I.M.* instead of *J.M.*; CANON LAW instead of CANON LAW; MATTH. instead of Matth.; *LONDON,* instead of *LONDON:*; and, of course, 1645 instead of 1644. (Two of these variants are neglected in the Columbia notes.) The text of the address to Parliament is in roman type in the second edition, but in italic in the third. The collation is the same in both editions; but the misnumbering of pages in 1644 resulted in some interesting mispagination in 1645. Thus, page 42 is misnumbered 44 (in 1644 the facing page was 45), page 43 is misnumbered 45 (as in 1644), page 44 is numbered correctly (in 1644 it was misnumbered 46, but the facing page was 45), and pages 46-47 are misnumbered 48-49 (as, indeed, they would be if the other pages of the inner forme were truly 44 and 45). In some copies page 36 is misnumbered 6. The third edition follows some of the manuscript corrections made in the second (see the paragraph above), and, oddly, repeats the list of *errata* (although in the copies which I have examined the last *erratum* has been corrected). Many copies contain an additional *erratum*—an odd misreading of the 1644 text. There are the usual minor variants besides; for example, line 24 on page 37 has either *neibours and* or *neighbors &*; and the single leaf, M1, in some copies seems identical with 1644. The printer of the second and third editions was almost certainly the same person (probably Matthew Simmons): some of the paper used is identical; the same ornamental block to contain the capital on page 1 occurs (only it is turned sideways in 1645); some of the type ornaments recur; and the two editions are remarkably similar in type and general format. Of the eighty-six catchwords, fifty-six are the same in both editions.

The fourth edition, also dated 1645, seems to be the work of another printer, and may have been an unauthorized edition, produced to capitalize on the growing notoriety of Milton's views on divorce. It was almost certainly set up in type from a copy of the third edition. No *errata* are noted, although the relevant misprints of the second edition are repeated, plus the new one of the third edition (see above). It is easily distinguished from the third edition by the absence of a border on the title-page. Like the third edition it follows some of the manuscript corrections made in the second. As in the third edition, pages 42-43 and 46-47 are misnumbered 44-45 and 48-49; but, in addition, pages 73-83 are misnumbered 69-78 consecutively. The collation is the same as that of the second and third editions, but the catchwords follow the third edition more than they follow the second. There are fewer ornaments than in the previous two, and all are new. The paper also seems to be different. In general, the spelling has been noticeably revised.

Between the publication of the second and third editions of *The Doctrine & Discipline*, a reply to Milton's tract appeared. This *Answer* was registered October 31, licensed November 14, and in the hands of Thomason November 19, 1644. Milton's comments on its publication in his *Colasterion* are important and provocative:

When as the *Doctrine of Divorce* had now a whole year bin publisht the second time, with many Arguments added, and the former ones better'd and confirm'd, this idle pamflet comes reeling forth against the first Edition only; as may appear to any by the pages quoted. Which puts me in minde of what by chance I had notice of to this purpos the last Summer, as . . . it was then told mee that *the Doctrin of divorce* was answerd, and the answer half printed against the first Edition; . . . But finding that it lay, what ever was the matter, half a year after unfinisht in the press, and . . . furder when I saw the stuff . . .

I was resolv'd, so soon, as leisure granted mee the recreation, that my man of Law should not altogether loose his soliciting.

The second edition of Milton's pamphlet is usually dated February 2, 1643/4, for this is the date which Thomason wrote on his own copy. But, unfortunately for Milton's argument, from February 2 to November 19 is not "a whole year," and he is rebuking his opponent dangerously if his facts are wrong. If, on the other hand, it can be shown that the second edition of *The Doctrine & Discipline* appeared in January, and the *Answer* reached Milton's hands in December, his rebuke will be reasonably accurate.

We have already seen that the second edition of Milton's tract experienced difficulties in going through the press. We may note, now, that the Thomason copy (B.M. E. 31) seems to be in a comparatively late state. It not only contains the cancel G2; pages 70-72 are numbered correctly; page 33 is printed correctly; the word *incidental*, page 65, line 22, is spelled correctly (it is not in most copies); certain typographical irregularities in the signatures (see C and E) have been corrected; and faulty punctuation in the headline on pages 27 and 69 has been removed. There are other slight variants, all of them suggesting that the copy which Thomason received February 2, 1644, was not among the first issued from the press. It seems probable, therefore, that the second edition was made available during the month of January 1644, and possibly early in the month. It could hardly have been published before.

What of the *Answer?* Note that Milton is doubly definite about its appearance in December or later: it reeled forth after the second edition of his tract had "a whole year bin publisht"; he had heard that it was "half printed" during the summer and lay "half a year after unfinisht in the press." As sometimes certainly happens, Thomason's dating may be wrong. But the book contains, on the page facing its title, an *imprimatur* dated November 14, and this Milton must have noticed. A more likely explanation, therefore, is that the book, like *The Doctrine & Discipline*, had its difficulties in the press (Milton, to be sure, suggests this strongly), and that Thomason received, in this instance, a copy in a very early state. I have found, however, but slight evidence to support this theory. In the

Thomason copy pages 2-3 and 6-7 lack the usual headline, being numbered at the top-center instead of at the top margin. But I have noticed no striking variants in the text. It is always possible, of course, that Milton, being busy with his *Tetrachordon*, may not have noticed the *Answer* until a few weeks after its appearance and may then have believed it just off the press.

The publisher of the *Answer*, William Lee, had been in business at the Turk's Head (or Great Turk's Head) in Fleet Street, next to the Mitre Tavern, since 1627, when he published Drayton's *Battaile of Agincourt*; and a stationer with this name was there as late as 1675. There is little clue to the authorship of the *Answer*. Milton says:

Only this I marvel'd, and other men have since, when as I, in a Subject so new to this age, and so hazardous to please, conceal'd not my name, why this Author defending that part which is so creeded by the people, would conceal his?

As a matter of fact, Milton concealed his name in the edition of the tract which his answerer was using, and his "marvelling" comes with dubious logic here. Nor is he helpful in assisting us to identify his opponent. The previous summer he had been told by someone that the *Answer* was written

not by one, but by a pack of heads; of whom the cheif, by circumstance, was intimated to mee, and since ratifi'd to bee no other . . . then an actual Servingman. This creature . . . transplanted himself, and to the improvement of his wages, and your better notice of his capacity, turn'd Soliciter.

Milton was always too easily satisfied with such loose gossip about his opponents; witness his attack on Morus. Furthermore, anyone reading the *Answer*, with its conspicuous use of legal precedents and instances, might guess it to be the work of a soliciter. But Milton has heard, let us notice, that his "man of Law" had been assisted "in the Divinity" by "a stripling Divine or two" newly out of the University, these to receive a share of the spoils if the *Answer* proved profitable. He had fully intended to ignore "such a Drones nest" until he further heard

for certain that a Divine of note, out of his good will to the opinion, had takn it into his revise, and somthing had put out, somthing put in, and stuck it heer and there with a clove of his own *Calligraphy*, to keep it from tainting

and, believing this, he resolved to administer a fitting *colasterion* (punishment). He wants the reader to note that he imputes "a share in the making to him whose name I find in the approbation"—in other words, the Rev. Joseph Caryl.

What part, if any, Caryl had in the composition of the *Answer*, it is impossible to say. He was a man about six years Milton's senior, a nonconformist leader, member of the Westminster Assembly, and, from 1645, minister of St. Magnus near London Bridge. An able and learned divine, he was even a moderate Independent in his thinking; but Milton does not spare him on this account. The recent defender of Smectymnuus is annoyed at the attitude which the clergy has publicly taken toward his divorce views; and the recent author of *Areopagitica* is particularly annoyed at the gratuitous comment which the licenser has appended to his *imprimatur*. Caryl at the time was busily at work on his commentary on the book of Job, and he suddenly learned what it was like to be visited by calamity which may or may not have constituted just punishment.

The author (or one of the authors) of the *Answer* seems to have identified the writer of the anonymous first edition, for he knows that Milton lived on Aldersgate Street. In another place he declares (page 16):

if every man were of your breeding and capacitie, there were some colour for this plea; for we believe you count no woman to due conversation accessible, as to you, except she can speak Hebrew, Greek, Latine, & French, and dispute against the Canon law as well as you, or at least be able to hold discourse with you. But other Gentlemen of good qualitie are content with meaner and fewer endowments, as you know well enough.

This may have been a hit in the dark, an inference from Milton's own argument, for there is nothing else in the *Answer* that so smacks of the personal. Milton's name is not once mentioned, and there is no suggestion of the fact that he has been deserted by his own wife. When one considers the usual language of controversy in this period, the Answerer is amazingly polite and does little to deserve the storm of abuse in the *Colasterion*. He ridicules some of Milton's expressions: **the** "frothie discourse" is "sugred over with a little neat language"; "the language is too sublime and Angelicall for mortall creatures to comprehend it"—but he is prompted to this because *The Doctrine and Discipline* has elsewhere been "commended" for its "fine language" (an interesting admission). The confuter is certainly no stylist himself, as the *Colasterion* makes devastatingly plain. The argument is a matter of *ergo* and *ipso facto*; Milton is often *he* and *you* in the same sentence; there are a few moments of satirical humor, but the tone is forced.

As C. L. Powell made clear in his *English Domestic Relations* (Columbia University Press, 1917), the *Answer* represents the orthodox viewpoint in 1644. On the other hand, quite apart from the validity of his rebuttal, the anonymous writer is amusingly confused in the pointing of his appeal. His book is "A Plea for Ladies and Gentlewomen, and all other Maried Women against Divorce" and, indeed, he defends the weaker sex against a wicked man who, "if shee prove not so meet as is expected," would "then put her away and take another." But he cannot conceal his horror over the fact that all Milton's arguments "prove as effectually, that the Wife may sue a Divorce from her Husband upon the same grounds" (page 13), and elsewhere he makes a typical statement of male superiority:

for then would it have been every wayes as much, yea more content and solace to *Adam*; and so consequently to every man, to have had another man made to him of his Rib instead of *Eve*: this is apparent by experience, which shews, that man ordinarily exceeds woman in naturall gifts of minde, and in delectablenesse of converse.

The whole point of Milton's idealistic conception of marriage has been lost on him.

The present text of the *Answer* reproduces a copy of the first edition in my own collection. The tract is here reprinted for the first time.

NOTES ON *OBSERVATIONS ON MILTON AGAINST SALMASIUS*

Milton closed his *Colasterion* (1645) by saying: if any man equal to the matter shall think it appertains him to take in hand this controversy, either excepting against ought writt'n, or perswaded hee can shew better how this question of such moment to bee throughly known may receav a true determination . . . if his intents bee sincere to the public, and shall carry him on without bitternes to the opinion, or to the person dissenting, let him not, I entreate him, guess . . . that I account it any displeasure don mee to bee contradicted in Print: but as it leads to the attainment of any thing more true, shall esteem it a benefit; and shall know how to return his civility and faire Argument . . .

But Milton, as he was soon to learn, lived in an age when such contributions to controversy were rare, and it was his own fate to be opposed but once by a man who argued ideas without acrimony. This unique experience came after the poet was blind, and during a period when, distressed and ill, he was waiting for Salmasius' reply to his *Defensio Prima*. What he thought of the quiet and respectful attack on his theories of government we do not know, for he offered no reply and made no reference to the criticism thereafter. If he relied on his friend George Thomason for information about his anonymous opponent, he may never have known the true author, for Thomason thought him to be Henry Hammond.

Sir Robert Filmer's "Observations on Master Milton against Salmasius" appeared on or before February 18, 1652, and was therefore one of the earliest replies to Milton's *Defensio*. The discussion formed pages 12-22 of a pamphlet of ninety-five pages entitled *Observations Concerning the Originall of Government*, "London: Printed for R. Royston, at the Angel in Ivie-Lane," 1652. The tract consists of four little essays, of which the one concerned with Milton is second; the first deals with Hobbes' *Leviathan* (1651), the third with Hugo Grotius' *De Jure Belli* (1625), and the fourth (which has separate pagination) with Philip Hunton's *Treatise of Monarchy* (1643).

The author was a studious gentleman who lived quietly in East Sutton, Kent, and about whom not much is known today.

He had been knighted by Charles I and was afterwards an ardent royalist, suffering greatly during the Civil War. He was in his sixties when he wrote his essay on Milton, and had already given expression to his political views in some anonymous pamphlets. Thomason attributed to him *The Necessity of the Absolute Power of all Kings* (August 21, 1648); and he certainly wrote *The Anarchy of a Limited or Mixed Monarchy* (April 19, 1648), for it is reprinted at the close of the 1652 *Observations* as "Upon Mr. Huntons *Treatise of Monarchy*." He may possibly have written *The Free-holders Grand Inquest* (February 1, 1648), which, however, Thomason attributed to Sir Robert Holbourne.

Filmer was the eldest son of Sir Edward Filmer, and he had married in 1618 Anne Heton, daughter of the late Bishop of Ely. His brothers were Edward, John, and Reginald, the last-named being a London merchant.[1] Filmer had six sons and two daughters; a younger son, Robert, married Elizabeth, daughter of Sir William Bevershal, in 1682. The political writer died May 26, 1653, only a little more than a year after the publication of his *Observations*.

Filmer's criticism of Milton is notable for more than its dignified and respectful tone, for it examines the poet's views on government not only in the *Defensio* but also in *The Tenure of Kings and Magistrates*, treating those views as they deserved to be treated—as a coherent whole. The *Tenure* is several times quoted,[2] and is considered without the pious horror which characterizes Walker's earlier attack upon it. Filmer does a tolerable job of criticizing Milton's ideas, especially in his insistence upon a definition of terms. He successfully isolates some of the more important doctrines of the lengthy *Defensio* (offering, by the way, some interesting translations), and ends on a note of half agreement. Taken all in all, it is a thoughtful, provocative reply from a man who has a carefully thought out theory of his own. That theory—of patriarchal government—was to enjoy a certain celebrity after 1680, thanks largely to attacks by Locke, James Tyrrell (an admirer of Milton), and Algernon Sidney.

---

[1] The genealogy of the Filmer family is contained in *The Visitation of London* (Harleian Society, 1880), I, 274. Filmer was licensed to marry Anne Heton August 8, 1618.

[2] *See*, particularly, the "Columbia" edition, V, 15-16.

Filmer's essay on Milton's political views is here reproduced from the British Museum copy of the *Observations* (100.K.7). It was reprinted in the 1679 edition of Filmer's *Reflections Concerning the Original of Government*, but has not, I believe, been reprinted since.

NOTES ON *THE CENSURE OF THE ROTA*

The Censure of the Rota has sometimes been ascribed to James Harrington by persons who have not read beyond the title-page. Its author cannot be Harrington, or any member of the debating club known as the Rota, for that famous but ephemeral society is satirized along with Milton in the pamphlet which cleverly pretends to be a report of the club's proceedings on a date after the club is known to have disbanded. The "censure" is of political visionaries in general, and of Milton and Harrington in particular. Milton bears the brunt of the attack.

The fullest and most revealing account of the Rota is that of John Aubrey, who was an auditor at the meetings and a good friend of Harrington, the directing spirit. Aubrey relates that Harrington's *Oceana* (1656),

together with his and H. Nevill's smart discourses and inculcations, dayly at coffee-houses, made many proselytes. In so much that, anno 1659, the beginning of Michaelmas-terme [i.e. October 10], he had every night a meeting at the (then) Turke's head, in the New Pallace-yard, where they take water, the next house to the staires, at one Miles's, where was made purposely a large ovall-table, with a passage in the middle for Miles to deliver his Coffee. About it sate his disciples, and the virtuosi. The discourses in this kind were the most ingeniose, and smart, that ever I heard, or expect to heare, and band[i]ed with great eagernesse: the arguments in the Parliament howse were but flatt to it. . . . Here we had (very formally) a *ballotting-box*, and balloted how things should be caried, by way of tentamens. The room was every evening full as it could be cramm'd. . . . We many times adjourned to the Rhenish-wine howse. . . . The doctrine was very taking, and the more because, as to human foresight, there was no possibility of the king's returne. But the greatest part of the Parliament-men perfectly hated this designe of *rotation by ballotting;* . . . 'twas death to them, except 8 or 10 to admit of this way, for H. Nevill proposed it in the Howse ... Now this modell upon rotation was:—that the third part of the Senate should rote out by ballot every yeare, so that every ninth yeare the Howse would be wholly alterd; no magistrate to continue above 3 yeares, and all to be chosen by ballot, then which manner of choice, nothing can be invented more faire and impartiall. Well: this meeting continued Novemb., Dec., Jan., till Febr. 20 or 21; and then, upon the unexpected turne upon generall Monke's comeing-in, all these aierie modells vanished. Then 'twas not fitt, nay treason, to have donne such ...

The membership of the Rota helps to explain the fascination which it had for Aubrey. Besides Harrington himself, the following seem to have been regular participants in the meetings: Cyriack Skinner, Milton's young friend and amanuensis; Henry Neville, political writer and member of Parliament; Dr. Robert Wood, physician and mathematician; Sir William Petty, political economist, who "troubled Mr. James Harrington with his arithmeticall proportions, reducing politie to numbers"; Sir John Wildman, politician, soldier, and writer; Sir Charles Wolseley, member of Parliament; Roger Coke, political writer; Sir William Poultney; Sir John Hoskins, barrister and later president of the Royal Society; James Arderne, later Dean of Chester but then a young man just out of the university; Maximilian Petty, "a very able man in these matters"; Michael Mallet; Philip Carteret; Francis Cradock, a merchant and later an admirer of Milton's verse; Sir Henry Ford, later Irish Secretary; Edward Bagshaw; Thomas Mariet; Richard Sackville, fifth Earl of Dorset; and Dr. William Croone, professor of rhetoric at Gresham College. This stimulating company of course attracted auditors, of whom Aubrey was one; others were Samuel Pepys, Sir John Birkenhead, Sir John Penruddock, and, probably, Andrew Marvell, who was an "intimate friend" of Harrington. The Rota also had its enemies, chief of whom seems to have been a Mr. Stafford, who on one occasion entered with his gang

in drink, from the taverne, and affronted the Junto (Mr. Stafford tore their orders and minutes). The soldiers [present as auditors] offerd to kick them downe stayres, but Mr. Harrington's moderation and persuasion hindred it.

It is most unlikely, however, that this Mr. Stafford, or any of his rowdy associates, was responsible for writing *The Censure of the Rota*.

The authorship of the pamphlet remains a secret, which is a pity, for of all the contemporary attacks on Milton it is probably the cleverest and most penetrating. The writer avoids abuse and name-calling; he uses the rapier of satire against the learned bludgeon of Milton, and with telling effect. There is a mock courtesy in his tone which makes the pamphlet amusing when it is most incisive. The author pretends to be none other than Harrington himself, and, as a kindred political theorist, he insists that he takes no pleasure in the task assigned him, which is "to give you an account of some Reflections that they [the members of the Rota] have lately made upon a Treatise of yours." He begs Milton's pardon, for the story he must tell is "not onely against mine own sense, but the Interesse which both you and I carry on." This particular touch of satire is dropped near the end, when "Harrington" himself attacks Milton in words which ridicule the theories of both.

The proceedings of the Rota are burlesqued throughout the pamphlet. Every opinion is solemnly voted on, resulting, of course, in a unanimous verdict against Milton. If the satirist's knowledge of Milton's writings is limited to the titles actually mentioned, he is acquainted with only five works: the *Ready and Easy Way* (which is his immediate subject), the *Eikonoklastes* and *Defensio Prima* (inevitable objects of attack), the recent *Considerations touching Hirelings*, and *Tetrachordon*. Oddly enough, it is *Tetrachordon*, and not *The Doctrine and Discipline*, for which Milton has "atchieved the honour to be Styld the Founder of a Sect." He taunts the reformer with the futility of his efforts, and declares: "though you have scribled your eyes out, your works have never been printed but for the Company of Chandlers and Tobacco-men, who are your Stationers, and the onely men that vend your Labors." This last slur is difficult to understand. The writer may have in mind the *Brief Notes* of 1660, which he does not mention, but which appeared without printer or bookseller's name in the imprint. The second edition of the *Ready and Easy Way* also contained no names in the imprint, being "Printed for the Authour." Milton's printer for the past six years had been Thomas Newcomb, a person of some importance in the business, who continued in favor after the Restoration. Milton's chief bookseller, on the other hand, was not so reputable a person: Livewell Chapman got into difficulties with the authorities during both Commonwealth and Restoration. Besides publishing for Milton, he had published in 1656 Harrington's *Oceana.*

I have discussed elsewhere (pages 55-58) the criticism of Milton's style which appeared in *The Censure of the Rota.* To the present writer this is one of the most interesting aspects of a pamphlet which is everywhere as shrewd as it is humorous. My own impression is that the critic does not know Milton personally, but combines rumor and reading with telling effect. He has heard that the Latin Secretary received £300 per annum for his services to the state, which is a fairly close guess (Milton actually received £288). He taxes the learned republican with wresting Scripture unmercifully. The *Defensio Prima* is called "that admired piece, which you writ to confute his [Salmasius'] Wife and his Maid." Masson admits that all this is "clever burlesque" but damns it with faint praise, declaring that *The Censure* is "of somewhat higher literary quality" than a scurrilous, shabby pamphlet of the same year called *The Character of the Rump.* This is understatement from one who loves Milton this side idolatry. The anonymous *Censure* is a fine piece of prose satire in the best Restoration tradition.

It enjoyed a certain celebrity in its own day. Thirteen years later, Richard Leigh apparently bowed to it in *A Censure of the Rota in Mr. Dryden's Conquest of Granada,* an attack which provoked a few printed replies. Leigh was a minor poet of the Restoration, and was probably the author of *The Transproser Rehearsed* (1673), which contained many violent attacks on Milton. Leigh will not do as the author of the earlier *Censure,* however, since he was only a boy of eleven when it appeared.

The Censure of the Rota against Milton was reprinted in the Harleian Miscellany (1745 edition, vol. IV; 1809 edition, by Thomas Park, vol. IV). It is here reproduced from the Thomason copy in the British Museum. I have in my own collection an unbound, uncut copy, the original stitching of which is still undisturbed.

NOTES ON *NO BLINDE GUIDES*

Dr. Matthew Griffith, a royalist divine, died at Bladon in Oxfordshire on October 14, 1665, having ruptured a blood vessel in preaching. He died at a time when the plague was beginning to abate in London, and when John Milton, living quietly in Chalfont St. Giles, was perhaps reflecting on young Ellwood's suggestion of a poem on *Paradise Regained*. The news of Griffith's violent end, if it finally reached the blind poet, must have brought an ironic smile to his lips. He had once caught Griffith in the most tactless move of the latter's blundering but well meaning life, and he had seized the occasion to publish a hasty commentary upon it—the next to the last of Milton's stubborn efforts to rally a dying commonwealth. The effort failed; in the overwhelming march of events the incident was quickly forgotten; but, at the moment, Milton's rapid attack was considered serious enough to warrant a published rebuttal.

Briefly, the facts are these. In March and April of 1660 public opinion was shifting with tremendous speed and power in favor of the restoration of Charles II. The fickle populace was making up its mind, but the issue was theoretically to be decided by a "full and free" Parliament, called for April 25. Meanwhile, General Monk and others in authority had to keep up the appearance of loyalty to their previous commitments. The leaders were in communication with Charles and were ready for the inevitable event, but their immediate policy was to watch and wait. They feared some last minute outburst of republican fervor which might disrupt their plans. Even more, they feared an imprudent outburst of royalist fervor which would force them to reveal their intentions before the right moment had arrived, thus inviting reaction.

On Sunday, March 25, the preacher at the Mercers' Chapel was Matthew Griffith, who had once been chaplain of Charles I, had been several times imprisoned under the Commonwealth, and was now excited over the near prospect of a Restoration. He chose for the text of his sermon *Proverbs* XXIV. 21: "My son, fear God and the King, and meddle not with them that be seditious or desirous of change." Other royalist sermons were being preached at the time, but Griffith's was both too impulsive and too tactless in tone. Besides urging loyalty to the exiled monarch, he attacked the Presbyterians and the Independents, comparing them to the Trojan Horse; and he went out of his way to extol Episcopacy as "the true *Protestant Religion.*" Charles II he likened to Samson, who would unexpectedly take his revenge. The sermon closed with an enthusiastic prophesy of sudden destruction for the seditious.

Griffith's intention was good but his action was ill-timed. Royalist sympathizers in London wrote immediately to the King in complaint, but before the Council of State could move, the clergyman blundered again, twice. On March 31 he registered his sermon for publication, and, printing it immediately, he appended a dedication to Monk and an openly political pamphlet entitled "The Samaritan revived . . . Historically applyed for the sound and speedy healing of our present dangerous Distractions." The dedication must have proved embarrassing to the General, who is there begged to carry on "what you have already so happily begun . . . till you have finish'd this great, and good work, and brought it to perfection." "It is a greater honour to make a *King*, then to be one," declared Griffith, with double tactlessness. His folly having become dangerous, the Council of State was forced to put him into prison.

Early in April, before the Convention Parliament had met, Milton published his *Brief Notes Upon a late Sermon.* He did not register the slim pamphlet at Stationers' Hall, and neither printer nor bookseller put his name in the imprint. Time was precious; and although the Council had punished Griffith (Milton refers to the fact with satisfaction), they would probably not have permitted anyone to answer him publicly. Milton's reply was, in effect, a frantic attempt to use Griffith's blunder and the subsequent action of the Council as a means of stemming the tide of royalist sympathy. He pronounced the clergyman's dedication to Monk "an impudent calumnie and affront to his Excellence." Griffith had charged the General

most audaciously and falsly with the renouncing of his own public promises and declarations both to the Parliament and the Army, and we trust his actions ere long will deterr such insinuating slanderers from thus approaching him for the future.

This was the politic line to take in the circumstances, and one looks for more. There is no more. The remainder of the pamphlet is a fruitless rehashing of old arguments, with no reference to the real problems of the crisis. Perhaps Milton failed to understand those problems completely. Perhaps Griffith's writing was so wretched that the scholarly Milton was distracted in his own endeavor, for he devotes a disproportionate amount of space to ridiculing his opponent's theology. He could not even resist striking a blow at Episcopacy in the person of Griffith. These digressions weaken his essential attack, which was probably foredoomed to failure in any case.

Nevertheless, some persons were disturbed by the persistent pamphleteering on the part of die-hard republicans, of which the *Brief Notes* was an example. Roger L'Estrange, royalist pamphleteer extraordinary, explains the situation:

> the whole Nation was as vigilant as possible to disappoint the Grand Conspiracy of the Phanaticks. About this time they made several Attempts in order to a general rising; but by the care and Conduct of the *Council*, the General, and the Militia, all came to nothing; the heart of the Design was almost broken: and yet they would not leave their Pamphleting. Particularly *Milton* put forth a bawling piece against Dr. *Griffith* and somebody else another scurrilous Libel, entituled, *EYE--SALVE:* I did not think it much material to reply upon these, the people being already convinc'd of the Right; but however, being excited to it by a private Friend, I return'd these following *Answers*.

This quotation is from page 157 of *L'Estrange His Apology*, 1660. What follow in the book are unsold original copies of his *No Blinde Guides* and *Physician Cure thy Self*, both of which had appeared more than a month earlier (the *Apology* reached Thomason's hands June 6; *Physician Cure thy Self* is dated on the title-page April 23). The *Apology* then concludes with two final paragraphs, a list of *errata,* and "A Catalogue of some Books Printed for *Henry Brome*" (pages 159-162 unnumbered). Charles II had entered London nine days before, and L'Estrange was busy calling attention to his valuable services.

No Blinde Guides bears the date April 20, 1660, in its imprint; and, although it is not so noted in the printed catalogue (1908), Thomason dated his copy April 25. Thus, L'Estrange managed to get his reply to Milton into print just before the meeting of Parliament on April 25. The pamphlet does not contain its author's name, although L'Estrange was glad enough to acknowledge it after the King's restoration. Milton's *Brief Notes* had been signed with initials, but L'Estrange, who had earlier commented upon Milton's distinctive style in *Treason Arraigned* (April 3), had no doubt about the author's identity.

L'Estrange's bookseller, Henry Brome, had been in business at the Gun in Ivy Lane from about 1659 (in which year he published Thomas Sprat's *The Plague of Athens*), and he remained there until the time of the Great Fire. After the fire Brome moved to the Star in Little Britain, which had once been the shop of John Saywell; but within a few years he relinquished the premises to Joseph Clarke and moved back to the neighborhood of St. Paul's. The Gun in Ludgate Street, at the west end of the Churchyard, was his address from September 1669 until 1681. Early in 1681, and shortly before he died, he published Milton's *Character of the Long Parliament and Assembly of Divines in MDCXLI*. Incidentally, his early address, the Gun in Ivy Lane, became the office of L'Estrange in August 1663, when he was appointed "Surveyor of the Imprimery."

No Blinde Guides, when read along with Milton's *Brief Notes*, speaks for itself, but perhaps a few observations are permissable here. The pamphlet gives no indication that L'Estrange had heard, or even read, Griffith's sermon; he is concerned, not with defending the foolish clergyman, but with discrediting Milton. As a matter of fact, in hastily ridiculing Milton's second paragraph — which "talks of *Purgatives, Myrrhe, Aloes, &c.*"—he is unintentionally ridiculing Griffith, of whom he elsewhere says: "I am not *bold* enough to be his *Champion*, in all particulars." Again he declares: "Let him [Griffith] acquit *himself*, in what concerns the *Divine*; and I'll adventure upon the most material parts of the *Rest*." This promise L'Estrange does not keep, for he argues with Milton's interpretations of a number of scriptural passages. It is noteworthy that L'Estrange carefully avoids the dangerous subject of Monk's attitude toward the Restoration—even avoids mentioning Monk by name. Coming to the relevant portion of Milton's pamphlet, he says that he will not concern himself with the latter's "unmannerly descant" upon Griffith's dedication, and then drops the subject. He is, however, openly royalist in sympathy: "*Is* there, or *is there not* at present, any King of *England?* You say, *No;* I'm of another mind."

L'Estrange does not confine his attack to the *Brief Notes.* In his introductory paragraphs he reminds the reader that Milton was the author of *Eikonoklastes* and the *Defensio Prima* and was even to his own wife " an *Incubus.*" Later there are attacks upon the *Readie and Easie Way* (which title L'Estrange misquotes), with four page-references to the text besides other allusions. He rather adroitly uses Milton's plan for a free commonwealth against the statements made in *Brief Notes.* In his eagerness to discredit his opponent, he resorts to many devices. Although accusing Milton of railing against Salmasius, he is himself abusive, in his opening sentence calling his opponent a devil in human shape. He does not hesitate to use Milton's earliest indiscretion against him: "you are for *Divorce,* I see, as well of *Governours,* as *Wives.*" When we recall Milton's own methods in controversy, however, it is difficult to condemn L'Estrange. The title of his pamphlet and the proverb on the title-page, "If the Blinde lead the Blinde, Both shall fall into the Ditch," seem to the modern student unnecessarily cruel—and, when one reflects on the proverb's implications as touching the English people, strangely tactless. L'Estrange was writing against time, and the title-page may have been a hasty after-thought suggested by the title of the second pamphlet which he was answering: *Eye Salve.* In the text itself there are only two allusions to blindness, neither of them offensive: the first is a common saying which might have been quoted if Milton had not been blind; the second implies that the poet lost his sight as a result of his attack on *Eikon Basilike.* L'Estrange could have been really cruel if he had wished; as a matter of fact, when one reads some of his other pamphlets, this one seems restrained and impersonal by comparison. He was perfectly sincere, and in *Treason Arraigned* he had called Milton "no Fool." Devil, yes, but no fool. This was grudging praise from a man so much in earnest, from one whose journalistic style has so annoyed later critics. In complete fairness we should remember that Sir Roger L'Estrange is listed among the "Names of the Nobility and Gentry That Encourag'd, by Subscription," the printing of the 1688 edition of *Paradise Lost.*

The following text of *No Blinde Guides* reproduces one of the two copies of the first edition in my own collection. When L'Estrange reissued his pamphlet as part of his *Apology*, he noted two errors in the printing:

Page 8	Line 11	For This Losse,	Read *his Losse*
	9	10	For these very Gentlemen are Pigeons, r.	*These Gentlemen are very Pigeons.*

No Blinde Guides was once before reprinted, as number five of *A Collection of Eighteen Rare and Curious Historical Tracts and Pamphlets,* Edinburgh (privately printed, the edition limited to 250 copies), 1884.

INDEX

INDEX

Following is an index of all persons and publications mentioned in the essay, notes, and list of allusions. It is recommended as a means of identifying persons who are incompletely identified in the quoted material or elsewhere. Abbreviations: pr. *for* printer, bks. *for* bookseller.

A., R. (Robert Austin, pr. 16⸺6?), 77.
Abbot, George (1562-1633), 115.
Abraham, 78.
Achitophel, 101.
Addison, Joseph, 54.
Agag, 82.
Aitzema, Leo de, 18.
Alarum to the Armies, 100, 102.
Allam, Andrew, 6.
Allen, William (pseud.), *Killing No Murder*, 96-97.
Allestry, James (bks., d. Nov. 3, 1670), 105, 111.
Allison, W. T., 82.
Allot, Robert (bks. 1626-36), 9.
Almoni, Peloni (pseud.), *Compendious Discourse*, 14-15, 71-72, 264.
Andrewes, Launcelot, *Moral Law Expounded, Private Devotions*, 8.
Annesley, Arthur (1614-86), 46.
Anonymous Biographer, 6, 29, 54.
Answer to a Book, 21, 74-75, 273-277.
Anti-Remonstrance, 263.
Apuleius, *Golden Ass*, 105-106.
Arber, Edward, *Term Catalogues*, 109-113, 116-117, 119.
Arbuthnot, Dr. John, 48.
Arderne, James, 281.
Areopagi, 268.
Aretine, the (Pietro Aretino), 116.
Aristotle, 59.
Arnold, Christopher, 26, 36, 108.
Arnold, Matthew, 65.
Ascham, Anthony, 103.
Ashton, John, 77.
Attaway, Mrs., 76.
Aubrey, John, 5-6, 54, 62, 280-281.
Aylmer, Brabazon (bks. 1670-1707), 49-50, 53, 119.

Bachiler, John, 76.
Bacon, Francis, 59.
Bagshaw, Edward, 281.
Baillie, Robert (1599-1662), *Dissuasive*, 75.
Baker, Colonel, *Blazing Star*, 104.
Banquet of Jests, 9.
Barebone, Praisegod (1596?-1679), 103.

Baron, Robert, *Cyprian Academy, Pocula Castalia*, 23.
Barrow, Dr. Samuel (1625?-82), 51.
Bedell, Gabriel (bks. 1646-68), 85.
Begley, Walter, 94.
Bellamy, John (bks. 1620-54), 92.
Be Merry & Wise, see R. L'Estrange.
Benham, A. R., 6.
Berge, Ernst Gottlieb vom, 54.
Best, John (pr. 1660-65), 109.
Bevershal, Elizabeth, 279.
Bevershal, Sir William, 279.
Birch, Thomas, 80.
Birkenhead, Sir John (1616-79), 97, 281.
Blackmore, Sir Richard, 54.
Blair, Robert (1593-1666), 263.
Bloody Tenet (by Roger Williams), 74, 76.
Blount, Edward (bks. 1594-1632), 9.
Blount, Thomas, *Glossographia*, 93.
Blunden, Humphrey (bks. 1637-54), 88.
Boulter, Robert (bks. 1666-83), 112.
Bourne, Nicholas (bks. 1609-57), 74.
Bradshaw, John (1602-59), 96, 98-99.
Bramhall, John, 14-15, 34, 86, 90-91; *Serpent Salve*, 73.
Brandenburg, Frederick William, the Great Elector of, 86.
Bridgewater, John Egerton, Earl of, 94.
Brief Description of Fanatics, 104.
Brome, Henry, 100-101, 103, 112, 286-287.
Brooke, Nathaniel (bks. 1646-77), 110.
Browne, Samuel (bks. at Hague 1643-60), 84.
Browne, Sir Thomas, 58.
Browne, William, 10.
Bucer, Martin, see J. Milton.
Buchler, John, *Thesaurus*, 109.
Bunny, Edmund (1540-1618), 77.
Burton, Robert, 57.
Bush, Douglas, 77.
Butter, Nathaniel (bks. 1604-64), 79, 265-266.

C., A. (Andrew Coe, Jr., pr. 1644-67), 109.
C., E. (Ellen Cotes or Edw. Crouch, prs.), 100.
C., T., 107.

293

C., T., *Glass for the Times*, 78.
Cadwell, J. (pr. 1659-62), 102.
Calamy, Edmund (1600-66), 265-266.
Calvert, Sarah, 108.
Carolus I Britanniarum Rex, 34, 90.
Carpentier, J., de Marigny, 96-97.
Carteret, Philip, 281.
Caryl, Joseph (1602-73), 21, 32, 49, 276.
Catalogue of Several Sects, 77.
Cecil, Sir Thomas, 270.
Censure of the Rota, 22, 28, 43, 55-58, 100, 280-283.
Certain Brief Treatises, 264.
Chapman, Livewell (bks. 1651-65), 97-98, 102, 283.
Chappell, William (1582-1649), 6, 90.
Character of the Rump, 43, 99, 283.
Charles IX of France, 82.
Chavance, Philibert, 105.
Christina, Queen, 87-89.
Cicero, 58-59, 105-106.
Clarendon, Edward Hyde, Earl of, 43.
Clarges, Sir Thomas, 46.
Clarke, Joseph (bks. 1670-3), 287.
Clementius, Antonius, 93.
Cobbet, Ralph, 104.
Coke, Roger, 281.
Collection of 18 Rare Tracts, 289.
Collinne, William, *Spirit of the Fanatics*, 43, 99-100.
Collins, James (bks. 1664-83), 117.
Colman, Walter, *La Dance Machabre*, 9.
Commonplace Book, 112, 118.
Constantine, 97-98.
Cook, John, 96, 104.
Cotes, Thomas (pr. 1627-41), 9.
Coverdale, Miles, 73.
Cowley, Abraham, 4, 48; *Poetical Blossoms*, 10.
Cradock, Francis, 281.
Cranmer, Thomas, 14, 72-73.
Crashaw, Richard, 23.
Creed, John (bks. 1670-85), 111.
Creyghton, Robert (1593-1672), 105-106.
Cripps, Henry (bks. d. 1663), 82.
Cromwell, Oliver, 40, 45, 53, 62-63, 82, 97, 101-102, 104, 115-116.
Cromwell, Richard, 41.
Crooke, John (bks. 1637-69), 102.
Croone, Dr. William, 281.

D., I. (John Dawson, pr. 1637-48), 73.
Daniel, Roger (pr. & bks. 1622-66), 72.
Dante, 98.
Dati, Carlo, 12, 64.
Davenant, Sir William, 9, 46, 48; *Gondibert*, 114.
David, 82.
Denham, Sir John, 48.
Denmark, Frederick III, King of, 89.

Dennis, John, 54.
Descartes, Rene, 87.
Dicas, Thomas (bks. 1660-69), 105.
Dignity of Kingship Asserted, see G. Sheldon.
Diodati, Charles, 56, 61, 63.
Discovery of Dangerous Tenets, 77.
Donne, John, 3-4, 113.
Dorislaus, Isaac (1595-1649), 103.
Dorset, Charles Sackville, Earl of, 48.
Double Your Guards, see R. L'Estrange.
Downame, George (d. 1634), 268.
Drayton, Michael, 275.
Dring, Thomas, Jr. (bks. 1668-94), 49, 117.
Dryden, John, 48, 51, 54, 59, 112, 283.
Du Bartas, Guillaume de Saluste, 4.
Dugard, William, 34, 90.
Du Moulin, Peter (1601-84), *Clamor*, 34, 37, 45, 69, 90, 92, 110; *Parerga*, 110-111.
Durie, John (1596-1680), 39, 108.

Eachard, John (1636?-97), *Contempt of the Clergy*, 24-25, 110.
Edwards, Thomas (1599-1647), *Gangraena*, 76-77.
Eglon, 81.
Ehud, 81.
Eikon Aklastos, see J. Jane.
Eikon Alethine, 30, 95.
Eikon Basilike, 17, 30, 32-33, 35, 47, 84, 86-88, 94-95, 98-99, 103-104, 108, 288.
Eikon e Piste, 30.
Electra, 84.
Elizabeth, Princess (1635-50), 84.
Ellwood, Thomas (1639-1713), 47, 59, 284.
Elzevier, 33, 39, 119.
English, Peter, *Survey of Policy*, 35.
Euripides, 65.
Evans, G. B., 24.
Eye Salve, 101, 103, 286, 288.

F., D., 84.
F., M., see M. Flesher.
F., T., see T. Forde.
Fabricius, Germanus, 54.
Featley, Daniel (1582-1645), *Dippers Dipt*, 20, 74.
Fell, Dr. John, 107.
Fevardentius, 15, 71.
Filmer, Edward, 279; Sir Edward, 279.
Filmer, John, 279.
Filmer, Reginald, 279.
Filmer, Robert, 279.
Filmer, Sir Robert, *Anarchy of Limited Monarchy*, 279; *Freeholders Grand Inquest*, 279; *Necessity of Absolute Power*, 279; *Observations*, 34, 89-90, **278-280**; *Reflections*, 280.

INDEX

Flesher, James (pr. 1652-70, son of Miles), 91.
Flesher, Miles (pr. 1619-64), 77, 79.
Fletcher, Giles, 4.
Fletcher, Phineas, 4.
Ford, Sir Henry (1619?-84), 281.
Forde, Thomas, *Letters*, 106-107.
Free Parliament Litany, 99.
French, J. Milton, 34, 69, 71, 80, 85-88, 91-95, 97-98, 105.
Fuller, Thomas, *Holy State*, 14, 72-73.

G., E. (Edward Griffin, Jr., pr. 1637-52), 72.
Garfield, John (bks. 1656-60), 88, 105.
Garthwait, Timothy (bks. 1650-69), 85.
Gellibrand, Samuel (bks. 1637-75), 76-77.
Gerbier, Sir Balthazar (d. 1667), 116.
Gilchrist, Octavius G., 110.
Gill, Alexander, Jr. (1597-1642), 6-9, 20, 56, 270.
Gilman, Wilbur E., 59.
Godbid, William (pr. 1656-77), 110.
Godwin, William, 109.
Goliath, 85.
Good, John Walter, *Studies in the Milton Tradition*, 54.
Goodwin, John, 73, 77; *Obstructors of Justice*, 28-29, 80-82, 96, 103-104; *Sion College Visited*, 78; *Twelve Serious Cautions*, 76.
Gott, Samuel, 94.
Grantham, William (bks. 1646-84), 107.
Grierson, Sir Herbert, 11, 13, 22, 27-28.
Griffith, Matthew (1599?-1665), 44, 101, 103, 284-287.
Grismond, John, II (pr. 1649?-64?), 265.
Grosart, A. B., 117.
Grotius, Hugo, *De Jure Belli*, 90, 278.
Guildhall Elegy, 98.
Güntzer, Christopher, 93-94.

Haak, Theodore (1605-90), 54.
Hacket, John (1592-1670), *Scrinia Reserata*, 17, 40.
Hakluyt, John, *Metropolitan Nuncio*, 82.
Hales, Sir James (d. 1554), 72.
Hall, John (1627-56), 101.
Hall, Joseph, 15-17, 19, 32, 40, 48, 59, 72, 94, 267-70; *Cases of Conscience*, 78; *Characters*, 15; *Defence*, 263, 265-266, 268; *Episcopacy by Divine Right*, 263, 265; *Humble Remonstrance*, 263, 265-266; *Remains*, 102; *Resolutions & Decisions*, 79; *Short Answer*, 264-266; *Toothless Satires*, 114, 267.
Hall, Robert, 267.
Haller, William, 2, 25, 76.
Hammond, Henry (1605-60), 77, 89, 278; *Letter of Resolution*, 91.

Hanford, James H., 10, 60.
Harrington, James, 43, 99, 280-282; *Oceana*, 280, 283.
Harrison, Thomas (1606-60), 104.
Hartlib, Samuel, 14, 23-24, 35, 117.
Haslerigg, Sir Arthur, 104.
Havens, Raymond D., 23-24, 54.
Hayes, John (pr. 1669-1705), 111.
Heath, James (1629-64), *Brief Chronicle*, 47, 108-109.
Heimbach, Peter, 55.
Heinsius, Nicolas, 39.
Herbert, George, 3.
Herrick, Robert, 4.
Herringman, Henry (pr. 1653-93), 49.
Heton, Anne, 279.
Heton, Martin (1552-1609), 279.
Hewson, John (d. 1662), 104.
Hickman, Spencer (bks. 1670-72), 49, 111-112.
Hobbes, Thomas, *Behemoth*, 40; *Leviathan*, 89, 278.
Hobson, John (1597?-1657), 14.
Hogg, William, 54.
Holbourne, Sir Robert, 279.
Hollandse Mercurius, 33-34, 85.
Holstenius, Lucas, 39.
Hooper, John, 73.
Hopkins, John, 54.
Hoskins, Sir John (1634-1705), 281.
Hotham, Charles (1615-72?), 84.
Houghton, Arthur A., 87.
Howell, James, 8; *Epistolae*, 92-93.
Hoyle, Thomas, Alderman of York (d. Jan. 30, 1650), 99, 103.
Hughes, Merritt Y., 11.
Hume, Patrick, 54.
Hunton, Philip (1604?-82), *Treatise of Monarchy*, 90, 278-279.
Hurd, Richard, 10.

Ibbitson, Robert (pr. 1646-61), 78, 92.
Irenaeus, 14-15, 71-72.
Ireton, Henry, 62.

Jane, Joseph, *Eikon Aklastos*, 31, 69, 86, 88, 105.
Jansson, J., 90.
Jehoram, 81.
Jehu, 81.
Job, 49, 276.
John, King, 268.
John (Buckhold) of Leyden, 83.
Johnson, Thomas (pr. & bks. 1642-77), 94.
Jonson, Ben, 3-4, 9-10.
Judas, 119.
Jus Divinum Ministerii, 265.
Juvenal, 111.

Kelley, Maurice, 34.

Keyes, Clinton W., 40.
Kiesser, Erhardus, 93-94.
King, Edward, 8, 11.
Kingdom's Scout, 80.
King's Book, see *Eikon Basilike*.
Knipperdolling, Bernard, 83.

L., F. (Francis Leach, pr. 1641-57), 73.
L., R., 110.
Labadie, Jean, 64.
Lamb, Charles, 57.
Latimer, Hugh, 72-73.
Laud, William, 263.
Lawes, Henry (1596-1662), 10-11, 14, 23-24.
Lawrence, Henry (1600-64), 26.
Lee, William, 74, 109, 275.
Leigh, Richard (b. 1649), *Transproser Rehearsed*, 25-26, 51, 113-117; *Censure of Dryden*, 283.
L'Estrange, Hamon, 89; *Smectymnuo-Mastix*, 264.
L'Estrange, Sir Roger (1616-1704), 43-44, 46, 52, 59, 112, 284-289; *Apology*, 98, 100-103, 286, 289; *Be Merry & Wise*, 98, 102; *Considerations*, 109; *Double Your Guards*, 100, 102; *No Blind Guides*, 46, 101-102, 284-289; *Physician Cure Thyself*, 101·102, 286; *Sir Politique*, 102; *Treason Arraigned*, 100, 102, 287-288.
Letter Intercepted, 102.
Ley, Lady Margaret, 14, 23.
Leybourn, Robert (bks. & pr. 1645-61), 107.
Leybourn, William (bks. & pr., 1645-65), 107.
Libri Theologici, etc., 97.
Life & Death of Vane, 108.
Life & Reign of Charles, 89.
Lilburne, John, 2, 25, 31.
Liljegren, S. B., 37.
Lilly, William, *Monarchy or No Monarchy*, 87-88.
Little Nonsuch, 21, 78.
Livius, Titus (Livy), 105-106.
Lloyd, Lodowick (bks. & pr. 1648-71), 82.
Locke, John, 279.
Lockyer, Robert (d. 1649), 103.
London, William (bks. 1653-60), 17, 94.

M., A. (Abraham Miller, pr. 1646-53), 78.
M., G. (George Miller, pr. 1625-46), 74.
Mabb, Thomas (pr. 1650-65), 102.
Mabbott, Gilbert, 26, 79-80.
Madan, F. F., 34-35.
Maggs Brothers, *Milton Catalogue*, 103.
Mallet, Michael, 281.
Man's Mortality (by Richard Overton), 73-74.

Mariet, Thomas, 281.
Marigny, J. Carpentier de, 96-97.
Markham (error for Marchamont?), 96.
Mar-prelate, Martin, 114.
Marriot, Richard (bks. 1645-79), 85.
Marshall, John (bks. 1645-47), 75.
Marshall, Stephen (1594?-1655), 40, 265-266, 268.
Martial, 106-107.
Martin, John (bks. 1649-80), 105.
Marvell, Andrew, 24-25, 46, 51, 112-119, 281.
Mary, Princess (1516-58), 72.
Mary, Princess (1631-60), 8.
Masson, David, 1, 20, 25, 39-41, 49, 52, 69-76, 78, 80, 82, 84-86, 89-90, 93-96, 98-100, 102-103, 105, 108-113, 116-117, 267-268, 283.
Maxey, Thomas (pr. 1640-56), 85.
Mercurius Librarius, 109.
Mercurius Politicus, 34-35, 39, 69, 71, 85-89, 92, 94-95, 97-98.
Mercurius Pragmaticus, 31, 84.
Mercurius Publicus, 104.
Metropolitan Nuncio, 82.
"Microcosmus, Theodorus," 104.
Miles, 280.
Milton, Christopher, 5.
Milton, John, Sr., 11.
MILTON, JOHN, *Ad Patrem*, 11; *Animadversions*, 15, 17, 48, 51, 59, 72, 94, 264, 266, 268-270; *Apology*, 15, 17, 32, 61, 94, 114-116, 264-267, 269-270; *Arcades*, 9-10; *Areopagitica*, 2, 19, 25-26, 29, 56, 70, 80, 108, 115-117, 276; *Brief Notes*, 44, 62, 101, 103, 282, 285-288; *Character of Long Parliament*, 287; *Colasterion*, 20-21, 26, 32, 59, 73, 77, 273, 276-278; *Comus*, 9-11, 54; *Considerations touching Hirelings*, 41-42, 97, 282; *Declaration*, 50; *De Doctrina*, 41; *Defensio Prima*, 4, 13, 18, 31, 33-35, 38-42, 45, 51, 53, 70, 84-97, 103-105, 107-108, 112-114, 116, 118-119, 267, 278-279, 282-283, 288; *Defensio pro Se*, 36-38, 61, 119; *Defensio Secunda*, 16, 18, 22, 28, 32-33, 36-38, 45, 57, 64, 92, 111, 119; *Doctrine & Discipline*, 14, 17-22, 26-27, 29, 31, 35, 43, 45, 51, 63, 70, 73-79, 82-84, 91-94, 98-99, 101-102, 104, 106-107, 110, 116, 118, 270-274, 277, 282, 288; *Eikonoklastes*, 4, 8, 28, 30-33, 35, 39, 43, 45, 53, 70, 84, 86, 88-89, 94-95, 99-101, 103, 105, 108, 114, 116, 282, 288; *Elegia Quarta*, 5; *Elegia Sexta*, 61; *Elegia Tertia*, 8; *Epistolarum*, 49-50, 119; *Epitaphium Damonis*, 4, 12; *Grammar*, 49, 51, 109, 112, 115; *History*, 49, 52-53, 111-112; *Hobson poems*, 9, 24; *Il Penseroso*, 63;

INDEX

L'Allegro, 1, 8; *Letter to Friend*, 42; *Letters of State*, 49, 53, 55; *Logic*, 49, 112; *Lycidas*, 1, 9-11, 54; *Marchioness of Winchester*, 9; *Martin Bucer*, 18-22, 26, 70; *Nativity Ode*, 23, 61; *Naturam non pati senium*, 8; *Observations*, 29-30; *Ode to Rouse*, 22; *Of Education*, 4, 24, 26, 49, 70, 110, 117; *Of Prelatical Episcopacy*, 15-16, 70-71, 94, 264; *Of Reformation*, 12, 14-15, 17, 70-73, 94, 98, 263; *Of True Religion*, 50, 113, 117; *On New Forcers*, 27; *On Shakespeare*, 9-10; *Paradise Lost*, 2, 24, 41, 48-54, 59-60, 109-110, 113-115, 119, 288; *Paradise Regained & Samson Agonistes*, 49-50, 54, 60, 64-65, 111-113, 284; *Paraphrases of Psalms*, 6, 23; *Passion*, 61; *Philosophus ad Regem*, 19-20; *Poems 1645*, 9, 11, 20, 23-24, 27, 39, 49, 85, 93-94, 119; *Poems 1673*, 49, 117; *Prolusions*, 6-7, 269; *Ready & Easy Way*, 43-44, 46, 62, 70, 98-100, 102, 282, 288; *Reason of Church Government*, 13, 15-17, 61, 70, 94, 264-265, 268; sonnets, 4; *Sonnet VII*, 10; *Sonnet VIII*, 20; *Sonnet to Vane*, 108; *Tenure*, 28-32, 45, 70, 80-82, 89, 109, 279; *Tetrachordon*, 20, 22, 77, 275, 282; *Treatise of Civil Power*, 41, 70, 95; *Vacation Exercise*, 7.
Miltonist, 83-84.
Modest Confutation, 72, 263-270.
Monk, George, 43, 45, 63, 100, 102, 281, 284-287.
More, Sir Thomas, 99.
Morrice, Sir William, 46.
Morus, Alexander, 36-38, 45, 90, 92, 110-111, 119, 275.
Moseley, Humphrey, 23-24, 49, 79, 93, 95.
Moses, 91.
Moulin, Peter du, see Du Moulin.

Needham, Marchamont, 2, 34, 58, 71, 84, 96, 99-102, 113.
Nero, Claudius, 82.
Nethercot, Arthur H., 10.
Neville, Henry (1620-94), 280-281.
Newcomb, Thomas (pr. 1649-81), 28, 92-93, 95, 99, 110, 282.
Newcomen, Matthew, (1610?-69), 265-266, 269.
Northumberland, John Dudley, Duke of, 72.
Norton, Sir Gregory, 103.
Nova Solyma, 94.

O., J. (John Owen), 115.
Okes, Mary (pr. 1643-45), 75.
Oldenburg, Henry, 38.
Orleans, Gaston Jean-Baptiste, Duke of, 86.

Overton, Henry (bks. 1629-48), 76.
Overton, Richard, 25, 58.

P., J., see J. Phillips.
P., T. (error for T.C.), 107.
Pagitt, Ephraim (1575?-1647), *Heresiography*, 75.
Paine, Thomas (pr. & bks. 1630-49), 270-271.
Palmer, Herbert (1601-47), *Glass of God's Providence*, 20, 74.
Palmer, William (bks. 1660-61), 100-101.
Park, Thomas, 83, 283.
Parker, John, 118.
Parker, Samuel (1640-88), 25-26, 47, 51, 113; *Reproof*, 116-117.
Parliamentary Intelligencer, 104.
Patrick, Dr. Simon, 115-116.
Peacham, Henry, *Paradox*, 264.
Pels, Peter, 35.
Pembroke, Mary Herbert, Countess of, 10.
Penruddock, Sir John, 281.
Pepys, Samuel, 53, 281.
Perfect Diurnal, 80.
Peters, Hugh (1598-1660), 101-102, 104.
Petty, Maximilian, 281.
Petty, Sir William, 281.
Phillips, Edward, 6, 50, 52, 54, 63; *Illustrious Shepherdess* and *Imperious Brother*, 30; *Tractatulus*, 109-110.
Phillips, John, 36, 88, 108-109; *Responsio*, 34, 90, 267.
Physician Cure Thyself, see R. L'Estrange.
Picture of the Good Old Cause, 103.
Pierson, David, 35.
Pierson, John, 90.
Plain English, 100, 102.
Pluto, 104.
Ponder, Nathaniel (bks. 1669-96), 119.
Poole, Joshua, *English Parnassus*, 23, 94.
Pory, Robert (1608?-69), 8.
Poultney, Sir William, 281.
Povey, Justinian, 270.
Powell, C. L., 277.
Powell, Mary, 28, 63, 264, 276.
Power, Thomas, 54.
Princely Pelican, 30.
Proclamation against Milton, 46.
Pro Rege et Populo Anglicano Apologia, see J. Rowland.
Prynne, William, 2, 20, 58; *Fresh Discovery*, 25; *Mount Orguil*, 113; *Republicans and Others*, 96; *Sword of Magistracy*, 92; *True Narrative*, 96; *Twelve Considerable Questions*, 73.
Public Intelligencer, 95, 104.

Rabshakeh, see M. Needham.
Rainolds, Dr. John (1549-1607), 263.
Ramus, Peter, 112.

Raymond, Dora N., 8, 69, 71, 77-78, 82, 93, 95, 98-99, 101-104, 107, 110.
Regii Sanguinis Clamor, see P. Du Moulin.
Richardson, Jonathan, 45.
Richter, George, *Letters*, 26, 108.
Richter, J. G., 108.
Ridley, Nicholas, 14, 72-73.
Robinson, Henry, 25.
Rogers, Daniel, *Matrimonial Honor* (1642), 22.
Roper, Abel (bks. 1638-79), 79.
Roscommon, Wentworth Dillon, Earl of, 54.
Ross, Alexander (1591-1654), *Pansebeia*, 91.
Rothwell, John, Jr. (bks. 1633-60), 16, 271.
Rouse, John (1574-1652), 22.
Rowe, Nicholas, 54.
Rowland, John (1606-60), 34, 86, 91; *Pro Rege et Populo Anglicano Apologia*, 86, 88, 90; *Polemica*, 92.
Roybold, William (bks. 1651-60), 89.
Roycroft, Thomas (pr. 1651-77), 105.
Royston, Richard (bks. 1629-86), 74, 90-91, 278.

S., G., *Britain's Triumph*, 101.
S., M., see Matthew Simmons.
Sackville, Richard, 281.
St. John, Oliver, 86.
Salmasius, Claudius, *Defensio Regia*, 24, 27, 33-40, 42-47, 53, 61, 70, 84-90, 93-94, 96, 103, 105, 107-108, 110, 112-113, 116, 118, 278, 283, 288; *Responsio*, 36, 46, 69, 105.
Salmasius his Dissection, 105.
Saltmarsh, John (d. 1647), 77; *Groans for Liberty*, 264.
Sambix, John à, 91.
Samson, 44, 64, 83, 97, 285.
Samuel, 97.
Sancroft, William (1617-93), 23.
Sanderson, Sir William, *Complete History*, 95.
Sanmase, Monsieur, see Salmasius.
Sarah, 78.
Sawbridge, George (pr. & bks. 1647-81), 93, 95, 109.
Sawbridge, Thomas (bks. 1669-92), 50, 116-117.
Saxony, Maurice, Duke of, 81.
Saywell, John (bks. 1646-58), 91, 287.
Schaller, Jakob, *Dissertatio*, 34, 91, 93.
Scholderer, Victor, 94.
Scott, Thomas (d. 1660), 104.
Scultetus, Abraham, 263.
Sedgewick, Obadiah (?), 99.
Seile, Henry (bks. 1619-61), 100.

Selden, John, *Uxor Hebraica*, 21-22, 26, 91.
Seneca, 73.
Serpent Salve, see J. Bramhall.
Seton, John (1498?-1567), 268.
Sexby, Edward (d. 1658), 96.
Sgouropolos, Sylvester, 105-106.
Shakespeare, William, 3-4, 9-10, 54.
Shaw, Dr. Ralph (d. 1484), 72.
Shaw, G. B., 62.
Sheldon, Gilbert (1598-1677), *Dignity of Kingship*, 46, 69, 100.
Sidney, Algernon (1622-83), 279.
Sikes, George, 108.
Simmons, Mary, 49.
Simmons, Matthew, 16, 28, 49, 76, 270-271, 273.
Simmons, Samuel, 48-49.
Skinner, Cyriack, 63, 281.
Sleidan, John Philip (1506-56), 81.
Smectymnuus, 8, 13, 15-17, 19, 22, 30, 32, 40, 45, 51, 72, 113-114, 263-270, 276; *Answer to a Book*, 263; *Vindication*, 264-265.
Smectymnuus Redivivus, 16, 265.
Smith, Dr. Richard (1500-63), 72.
Smith, Ralph (bks. 1642-84), 76.
Sobieski, John, 50.
Solomon, 81.
Sophocles, 84.
Soul's Mortality, see *Man's Mortality*.
Sparke, Michael, Sr. (bks. 1620-53), 73.
Spencer, Sir Edward, 92.
Spenser, Edmund, 4.
Spoor, Friderici, 94.
Sprat, Thomas, 287.
Spurstow, William (1605?-66), 265-266, 269.
Stafford, Mr., 281.
Stanley, Sir Edward, 10.
Starkey, George, *Royal Blood*, 103.
Starkey, John (bks. 1658-89), 109, 112.
Stern, Alfred, 69, 71, 87, 89, 92, 96, 104, 107.
Sterry, Peter (d. 1672), 104.
S'too him Bayes, 112.
Strickland, Walter, 86.
Stubbe, Henry, 17, 98.
Suckling, Sir John, 23.
Sweeting, John (bks. 1639-61), 79.
Swift, Jonathan, 48.
Sylvester, Joshua, 4.

Taylor, Jeremy, 48.
Taylor, John, *Traitors Perspective Glass*, 107.
Term Catalogues, see E. Arber.
Testimony to the Truth, 78.
These Tradesmen are Preachers, 77.

INDEX

Thomas, William, 14.
Thomason, George, 2, 14, 25-26, 70-71, 73-78, 80, 85-87, 89-104, 270, 273-275, 278-279, 283, 286.
Thurloe, John, 43.
Tillyard, E. M. W., 11, 40-41.
Titus, Silas, 96.
Todd, Henry John, 10, 23, 69, 71, 73, 75-76, 78, 83-84, 93, 101-102, 104, 107, 110, 117, 119.
Toland, John, 26, 45, 47, 55.
Tomlins, Richard (bks. 1644-72), 95.
Tonson, Jacob, 49.
Treason Arraigned, see R. L'Estrange.
Trot, Robert (bks. 1645-9), 75.
Tullius, Marcus, see Cicero.
Tyrrell, James (1642-1718), 279.

Ulac, A., see A. Vlaccus.
Underhill, Thomas (bks. 1641-59), 24, 74, 78.
Ussher, James, 16, 40, 94, 263.

Vane, Lady Frances, 108.
Vane, Sir Henry, 35, 104, 108.
Vaughan, Henry, 24.
Venn, Col. John, 103.
Verax, Theodorus, see C. Walker.
Verax Prodromus in Delirium, 93.
Verdussen, Hieronymus, 88, 90.
Victor I, Bishop of Rome, 71.
Vindication of Royal Commission, 74.
Vlaccus, Adrian, 37-38, 90, 92, 106.

Walker, Clement (d. 1651), *History of Independency*, 29, 82-83, 279.
Waller, Edmund, 23.
Wallis, F. (Elisha?), 100.
Walton, Izaak, 3.
Walwyn, William, 58.
Warren, Alice (pr. 1660-62), 103.
Warton, Thomas, 23-24.
Wase, Christopher, 21, 83-84, 101.
Whitaker, Richard (bks. 1619-48), 72.
White, Daniel (bks. 1659-60), 103.
Whiting, G .W., 15, 71.
Wildman, Sir John, 281.
Wilkins, John (1614-72), 22, 77.
Willems, Alphonse, *Les Elzevier* (1880), 90.
Williams, John (1582-1650), 17.
Williams, John (bks. 1635-83), 72.
Wilson, William (pr. 1640-65), 75.
Winstanley, William, 52.
Wither, George, 8, 48.
Wit Restored, 9.
Wolseley, Sir Charles, 281.
Wood, Anthony à, 6, 29, 53-54, 113.
Wood, Dr. Robert, 281.
Woodcock, Katharine, 40.
Wotton, Sir Henry, 11, 24, 85.
Wyngaerden, Adrian, 93.

Young, Patrick (1584-1652), 14.
Young, Thomas (1587-1655), 5, 7, 12-13, 40, 265-266.

Zesen, Filip von, *Charles II*, 107.
Ziegler, Caspar, 91.

SCHEELE MEMORIAL LIBRARY

3 6655 00003275 6
PR3583 .P3 1971
Parker, William Ril/Milton's c

PR
3583   Parker
.P3   Milton's contemporary
1971   reputation

Date Due

PR
3583   Parker
.P3   Milton's contemporary
1971   reputation

DATE	ISSUED TO
DEC 6 1977	C Rusciano 303
JAN 29 1985	E. Jellinger
MAR 28 1989	J. War Cap 205

Concordia College Library
Bronxville, New York 10708

 PRINTED IN U.S.A.